Trumping Truth

Trumping Truth

*Essays on the Destructive Power
of "Alternative Facts"*

Edited by
SALVADOR JIMÉNEZ MURGUÍA

McFarland & Company, Inc., Publishers
Jefferson, North Carolina

LIBRARY OF CONGRESS CATALOGUING-IN-PUBLICATION DATA

Names: Murguía, Salvador Jiménez, editor.
Title: Trumping truth : essays on the destructive power of "alternative
   facts" / edited by Salvador Jimenez Murguía.
Description: Jefferson, North Carolina : McFarland & Company, Inc.,
   Publishers, 2019 | Includes bibliographical references and index.
Identifiers: LCCN 2019017080 | ISBN 9781476679099 (paperback :
   acid free paper) ∞
Subjects: LCSH: Trump, Donald, 1946– | Truthfulness and false-
   hood—Political aspects—United States—History—21st century. |
   Communication in politics—United States—History—21st century.
   | Journalism—Corrupt practices—United States—History—21st
   century. | Press and politics—United States—History—21st century.
   | Fake news—United States—History—21st century.
Classification: LCC E912 .T78 2019 | DDC 973.933092—dc23
LC record available at https://lccn.loc.gov/2019017080

BRITISH LIBRARY CATALOGUING DATA ARE AVAILABLE

ISBN (print) 978-1-4766-7909-9
ISBN (ebook) 978-1-4766-3765-5

Front cover: President Donald Trump speaking at the Conservative
Political Action Conference (CPAC) in National Harbor, Maryland,
on February 23, 2018 (photograph by Gage Skidmore)

Printed in the United States of America

McFarland & Company, Inc., Publishers
   Box 611, Jefferson, North Carolina 28640
   www.mcfarlandpub.com

To *Fact*—may you endure, survive and
return to the United States of America safely.

Acknowledgments

I would like to thank Susan Kilby, Managing Editor—Development, of McFarland for her consideration, support and advice in getting this project off the ground. She and her fellow staff were professional and a pleasure to work with.

This volume would not have been possible without the hard work and focus of its contributors, who kept pace with the monthly, weekly, and eventual daily flood of alternative facts from the news coverage on the Trump administration. In a peculiar fashion, I know it was as interesting as it was daunting and demoralizing, yet each of you did a remarkable job in meeting demands for deadlines and documents—for this, I applaud each of you, your courage and your efforts!

I would also like to express my gratitude and appreciation for all of the advice, insight, encouragement and inspiration of the many people that both watched and helped with seeing this project through to completion. I include among these individuals Dr. Peter McCagg, Dr. Chris Carl "Enrique" Hale, Dr. Mark Juergensmeyer, Dr. Adam Dodd, Dr. Amie Miller, Boar Pants, and Counselor Robert F. Alvarenga.

Finally, as always, I appreciate the support of family and friends that gave me a pass, rescheduled dates and events, filled in as baby-sitters, and simply understood that I needed time to read, write and edit. In this light, some very special thanks go out to Hide Murguía, Paul and Jan Jiménez, Adrienne Morales, Yoko Naganishi, Tomie Shiraishi, Debbie Lemos, Ernie Lemos, Gerald Villarreal, Christine and Terrance Plumb, Heather and Stephen Plumb, Kei-Sempei and Kaya Suzuki, Yukari McCagg, Bart Scott, Dori and John Ramirez, Jaime Mireles, John Ortiz, and Roberto Amador.

Table of Contents

Preface

The topic for this volume emerged in the moments just after the election of President Donald J. Trump on November 8, 2016. Throughout his campaign, it became more and more clear that truth had gradually become secondary to lies. The racism, sexism, fear-mongering and the like that stoked the flames within the engine of Trump's campaign were always one or more positions removed from the truth, and due to the ceaseless barrage of what can only be characterized as blatant lies, it appeared that no person, outfit or otherwise was able to keep up with all of the falsehoods, assess the damage of their impact, or even challenge, much less correct them. The task was simply too daunting, and so what was lost in the milieu of shock and confusion that this particular election brought about was how truth—a pillar of modern critical thought—could become such a trivial item to be tossed about, disregarded and even rendered impotent.

In reaction, I put out a call for contributors to this volume, asking them to take up the topic of truth and its otherwise indelible position and place in our society. Sorting through the various proposals I realized that it was not lost on any of them that truth was indeed under attack and merited an analysis that would ground the issue at hand, rather than simply follow the many bizarre antics of Trump and his administration that characterized so much of the mainstream media's coverage of U.S. politics. The contributors herein had no trouble adhering to this focus on truth and what we agreed upon was its new state of triage.

Along these lines, this volume deals with the precarious situation in which truth has been compromised in a variety of political spheres within the United States. Although this work is guided largely by the current Trump administration's abuse of factual information—harkening back to a specific incident in 2017 when Kellyanne Conway uttered the term "alternative facts"—contributors to the volume have branched out in their interpretations of veracity, some making historical links to the current political climate, while others have anticipated a new (ab)normal future where truth will

1

simply be something of an antiquated feature of our past. In this way, this volume is less of a critique of the Trump administration and more of a broad exploration of the fragility of truth and the potential implications, consequences and even the significance of why and, more importantly, how truth can matter.

Introduction

On January 22, 2017, Kellyanne Conway, counselor to the president under the newly inaugurated Trump administration, was featured on NBC's Sunday morning talk show *Meet the Press* with Chuck Todd. In what became a somewhat heated exchange, Todd probed into then–press secretary Sean Spicer's comments to the press on the day after the inauguration in which he stated that the viewers of the event were the "largest audience to ever ... to [*sic*] witness an inauguration, period—both in person and around the globe."[1] As Todd inquired about why Spicer, in his very first official public appearance, would "utter a provable falsehood," Conway remarked, "Don't be so overly dramatic about it, Chuck. You're saying it's a falsehood, and ... our press secretary, Sean Spicer, gave alternative facts to that."[2] In that moment, alternative facts were born and a somewhat new era fostering the irrelevance of veracity was forged.

Packed into this example are Trump's illusions of grandeur, Spicer's angry embellishment, and finally Conway's defense of a lie, all culminating in the administration's earliest issue of alternative facts—an apparent semantic strategy that challenges substantiated facts and argues against them by offering up alternative *factoids*. Although the use of falsehoods is nothing new within politics, nor is the critical examination of them—academic and otherwise—the concerted effort to defend falsehoods in this way appears novel, increasing in use and of growing concern.

This volume explores alternative facts, some of their parallels in history, and implications for their future impact on American society. Drawing attention to the precarity of what constitutes truth in the era of the Trump administration, the 13 essays herein provide various interpretations of how it could ever be acceptable to be seemingly indifferent to the facts and, more important, why now? Given the ceaseless flow of falsehoods engendered by this administration, a major challenge for a volume like this is where to begin. As of December 2018, the *Washington Post* reported that President Trump had uttered more than 7,640 lies in his 710 days in office. The "Fact-Checker

Blog" keeps strict track of every one of his false claims, noting at that time that he was "averaging nearly 6.5 claims a day," up from "4.9 claims a day" during his first 100 days in office.[3] This, however, is merely one person; forging ahead and accounting for his entire administration, including his public affairs apparatus, the phenomena of generating falsehoods has become more of a cultural practice as opposed to some isolated instances.

Of course, giving the benefit of the doubt to President Trump and his administration, there could be something said for simply getting the facts wrong, yet only in a limited number of cases has there ever been an attempt to correct these falsehoods. One such instance took place on February 2, 2017, when Kellyanne Conway made headlines once again for her appearance on MSNBC's *Hardball* with Chris Matthews. Defending President Trump's suspension of immigration from seven countries with Muslim-majority populations, Conway stated, "Two Iraqis came here to this country, were radicalized and were the masterminds behind the Bowling Green massacre"[4]—an event that never actually took place. Five days later, Conway returned to the spotlight on CNN offering a *mea culpa* in an interview with Jake Tapper. As Conway stated, "I regretted it tremendously because I used the wrong word to describe something several times" and "I felt badly about that and I apologize and I rectify.... Let me just say we have a very high respect for the truth and I can only speak for me and I'm sorry that I misspoke."[5] Again, however, these apologies are very few and certainly far between. More, it is important to note that Conway spent the majority of that segment with Jake Tapper defending other Trump falsehoods and criticizing CNN and other news outlets for their lack of coverage of important events—only passively admitting that CNN *did not* cover the "Bowling Green Massacre" that never took place, and for that simple fact was impossible to actually report on.

There is certainly a range of interpretations regarding the motives for maintaining such dishonesty and deceit. Some might argue that the Trump administration truly believes that their statements are on par with the truth— even if only *alternatively* speaking. There are also some that would characterize this administration's manipulation of facts as deliberate or "smoke-and-mirrors" to distract from its overall incompetency. Others still may contend that the Trump administration is simply ignorant to the importance of factual information, and in a series of blunders, they are merely executing damage control—in the face of ill-preparedness that the administration is experiencing the growing pains of learning on the job.

Nonetheless, what is for sure is that the alternative facts continue. From verbal *faux pas* implying that Frederick Douglass was still alive more than a century after his death[6] and Trump's impassioned remark about a tragedy that never happened in Sweden[7] to the more egregious suggestions that hate-filled white supremacists may also somehow include some "very fine people,"[8] the bizarre subjectivity of President Trump trickles into his speech and lights up the trend barometers across the Internet. It is no secret that President Trump understands the power of publicity. During the Republican National Convention, Melania Trump was embroiled in media flap that characterized her speech as uncannily similar to that of former first lady Michelle Obama. Seemingly unrattled by the accusations that his wife riffed on Obama's work, Trump tweeted, "Good news is Melania's speech got more publicity than any in the history of politics especially if you believe that all press is good press!"[9] As citizen Trump too, he made quite clear his intentions to attract the attention of the media as part of his strategy for making ideal business deals. In this candid excerpt from his 1987 book *The Art of the Deal*, Trump is explicit on this point:

> One thing I've learned about the press is that they're always hungry for a good story, and the more sensational the better. It's in the nature of the job, and I understand that. The point is that if you are a little different, or a little outrageous, or if you do things that are bold or controversial, the press is going to write about you. I've always done things a little differently, I don't mind controversy and my deals tend to be somewhat ambitious. Also, I achieved a lot when I was very young, and I chose to live in a certain style. The result is that the press has always wanted to write about me.
> I'm not saying they necessarily like me. Sometimes they write positively and sometimes they write negatively. But from a pure business point of view, the benefits of being written about have far outweighed the drawbacks…. The funny thing is that even a critical story that can be hurtful personally, can be very valuable to your business.[10]

In this way, it almost goes without stating that at least some of President Trump's controversial remarks are intentional. However, generating lies in order to direct the spotlight toward oneself does not preclude the conventional practices of the highest office where, throughout much of history, stating non-facts and largely escaping public scrutiny has been unacceptable, unfathomable and unconscionable.

One case in point is the May 2018 revelation that candidate Trump's health assessment was fabricated by his personal physician, Dr. Harold Bornstein. The shaken Bornstein recounted an incident in which President Trump's ex-bodyguard and an attorney removed Trump's medical records from his office, after Bornstein avowed that Trump was using Propecia to stimulate hair growth. Bornstein then went on to state that Trump "dictated that whole letter," adding, "I didn't write that letter … I just made it up as I went along."[11] Although the assessment really was cut from the ostentatious cloth of Trump's other self-characterizations—and few might have doubted that Bornstein was only the M.D. signatory—the story was just another *story*, and the public seemed to move on as there was nothing there to see.

Bornstein is only one member of a long list of characters that we might now safely conclude as having done Trump's bidding by disseminating lies. Others, like current White House Press Secretary Sarah Huckabee Sanders, seem to smugly defend Trump, never conceding any territory to scrutiny without some reference to such criticism as "fake news"—yet anyone with even the most rudimentary critical thinking skills can see through this veil. Of course, some critics might argue that the use of these trope-like references to fake news are really more of the president's M.O. and for this reason his staff are only employing similar rhetorical strategies in an effort to be more consistent with his style of communication. It may be argued, then, that the use of the term fake news is nothing more than figurative speech, isolated to the White House and commanding no real influential qualities. Yet this is not the case, as evidence has come to bear that this strategy has permeated well beyond the walls of the White House. For example, in early April 2018, several news outlets broke a story about how Sinclair Broadcasting, owner of 193 television stations nationwide, distributed an actual script to various stations to be read on their broadcasts, denouncing the use of fake news by other networks. Written for co-anchors to alternate its reading, the first portion of the script obtained by the *Seattle Post-Intelligencer* read:

Hi, I'm (A) _____, and I'm (B) _____

(B) Our greatest responsibility is to serve our Northwest communities. We are extremely proud of the quality, balanced journalism that KOMO News produces.

(A) But we're concerned about the troubling trend of irresponsible, one sided news stories plaguing our country. The sharing of biased and false news has become all too common on social media.

(B) More alarming, some media outlets publish these same fake stories ... stories that just aren't true, without checking facts first.

(A) Unfortunately, some members of the media use their platforms to push their own personal bias and agenda to control "exactly what people think." This is extremely dangerous to a democracy.[12]

This, and other examples like it, seem to suggest the existence of a culture of deliberate control over information flows. It smacks of propaganda, has serious social and political implications, and is, like the characteristics of alternative facts, becoming the new normal.

Farhad Manjoo's 2008 book *True Enough: Learning to Live in a Post-Fact Society* was seminal in articulating the dimensions of this post-fact condition we find ourselves in nearly a full decade after its publication. Sadly, it seems that side-stepping truth and bolstering lies has become rather effective and we may only now find ourselves facing a serious crisis of legitimacy in terms of how we wish to challenge the ubiquity of large-scale cognitive dissonance. It may very well be the greatest challenge of our time.

This volume is meant to explore the establishment of alterative facts as a definitive point of departure among the new political dimensions within the United States. Comprised of 13 essays, this volume is organized into the following parts: (1) Trump Administration Observations; (2) Philosophical Observations; (3) Historical Observations; and (4) Pop Cultural Observations.

In the first part of this book, four contributing authors establish the tenor for the volume, revolving around how the Trump administration has engendered, allowed for, and, at times, complemented the practice of compromising truth. In addition to operating within the political sphere, the dismissal of facts and the downgrading of their importance to mere semantics of discourse have spilled into other arenas of social interaction. From campaign rhetoric and the frenzy of unbridled support that arose during rallies to the reality-television model of organizing public affairs and the way in which the rest of the country appeared to be granted license in breaching moral and ethical conventions, the United States had seemingly begun its trek into a crisis of legitimacy associated with how truth could be alternatively constructed.

In "(Not So) White Lies," Justin D. García introduces how the Trump campaign made immigration its primary focus in soliciting media attention and later votes. The conflated fear-mongering and demonizing of Latinos became central in generating anxieties about a generalized and misrepresented population said to be on the doorstep of the United States—something Trump used as a rhetorical mechanism in situating himself as the only candidate willing to face the encroaching threat of, in so many of his words, "rapists," "drug dealers," "illegal aliens" and "bad hombres." García's essay demonstrates how alternative facts were already an integral part of Trump's larger political agenda well before he ever entered the office of the presidency and he has continued to use it as the one consistent means for engendering support of his chaotic agenda.

In "The Irony at the Heart of Fake News and Alternative Facts," Robin Blom argues that an irony exists within the debate about a piece of "fake news," as it is not much different than the discussion about a piece of "true news"—except that the parties agreeing or disagreeing in the dispute are reversed. Focusing on this irony, Blom explores why people believe information that is false (alternative facts) and reject information that is true (the actual facts), demonstrating how their own cognitive biases lead to misinterpretation of information.

In "'Rope. Tree. Journalist. Some Assembly Required,'" Jim Clarke details some of the more pronounced efforts to undermine and derail news reporting media by the Trump campaign, its subsequent administration, and its allied constituency. From online propaganda and unapologetic deceit to the peculiar condition of actual fact-checking that appears to be working counter-productively for media outlets, Clarke reveals how these different assaults on truth have contributed to nothing less than a rather popular war on journalism.

The last essay in this part, "Departing from the Truth and Alternative Realities," is a case study that sheds light on how facts have long been wound up with the trajectory of the arguments they attempt to "prove." Sig Langegger's essay tells the 2010 story of Denver, Colorado, resident Marvin Booker, who died from excessive force in an onslaught of aggression by sheriff's deputies while in custody. As Langegger's analysis of the four-year trial indicates, the defendants, the City of Denver, rejected the Booker family's allegations, claiming that their alternative accounts of the death of Marvin merely "departed from the truth." In the end, the Booker family was awarded a $6 million settlement in late 2014, and although the trial took place well before Trump's election, the case study is a telling reminder of the admissibility, if not acceptability, of false claims and the semantics game that can be played when even the most serious of facts are under consideration.

In the second part of this volume, contributing authors provide insight into some of the more philosophical issues associated with truth, Trump and politics. These three essays address various characteristics associated with alternative facts, including their efficacy and how they may transform epistemology as well as the dimensions roles, symbols and expectations assigned to the people that avow them.

In "Sophistry Redux," Andrew Grossman draws parallels between the post-fact condition so closely epitomized by the Trump administration and the classical antiquity of Greek mythology and sophistry. Using Plato's dialogues *Gorgias* and *Protagoras* as springboards, Grossman seeks to frame the politics of alternative facts not as a postmodern dissolution of an objective reality but as a contemporary version of old Gorgian rhetoric, which emphasizes the ethos of pleasure-seeking and power-holding above any truths, whether factual or ethical.

In "On Faith/Trust and Credibility in an Alterfactual Sense," Sabatino DiBernardo provides an analysis of *alterfactual* statements made by Donald Trump and company—and the maddened responses engendered in the media—arguing that the epistemological problematic addressed by philosophers for well over two millennia has now become "breaking news" (fake or otherwise). DiBernardo goes on to employ a poststructuralist questioning of various binary oppositions presupposed by media discourse (e.g., fact/fiction and real/fake [news], among others), in what concludes as a complex critique of alternative facts.

In "What Is a Politician?" Christopher W. Thurley explores the role and purpose of politicians as they are known today in American culture and society. Thurley attempts to define these democratically elected positions etymologically and historically, all while juxtaposing their powers and abilities to the standards set for other positions of power, leadership, and knowledge dissemination that societies have relied upon for centuries, such as doctors, professors, and researchers. The argument concludes that the role of politicians, as they exist now and as defined by how they act when confronted with facts, runs contrary to the matrices in place for experts who impact policy and are not congruent with the merits and expertise needed for all other positions in developed societies that act as paragons of truth, investigators of facts, and protectors of knowledge.

Part 3 offers a number of historical observations about how alternative facts have sprung up as mechanisms to instill anxiety, fear, loathing, and, in one case, delusions of grandeur. Two of these essays are not *necessarily* bound to the Trump campaign or presidency, but rather various events characterized by the use of alternative facts—a segue transition from several earlier essays that alluded to how the construction of alternative facts may not be something entirely new.

"Of Crowd Sizes and Casualties," by Sean D. O'Reilly, traces a trail of alternative facts that lead back to World War II. O'Reilly compares the 2017 Trump administration to the regimes controlling Japan during the war against the United States, focusing upon the issue of *efficacy*. Ultimately, O'Reilly's essay is a stark warning about the dangers of manipulating facts, especially when the stakes are potentially high and the cost of human casualties may be incurred.

In "Wild Irishmen, Alternative Facts and the Construction of America's First 'Wall,'" Debra Reddin van Tuyll characterizes the Trump administration's use of alternative facts as pages taken from an old playbook originating in the 18th century. Van Tuyll recounts the passage of the Alien and Sedition Acts in 1798 that may not have resulted in the construction of a physical barrier to immigration, but instead provided for a legal one—the sort that perhaps proved even more effective in the long run. To drum up support for the Acts, Federalist newspapers slugged away at portraying the Irish as the worst kind of disruptive forces, a strategy that van Tuyll argues is all too similar to how Trump's own use of alternative facts has stirred up meritless angst about Latinos along the southern border of the United States.

"The Alternative Electorate" by Jacopo della Quercia compares the official results of the 2016 U.S. presidential election to the "alternative" results presented by President Trump and members of his administration. In a clear and practical fashion, della Quercia's analysis reveals that Trump's narrative of the 2016 election is a falsehood that underscores how modest his actual electoral performance was. Comparing the official results of the 2016 election to Trump's descriptions of it is an intriguing look at how taking the time to examine these falsehoods can really reinstate a true appreciation and abiding respect for the facts.

In part 4, contributing authors take up the topic of popular culture and alternative facts. For this part, the mediums of television and the Internet are brought to the fore in three insightful explorations of satire, conspiracy theory and cultural drama. The relevance of these three essays to the rest of this volume is enormous, as the constantly changing landscape of popular culture appears to *only* be out-paced by the alternative facts that run rampant throughout it. These essays demonstrate just how quickly today's news and events can become passé in this seeming avalanche of alternative facts.

In "Speaking Post-Truth to Power," Melanie Piper looks at how *Saturday Night Live* creates its satirical alternative to the Trump administration through the mode of "docucomedy," which uses factual material as the template for its comedic sketch characters. In contrast to the past model of the culturally relevant *SNL* political impersonation—such as Tina Fey's Sarah Palin—the humor of Alec Baldwin's Trump does not rely on comedically fabricating a disruption of political norms. Rather, these sketches highlight the way that the Trump administration has already disrupted political norms. Through an analysis of political sketch comedy as grounded in the material of factuality, this essay argues that *SNL* presents its own alternative facts to the Trump administration and an ever-increasing audience of the American public and viewers worldwide.

"The Oven That Cooked Up Pizzagate," by Jeffrey J. Hall, explores the culture of 4chan's *Politically Incorrect* board, commonly referred to as "/pol/," a web forum that gained widespread attention in 2016 as a major online community for members of the Alt-Right—a political movement that supported Donald Trump's presidential campaign. One of /pol/'s most infamous contributions to the campaign was the creation of the "Pizzagate" conspiracy theory, which alleged that a pizza restaurant in Washington, D.C., was the center of a secret pedophile ring linked to one of Hillary Clinton's top advisors. Based on a one-year online ethnography (netnography) of /pol/, Hall explains how this online community maintains its solidarity through strong distrust of all mainstream media and the embrace of numerous conspiracy theories from Pizzagate to Holocaust denial. Hall argues that to the Alt-Right users of /pol/, the mainstream media, academia, and the old political establishment are the true creators of false news, and those who question pro–Trump alternative facts are denounced as "shills." As Hall concludes, by mixing anonymity, Internet prank/trolling culture, and right-wing ideology, the users of /pol/ have created a powerful engine for the promotion of Alt-Right alternative facts.

In "From Mary Tyler Moore to Kellyanne Conway," Terri Toles Patkin draws readers to the possibility of Mary Tyler Moore's influence on Kellyanne

Conway and her use of alternative facts. As Patkin argues, Moore shaped a half century of television programming, which ultimately constructed the environment that nurtured reality television, 24/7 news cycles, and the era of alternative facts. Drawing on the scholarship of Rose K. Goldsen, whose critical examination of the "consciousness industry" was foundational in identifying the systematic effects of communication technologies, this essay connects the psychological and sociological influences of the media environment to the contemporary surreal political masquerade where style trumps substance and "truthiness" passes for news. The narcotization of the audience via popular culture, desensitization and information overload, and the false transparency of the surveillance society have led to the comingling of medium and message, where audiences have become characters in their own cultural drama.

These 13 essays, different though they may be, are all centered on opening up a dialogue about how the manipulations of truth can emerge so subtly that they may go unnoticed, be considered acceptable, characterized as harmless, or even become reduced to minor errors of irrelevance. In one of the most clever and insightful short reads I have ever come across, Princeton philosophy professor Harry Frankfurt's 2005 book *On Bullshit* brings to light how we as a society operate within a deprived repertoire for dealing with what can only be described as "bullshit"—something I would argue that, without a challenge to it, makes us complicit in the abandonment of truth. It is in the spirit of regarding truth as something that matters and should be appreciated that these essays have been written. It is our hope that the contextualization of alternative facts herein reminds readers that facts have an elementary quality to them: they cannot be broken down into other subfactual parts; they do not, or should not, require appending a modifier like "alternative" to them; and they are substantiated by the sheer virtue of their own factual substance. Alternative facts, as they are depicted in the pages that follow, are simply not facts, as only *facts* can be *facts*.

Notes

1. Daniel Trotta, "Crowd Controversy: The Making of an Inauguration Day Photo," Reueters.com, 24 January 2017, https://www.reuters.com/article/us-usa-trump-inauguration-image/crowd-controversy-the-making-of-an-inauguration-day-photo-idUSKBN1572VU (1 Feb. 2017).

2. Rebecca Sinderbrand, "How Kellyanne Conway Ushered in the Era of Alternative Facts," *Washington Post*, 22 January 2017, https://www.washingtonpost.com/news/the-fix/wp/2017/01/22/how-kellyanne-conway-ushered-in-the-era-of-alternative-facts/?utm_term=.f2a7c490ee21 (25 Jan. 2017).

3. Glenn Kessler, Salvador Rizzo and Meg Kelly, "President Trump Has Made 3,001 False or Misleading Claims So Far," *Washington Post*, 1 May 2018, https://www.washington-post.com/news/fact-checker/wp/2018/05/01/president-trump-has-made-3001-false-or-mis-leading-claims-so-far/?utm_term=.7e6bea98db31 (5 May 2018).

4. Steve Contorno and Louis Jacobson, "Fact-Checking Kellyanne Conway on the 'Bowling Green Massacre,'" Politifact.com, 3 February 2017, http://www.politifact.com/truth-o-

meter/statements/2017/feb/03/kellyanne-conway/fact-checking-kellyanne-conways-bowling-green-mass/ (10 Feb. 2017).

5. Alex Stedman, "Kellyanne Conway Apologizes for Bowling Green 'Massacre' Remarks, Spars with CNN's Jake Tapper," Variety.com, 7 February 2017, http://variety.com/2017/tv/news/kellyanne-conway-bowling-green-massacre-cnn-jake-tapper-1201980910/ (10 Jan. 2017).

6. Cleve R. Wootson, Jr., "Trump Implied Frederick Douglass Was Alive. The Abolitionist's Family Offered a 'History Lesson,'" *Chicago Tribune*, 2 February 2017, http://www.chicago tribune.com/news/nationworld/ct-trump-frederick-douglass-remark-20170202-story.html (4 Feb. 2017).

7. Mary Papenfuss, "'Pray for Sweden,' Twitter Uses Giggle After Trump's Latest Stumble," HuffingtonPost.com, 20 February 2017, https://www.huffingtonpost.com/entry/trump-sweden-twitter_us_58aa36f6e4b037d17d291bea (22 Feb. 2017).

8. Rosie Gray, "Trump Defends White Nationalist Protesters," *The Atlantic*, 15 August 2017, https://www.theatlantic.com/politics/archive/2017/08/trump-defends-white-national-ist-protesters-some-very-fine-people-on-both-sides/537012/ (18 Aug. 2017).

9. Dara Lind, "Donald Trump Perfectly Explains His Entire Campaign Strategy, in One Bizarre Tweet," Vox.com, 20 July 2016, https://www.vox.com/2016/7/20/12237172/donald-trump-tweet-melania (12 June 2017).

10. Donald J. Trump with Tony Schwartz, *The Art of the Deal* (New York: Ballantine, 1987), 56–57.

11. Alex Marquardt, "Exclusive: Bornstein Claims Trump Dictated the Glowing Health Letter," CNN.com, 2 May 2018, https://edition.cnn.com/2018/05/01/politics/harold-born-stein-trump-letter/index.html (2 May 2018).

12. Stephen Cohen, "KOMO Attacks 'Biased and False News' in Sinclair-Written Promos," *The Seattle Post-Intelligencer*, 3 April 2018, https://www.seattlepi.com/seattlenews/arti-cle/KOMO-fake-news-Sinclair-promos-12792032.php (21 April 2018).

PART 1

Trump Administration Observations

(Not So) White Lies

"Rapists," "Bad Hombres" and Donald Trump's Conflation of "Mexicans" with "Illegal Immigration" During an Era of Declining Migration from Mexico

Justin D. García

Donald J. Trump began his candidacy for the Republican Party's presidential nomination on June 16, 2015, with the following inflammatory quote: "When Mexico sends its people [to the United States], they're not sending their best.... They're sending people that have lots of problems, and they're bringing those problems with us. They're bringing drugs. They're bringing crime. They're rapists. And some, I assume, are good people."[1] This was the first of numerous statements from the business magnate and reality television star targeting Mexico and singling out Mexicans for the nation's alleged failure to control its borders and stem illegal immigration. In fact, on perhaps no other political issue did Trump stake his presidential ambitions higher than on immigration policy. From his initial speech accusing Mexicans of bringing crime, drugs, and rape to the United States to his unyielding promises to build a border wall that would be funded entirely by the Mexican government, Trump made harsh, controversial, and stringent immigration policies central to his campaign more so than any other presidential nominee in recent American political history. Not content with limiting his criticism of U.S. immigration policy to illegal immigration, Trump also targeted the influx of refugees from various Muslim-majority nations (who, by the very legal definition of the status "refugee" under U.S. immigration law are in the country lawfully) as a dire threat to national security and the safety of American citizens.

Just three days into his presidential administration, Trump's counselor Kellyanne Conway cavalierly revealed during a televised interview with Chuck Todd on NBC's *Meet the Press* that White House Press Secretary Sean Spicer presented "alternative facts" a day earlier when he made a patently absurd and visibly false claim that the crowd size for Trump's inauguration equaled, or exceeded, that of President Obama's 2009 inauguration.[2] With Conway's interview, a new term entered the political lexicon and public parlance—with alternative facts understood to imply falsehoods and outright lies that are presented straight-faced as unimpeachable truths. In other words, alternative facts refers to complete and utter gaslighting nonsense that is repeated so frequently with such gumption that it begins to take on a life of its own.

The purpose of this essay is to highlight Trump's alternative facts and deliberate misconstruing of empirical, quantitative statistical data pertaining to U.S. immigration policy, including his emotionally-charged and polarizing statements regarding illegal immigration and, particularly, Mexican immigrants. This essay primarily focuses on this phenomenon during Trump's campaigns in the presidential primaries and general election in 2015–2016, although some attention is devoted to Trump's immigration policies during the first year of his presidential administration. An exhaustive examination of the Trump administration's policy initiatives, agenda, and executive orders pertaining to immigration far exceed the limits of this essay—although at the time of this writing, the nation finds itself in the midst of a partial government shutdown stemming from a political stalemate over President Trump's insistence that the U.S. Congress provide $5 billion of funding for the construction of a wall along the U.S.-Mexico border.

Admittedly, immigration is an extremely broad subject and Trump's rhetoric and policy initiatives pertaining to immigration are not confined to just Mexican immigration or even illegal immigration more generally. Given the vast nature, centrality, and significance of immigration to Trump's political endeavors, this essay strictly limits its focus to Trump's alternative facts relating to Mexican migration, even though Trump has also targeted Muslim refugees and seeks steep reductions in the nation's legal immigration system and refugee admissions program. Of important note, for the purpose of this essay, is Trump's relentless rhetoric conflating "illegal immigrants" and "illegal immigration" with "Mexicans," despite the fact that immigration from Mexico has declined precipitously over the past decade and undocumented migration from other nations has increased dramatically over this same time period. Such rhetorical tactics and Mexican-centered discourses reflect a conscious effort on the part of Trump to eschew an accurate, empirically data-driven analysis of immigration policy in favor of pandering to explicitly nativist anti–Mexican sentiments fueled by the simplistic conflations of "illegal aliens" as "Mexicans" and illegal immigration as a predominantly "Mexican issue" and "southern border issue." However, explicit demagoguing of illegal immigration and conflation of the phenomenon with Mexicans did not begin with Donald Trump and the 2016 presidential campaign. Therefore, a brief examination of the history of this anger-arousing political tactic is necessary before investigating Trump's immigration platform and its extensive use of alternative facts.

Mexicans and Illegal Immigration in U.S. Politics in Recent Decades

A thorough analysis of political discourse surrounding the interplay between Mexico, Mexicans, and illegal immigration in U.S. history is an extremely long and complex topic that far exceeds the length and scope of this essay. As such, the overview provided here is strictly limited to the past 40 years. By the late 1970s and throughout the early 1980s, the number of undocumented Mexican immigrants in the United States increased sharply as a result of a deepening economic crisis and rising unemployment in Mexico. After years of intense debate, President Reagan signed the Immigration Reform and Control Act (IRCA) into law in 1986, which offered amnesty and permanent alien residency (better known as "green card") status to approximately three million undocumented immigrants while also making it a federal offense—with civil and criminal penalties—for employers to hire undocumented workers.

However, the nature of political discourse on this topic has shifted considerably since the early 1990s. A watershed moment in immigration politics occurred in 1994. That year Californians approved the controversial ballot referendum Proposition 187, which sought to exclude undocumented immigrants from attending public schools and receiving medical treatment at public hospitals. Proposition 187 also encouraged citizens and legal residents to report persons they suspected of being present in California illegally to authorities, thus sending a message that it was the entire public's duty to safeguard against undocumented immigrants. Also of important note is the degree to which the debate over illegal immigration in California in the early to mid–1990s embraced explicitly anti–Mexican/anti–Latino rhetoric, stereotypes, and misinformation. For example, in 1994 California Republican state assemblyman Richard Mountjoy baselessly called for a crackdown on undocumented immigrants from Puerto Rico[3] (despite Puerto Ricans being U.S. citizens since 1917, when the Jones Act conferred American citizenship upon all inhabitants of the Caribbean island). Also in 1994, California state senator William Craven, also a Republican, recommended that "all persons of Hispanic descent" should carry special identification to verify that they are legally present in the United States.[4]

One of the most overt examples of the burgeoning conflation of illegal immigration with Mexico, which allegedly serves to justify Americans' fear, anger, and animosity towards Mexicans, was expressed by Linda Hayes, a media director for Proposition 187. In an October 1994 letter to the editor published in *The New York Times*, Hayes forewarned that Mexican-origin persons were on pace to outnumber non–Mexicans in California within a decade, which would provide Mexican Americans with enough cultural and political power to establish Spanish as California's official language.[5] Hayes also asserted that once Mexican Americans became a majority of Californians, nothing could prevent them from voting to secede from the United States and reunify California with Mexico.[6]

Hayes's letter to the editor thus indicates that the primary concern with illegal immigration was discomfort with impending racial/ethnic demographic change, along with presumed permanent cultural, linguistic, and national loyalty shifts. Such ethnically-tinged paranoia represents an early display of immigration alternative facts. Mexicans (and Latin Americans more broadly) were not the only group of undocumented immigrants residing in California in the 1990s, and linguists have noted that the U.S.-born children and grandchildren of Mexican immigrants exhibit a rapid acquisition of English fluency across generational lines while steadily exhibiting a loss of Spanish-language competency.[7]

Nevertheless, the alleged dire threats posed to American society by a growing Mexican American/Latino population has proven so politically salient since the 1990s that anthropologist Leo Chavez has termed this paranoia the "Latino Threat Narrative."[8] Circulated in mainstream conservative and alt-right media sources, such as talk radio, Internet, and print publications, this "Latino Threat Narrative" constructs Mexicans/Latinos as inherently foreign and largely undocumented, excessively fertile, unable or unwilling to assimilate into American society, disloyal to the United States while retaining allegiance to their ethnic and national origins, vastly different from the waves of European immigrants who settled during the 19th and early 20th centuries, and poised to overrun the nation unless dramatic action to control the borders occurs now.[9]

A prominent illustration of the "Latino Threat Narrative" is found in Harvard political science professor Samuel Huntington's 2004 book *Who Are We? The Challenges to America's National Identity*. Although Huntington does not focus solely on Mexican/Latino immigration, in a chapter titled "Mexican Immigration and Hispanization" Huntington engages in his own share of alternative facts. Addressing the allegedly problematic nature of Mexican immigration and the nation's rapidly growing Latino population, Huntington declares that no other immigrant/ethnic group in U.S. history has been as geographically concentrated as are Mexicans and Mexican Americans today in the southwestern states.[10] Such a statement overlooks the fact that German immigrants between the Civil War and World War I were overwhelmingly concentrated in the present-day Rust Belt region between Pennsylvania and Wisconsin. Likewise, the vast majority of Italian immigrants in the early 20th century settled in the Mid-Atlantic and eastern upper-Midwest states—geographic regions that are comparatively smaller than the expansive territorial range of the southwestern states.

Furthermore, Huntington points to the alleged reluctance of Mexicans and Mexican Americans to marry outside their respective ethnic group as evidence of their low rates of assimilation and acculturation.[11] However, the Pew Research Center found that 26 percent of all Hispanics (the term used by Pew in their report, in place of "Latino") who married in 2010 wed a non–Hispanic spouse—a rate that was slightly exceeded only by Asian Americans.[12] Furthermore, the Pew Research Center reported in 2017 that 42 percent of all intermarriages in the United States are between a Hispanic and non–Hispanic white spouse—the most common intermarriage pairing.[13] Additionally, 5 percent of all intermarriages are between a Hispanic and non–Hispanic black spouse.[14] That just under half of all intermarriages in the United States involve a Hispanic spouse strongly refutes Huntington's "alternative fact" of alleged Mexican/Latino aversion to intermarriage as a testament to their presumed low degree of assimilation to American society.

Just two weeks before Trump formally declared his candidacy, conservative pundit Ann Coulter's nativist tome controversially-titled *¡Adios, America! The Left's Plan to Turn Our Country into a Third World Hellhole*, hit the market. Coulter is a longtime critic of both legal and illegal immigration, largely on the grounds that post–1965 immigration from Latin America, Asia, Africa, and the Middle East threatens to greatly diminish the white population of the United States. Her book was a *New York Times* best-selling, 300-page screed against the influx of non–European immigrants replete with distortions, hyperbolic rhetoric, sweeping generalizations, blatant stereotypes, and outright lies. As an example of the sensationalist and hyperbolic tone of her prose throughout, Coulter declares when discussing the nature of Latino identity, "The notion of Hispanic unity—much less Hispanic-black unity—is pure liberal fantasy. Puerto Ricans and Dominicans hate one another, blacks and Mexicans hate one another, Haitians and African Americans hate one another, and everyone hates the Cubans."[15] Such discourse obviously ignores the highly nuanced, fluid, and dynamic nature of interethnic social relations found in local communities throughout the United States, as empirically and qualitatively researched by urban sociologists, cultural anthropologists, and social psychologists. Coulter also declares that "the rape of little girls isn't even considered a crime in Latino culture" and "another few years of our current immigration policies, and we'll all have to move to Canada to escape the rapes."[16] Nevertheless, Trump praised Coulter's book as a "great read,"[17] while Coulter quickly embraced Trump as her preference for the Republican Party's 2016 presidential nominee and occasionally spoke at his campaign rallies.[18]

Thus, when Donald Trump announced his presidential candidacy in June 2015, he entered a political arena in which the groundwork for overtly anti–Mexican half-truths, distortions, and alternative facts with respect to immigration policy had already been laid during the prior 25 years. Shrill immigration rhetoric had long characterized numerous campaigns at the local, state, and Congressional levels. However, Trump established himself as the first presidential nominee from either of the two major parties to make immigration policy a central plank of his platform in the post–Civil Rights era.

Trump's Immigration Alternative Facts

From the outset, Trump established a hardline stance on immigration—particularly staunch opposition to illegal immigration and, to a somewhat lesser extent, outspoken criticism of the influx of immigrants and refugees from Muslim-majority nations—as the cornerstone of his presidential ambitions. His controversial statement about Mexican "criminals" and "rapists," made during his campaign announcement, foreshadowed the tone towards, and centrality of, illegal immigration from Mexico throughout the 2016 campaign and during his administration. Four days after Trump officially announced his candidacy, Coulter appeared on HBO's *Real Time with Bill Maher* and praised Trump's courage to confront U.S. immigration policy, which she chided for dramatically shifting the nation's ethnic composition.[19] That night Coulter also accurately predicted that Trump stood the best chance of winning the Republican presidential nomination[20] in large part because of his tough-minded approach towards immigration. Trump chose immigration as the topic of his first policy position report, which his campaign issued on August 16, 2015.[21] Since declaring his candidacy, Trump's alternative facts on immigration—comprised from an emotionally-charged blend of sensationalist rhetoric, half-truths, misunderstanding of actual U.S. immigration law, and outright lies—have produced an alarmist narrative based on several deceptive talking points and insinuations:

- Illegal immigration is an overwhelmingly Mexican phenomenon
- Illegal immigration from Mexico is out of control and at epidemic levels

- Undocumented immigrants drain taxpayer dollars without paying into the system
- A wall constructed along the U.S.-Mexico border will severely curtail illegal immigration
- Mexico (the nation whose citizens the border wall is intended to deter from entering illegally) will fully fund the construction of the border wall
- Mass deportations of undocumented immigrants, increased border enforcement, and enhanced restrictions on legal immigration will reduce crime and improve job opportunities for native-born U.S. citizens

In Trump's immigration narrative, these themes often intersect and aim to buttress one another. However, these alternative facts are easily debunked through a quick examination of empirical data compiled by the U.S. Census Bureau (USCB), Immigration and Customs Enforcement (ICE), the Department of Homeland Security (DHS), the Internal Revenue Service (IRS), and numerous scholars. Nevertheless, it is important to bear in mind that Donald Trump did not invent the aforementioned myths about immigration. Such perceptions have existed for some time, and Trump merely exploited these perceptions effectively for his own political gain. Also, since these perceptions are so deeply engrained in the minds of many of the most passionate hardline immigration control advocates, simply pointing out the faulty logic and false nature of these myths will probably not change the views of many of Trump's most loyal supporters—especially among those who embraced his candidacy *because of* (rather than despite) his shrill rhetoric on illegal immigration and Mexico. Psychologists note the tremendous power of "motivated reasoning" in influencing political ideology and voting behavior, by which many individuals who feel strongly about a specific topic often pre-determine a conclusion about that respective topic, regardless of the facts and objective data pertaining to the topic.[22,23] Even more troubling, Gleb Tsipursky of *Scientific American* warns that "when presented with accurate information that contradicts their current political perspective, people tend to invest more strongly into their current political beliefs instead of changing their mind, a thinking error known as the backfire effect."[24]

To put it another way, chances are good that if a die-hard Trump supporter who subscribes to Ann Coulter's line of thinking on immigration stumbles upon this book and reads this essay (written by a presumably elitist, East Coast professor with a Hispanic surname, mind you), he or she will instantly become furious, dismiss its points as "complete bullshit," and accuse the author of automatically harboring racially/ethnically biased views that preclude any objective discussion of immigration—perhaps even prompting angry emails, possibly laced with profanity and/or slurs, demanding him to "Go back to Mexico!" and "Get out of my country!" As unpleasant as that sounds, however, it is imperative to confront and refute alternative facts whenever they arise, lest empirical data and demonstrable truth be ceded to the manipulative power of emotions and the political opportunism of a given moment.

Quantitative data indicate that illegal immigration was a significant concern for Trump voters throughout the 2016 campaign. An August 2016 survey of registered voters conducted by the Pew Research Center found that 66 percent of Trump supporters felt that immigration was a "very big problem" in the United States.[25] Two weeks before the presidential election, that number had increased to 79 percent of Trump backers.[26] The Pew Research Center also found in late October 2016 that 86 percent of Trump supporters felt that immigration had "gotten worse" since 2008[27]—that is, the immigration situation in the United States had deteriorated during the Obama administration. In August 2016, 79 percent of Trump-leaning voters supported their preferred candidate's promise to build a wall along the U.S.-Mexico border,[28] while half of Trump supporters felt that undocumented immigrants are more likely to commit serious crimes than U.S. citizens.[29] As early as March 2016, while the Republican Party presidential primaries were still in process, 42 percent of Trump supporters favored a nationwide effort to deport all undocumented immigrants residing in the United States.[30] This latter statistic may be more indicative of the intensity of anti-illegal immigrant sentiments among Trump's most ardent loyalists, as the data was compiled while the Republican nomination was still ongoing and featured a divided field with rival candidates, such as Florida senator Marco Rubio and Ohio governor John Kasich—both of whom espoused more moderate tones on immigration policy—still in the race. Some voters who supported Trump after he secured the Republican nomination may have reluctantly backed him out of party loyalty and/or opposition to his Democratic opponent, former secretary of state Hillary Clinton, while disagreeing with an all-out effort to deport the entire undocumented population.

Almost immediately, Trump's controversial and hardline positions on illegal immigration prompted other candidates seeking the 2016 Republican presidential nomination to adopt more restrictive stances on undocumented migrants. This was quite ironic, considering that after the 2012 election, the Republican Party conducted a self-analysis that recommended it soften its tone on illegal immigration and adopt a more moderate policy towards undocumented immigrants in effort to appeal to a growing number of Latino voters.[31] In August 2015, Wisconsin governor Scott Walker—originally considered one of the frontrunners for the party's 2016 presidential nomination before Trump's meteoric rise—adopted Trump's pledge to build a border wall as part of his own campaign platform, while also calling for an end to birthright citizenship to children born on U.S. soil to undocumented parents.[32] Former Pennsylvania senator Rick Santorum and Louisiana governor Bobby Jindal also advocated immediately terminating U.S. citizenship for such children,[33] who are derisively referred to as "anchor babies" by staunch critics of illegal immigration.[34] Jindal (himself the son of Indian immigrants) upped the ante regarding undocumented immigrants' alleged laziness and refusal to acculturate to American society during an August 30, 2015, interview on CBS's *Face the Nation*, when he declared, "We need to insist [that] people who want to come to our country should come legally, should learn English and adopt our values, roll up their sleeves, and *get to work* [emphasis original]. One of the things I've been emphasizing, as the son of immigrants who came here legally, [is that] we need to insist, on assimilation.... Immigration without assimilation is invasion."[35] Walker, Santorum, and Jindal each adopted hardline stances on immigration shortly after the Trump campaign issued an immigration policy paper that declared, "[Granting citizenship to U.S.-born children of undocumented immigrants] remains the biggest magnet for illegal immigration"[36]—a particularly egregious "alternative fact" that will be discussed more thoroughly below.

Before deconstructing the narrative of so-called anchor babies, however, it is useful to scrutinize the alternative facts surrounding the narrative of illegal immigration from Mexico. Given the realities that Mexico and the United States share a 2,000-mile border, that the United States has long boasted of higher wages and a lower unemployment rate than Mexico, that Mexicans historically comprised the single-largest nationality of undocumented migrants in the United States, and striking visual power of photographs and televised footage illustrating undocumented migrants crossing the U.S.-Mexico border and Border Patrol agents apprehending them, it is not difficult to understand why many Americans so easily conflate "illegal immigration" with "Mexicans." However, critical developments in recent years have dramatically shifted the nature of contemporary illegal immigration and the demographics of the current undocumented population residing in the United States. Nevertheless, the simplistic notion of undocumented immigrants as "illegal aliens from Mexico" who "crash the border" remains extremely powerful in the national psyche, which Donald Trump successfully tapped into with his immigration rhetoric targeting Mexicans. Interestingly, despite Trump's incessant harping about illegal immigration throughout the campaign and during the early months of his presidency, he rarely discussed the influx of undocumented immigrants from Canada, Asia, Africa, or Europe.

Reflecting his propensity to characterize illegal immigration as a specifically "Mexican problem," Trump ominously warned at a campaign rally held in Phoenix on July 12, 2015, "I love the Mexican people.... I respect Mexico ... but the problem we have is that their leaders are much sharper, smarter, and more cunning than our leaders, and they're killing us at the border.... They're taking our manufacturing jobs. They're taking our money. They're killing us."[37] The following month, the Trump campaign issued its first policy position paper in which it asserted, "In short, the Mexican government has taken the United States to the cleaners [because of illegal immigration]. They are responsible for this problem, and they must help pay to clean it up."[38] One week into his administration, Trump connected the threat posed by an alleged porous Mexican border to the violence of Mexican drug cartels in a testy phone call with Mexican president Enrique Peña Nieto. In colorful mock Spanish, Trump warned the Mexican head of state, "You have a bunch of bad hombres[39] down there. You aren't doing enough to stop them. I think your military is scared. Our military isn't, so I just might send them down there to take care of it."[40] Trump had previously used the "bad hombres" reference during his third presidential debate with Clinton on October 19, 2016, when, discussing his immigration views, he vowed, "We have some bad hombres here and we're going to get them out."[41]

One of the most curious lines of the 2016 campaign, however, came from Trump's vice presidential nominee, Indiana governor Mike Pence, during the vice presidential debate with Virginia senator Tim Kaine on October 5. When Kaine challenged Trump's infamous quote about Mexican rapists, Pence retorted with a thinly-veiled double entendre about Mexican male anatomy while tying it to crime. "Senator, you whipped out that Mexican thing again," Pence responded. "[There] are criminal aliens in this country ... who have come to this country illegally, who are perpetrating violence and taking American lives."[42] Thus Pence, like Trump, conflated illegal immigration with Mexicans and Mexicans with violent crime; under such logic, "Mexicans" are interchangeable with "illegal aliens."

And yet, empirical data collected from both U.S. and Mexican sources reveals a vastly different picture of illegal immigration. Despite Trump's bombastic oratory on the topic, the estimated number of unauthorized immigrants residing in the United States has actually *declined* over the past decade—from a record high of 12.2 million in 2007 to 11.1 million in 2014, according to information from the U.S. Census Bureau and the Pew Research Center.[43] During that time, the number of undocumented migrants from Mexico declined dramatically, but was somewhat offset by sizable increases in undocumented migrants from other Central American, Asian, and African nations.[44] The 2014 Mexican National Survey of Demographic Dynamics, conducted by the government of Mexico, found that one million Mexican nationals and their U.S.-born children left the United States and returned to live in Mexico between 2009 and 2014.[45]

By contrast, the U.S. Census Bureau estimated that only 870,000 Mexican migrants settled in the United States during the same time period, resulting in a net loss of 140,000 Mexican nationals and their family members over the five-year period.[46] Even more dramatic, the Pew Research Center notes that the undocumented Mexican population in the United States declined by more than one million in less than a decade, falling from a record high of 6.9 million in 2007 to 5.6 million in 2014.[47] The number of undocumented Mexicans arrested by the Border Patrol has steadily declined since the mid–2000s, with the 188,122 apprehensions of Mexican nationals in 2015 representing the lowest number of arrests along the U.S.-Mexico border since 1969.[48] Illegal immigration from Mexico has declined to such an extent over the past ten years that by 2016, the number of undocumented immigrants from nations other than Mexico surpassed the undocumented Mexican population.[49]

Today, China and India have each surpassed Mexico in numbers of immigrants currently entering the United States.[50] In fact, an estimated 130,000 undocumented migrants from India entered the United States between 2009 and 2014, bringing the total number of undocumented migrants from that nation to approximately 500,000.[51] A 2015 report issued by the Migration Policy Institute revealed that the number of undocumented immigrants from Asia increased 202 percent between 2000 and 2013,[52] during the time in which illegal immigration from Mexico peaked and then declined precipitously. While so much emotion and attention on illegal immigration is devoted to concern with the U.S.-Mexico border, a large share of undocumented migrants did not enter the country by crossing the border illegally, but rather entered the United States legally on student or tourist visas and simply remained after their visas expired. Approximately two-thirds of undocumented immigrants who settled in the country in 2014 were visa overstayers, according to the New York–based Center for Migration Studies.[53] According to statistics from the U.S. Department of Homeland Security, approximately 416,500 foreigners overstayed their visas in 2015,[54] with Canadians comprising the single-largest nationality of this segment of the undocumented population that year.[55] Needless to say, a border wall and an infinite number of Border Patrol agents will do nothing to stem the flow of visa overstays.

Importantly, this steep decline in illegal immigration from Mexico occurred well before Donald Trump emerged as a viable presidential candidate, so he cannot claim credit for this momentous trend. Moreover, demographers and immigration scholars doubt that the profound decline in Mexican migration over the past decade is merely a fleeting, temporary aberration. The downturn in Mexican migration since the mid–2000s corresponds with an improving economy and decreased unemployment in Mexico, along with a dramatically declining birthrate among Mexican women.[56] Whereas

Mexican women in the 1960s gave birth to an average of six children, today that figure has declined to two—roughly equivalent to the birth rate of the United States.[57] Furthermore, a 2015 Pew Research Center report found that 33 percent of adults in Mexico now believe that life in the United States is neither better nor worse than life in Mexico, a 10-point surge in opinion on this question since 2007.[58] Consequently, a strengthening Mexican economy and a shrinking birthrate means that there is significantly less pressure on Mexicans to leave their homeland in search of employment, while fading romanticism of life north of the border will deter a growing number of Mexicans from seeking to enter the United States. Although demographers and immigration analysts point out that an uptick in Mexican migration might occur in the future, should the Mexican economy falter, it is extremely unlikely to parallel the massive Mexican migration that occurred between the mid–1960s and mid–2000s.[59]

Nevertheless, in Donald Trump's alternate reality, illegal immigration from Mexico is at epidemic levels and nothing short of a massive, impenetrable wall along the U.S.-Mexico border is required to stem the flow. In fact, the promise of constructing a wall on the Mexican border (for which the Mexican government would foot the bill) may be the best-known policy proposal of the Trump campaign—other than, of course, his vow to "Make American Great Again." Trump first declared his intent to erect a "great, great wall on our southern border"[60] during his June 2015 candidacy announcement. His campaign rallies often featured raucous throngs of supporters erupting into loud chants of "Build the wall! Build the wall!" as Trump rhythmically pumped his fist in tune. These feisty rallies also commonly featured Trump initiating passionate call-and-response exchanges with audiences as he would rhetorically ask, "Whose gonna pay for the wall?" to which the crowd would ecstatically scream, "MEXICO!" While such a spectacle makes for good television, the practicality of such a proposal is an entirely different matter.

Trump initially implied that his wall would span the entire 2,000-mile length of the southern border, but he downsized his plans considerably when pressed for details in an interview with MSNBC's Tamron Hall on February 9, 2016. Trump assured Hall that building the wall would be a relatively simple and inexpensive task because "of the two thousand [miles of U.S.-Mexico border] ... we [only] need one thousand [miles of fencing] ... and I'm taking it price per square foot."[61]

Despite such bold assurances, uncertainty abounds as to the actual size, cost, and structure of Trump's proposed "great wall." On the campaign trail Trump initially estimated that its construction would cost approximately $8 billion,[62] which Mexico would pay for entirely through a variety of means—including renegotiating the terms of the North American Free Trade Agreement (NAFTA), taxing or seizing remittances from undocumented Mexican immigrants to their homeland, imposing a tax on Mexican nationals who legally enter the United States through an official port of entry, and/or imposing special fees on U.S. visas issued to Mexican diplomats and businesspersons.[63] However, during a Republican primary debate in Houston on February 25, 2016, Trump considerably upped the projected cost of building "a real wall" to between $10 and $12 billion.[64] Needless to say, the Mexican government repeatedly dismissed Trump's pledge that they will pay for the wall as a delusion of grandeur. Trump also fluctuated widely on the size of his border wall throughout the campaign season, as its proposed height ranged from 30 to 55 feet tall.[65] However, when push came to shove once Trump assumed office, reality set in. The Department of Homeland Security (DHS) estimated that the wall would cost approximately $21.6 billion to build and would take at least three and a half years to complete.[66] Furthermore, Trump quickly retreated from his stance demanding Mexico front the cash for the wall by redirecting $20 million from other DHS operations to begin construction on the wall while requesting $1.4 billion from Congress to supplement initial construction.[67] In February 2017 the Trump administration suggested imposing specific tariffs on products imported from Mexico to fund the wall,[68] which, in a convoluted twist of alternative facts, would leave American citizen consumers directly paying for the wall's construction by cutting out the Congressional middlemen who redistribute and allocate tax money for budgetary purposes!

Aside from building a "great border wall" and exponentially bolstering deportations (which is discussed below), Trump's strategy to stem the already subdued flow of illegal immigration from Mexico consisted of terminating birthright citizenship to anchor babies.[69] The current practice of granting U.S. citizenship to infants born within the United States stems from the 14th Amendment to the U.S. Constitution, which declares, "All persons born or naturalized in the United States and subject to the jurisdiction thereof, are citizens of the United States and of the State wherein they reside." This practice of granting American citizenship is today extended to children born on U.S. soil to mothers who are themselves citizens as well as legal immigrants, undocumented migrants, and refugees. Critics of illegal immigration have long contended that granting birthright citizenship serves as an incentive for undocumented immigrants, particularly women, to enter the country illegally to give birth to an anchor baby who allegedly gives the mother a permanent right to remain in the country.[70] The specific narrative of undocumented parents and their anchor babies manifests differently among illegal immigration critics, though—some presume that the giving birth to a U.S. citizen automatically transforms an undocumented parent's immigration status from "illegal alien" to "U.S. citizen," while others presume that the parent remains undocumented but is otherwise awarded immunity from deportation.

Another common claim is that undocumented parents of anchor babies become entitled to receive a host of taxpayer-funded welfare benefits, thus allegedly providing additional incentives to thwart the nation's immigration laws.[71] However, none of these allegations are true.

Trump made extensive use of the Mexican anchor baby trope during his presidential campaign. At a September 2015 Republican primary debate he scoffed, "A woman gets pregnant. She's nine months [pregnant], she walks across the border, she has the baby in the United States, and we take care of the baby for 85 years. I don't think so!"[72] He warned his supporters at a Dallas rally that same month that the United States had become a "dumping ground" for anchor babies.[73] During an interview on the Fox News Channel with Bill O'Reilly on August 18, 2015, Trump attempted to explain the sinister dynamics of anchor babies, claiming, "What happens is [pregnant women are] in Mexico, they're going to have a baby, they move over here for a couple of days, they have the baby.... I'd much rather find out whether or not 'anchor babies' are citizens because a lot of people don't think they are."[74] In addition to bemoaning an alleged tidal wave of anchor baby births, Trump also treats the citizenship status of such children as if it is an unsettled, open issue—not as a policy that he is in favor of changing, but as a mysterious and unresolved question at the present moment.

Empirical data and a quick examination of U.S. immigration laws quickly and decisively refute the anchor baby trope, however. As is the case with border crossings from Mexico, the number of children born to at least one undocumented parent has steadily decreased since the mid–2000s. The number of such births peaked in 2007 at 360,000, but the number had fallen to 295,000 in 2013.[75] This figure represented approximately 8 percent of all births in the United States in 2013,[76] but this overrepresentation does not indicate that the majority of undocumented immigrants enter the country just for purposes of having a child. Rather, undocumented immigrants tend to be much younger on average than the overall U.S. population, so their arrival during their peak childbearing years would correspond with an overrepresentation among total U.S. births.[77] Moreover, rather than serving as the catalyst for illegally entering the United States, qualitative data indicate that the likelihood of an undocumented woman giving birth increases the longer she has been in the United States, and giving birth to a child in the United States profoundly shifts an undocumented immigrant's orientation away from their homeland.[78] Even Mark Krikorian, the executive director of the immigration restrictionist advocacy group Center for Immigration Studies, acknowledges this point, conceding, "[Birthright citizenship] is not birth tourism. It's not so much about inducement or enticement, but about people coming here to work, meeting someone, then the birds and the bees happen, and they have kids."[79]

Even more to the point, and to the surprise of many critics of illegal immigration, simply being the parent of a child born on U.S. soil does not confer legal "permanent alien residency" status on undocumented migrants, let alone U.S. citizenship. Being the parent of a citizen in no way alters one's immigration status, and undocumented parents of citizens are eligible for deportation if they are apprehended by ICE agents or other authorities.[80] In 2013, for example, ICE deported more than 72,000 undocumented migrants who were the parents of U.S. citizens.[81] If an undocumented parent of a U.S. citizen minor is apprehended and deported, he or she has the choice of either taking their child with them to their homeland, placing the child in the custody of another relative residing in the United States, or placing their child in foster care. Additionally, since their immigration status does not change through childbirth, such parents remain ineligible to receive publicly-funded welfare programs, such as the Supplemental Nutrition Assistance Program (SNAP). Although it is true that undocumented parents can claim such benefits for their citizen children, undocumented migrants themselves are barred from receiving such benefits and are excluded from any calculation of allocated benefits.[82]

Perhaps the most ridiculous "alternative fact" in Trump's immigration platform, however, remains his boastful claim made in September 2015 that he could deport the entire undocumented population of 11 million people (roughly equivalent to the population of Ohio) within a time frame of 18 months to two years.[83] To carry out such an arduous task, Trump vowed to create a "deportation force"[84] by tripling the number of Immigration and Customs Enforcement (ICE) agents.[85] Even the most adamant right-wing advocates of stricter immigration enforcement in the U.S. Congress never made such phenomenal claims, which fly in the face of any sense of reality. The conservative think tank American Action Forum analyzed Trump's "deport-them-all" plan and found that in order for such an idea to be remotely feasible, ICE would need to multiply its number of agents *18 times* (from 5,000 to 90,000) to meet the minimal level of necessary staffing![86] The forum estimated that the total cost of deporting all undocumented immigrants would cost between $100 and $300 billion in order to account for the necessary construction and staffing of new immigration detention centers and the ramped-up chartered buses and planes that would be needed to return migrants to their nations of origin.[87]

Nevertheless, despite the absurdity of the multitude of alternative facts that Trump has presented on immigration, the issue remains at the top of his domestic agenda more than six months into his administration. Although the number of apprehensions along the U.S.-Mexico border have fallen sharply over the past decade and are now at near-historic lows, Trump has requested a 21 percent budget increase for Customs and Border Protection

(CBP) to begin building the wall and hire an additional 5,000 Border Patrol officers.[88] Trump has also sought to increase the ICE budget by almost 30 percent to hire new agents and build new detention centers.[89] By making immigration enforcement the Department of Homeland Security's central mission, Trump's proposed budget for DHS would lead to allocation cuts to the United States Coast Guard (USCG) and depleted resources for the Transportation Security Administration (TSA).[90]

The disturbing nature of alternative facts notwithstanding, immigration may be the perfect issue for Donald Trump to project a winning image to his loyal base. Hindered by the inability to push a major piece of legislation through Congress and sign it into law (as best exemplified by his failed campaign promise to immediately repeal and replace the Affordable Care Act), Trump has relative autonomy with respect to immigration and does not need Congressional authorization to bolster enforcement and deportations. Thus, a tough tone on Mexican illegal immigration represents a no-lose scenario for Trump. If the number of undocumented Mexicans declines substantially due to external factors (as has been the case for years), Trump can claim credit and declare victory. On the other hand, if illegal immigration increases, Trump can point to his hardline rhetoric and restrictionist policies as evidence that he means business and is working hard to solve the problem on behalf of beleaguered American citizens. On this issue, perhaps more than any other, overheated and alarmist rhetoric may matter more than actual results in the minds of voters for whom stringent immigration control is important.

Wrestling with Reality in the Age of Trump

Given his litany of inflammatory statements about Mexico and Mexicans, alongside his half-truths and outright lies about immigration, it is no surprise that Trump is deeply unpopular south of the border. During the 2016 presidential election, anti–Trump resentment in Mexico steadily escalated and manifested in an unusual pop culture icon. Sam Polinsky—a white American citizen living in Mexico, where he performs with the Mexican professional wrestling league *Consejo Mundial de Lucha Libre* (World Wrestling Council)—capitalized on the Mexican public's animosity towards Donald Trump by adopting the persona of an ardent Trump supporter as his wrestling gimmick. Polinsky, known in the ring as "Sam Adonis," is a Pittsburgh native and the younger brother of noted World Wrestling Entertainment (WWE) wrestler-turned-commentator Corey Graves.[91] He relocated to Mexico to pursue his wrestling career after an injury sustained in 2011 hindered his prospects of landing a contract with WWE.[92] Polinsky claims that he developed the idea for his villainous Sam Adonis character in July 2016, at the height of the U.S.

presidential campaign.[93] His tall stature, blond hair, and handsome looks accentuate his *gringo* identity south of the border, and he enters the ring carrying a giant American flag with Trump's smiling face superimposed in the center. Polinsky's in-ring antics include taunting his opponents and Mexican spectators with pro–Trump and jingoistic rhetoric. While discussing his Sam Adonis alter ego, Polinsky acknowledged, "[Mexican fans] were so angry! I'm a flamboyant loudmouth. I'm willing to shove my president down your throat. I'm just such an ass that I want to be Trump. I'm the high school quarterback that picked on you."[94] Yahoo! Sports columnist Eric Adelson has even referred to Adonis as "possibly the most reviled man in all of Mexico."[95]

Although he is not an elected U.S. government official, Sam Polinksy/Sam Adonis nonetheless plays an important cultural role in Mexican society during this current political moment of strained U.S.-Mexico relations under the Trump administration. As anthropologist Heather Levi has documented, professional wrestling (known in Mexico as *lucha libre*) is extremely popular among working-class urban Mexican citizens,[96] and since the 1980s, *luchadores*[97] have increasingly emerged as symbols of political mobilization. Meanwhile, professional wrestling in the United States and Mexico alike has long used the gimmick of evil, foreign *heels* (wrestling lingo for the "villains" or "bad guys" whom the audience jeers, known as *rudos* in Mexican *lucha libre*) to arouse the anger and hatred of fans.

As political commentator Chris Cillizza has argued, professional wrestling may actually be "the perfect metaphor for Donald Trump's presidency."[98] Trump is an avid wrestling fan and has occasionally participated in various WWE events. Trump hosted the WWE's signature annual event, Wrestlemania IV and V, at the Trump Plaza Hotel and Casino in Atlantic City in 1988 and 1989, respectively, and he also served as a manager for a match dubbed "the Battle of the Billionaires" against WWE chairman Vince McMahon at Wrestlemania XXIII in 2007. In 2013 McMahon inducted Trump into the WWE Hall of Fame for his longtime corporate support for the wrestling company.[99] The McMahon family and Trump maintain a close friendship in real life, and Trump appointed Vince's wife Linda (the former CEO and president of WWE) as head of the Small Business Administration three weeks into his presidency.[100] Much more significantly, however, is the very nature of professional wrestling and how it resembles Trump's approach towards his political agenda.

As a scripted medium euphemistically known as "sports entertainment," professional wrestling is choreographed and the outcomes of matches are predetermined. To put it another way, for purposes of remaining consistent with Trump's frequently uttered description of the mainstream media, professional wrestling is "fake." Wrestlers create intriguing characters with colorful personalities that they portray onscreen, as they engage in scripted and rehearsed storyline "feuds" with one another. Thus, professional wrestling deliberately creates an alternate reality in which its workers exist and perform for the entertainment of fans. This alternate reality (known in wrestling parlance as *kayfabe*) blurs the boundary between truth and fantasy while stoking fans' passions and, sometimes, prejudices. Cilliza notes:

> This basic divide [in wrestling] between fake and real is what Trump capitalizes on … there isn't a more attentive media consumer than Donald Trump. He watches cable TV constantly—as evidenced by the installation of a 60-plus inch TV in his dining room near the Oval Office.… Most people—particularly in the media know this fact. But lots of other people, including many of Trump's supporters, truly believe he hates the media. That he is the fighter against "fake news" they have been waiting for their entire lives. They don't get that Trump is playing a role, that he is doing a schtick because he knows there is political gain to be had there.… If Trump was running the WWE, he would create a wrestler who was a reporter. That character—call him Clark Can't—would have gone to Harvard, would work for CNN or *The New York Times*, would wear glasses, and would spend the time before each match lecturing the crowd about how they need to be more politically correct. In truth, the character would likely be a huge success as a villain.[101]

While Trump's staged hatred of the mainstream media might be reminiscent of the kayfabe found in professional wrestling, so too is another aspect of Trump's political demeanor that is arguably far more sinister and dangerous in its potential real-life consequences. As mentioned above, the gimmick of the intimidating, evil, menacing foreigner who espouses anti–American sentiments and seeks to inflict suffering on good-natured, all-American *babyfaces* (pro wrestling slang for the popular "heroes" or "good guys" whom the spectators cheer) is one of the oldest and most widely-utilized tropes in professional wrestling programming. Such characters—from Nikolai Volkoff's pro-communist Soviet loyalties and The Iron Sheik's pro–Iranian/anti–American fanaticism of the 1980s to Muhammad Hassan's implied affiliation with Islamic terrorists in the early 2000s—serve a direct purpose: to enrage fans and arouse strong negative reactions from them (often in the form of deafening "U-S-A!" chants) by embodying the absolute worst of popular stereotypes about the respective identity being portrayed. Trump's continual assertion of alternative facts about Mexican and Muslim immigrants, which allude to alleged criminal inclinations and grossly inflate the extent of illegal immigration and the propensity for terrorism by Muslim refugees, is reminiscent of professional wrestling promoters who peddle negative stereotypical constructions of foreign and ethnic minority heels to arouse the wrath of their fanbase. Like enticing spectators to jeer a foreign heel at a WWE event, Trump routinely and deliberately prompts throngs of supporters at campaign rallies to erupt into choruses of boos and thunderous chants of "Build the Wall!" and "U-S-A!" at the slightest mention of his respective foreign heels—"Mexican illegal aliens" and "Muslim refugee terrorists."

The major difference, of course, is that Sam Polinsky and Vince McMahon are strictly entertainers who freely acknowledge that their occupation—professional wrestling—is a scripted and rehearsed artform. Their words and actions do not carry political authority, and they are in no position to implement public policy. Donald Trump, on the other hand, is the president of the United States, the leader of the free world, and the international face of the nation. The alternate reality he seeks to create through continual use of alternative facts is not confined to a wrestling arena; it carries real-life ramifications. Such ramifications include, among other things, Trump supporters potentially acting out their enflamed passions in acts of incivility or worse towards others—such as occurred when a Trump supporter told Mexican American journalist Jorge Ramos, a naturalized U.S. citizen, to "get out of my country!" after a testy exchange between Ramos and Trump at an August 2015 rally in Iowa.[102] Also in August 2015, two white men beat up and urinated on a 58-year-old Mexican man in Boston, whom they suspected of being an undocumented immigrant.[103] Although the victim was a permanent resident and thus a legal immigrant, the perpetrators told police, "Donald Trump was right: All these illegals need to be deported."[104]

Lest Trump's targeted criticism of "Mexicans" be limited to undocumented immigrants, Trump also garnered significant media attention in the spring of 2016 when he repeatedly accused federal judge Gonzalo P. Curiel of harboring an inherently anti–Trump bias in the Trump University class-action lawsuit case because "he's a Mexican" and, therefore, naturally opposes Trump because of Trump's tough stance on illegal immigration—even though Curiel is an American citizen who was born in Indiana.[105] Ironically, Trump's assertions that Curiel's Mexican American heritage precluded his ability to treat Trump impartially occurred in the midst of Trump posting an infamous Cinco de Mayo 2016 tweet declaring his love for "Hispanics." The tweet consisted of a photograph of a smiling Trump giving a thumbs-up gesture to the camera, as he prepares to eat a taco salad at his desk in Trump Tower.[106] The tweet's text read "Happy #CincoDeMayo! The best taco bowls are made in Trump Tower Grill. I love Hispanics!"[107] This tweet turned out to be an alternative fact in its own right, as the Trump Tower Grill does not offer taco bowls on its menu.[108]

On a much more serious note, Trump's attempt to conflate a U.S.-born citizen of Mexican descent with Mexico and illegal immigration demonstrates a disturbing willingness to "other" individuals different from himself. The allegations of an inherently biased Mexican American professional followed almost a year of non-stop Trumpian alternative facts regarding Mexico and Mexican migration. As Jia Tolentino of *The New Yorker* points out, "By 2016, the label 'Mexican' had taken on such a *mythologically* corrupt quality for Trump that it could be used as an aspersion on an American judge—a racist shorthand that, for many of Trump's supporters, made total sense."[109]

Notes

1. Michelle Ye Hee Lee, "Donald Trump's False Comments Connecting Mexican Immigrants and Crime," *Washington Post*, 8 July 2015, https://www.washingtonpost.com/news/fact-checker/wp/2015/07/08/donald-trumps-false-comments-connecting-mexican-immigrants-a nd-crime/?utm_term=.ecc36c8b1d38 (21 July 2017).

2. Alexandra Jaffe, "Kellyanne Conway: WH Spokesman Gave 'Alternative Facts' on Inauguration Crowd," NBCNews.com, 22 January 2017, http://www.nbcnews.com/meet-the-press/wh-spokesman-gave-alternative-facts-inauguration-crowd-n710466 (21 July 2017).

3. Elizabeth Kadetsky, "Bashing Illegals in California," *The Nation*, 17 October 1994, 419.

4. Leo R. Chavez, *Shadowed Lives: Undocumented Immigrants in American Society*, 2d ed. (Orlando: Harcourt Brace, 1998), 191.

5. Chavez, *Shadowed Lives*, 193.

6. Chavez, *Shadowed Lives*, 193.

7. "Massey Study Shows Rapid Loss of Spanish Among Mexican Immigrants in the United States," *Princeton.edu*, 13 September 2006, https://www.princeton.edu/news/2006/09/13/massey-study-shows-rapid-loss-spanish-language-among-mexican-immigrants-united (21 July 2017).

8. Leo R. Chavez, *The Latino Threat: Constructing Immigrants, Citizens, and the Nation* (Stanford: Stanford University Press, 2008), 2–4.

9. Chavez, *The Latino Threat*, 2–4.

10. Samuel P. Huntington, *Who Are We? The Challenges to America's National Identity* (New York: Simon & Schuster Paperbacks, 2004), 226–227.

11. Huntington, *Who Are We?*, 239–241.

12. Wendy Wang, "The Rise of Intermarriage," *Pew Research Center*, 16 February 2012, http://www.pewsocialtrends.org/2012/02/16/the-rise-of-intermarriage/ (21 July 2017).

13. Kristen Bialik, "Key Facts About Race and Marriage, 50 Years After Loving v. Virginia," *PewResearch.org*, 12 June 2017, http://www.pewresearch.org/fact-tank/2017/06/12/key-facts-about-race-and-marriage-50-years-after-loving-v-virginia/ (21 July 2017).

14. Bialik, "Key Facts About Race and Marriage."

15. Ann Coulter, *¡Adios, America! The Left's Plan to Turn Our Country into a Third World Hellhole* (Washington, D.C.: Regnery, 2015), 6.

16. Gregory Reid, "The Republican Party's White Strategy," *The Atlantic*, July/August 2016, https://www.theatlantic.com/magazine/archive/2016/07/the-white-strategy/485612/ (21 July 2017).

17. Reid, "The Republican Party's White Strategy."

18. Reid, "The Republican Party's White Strategy."

19. "Real Time with Bill Maher: Ann Coulter on Immigration (HBO)," YouTube.com, 19 June 2015, https://www.youtube.com/watch?v=tW0GowO_MaM (21 July 2017).

20. "Real Time with Bill Maher: Overtime—June 19, 2015 (HBO)," YouTube.com, 19 June 2015, https://www.youtube.com/watch?v=0–2uSG1xUEg (21 July 2017).

21. Nick Corasaniti, "Donald Trump Releases Plan to Combat Illegal Immigration," *The New York Times*, 16 August 2015, https://www.nytimes.com/2015/08/17/us/politics/trump-releases-plan-to-combat-illegal-immigration.html?hp&action=click&pgtype=Homepage&module=first-column-region&region=top-news&WT.nav=top-news&_r=0 (21 July 2017).

22. Julie Beck, "This Article Won't Change Your Mind," *The Atlantic*, 13 March 2017, https://www.theatlantic.com/science/archive/2017/03/this-article-wont-change-your-mind/519093/ (21 July 2017).

23. Gleb Tsipursky, "Sometimes, Facts Can Actually Trump Ideology," *Scientific American*, 19 May 2017, https://blogs.scientificamerican.com/observations/sometimes-facts-can-actually-trump-ideology/ (21 July 2017).

24. Tsipursky, "Sometimes, Facts Can Actually Trump Ideology."

25. Carroll Doherty, "5 Facts About Trump Supporters' Views of Immigration," *PewResearch.org*, 25 August 2016, http://www.pewresearch.org/fact-tank/2016/08/25/5-facts-about-trump-supporters-views-of-immigration/ (21 July 2017).

26. John Gramlich, "Trump Voters Want to Build the Wall, but Are More Divided on Other Immigration Questions," *PewResearch.org*, 29 November 2016, http://www.pewresearch.org/fact-tank/2016/11/29/trump-voters-want-to-build-the-wall-but-are-more-divided-on-other-immigration-questions/ (21 July 2017).

27. Gramlich, "Trump Voters Want to Build the Wall."

28. Gramlich, "Trump Voters Want to Build the Wall."

29. Gramlich, "Trump Voters Want to Build the Wall."

30. Doherty, "5 Facts About Trump Supporters' Views of Immigration."

31. Taegan Goddard, "2016 Republicans are Completely Ignoring the Lessons of Their 2012 'Autopsy,'" TheHill.com, 1 June 2015, http://theweek.com/articles/557753/2016-republicans-are-completely-ignoring-lessons-2012-autopsy (21 July 2017).

32. David A. Fahrenthold, "Trump Driving Migrant Debate Among GOP Field," *Washington Post*, 17 August 2015, https://www.washingtonpost.com/politics/with-trumps-rise-hard-line-immigration-ideas-take-hold-in-gop/2015/08/17/85dbbf3e-4506-11e5-846d-02792f854297_story.html (21 July 2017).

33. Fahrenthold, "Trump Driving Migrate Debate Among GOP Field."

34. Janell Ross, "The Myth of the 'Anchor Baby' Deportation Defense," *Washington Post*, 20 August 2015, https://www.washingtonpost.com/news/the-fix/wp/2015/08/20/the-myth-of-the-anchor-baby-deportation-defense/?utm_term=.0ed663c12b7d (21 July 2017).

35. Rebecca Kaplan, "Bobby Jindal: 'Immigration Without Assimilation is Invasion,'" CBSNews.com, 20 August 2015, http://www.cbsnews.com/news/bobby-jindal-immigration-without-assimilation-is-invasion/ (21 July 2017).

36. Fahrenthold, "Trump Driving Migrant Debate Among GOP Field."

37. Daniel Politi, "Donald Trump in Phoenix: Mexicans Are 'Taking Our Jobs' and 'Killing Us,'" Slate.com, 12 July 2015, http://www.slate.com/blogs/the_slatest/2015/07/12/donald_trump_in_phoenix_mexicans_are_taking_our_jobs_and_killing_us.html (21 July 2017).

38. Rick Wilking, "Trump Proposes Ways to Make Mexico Pay for Immigrants," *CBSNews*.com, 1 August 2015, http://www.cbsnews.com/news/donald-trump-border-wall-immigration-plan-mexico-pay/ (21 July 2017).

39. Spanish for "men."

40. David Agren, "'Bad Hombres': Reports Claim Trump Spoke of Sending Troops to Mexico," TheGuardian.com, 1 February 2017, https://www.theguardian.com/us-news/2017/feb/02/bad-hombres-reports-claim-trump-threatened-to-send-troops-to-mexico (21 July 2017).

41. Maya Rhodan, "Donald Trump Raises Eyebrows with 'Bad Hombres' Line," Time.com, 19 October 2016, http://time.com/4537847/donald-trump-bad-hombres/ (21 July 2017).

42. Daniella Diaz, "Pence to Kaine: 'You Whipped Out that Mexican Thing Again,'" CNN.com, 5 October 2016, http://www.cnn.com/2016/10/05/politics/mike-pence-mexican-thing-time-kaine-vp-debate/index.html (21 July 2017).

43. Jeffrey S. Passel and D'Vera Cohn, "Overall Number of U.S. Unauthorized Immigrants Holds Steady Since 2009," *PewHispanic.org*, 20 September 2016, http://www.pewhispanic.org/2016/09/20/overall-number-of-u-s-unauthorized-immigrants-holds-steady-since-2009/ (21 July 2017).

44. Passel and Cohn, "Overall Number of U.S. Unauthorized Immigrants Holds Steady Since 2009."

45. Ana Gonzalez-Barrera, "More Mexicans Leaving than Coming to the U.S.," *PewHispanic.org*, November 19, 2015, http://www.pewhispanic.org/2015/11/19/more-mexicans-leaving-than-coming-to-the-u-s/.

46. Gonzalez-Barrera, "More Mexicans Leaving than Coming to the U.S."

47. Gonzalez-Barrera, "More Mexicans Leaving than Coming to the U.S."

48. Ana Gonzalez-Barrera, "Apprehensions of Mexican Migrants at U.S. Borders Reach Near-Historic Low," *PewResearch.org*, 14 April 2016, http://www.pewresearch.org/fact-tank/2016/04/14/mexico-us-border-apprehensions/ (21 July 2017).

49. Hansi Lo Wang, "Mexicans No Longer Make Up Majority of Immigrants in U.S. Illegally," *NPR.org*, 25 April 2017, http://www.npr.org/sections/thetwo-way/2017/04/25/525563818/mexicans-no-longer-make-up-majority-of-immigrants-in-u-s-illegally (21 July 2017).

50. Gonzalez-Barrera, "More Mexicans Leaving than Coming to the U.S."

51. Passel and Cohn, "Overall Number of U.S. Unauthorized Immigrants Holds Steady Since 2009."

52. Phippen J. Weston, "Asians Now Outpace Mexicans in Terms of Undocumented Growth," *The Atlantic*, 20 August 2015, https://www.theatlantic.com/politics/archive/2015/08/asians-now-outpace-mexicans-in-terms-of-undocumented-growth/432603/ (21 July 2017).

53. Hansi Lo Wang, "How America's Idea of Illegal Immigration Doesn't Always Match Reality," *NPR.org*, 8 March 2017, http://www.npr.org/sections/thetwo-way/2017/03/08/51756 1046/how-americas-idea-of-illegal-immigration-doesnt-always-match-reality (21 July 2017).

54. Wang, "How America's Idea of Illegal Immigration Doesn't Always Match Reality."

55. Wang, "How America's Idea of Illegal Immigration Doesn't Always Match Reality."

56. John Cassidy, "The Facts About Immigration," *The New Yorker*, 31 March 2017, http://www.newyorker.com/news/john-cassidy/the-facts-about-immigration (21 July 2017).

57. Cassidy, "The Facts About Immigration."

58. Gonzalez-Barrera, "More Mexicans Leaving than Coming to the U.S."

59. Wilking, "Trump Proposes Ways to Make Mexico Pay for Immigrants." CBSNews.com.

60. David Bier, "A Wall Is an Impractical, Expensive, and Ineffective Border Plan," *Cato.org*, 28 November 2016, https://www.cato.org/blog/border-wall-impractical-expensive-ineffective-plan (21 July 2017).

61. Anna Brand, "Trump Puts a Price on His Wall: It Would Cost Mexico $8 Billion," MSNBC.com, 9 February 2016, http://www.msnbc.com/msnbc/donald-trump-says-his-wall-would-cost-8-billion (21 July 2017).

62. Brand, "Trump Puts a Price on His Wall."

63. Wilking, "Trump Proposes Ways to Make Mexico Pay for Immigrants."

64. Philip Bump, "Donald Trump's Mexico Border Wall Will Be as High as 55 Feet, According to Donald Trump," *Washington Post*, 26 February 2016, https://www.washingtonpost.com/the-fix/wp/2016/02/26/so-how-high-will-donald-trumps-wall-be-an-investigation/?utm_term=.c636c3515741 (21 July 2017).

65. Bump, "Donald Trump's Mexico Border Wall Will Be as High as 55 Feet."

66. Philip Bump, "The Initial Estimate is Here: Trump's Wall Will Cost More Than a Year of the Space Program," *Washington Post*, 10 February 2017, https://www.washingtonpost.com/news/politics/wp/2017/02/10/the-initial-estimate-is-here-trumps-wall-will-cost-more-than-a-year-of-the-space-program/?utm_term=.d973316f10b9 (21 July 2017).

67. Ron Nixon, "Border Wall Could Cost 3 Times Estimates, Senate Democrats' Report Says," *The New York Times*, 18 April 2017, https://www.nytimes.com/2017/04/18/us/politics/senate-democrats-border-wall-cost-trump.html (21 July 2017).

68. Bump, "The Initial Estimate Is Here."

69. Wilking, "Trump Proposes Way to Make Mexico Pay for Immigrants."

70. Ross, "The Myth of the 'Anchor Baby' Deportation Defense."

71. Ross, "The Myth of the 'Anchor Baby' Deportation Defense."

72. Pamela Constable, "For Illegal Immigrants with Babies, the Anchor Pulls in Many Directions," *Washington Post*, 20 September 2015, https://www.washingtonpost.com/local/social-issues/for-illegal-immigrants-with-babies-the-anchor-pulls-in-many-directions/2015/09/20/d5d7a2f0–570d-11e5-b8c9–944725fcd3b9_story.html?utm_term=.8466e5710558 (21 July 2017).

73. Constable, "For Illegal Immigrants with Babies."

74. Reena Flores, "Donald Trump: 'Anchor Babies' Aren't American Citizens," CBSNews.com, 19 August 2015, https://www.cbsnews.com/news/donald-trump-anchor-babies-arent-american-citizens/ (21 July 2017).

75. Constable, "For Illegal Immigrants with Babies."

76. Jeffrey S. Passel and D'Vera Cohn, "Number of Babies Born in U.S. to Unauthorized Immigrants Declines," *PewResearch.org*, 11 September 2015, http://www.pewresearch.org/fact-tank/2015/09/11/number-of-babies-born-in-u-s-to-unauthorized-immigrants-declines/ (21 July 2017).

77. Passel and Cohn, "Number of Babies Born in U.S. to Unauthorized Immigrants Declines."

78. Constable, "For Illegal Immigrants with Babies."

79. Constable, "For Illegal Immigrants with Babies."

80. Ross, "The Myth of the 'Anchor Baby' Deportation Defense."

81. Ross, "The Myth of the 'Anchor Baby' Deportation Defense."

82. Rick Newman, "5 Trump Myths About Illegal Immigration," Yahoo.com, 23 February 2017, https://finance.yahoo.com/news/5-trump-myths-about-illegal-immigration-193622157.html (21 July 2017).

83. Heather Haddon, "Donald Trump Says Immigrant Deportations Done in Two Years," *Wall Street Journal*, 11 September 2015, https://blogs.wsj.com/washwire/2015/09/11/donald-trump-says-immigrant-deportations-done-in-two-years/ (21 July 2017).

84. Tom LoBianco, "Donald Trump Promises 'Deportation Force' to Remove 11 Million," CNN.com, 12 November 2015, http://www.cnn.com/2015/11/11/politics/donald-trump-deportation-force-debate-immigration/index.html (21 July 2017).

85. LoBianco, "Donald Trump Promises 'Deportation Force' to Remove 11 Million."

86. Ian Salisbury, "The Insane Numbers Behind Trump's Deportation Plan," Time.com, 14 November 2016, http://time.com/money/4566401/trumps-deportation-immigration-plan-numbers/ (21 July 2017).

87. Salisbury, "The Insane Numbers Behind Trump's Deportation Plan."

88. Ron Nixon, "Job One at Homeland Security Under Trump: Immigration," *The New York Times*, 13 July 2017, https://www.nytimes.com/2017/07/13/us/politics/dhs-immigration-trump.html (21 July 2017).

89. Nixon, "Job One at Homeland Security Under Trump: Immigration."

90. Nixon, "Job One at Homeland Security Under Trump: Immigration."

91. Eric Adelson, "How President Donald Trump Led to a Wrestler Becoming the Most Reviled Man in Mexico," *Yahoo Sports*, 15 June 2017, https://president-donald-trump-led-wrestler-becoming-reviled-man-mexico-191510838.html (21 July 2017).

92. Adelson, "How President Donald Trump Led to a Wrestler Becoming the Most Reviled Man in Mexico."

93. Adelson, "How President Donald Trump Led to a Wrestler Becoming the Most Reviled Man in Mexico."

94. Adelson, "How President Donald Trump Led to a Wrestler Becoming the Most Reviled Man in Mexico."

95. Adelson, "How President Donald Trump Led to a Wrestler Becoming the Most Reviled Man in Mexico."

96. Heather Levi, *The World of Lucha Libre: Secrets, Revelations, and Mexican National Identity* (Durham: Duke University Press, 2008), 177–180.

97. Spanish for "wrestlers."

98. Chris Cillizza, "Why Pro Wrestling Is the Perfect Metaphor for Donald Trump's Presidency," CNN.com, 2 July 2017, http://www.cnn.com/2017/07/02/politics/trump-wrestling-tweet/index.html (21 July 2017).

99. Aaron Oster, "Donald Trump and WWE: How the Road to the White House Began at 'Wrestlemania,'" RollingStone.com, 1 February 2016, http://www.rollingstone.com/sports/features/donald-trump-and-wwe-how-the-road-to-the-white-house-began-at-wrestlemania-20160201 (21 July 2017).

100. Jason Diamond, "WWE's Linda McMahon Approved to Lead Small Business Administration," RollingStone.com, 14 February 2017, http://www.rollingstone.com/sports/news/wwe-linda-mcmahon-joins-trump-administration-small-business-w466987 (21 July 2017).

101. Cillizza, "Why Pro Wrestling is the Perfect Metaphor for Donald Trump's Presidency."

102. Maxwell Tani, "Man at Donald Trump Rally Tells Univision Anchor Jorge Ramos: 'Get Out of My Country,'" *Business Insider*, 26 August 2015, http://www.businessinsider.com/donald-trump-jorge-ramos-get-out-video-2015-8 (21 July 2017).

103. "Boston Men Jailed for Trump-Inspired Hate Crime Attack," Reuters.com, 16 May 2016, http://www.reuters.com/article/us-usa-mexico-beating-idUSKCN0Y805K (21 July 2017).

104. "Boston Men Jailed for Trump-Inspired Hate Crime Attack."

105. Theodore Schleifer, "Trump Defends Criticism of Judge with Mexican Heritage," CNN.com, 5 June 2016, http://www.cnn.com/2016/06/03/politics/donald-trump-tapper-lead/index.html (21 July 2017).

106. Ashley Parker, "Donald Trump's 'Taco Bowl' Message: 'I Love Hispanics,'" *The New York Times*, 5 May 2016, https://www.nytimes.com/politics/first-draft/2016/05/05/donald-trump-taco-bowl/ (21 July 2017).

107. Parker, "Donald Trump's 'Taco Bowl' Message."

108. Parker, "Donald Trump's 'Taco Bowl' Message."

109. Jia Tolentino, "Trump and the Truth: The 'Mexican' Judge," *The New Yorker*, 20 September 2016, http://www.newyorker.com/news/news-desk/trump-and-the-truth-the-mexican-judge (21 July 2017).

The Irony at the Heart
of Fake News
and Alternative Facts

ROBIN BLOM

In 1835, the *New York Sun* published several articles about life on the moon. The fantastic drawings of flying creatures in a landscape full of cascades and caverns were officially discredited more than a century later by Neil Armstrong and Buzz Aldrin. However, the skeptics have been loud and clear: That moon landing was also fake. Labeled as a hoax and fraudulent before, nowadays, those same doubters would probably describe the press coverage of the Apollo 11 mission as fake news or propose alternative facts about what *actually* happened.[1]

The terms "fake news" and "alternative facts" have become staples in the political lexicon to explain away any type of negative and inconvenient information after being mentioned numerous times by Donald Trump and family members,[2] his counselor Kellyanne Conway,[3] other campaign officials,[4] and White House press secretaries[5] as well as others associated with the Trump administration[6] and supportive right-wing media organizations.[7]

Trump's first tweet with a reference to "fake news" was posted a few weeks after the 2016 presidential elections.[8] Another month later, there was a second tweet—in all caps—with that term ("FAKE NEWS—A TOTAL POLITICAL WITCH HUNT!"),[9] which he has since mentioned over 300 times on Twitter as of December 2018, in addition to numerous other occasions. The other phrase, "alternative facts," became a prominent expression around the same time, after Kellyanne Conway used it to defend White House Press Secretary Sean Spicer's false statement about the attendance numbers at the presidential inauguration.[10]

Both terms are a bit of a misnomer. Much news content does not consist of hoaxes nor fiction, although they can still contain falsehoods: a news story could be exclusively dedicated to a tweet that is one big lie, which does not make the news automatically false because the tweet is real. For instance, several news outlets around the world, such as *Politico*[11] and *The Independent*,[12] have reported on Trump's vaccination tweets for which there is no medical evidence substantiating his claims (e.g., "Healthy young child goes to doctor, gets pumped with massive shot of many vaccines, doesn't feel good and changes—AUTISM. Many such cases!").[13]

By mentioning the content of the tweet in stories about vaccination conspiracy theories, the press (and, ironically, this essay) disseminated misinformation—more or less the journalistic version of collateral damage. A report with a source making the case that vaccines are safe and a source claiming the opposite is—by default—not fully representing the truth, especially when those claims are balanced in news reports when in actuality an overwhelming amount of scientists and other experts support one position over others. This exhibits a classic zero-sum game: when one position is true, the opposing positions are certainly wrong—although people in denial of the truth may adhere to different explanations and interpretations of that.[14]

The real irony is that the debate about a piece of "fake news" and "alternative facts" is not much different than the discussion about a piece of truthful news and the actual facts, except that some parties agreeing or disagreeing with the report are reversed. That is because many citizens, armed with motivated skepticism and other types of cognitive biases, will find ways to denounce (and, in their mind, debunk) factual information that is different from their beliefs or, at least, inconvenient for a narrative that they want to maintain. Such cognitive dissonance makes clinging onto falsehoods and denialism very expedient options.[15]

Groups of people divided on partisan lines—but not necessarily on political party lines—are disputing all kinds of factual information each day. Even worse, as James Kuklinski pointed out, the public holds "grossly inaccurate factual beliefs but confidently assume to know the facts."[16] That phenomenon led Kahan and colleagues to conclude that there is a culture war in America about "facts, not values."[17] In that battle, sticking to alternative facts is the new way of saying, "I'm definitely right and you are not" with the regrettable twist that many of the parties involved in that debate cannot fathom that they are actually in the wrong. Even when the parties may agree at times on the facts underlying a debate, they have different explanations for those facts, which is still undesirable: "widespread misinformation can lead to collective preferences that are far different from those that would exist if people were correctly informed."[18]

This essay focuses on the different levels of political knowledge among partisans in the United States as well as motivations for people to counter-argue information that opposed their world views rather than aiming for being rightly informed. This motivated skepticism explains to a large extent why large groups of people accept different types of false information as factual, but also how it influences what types of news sources are trusted and distrusted. Yet, those two aspects—(dis)trust perceptions of messages as well as the messengers—do not arise in a vacuum. They are interconnected and, only occasionally, lead people to believe news reports from highly distrusted sources. Yet, this indicates that the actual facts are only accepted in certain situations and, as a result, blame or praise toward particular news sources is frequently inconsistent and paradoxical. Hence, the designations of "fake news" and "alternative facts" are often an indication of personal preference rather than an objective evaluation of a message and its source.

Being Misinformed

As a junior senator from Illinois, Barack Obama was anticipating tough election debates about numerous social and economic issues after announcing his bid for the presidency. But he had not fully expected that a tiny biographical detail—his birthplace—would become a hot-button topic during his two-year run for office, let alone that his American citizenship would be contested well after he was inaugurated as the 44th president of the United States.

About three years later, in April 2011, Obama provided a copy of his original long-form birth certificate to the public. It stated that he was born at Honolulu's Kapiolani Hospital on August 4, 1961. "We do not have time for this kind of silliness. We've got better stuff to do. I've got better stuff to do," the president said, visibly irritated, during a press conference about the claim that he was born abroad and, conceivably even more, for the extensive press coverage the accusation received. Nonetheless, Obama had hoped that the release of the copy of his birth certificate would put an end to the persistent rumors.[19]

It did not.

Donald Trump took credit for forcing Obama to release his birth certificate yet continued to claim that Obama was born outside the United States. "An 'extremely credible source' has called my office and told me that @BarackObama's birth certificate is a fraud," he assured his followers on Twitter.[20] Others have also suggested for years that there was "evidence" of fraud. They argued that the document was fabricated and, thus, could not be a copy of an original birth certificate. These accusations quickly found their way around the country and the rest of the world through the Internet.[21]

Several public opinion polls indicated that about one out of six U.S. adults were still unconvinced that Obama was born in Honolulu, or any other place in the United States. Even though this was a decrease from the 27 percent that did not believe him a year earlier, this dispute made one thing very clear: at least two out of ten Americans were wrong on the issue. That percentage could have been even higher—about 80 percent—but only when critics had been able to prove that Obama was born outside of Hawaii, which has yet to happen.[22]

Regardless, the "Birther Conspiracy," as it was known, demonstrated that large groups of people were motivated to counter-argue facts that were inconvenient and disseminate alternative theories about the alleged false paperwork. This has been similar to people claiming that the moon landing footage was recorded in a Hollywood film studio and directed by Stanley Kubrick.[23] Not only that, someone watching the broadcast in Australia claimed to have seen a Coca-Cola bottle as part of the live footage—allegedly indicating a staged recording.[24]

There will always be people believing information that is false and reject information that is true, especially in the current "post-fact" political climate in which homogeneous communities promote rumor, misinformation, propaganda, and disinformation on social media that foster all kinds of speculation, guesswork, and hearsay.[25] As a result, many people still claim that Barack Obama has been a devout Muslim (in addition to the claim that he was born abroad), the U.S. government orchestrated the 9/11 attacks, and Osama Bin Laden was not killed during a raid of a villa in Abbottabad, Pakistan. Also add in the aforementioned fake moon landing, Bigfoot, Paul McCartney's death, Elvis faking his own death, and, in recent times, #PizzaGate, and you have a long list of popular mystery cases that will be investigated for eternity. *The X-Files* come to life.

Yet, this is not to suggest that alternative facts are solely part of conversations about conspiracy theories. Polarizing political climates also fuel an information environment that disguises hoaxes and fabrications as valid information sources to rally likeminded individuals and, potentially, convert nonbelievers in regards to a variety of public affairs. The result is a myriad of falsehoods and omissions of facts that underlie public debates that should, fundamentally, be aimed at solving eminent social issues.

There have been many examples of citizens being skeptical about important political facts. For instance, the invasions of Iraq and Afghanistan in the early 2000s have led to much confusion about whether weapons of mass destruction have been found; the number of allied casualties during those wars; and the alleged role of the Saddam Hussein administration in plotting the 9/11 attacks.[26] Similar knowledge discrepancies have been noticed on domestic affairs as well. For example, there has been much confusion about the direction of important economic indicators, such as inflation and unemployment levels.[27] Additionally, many people have been misinformed about the proportion of the federal budget that has been spent on foreign aid,[28] roll call voting of members of Congress,[29] and social security.[30]

These examples indicated that most people were not necessarily uninformed about important issues in their personal environment or somewhere else on the planet (i.e., they were aware that the issues existed), but it has become clear that many citizens are not accepting all vital details surrounding those matters of public concern to be true when they are.[31]

As Delli Carpini and Keeter elegantly explained, "Political information is to democratic politics what money is to economics: it is the currency of citizenship."[32] Additionally, citizens need access to factual information and, equally important, must use it to make decisions about public policies: "They must absorb and apply the facts to overcome areas of ignorance or to correct mistaken conceptions. The more facts they bring to bear, the better, and some facts are always better than no facts. What is crucial is that preferences stem from facts, objective data about the world."[33]

Alternative Explanations

It is not necessarily a surprise that "alternative facts" are deemed the actual facts by large groups of people, because overall levels of political knowledge are low in the United States.[34] Bartels even declared that political ignorance is "one of the best-documented features of contemporary politics."[35] In some sense, the lack of knowledge about public affairs is somewhat understandable, because most critical social issues are so complex that they require advanced skills and comprehension of data processing from a variety of disciplines as well as a well-rounded understanding of scientific inquiry. In general, such literacy is minimal among the U.S. population. Only a small minority grasps the basic vocabulary of scientific terms and research protocols.[36] For instance, Stamm, Clark, and Eblacas surveyed adults in the Seattle metropolitan area about their knowledge of global warming and found that misconceptions were widespread. Many participants knew little about causes, consequences, and potential solutions for global warming—even though they were very well aware that the problem existed as they had been exposed to a great deal of information discussing the subject for years. News consumption, in this case, did not lead to increased knowledge for all people.[37]

The same has been the case for many other scientific topics, including the alleged link that measles-mumps-rubella (MMR) vaccinations for young children increase the odds for them to become autistic at later age. The unsubstantiated claims were made in a 1988 peer-reviewed journal article,[38] which was later denounced by several co-authors of the manuscript and eventually retracted by the editorial board of *The Lancet*. Nonetheless, many parents have decided not to immunize their children after publication of the article and the subsequent press coverage that alerted people all around the world that there may have been a problem. This led to an increase in vaccine-preventable diseases and, in some cases, young children passing away. In addition, large sums of money were needed for follow-up research and information campaigns to correct the misperceptions that existed among the public.[39] In this last example, there are essentially two camps: one claims the vaccines cause autism and the other claims that vaccines are not to blame. The partisan groups simply disagreed on the facts.

Yet, there have been occasions that partisan groups agreed on the facts and had different explanations for those facts. For instance, Gaines and colleagues found that Democrats were more likely to interpret the lack of weapons of mass destruction found after the invasion of Iraq as evidence that the Weapons of Mass Destruction (WMD) were not there in the first place, whereas Republicans were more likely to argue that the WMD must have been moved or destroyed, or that the weapons are still out there to be found. The researchers, therefore, concluded that "partisan groups differed considerably in how they mapped casual beliefs into interpretations."[40]

Motivated Skepticism

Several studies have found that partisans remember more information when it supported their side rather than that it contradicted their position.[41] Therefore, Turner initially expected that liberals would remember more arguments made in a news segment attributed to a news source that was perceived as having a liberal perspective (e.g., CNN) than when the news source was perceived as having a conservative perspective (e.g., Fox News), and vice versa for conservative voters. However, his data demonstrated the opposite: The participants recalled more information from a news outlet that they considered incongruent with their ideology.[42]

Earlier research demonstrated similar results. For instance, Priester and Petty found that a higher source trustworthiness led to lower message elaboration,[43] and Gillig and Greenwald demonstrated that higher source credibility led to less discounting and counter arguing.[44] Additionally, positive information has usually been cognitively processed less heavily than negative information.[45] The more information is inconsistent with what an individual believes to be true (i.e., the larger the discrepancy between the position argued in a news message statement and one's own position on the issue), the larger the amount of counter-arguing, in particular for overt persuasive attempts to change opinions.[46] This demonstrated that people put more effort in causal reasoning (asking themselves the "why" question) when an outcome is negative, especially when the outcome was unexpected.[47]

Huckfeldt, Johnson, and Spraque pointed out that "attitudes and opinions are resistant, but not invulnerable, to political change,"[48] but after reviewing a large amount of persuasion literature, they concluded that information threatening one's viewpoints or perceived knowledge will likely be highly scrutinized—and, when possible, disregarded. Taber and Lodge, therefore, proposed a model of motivated skepticism that explained such biased information processing: individuals counter-argue contrary arguments and evidence to a much higher extent than supporting messages, if at all, in the latter cases.[49]

To do so, they adopt several strategies to delegitimize opposing messages by identifying flaws in those arguments or their sources. "People can thus defend current beliefs and attitudes against discordant information by some combination of avoiding, disbelieving, misperceiving, forgetting, or misremembering it."[50] This suggests "that a core component of self-serving bias is the differential quantity of cognitive processing given to preference-consistent and preference-inconsistent information."[51] Hence, supporting arguments are usually uncritically accepted, which allows individuals to "arrive at conclusions that they want to arrive at."[52]

This circumvents cognitive dissonance, because there would be no tension between the drive to be accurate and belief perseverance.[53] Such attitude congruency bias is moderated by strength of prior attitudes, which may lead to further issues of polarization as partisan groups with strong attitudes will be more confident in their own positions.[54] This could be accounted for as a sense of closure whereby citizens desire certainty toward the conclusion of an issue that is consistent with their dispositions.[55]

A classic example of cognitive dissonance leading to biased eyewitness accounts was provided by Hastorf and Cantril, who observed that football fans from Dartmouth College and Princeton University disagreed on the amount of infractions on the field. The matchup between the two institutions in 1951 was vicious. Princeton's star player left the game in the second quarter with a broken nose and an opposing player broke his leg in the third quarter. Dartmouth fans argued that their players committed as many infractions as the Princeton team, yet Princeton fans argued that the other team had twice as many infractions. Hence, the supporters from both sides "counted" a particular number of infractions that made their own team look more positive and the other team more negative.[56]

Cognitive bias is not only apparent when it comes to debating sporting events. Even scientists are prone to the same prejudice when it comes to taking side in academic discussions. In an experiment, a sample of scholarly researchers considered studies that confirmed their position on a controversial issue to be of higher quality (e.g., methodological quality and relevance of topic) than papers that did not confirm their position, especially among scientist that had strong beliefs on the issue.[57]

To avoid dissonance in the political realm, partisan motivations often prevail over accuracy and many people do not want "further information to disturb the images and opinions that they had already formed."[58] For example, capital punishment proponents argued that a study abstract in support of their viewpoint was better conducted and contained more believable evidence than an abstract that discredited their position. This belief was reversed for opponents of the death penalty. When asked whether respondents had changed their overall opinion on the issue, three-quarters of them demonstrated further attitude polarization rather than ambivalence or moderation (only 6 percent depolarized), while the two abstracts contained mixed data.[59]

In a replication of this study, it became apparent that when there was balance in the pro and con statements, participants were overall resistant to change toward the opposite position of their initial opinion. More specifically, this process did not deter participants from choosing the one study supporting their prior beliefs as more convincing than the other. Both groups accepted evidence that validated its position at face value and regarded the other piece of lesser value.[60]

The latter two studies did not manipulate source identification or strength, while Cook speculated that higher persuasiveness by trusted sources over distrusted sources could be explained by a difference in the amount of counter arguing that is stimulated by the level of source credibility: the number of rebuttals would decline when source credibility increases. He found that decreased counter arguing mediated the attitude change that was caused by the level of source credibility.[61] This was what Turner, whose work was mentioned at the beginning of this section, also concluded after all: liberals barely counter-argued news segments attributed to CNN or when it was not attributed to a news source, but considerably questioned the same footage when attributed to Fox News. Similarly, conservatives barely counter-argued news segments attributed to Fox News or when it is not attributed to a news source, but considerably questioned the same footage when attributed to CNN. Contrarily, political moderates did not differ in the number of counterarguments for those news networks.[62]

Expectancy Violations

Source affiliation is an important aspect in assessing the believability of each story. If *USA Today* would report that "global warming is based on faulty science and manipulated data" (which is what Donald Trump tweeted in November 2012),[63] readers will rely on their prior knowledge about science in general and climate change specifically as well as their knowledge about the newspaper—either through personal experiences or third-person accounts (e.g., commentators on talk radio or news networks talking about the credibility and trustworthiness of USA Today). And eventually, all readers will determine for themselves to what degree they believe the news story.

The same process—focusing on a combination of the source and the content—is true when a commentator of a liberal-leaning news network (let's say Rachel Maddow of MSNBC) claims that White House Press Secretary Sean Spicer lied about the attendance figures of this year's inauguration. For staunch Hillary Clinton supporters, the assessment is probably fairly simple: the message sounds about right ("Obama had more people in attendance") and the source is likely deemed favorable. But what if that same information was coming from one of the commentators of Fox News—let's say Laura Ingraham, Tucker Carlson, Sean Hannity, or Jesse Watters. The Clinton supporters would probably still agree with the message opposing Sean Spicer. But simultaneously, they would have to agree with a news source that they usually distrust, as it would be very rare that they agree with any commentary coming from that network. But it would not take long to clear any state of cognitive dissonance: the sheer distrust of Fox News now suddenly becomes its biggest asset in determining the validity of the claim that the administration is lying about the attendance figures. The potential rationale of this hypothetical scenario could be "Even Fox News says it's false, so it really must be false!" (In fact, Fox News Channel did report just that by publishing an Associated Press fact check story on its website.)[64]

People make attribution decisions like these every day: Is the smiling salesperson really friendly? Or is it a clever trick to boost sales? Most people would probably think the latter and may not take all recommendations from the welcoming salesperson at face value.[65] However, the reaction may be different when people say something unexpectedly, such as manufacturers revealing negative side effects of their products, scientists pointing out limitations of their research, or politicians taking issue positions that are different from their party's platform.[66]

In those cases, through the expectancy violations, we learned something new: the manufacturers, scientists, and politicians were arguing against their self-interest. This likely enhanced their believability as the honest disclosures could have negative consequences, for instance not selling products, fewer people taking the study results seriously, or lower campaign contributions. Hence, the message recipient may trust that the information from those sources to be true because of the authentic admissions.[67]

To provide additional empirical evidence for that proposition, Blom attributed a headline about an environmental topic to either CNN or Fox News and found that an interaction between source trust and the extent to which a person was surprised or unsurprised about the content of a news headline predicted the level of believability for that headline.[68] The results were similar in a follow-up study with illegal immigration as the topic of the headline.[69] This was also the case when headlines about religious topics were attributed to the Religion News Service and the *Washington Post*[70] as well as the Christian Broadcast Network.[71]

There is also anecdotal evidence for this phenomenon in Trump's own Twitterverse. Whereas he often has made mentions of the "failing New York Times"[72] in his online posts to argue that negative news reports about him were allegedly inaccurate of fabricated, he eagerly linked to *The New York Times* reports that were positive for him during the presidential campaign. In fact, occasionally, his tweets even contain some praise: "Such a nice article in the New York Times about a wonderful developer, Arthur Zeckendorf."[73] Similarly, Trump retweeted a link to a CBS News story that supposedly contained positive information about the tax cuts he had signed into law.[74] Yet, when news networks provide negative coverage about him, they were considered the "enemy of the American People!"[75]

Conclusion

This essay has examined the role of motivated skepticism in biased information processing and to what extent highly distrusted sources could be very believable on some occasions, and vice versa. This showed that there is an important relation between source trust and content expectancy. This has become very clear in recent debates about "fake news" and "alternative facts" as well. Yet, the contemporary use of the terms may just reflect situations in which a disliked source says something that is found disagreeable or undesirable, as shown with Donald Trump's own tweets. However, those same sources would suddenly be considered *not so fake* when the content can be agreed upon. No "alternative facts" are needed at such moments.

NOTES

1. Kevin Young, "Moon Shot: Race, a Hoax, and the Birth of Fake News," *The New Yorker*, 21 October 2017, https://www.newyorker.com/books/page-turner/moon-shot-race-a-hoax-and-the-birth-of-fake-news (21 Jan. 2018).

2. Donald J. Trump, Jr., *Twitter* post, 2017, https://twitter.com/donaldjtrumpjr/status/853341481175789571 (15 April 2017).

3. Tessa Berenson, "Kellyanne Conway Said She's 'Never Uttered' the Words 'Fake News.' She Has," 11 October 2017, http://time.com/4977924/kellyanne-conway-said-shes-never-uttered-the-words-fake-news-she-has (21 Jan. 2018).

4. Stephen K. Bannon, *Twitter* post, 2018, https://twitter.com/stevekbannon/status/948609554270564354 (3 Jan. 2018).

5. Marina Fang, "Reporter Challenges Sarah Huckabee Sanders After She Rants About 'Constant Barrage of Fake News,'" *Huffington Post*, 2017, https://www.huffingtonpost.ca/2017/06/27/reporter-challenges-sarah-huckabee-sanders-after-she-rants-about_a_23005163/ (27 June 2017).

6. Michael D. Cohen, *Twitter* post, 2017, https://twitter.com/michaelcohen212/status/897433698404098050 (15 Aug. 2017).

7. Erik Wemple, "Fox News's Sean Hannity Is Suddenly an Expert on Trump and Mueller," *The Washington Post*, March 19, 2018, https://www.washingtonpost.com/blogs/erik-wemple/wp/2018/03/19/fox-newss-sean-hannity-is-suddenly-an-expert-on-trump-and-mueller (20 March 2018).

8. Donald J. Trump, *Twitter* post, 2016, https://twitter.com/realdonaldtrump/status/807588632877998081 (10 Dec. 2016).

9. Donald J. Trump, *Twitter* post, 2017, https://twitter.com/realdonaldtrump/status/818990655418617856 (10 Jan. 2017).

10. Alexandra Jaffe, "Kellyanne Conway: WH Spokesman Gave 'Alternative Facts' on Inauguration Crowd," *NBC News*, 2017, https://www.nbcnews.com/storyline/meet-the-press-70-years/wh-spokesman-gave-alternative-facts-inauguration-crowd-n710466 (22 Jan. 2017).

11. Tara Haelle, "Why Trump's Meeting with RFK Has Scientists Worried," *Politico*, 2017, https://www.politico.com/magazine/story/2017/01/trump-robert-kennedy-jr-vaccines-meeting-autism-214626 (12 Jan. 2017).

12. Katie Foster, "Donald Trump Raises Concern about Autism Myth Used by Anti-Vaccination Campaigners," *The Independent*, 2017, https://www.independent.co.uk/news/world/americas/us-politics/donald-trump-autism-anti-vaccination-vaxxer-myth-injection-health-campaigners-a7580941.html (15 Feb. 2017).

13. Donald. J. Trump, *Twitter* post, 2014, https://twitter.com/realDonaldTrump/status/449525268529815552 (28 March 2014).

14. Maxwell T. Boykoff and Jules M. Boykoff, "Climate Change and Journalistic Norms: A Case-Study of U.S. Mass-Media Coverage," *Geoforum* 38, no. 6 (2007): 1190–1204.

15. Pascal Diethelm and Martin McKee, "Denialism: What It Is and How Should Scientists Respond?" *European Journal of Public Health* 19, no. 1 (2009): 2–4.

16. James H. Kuklinski, "The Limits of Facts in Citizen Decision-Making," *Extensions* 15, no. 2 (2007): 5–8.

17. Dan M. Kahan, Donald Braman, Paul Slovic, John Gastil, and Geoffrey L. Cohen, "The Second National Risk and Culture Study: Making Sense of—and Making Progress in—the American Culture War of Fact," *SSRN*, 2007, https://papers.ssrn.com/abstract=1017189 (26 Sept. 2007).

18. James H. Kuklinski, Paul J. Quirk, Jennifer Jerit, David Schwieder, and Robert F. Rich, "Misinformation and the Currency of Democratic Citizenship," *The Journal of Politics* 62, no. 3 (2000): 790–816.

19. Alan Silverleib, "Obama Releases Original Long-Form Birth Certificate," *CNN*, 2011, http://www.cnn.com/2011/POLITICS/04/27/obama.birth.certificate/index.html (last modified 27 April 2011).

20. Donald J. Trump, *Twitter* post, 2012, https://twitter.com/realdonaldtrump/status/232572505238433794 (6 Aug. 2012).

21. Megan Cassidy, "Sheriff Joe Arpaio Renews Birther Claims about Obama's Birth Certificate," *The Arizona Republic*, 2016, https://www.usatoday.com/story/news/nation-now/2016/12/15/sheriff-joe-arpaio-probe-proves-obama-birth-certificate-fake/95500958 (15 Dec. 2016).

22. CNN Political Unit, "Birth Certificate Eases Most—But Not All—Obama Doubts," *CNN*, 2011, http://politicalticker.blogs.cnn.com/2011/05/06/birth-certificate-eases-most-but-not-all-obama-doubts (6 May 2011).

23. Jacob Stolworthy, "Stanley Kubrick's Daughter Debunks Moon Landing Conspiracy Theory," *The Independent*, 2016, http://www.independent.co.uk/arts-entertainment/films/news/stanley-kubrick-daughter-vivian-kubrick-apollo-11-moon-landing-conspiracy-theory-a7122186.html (6 July 2016).

24. Mary Bennett, David Percy, and Mary Bennet, *Dark Moon: Apollo and the Whistle-Blowers*, 3d ed. (Kempton, IL: Adventures Unlimited Press, 2001).

25. Anthony Perl, Michael Howlett, and M. Ramesh, "Policy-Making and Truthiness: Can Existing Policy Models Cope with Politicized Evidence and Willful Ignorance in a 'Post-Fact' World?" *Policy Sciences* 51, no. 4 (2018): 581–600.

26. Gary C. Jacobson, "Perception, Memory, and Partisan Polarization on the Iraq War," *Political Science Quarterly* 125, no. 1 (2010): 31–56; Steven Kull, Clay Ramsay, and Evan Lewis, "Misperceptions, the Media, and the Iraq War," *Political Science Quarterly* 118, no. 4 (2003): 569–98; Monica Prasad, Andrew J. Perrin, Kieran Bezila, Steve G. Hoffman, Kate Kindleberger, Kim Manturuk, and Ashleigh Smith Powers, "'There Must Be a Reason': Osama, Saddam, and Inferred Justification," *Sociological Inquiry* 79, no. 2 (2009): 142–62.

27. Larry M. Bartels, "Beyond the Running Tally: Partisan Bias in Political Perceptions," *Political Behavior* 24, no. 2 (2002): 117–50.

28. Martin Gilens, "Political Ignorance and Collective Policy Preferences," *American Political Science Review* 95, no. 2 (2001): 379–96.

29. J. Matthew Wilson and Paul Gronke, "Concordance and Projection in Citizen Perceptions of Congressional Roll-Call Voting," *Legislative Studies Quarterly* 25, no. 3 (2000): 445–67.

30. Jennifer Jerit and Jason Barabas, "Bankrupt Rhetoric: How Misleading Information Affects Knowledge about Social Security," *Public Opinion Quarterly* 70, no. 3 (2006): 278–303.

31. Philip E. Converse, "Assessing the Capacity of Mass Electorates," *Annual Review of Political Science* 3, no. 1 (2000): 331–53; Stephan Lewandowsky, Ullrich K. H. Ecker, Colleen M. Seifert, Norbert Schwarz, and John Cook, "Misinformation and Its Correction: Continued Influence and Successful Debiasing," *Psychological Science in the Public Interest* 13, no. 3 (2012): 106–31; Ariel Malka, Jon A. Krosnick, and Gary Langer, "The Association of Knowledge with Concern About Global Warming: Trusted Information Sources Shape Public Thinking," *Risk Analysis* 29, no. 5 (2009).

32. Michael X. Della Carpini and Scott Keeter, *What Americans Know about Politics and Why It Matters* (New Haven: Yale University Press, 1997), 8.

33. Kuklinski et al., 791.

34. Jason Barabas and Jennifer Jerit, "Estimating the Causal Effects of Media Coverage on Policy-Specific Knowledge," *American Journal of Political Science* 53, no. 1 (2009): 73–89.

35. Larry M. Bartels, "Uninformed Votes: Information Effects in Presidential Elections," *American Journal of Political Science* 40, no. 1 (1996): 194–230.

36. Arthur G. Miller, John W. McHoskey, Cynthia M. Bane, and Timothy G. Dowd, "The Attitude Polarization Phenomenon: Role of Response Measure, Attitude Extremity, and Behavioral Consequences of Reported Attitude Change," *Journal of Personality and Social Psychology* 64, no. 4 (1993): 561–74.

37. Keith R. Stamm, Fiona Clark, and Paula Reynolds Eblacas, "Mass Communication and Public Understanding of Environmental Problems: The Case of Global Warming," *Public Understanding of Science* 9, no. 3 (2000): 219–37.

38. Andrew J. Wakefield, Simon H. Murch, Andrew Anthony, John Linnell, D. M. Casson, Mohsin Malik, Mark Berelowitz et al., "RETRACTED: Ileal-Lymphoid-Nodular Hyperplasia, Non-Specific Colitis, and Pervasive Developmental Disorder in Children," *The Lancet* 351, no. 9103 (1988): 637–41.

39. Heidi J. Larson, Louis Z. Cooper, Juhani Eskola, Samuel L. Katz, and Scott Ratzan, "Addressing the Vaccine Confidence Gap," *The Lancet* 378, no. 9790 (2011): 526–35.

40. Brian J. Gaines, James H. Kuklinski, Paul J. Quirk, Buddy Peyton, and Jay Verkuilen, "Same Facts, Different Interpretations: Partisan Motivation and Opinion on Iraq," *The Journal of Politics* 69, no. 4 (2007): 957–74.

41. Roger Giner-Sorolla and Shelly Chaiken, "The Causes of Hostile Media Judgments," *Journal of Experimental Social Psychology* 30, no. 2 (1994): 165–80; Kathleen M. Schmitt, Albert C. Gunther, and Janice L. Liebhart, "Why Partisans See Mass Media as Biased," *Communication Research* 31, no. 6 (2004): 623–41.

42. Joel Turner, "The Messenger Overwhelming the Message: Ideological Cues and Perceptions of Bias in Television News," *Political Behavior* 29, no. 4 (2007): 441–64.

43. Joseph R. Priester and Richard E. Petty, "The Influence of Spokesperson Trustworthiness on Message Elaboration, Attitude Strength, and Advertising Effectiveness," *Journal of Consumer Psychology* 13, no. 4 (2003): 408–21

44. Paulette M. Gillig and Anthony G. Greenwald, "Is It Time to Lay the Sleeper Effect to Rest?" *Journal of Personality and Social Psychology* 29, no. 1 (1974): 132–39.

45. Felicia Pratto and Oliver P. John, "Automatic Vigilance: The Attention-Grabbing Power of Negative Social Information," *Journal of Personality and Social Psychology* 61, no. 3 (1991): 380–91.

46. Timothy C. Brock, "Communication Discrepancy and Intent to Persuade as Determinants of Counterargument Production," *Journal of Experimental Social Psychology* 3, no. 3 (1967): 296–309; Kari Edwards and Edward E. Smith, "A Disconfirmation Bias in the Evaluation of Arguments," *Journal of Personality and Social Psychology* 71, no. 1 (1996): 5–24.

47. Reid Hastie, "Causes and Effects of Causal Attribution," *Journal of Personality and Social Psychology* 46, no. 1 (1984): 44–56; Paul T. Wong and Bernard Weiner, "When People Ask 'Why' Questions, and the Heuristics of Attributional Search," *Journal of Personality and Social Psychology* 40, no. 4 (1981): 650–63.

48. Robert Huckfeldt, Paul E. Johnson, and John Sprague, *Political Disagreement: The Survival of Diverse Opinions within Communication Networks* (Cambridge: Cambridge University Press, 2004), 25.

49. Charles S. Taber and Milton Lodge, "Motivated Skepticism in the Evaluation of Political Beliefs," *American Journal of Political Science* 50, no. 3 (2006): 755–69.

50. Gary C. Jacobson, "Perception, Memory, and Partisan Polarization on the Iraq War," *Political Science Quarterly* 125, no. 1 (2010): 31–56.

51. Peter H. Ditto and David F. Lopez, "Motivated Skepticism: Use of Differential Decision Criteria for Preferred and Nonpreferred Conclusions," *Journal of Personality and Social Psychology* 63, no. 4 (1992): 568–84.

52. Ziva Kunda, "The Case for Motivated Reasoning," *Psychological Bulletin* 108, no. 3 (1990): 480–98.

53. Leon Festinger, *A Theory of Cognitive Dissonance* (Stanford: Stanford University Press, 1957).

54. Charles S. Taber, Damon Cann, and Simona Kucsova, "The Motivated Processing of Political Arguments," *Political Behavior* 31, no. 2 (2009): 137–55.

55. Arie W. Kruglanski and Donna M. Webster, "Motivated Closing of the Mind: 'Seizing' and 'Freezing,'" *Psychological Review* 103, no. 2 (1996): 263–83.

56. Albert H. Hastorf and Hadley Cantril, "They Saw a Game; a Case Study," *The Journal of Abnormal and Social Psychology* 49, no. 1 (1954): 129–34.

57. Jonathan J. Koehler, "The Influence of Prior Beliefs on Scientific Judgments of Evidence Quality," *Organizational Behavior and Human Decision Processes* 56, no. 1 (1993): 28–55; Michael J. Mahoney, "Publication Prejudices: An Experimental Study of Confirmatory Bias in the Peer Review System," *Cognitive Therapy and Research* 1, no. 2 (1977): 161–75.

58. Doris A. Graber, *Processing the News: How People Tame the Information Tide* (New York: Longman, 1988), 125.

59. Charles G. Lord, Lee Ross, and Mark R. Lepper, "Biased Assimilation and Attitude Polarization: The Effects of Prior Theories on Subsequently Considered Evidence," *Journal of Personality and Social Psychology* 37, no. 11 (1979): 2098–2109.

60. Arthur G. Miller, John W. McHoskey, Cynthia M. Bane, and Timothy G. Dowd, "The Attitude Polarization Phenomenon: Role of Response Measure, Attitude Extremity, and Behavioral Consequences of Reported Attitude Change," *Journal of Personality and Social Psychology* 64, no. 4 (1993): 561–74.

61. Thomas D. Cook, "Competence, Counterarguing, and Attitude Change," *Journal of Personality* 37, no. 2 (1969): 342–58.

62. Turner.

63. Donald J. Trump, *Twitter* post, 2012, https://twitter.com/realdonaldtrump/status/264441602636906496 (2 Nov. 2012).

64. Associated Press, "Fact Check: Trump Overstates Crowd Size at Inaugural," *Fox News*, 2017, http://www.foxnews.com/us/2017/01/21/fact-check-trump-overstates-crowd-size-at-inaugural.html (21 Jan. 2017).

65. Gary F. Koeske and William D. Crano, "The Effect of Congruous and Incongruous Source-Statement Combinations upon the Judged Credibility of a Communication," *Journal of Experimental Social Psychology* 4, no. 4 (1968): 384–99; Matthew D. Lieberman, Ruth Gaunt, Daniel T. Gilbert, and Yaacov Trope, "Reflection and Reflexion: A Social Cognitive

Neuroscience Approach to Attributional Inference," in *Advances in Experimental Social Psychology*, ed. Mark. P. Zanna (San Diego: Elsevier, 2002), 199–249.

66. Daniel E. Bergan, "Partisan Stereotypes and Policy Attitudes," *Journal of Communication* 62, no. 6 (2012): 1102–20; Adam J. Berinsky, "Rumors and Health Care Reform: Experiments in Political Misinformation." *British Journal of Political Science* 47, no. 2 (2017): 241–62; Jarret T. Crawford, Lee Jussim, Stephanie Madon, Thomas R. Cain, and Sean T. Stevens, "The Use of Stereotypes and Individuating Information in Political Person Perception," *Personality and Social Psychology Bulletin* 37, no. 4 (2011): 529–42.

67. Alice H. Eagly, Wendy Wood, and Shelly Chaiken, "Causal Inferences about Communicators and Their Effect on Opinion Change," *Journal of Personality and Social Psychology* 36, no. 4 (1978): 424–35; Edward E. Jones, Keith E. Davis, and Kenneth J. Gergen, "Role Playing Variations and Their Informational Value for Person Perception," *The Journal of Abnormal and Social Psychology* 63, no. 2 (1961): 302–10; Harold H. Kelley, "The Processes of Causal Attribution," *American Psychologist* 28, no. 2 (1973): 107–28.

68. Robin Blom, "Fact or Fiction: Believability of Statements Made by News Networks" (doctoral dissertation, Michigan State University, 2013).

69. Robin Blom, "Believing False News and Ignoring True News about Illegal Immigration? The Interaction between News Source and Message Expectancy," *Journalism* (2018, in press).

70. Robin Blom, "Believing News Headlines about Illegal Immigrants That Are True and News Headlines That Are False" (presentation, Bi-Annual Convention of the InterAmerican Society of Psychology, Lima, Peru, July 12–16, 2015).

71. Robin Blom, "Believing News from the Christian Broadcast Network: The Intersection between Source Trust, Content Expectancy, and Religiosity" (presentation, Annual Convention of the Association for Education in Journalism and Mass Communication, Minneapolis, Minnesota, August 4–7, 2016).

72. Donald J. Trump, *Twitter* post, 2018, https://twitter.com/realdonaldtrump/status/1050008315286171648 (10 Oct. 2018).

73. Donald J. Trump, *Twitter* post, 2013, https://twitter.com/realdonaldtrump/status/403963068167643136 (22 Nov. 2013).

74. Donald J. Trump, *Twitter* post, 2016, https://twitter.com/realdonaldtrump/status/700295391842058240 (18 Feb. 2016).

75. Donald J. Trump, *Twitter* post, 2017, https://twitter.com/realdonaldtrump/status/832708293516632065 (17 Feb. 2017).

"Rope. Tree. Journalist. Some Assembly Required"

Donald Trump's War on Journalism

JIM CLARKE

In an aircraft cargo hangar at Minneapolis-Saint Paul International Airport on November 6, 2016, Republican candidate Donald Trump held a rally two days before the presidential election. At this rally, a supporter was photographed by Reuters wearing a t-shirt which bore the slogan "Rope. Tree. Journalist. Some Assembly Required." The image went viral almost immediately, due to the highly controversial nature of the sentiment expressed. Even as a joke, the concept of lynching, and particularly the lynching of journalists, was considered deeply unpleasant by many. The t-shirt design was swiftly removed from a number of online retailers, including Teespring, which is owned by Walmart. The designer was subsequently tracked down by a journalist from *The Daily Beast*. "What monster," pondered Brandy Zadrozny, "would at best joke, and at worst advocate, for the lynching of journalists, the very people encapsulated by the First Amendment to the U.S. Constitution, the document that conservatives claim to hold so dear?"[1] Her investigation revealed that the man wearing the design was a 58-year-old, retired Navy veteran living on the Tennessee/Georgia border—a grandfather with an interest in hunting, fishing, weaponry, distilling and playing the blues on his guitar.

For Zadrozny, this rural grandfather, with his expressed antipathy to the "fake news" propagated by the media, was in complete alignment with the candidate he espoused. Negativity towards journalism had become a hallmark of the Trump presidential campaign, with journalists corralled into a gated area during his rallies, where he would persistently point at them and critique their honesty. Further investigation revealed that the design was a decade old, the creation of a conservative blogger known as "Misha," who writes for the website Anti-Idiotarian Rottweiler. When the Reuters photograph went viral, Misha wrote to claim the credit for its creation on his blog, where he defended it as hyperbole, though also warned that journalists "deserve far, far worse at this point in history."[2]

Misha's blog detailed a lengthy list of complaints about what he perceived as a partisan media, in thrall to "social justice warriors" and inclined to destroy the lives of Republican politicians, conservatives and gun owners. That these arguments are all disputable is not the point. Indeed, as I intend to demonstrate, engaging the arguments on an empirical level with the intent of defeating them with proven fact is not merely pyrrhic, but utterly misses the point. The lesson to be learned from the Minnesota t-shirt, and its decade-long history, is that a constituency of Mishas has existed for at least the entirety of that time which idolizes Ronald Reagan; which voted reluctantly at best for the two George Bushes; which considers Democrats to be traitors to the nation; and which identifies the mainstream media as the catalyst and facilitator for their political opposition in all forms. Like the Navy vet photographed in Minneapolis airport, this constituency is white, often rural, conservative, gun-owning and blames the media for many of the setbacks they perceive they have experienced since the departure of Reagan as president. The story of the 2016 presidential election is that an inexperienced anti-politician was able to identify this constituency, radicalize them and leverage their votes to get elected.

However, the sub-text of this narrative is *how* he did it. Trump attained the presidency not by courting the media, nor by adapting to the web 2.0 social media world as Barack Obama had, but by opposing the media which had made him a star at every step, in keeping with the prejudices and antipathies espoused by this hidden electorate. He used Twitter to circumvent the media and project his message past them directly to the public, positing an alternative reportage of events in 140-character microblogs. This alternative reportage, designed to appeal to the hidden electorate, has had two significant effects. Firstly, it has vastly widened the chasm between progressives and conservatives in the United States, creating an overt cultural battlefield where politics used to exist. Secondly, it has deliberately been aimed at undermining the credibility of the media by amplifying the discontent espoused by the hidden electorate, largely located in flyover states, towards what they perceived as coastally-located liberally biased, big city reportage. As these schisms grew, and they have grown during the Trump campaign and into his presidency, an ontological double vision has developed. Words like 'American,' 'citizen,' 'immigrant,' and 'President' have become polysemous battlefields. Different cohorts within and without the United States now use the same words to mean vastly different things. When that Navy vet wore his t-shirt two days before the election, the cold war between these constituencies came to an end. That t-shirt was the open declaration of Trump's war on journalism, a salvo against the investigatory, fact-checking methodology of the media itself. There were, it soon became evident, two superimposed ontological realities in America, each with their own set of facts. And one day into Trump's presidency, this was codified by his administration.

On Friday January 20, 2017, Donald J. Trump was inaugurated as the 45th President of the United States of America. The following day, his Press Secretary Sean Spicer told the media that "this was the largest audience to ever witness an inauguration, period, both in person and around the globe."[3] However, this was swiftly and hotly debated by many observers, especially journalists and photographers, who compared images of a crowded National Mall during President Barack Obama's inauguration in 2009 to similar images of Trump's inauguration which appeared to indicate a significantly smaller crowd in attendance. In response to this burgeoning controversy, Trump's Counselor Kellyanne Conway made an appearance on NBC's *Meet the Press* on Sunday 22 January where she was quizzed by presenter Chuck Todd on Spicer's comments. Todd proposed to Conway that Spicer had "uttered a falsehood" about Mr. Trump having the "largest crowd in inauguration history." Conway characterized Todd's term "falsehood" as "overly dramatic," and in a now infamous misstatement, she went on to say, "Sean Spicer, our press secretary, gave alternative facts to that."[4]

Less commonly known is that, on the same day that Spicer was offering his 'alternative facts' to the press, the President himself was expressing similar sentiments in a speech he delivered at the CIA headquarters in Langley, Virginia. In the company of Vice-President Mike Pence, the newly-inaugurated President Trump took the opportunity of his first event as President to lambaste the media for alleged misreporting of the inauguration crowd numbers. In an apparently off-the-cuff speech, Trump told the assembled CIA gathering that his purpose for visiting them in his first formal appointment as President was in order to correct what he felt was a media misrepresentation that he had a feud with the intelligence community. He then went on to address the issue of attendance at the inauguration and its reportage, already emerging in the press that day:

> And the reason you're my first stop is that, as you know, I have a running war with the media. They are among the most dishonest human beings on Earth. And they sort of made it sound like I had a feud with the intelligence community. And I just want to let you know, the reason you're the number-one stop is exactly the opposite—exactly. And they understand that, too.
>
> And I was explaining about the numbers. We did a thing yesterday at the speech. Did everybody like the speech? I've been given good reviews. But we had a massive field of people. You saw them. Packed. I get up this morning, I turn on one of the networks, and they show an empty field. I say, wait a minute, I made a speech. I

looked out, the field was—it looked like a million, million and a half people. They showed a field where there were practically nobody standing there. And they said, Donald Trump did not draw well.[5]

In one sense it is impossible to be absolutely sure about the relative inauguration attendance figures. Neither the 2009 nor the 2017 inaugurations were ticketed events. Additionally, large crowds are notoriously difficult to estimate, and the most reliable method for doing so—via an overhead image—was frustrated both by the fact that the FAA enforces a no-fly zone over central Washington, D.C., during presidential inaugurations and by the fact that low cloud cover rendered satellite images unusable for this purpose. However, an analysis of available imagery conducted by crowd safety consultant Professor Keith Still of Manchester Metropolitan University on behalf of *The New York Times* estimated that the crowd which attended Trump's inauguration was approximately one-third the size of that which had attended the inauguration of Barack Obama.[6] On the one hand, it seemed patently obvious to most people who viewed images from both inaugurations that the attendance in 2017 was significantly lower. However, on the other hand, because of the lack of a formal attendance figure, this was not actually provable beyond all doubt.

Trump's boastful rhetoric, a characteristic of his entire electoral campaign as well as his career to date as property mogul and reality television star, coupled with his antipathy for the national media, had instigated at the very outset of his presidency a new era in hermeneutics. Thanks to Trump's hubristic insistence that his inauguration attendance was bigger than that of President Obama, his spokespersons, Spicer and Conway, had been forced to defend an apparently false assertion. Furthermore, though Spicer did subsequently acknowledge that some of what he had said to the media was incorrect, a new phrase with ominous Orwellian overtones entered public discourse, along with its concomitant implications. Empirical facts were now open to interpretation, according to the Trump administration, due to what they insisted was an inherently untrustworthy and hostile media. Conway's slip of the tongue to Chuck Todd inadvertently opened up a new paradigm in critique of media reportage. The concept of "fake news," a constant accusation levied by Trump on the campaign trail against the media in general and CNN and *The New York Times* in particular, had evolved into "alternative facts."

Michael Wolff's exposé of the first year of the Trump White House, *Fire and Fury: Inside the Trump White House,* correctly identifies this accidental evolution from "fake news" to "alternative facts" as a staging post in the Trump team's ongoing war against journalism. According to Wolff,

The next day Kellyanne Conway, her aggressive posture during the campaign turning more and more to petulance and self-pity, asserted the new president's right to claim "alternative facts." As it happened, Conway meant to say "alternative information," which at least would imply there might be additional data. But as uttered, it certainly sounded like the new administration was claiming the right to recast reality. Which, in a sense, it was. Although, in Conway's view, it was the media doing the recasting, making a mountain (hence "fake news") out of a molehill (an honest minor exaggeration, albeit of vast proportions).[7]

Conway's belligerent response to media incredulity at Spicer's claims, which could be characterized as running offense in lieu of a good defense, was to become typical of the White House's interactions with the media in the early days of Trump's presidency. During that first month in office, Trump spoke of his "running war" with the media, who had also identified by his then advisor Steve Bannon as "the opposition party."[8] This confrontation had its origins much earlier in Trump's political career, when he identified firstly CNN and later the national media in general as a source of vexation for their largely negative reporting on his electoral campaign. This general attitude of a war footing early in the administration's tenure appears to be what Conway was referring to in her interview with Todd, when she spoke of rethinking the Trump administration's relationship with the media.

Such was Trump's antipathy to the national press that he actually claimed in a rare media interview to have invented the term "fake news." In conversation in October 2017 with two-time Republican presidential candidate Mike Huckabee, father to Trump's own press secretary Sarah Huckabee Sanders, he took credit for inventing the phrase which Collins Dictionary was to anoint a week later as the "word of the year." "The media is really, the word, one of the greatest of all terms I've come up with, is 'fake,'" Trump stated on the TBN show *Huckabee*. "I guess other people have used it perhaps over the years but I've never noticed it."[9]

However, the phrase predates Trump by many decades, and indeed the concept predates Trump by millennia. For as long as information has been a battleground, combatants seeking to control narratives have sought to spin stories or accused their opponents of doing so. A brief diversion into the history of fake news is useful in order to historicize and inform the nature of the Trump administration's evolution of the concept.

In the 12th century BCE, the forces of Ramesses II faced the Hittites in the Battle of Kadesh. Two forms of information, somewhat contradictory, arose from that battle. The first are the Kadesh inscriptions, which are hieroglyphic reliefs found in multiple temple locations in ancient Egypt. The second is the text of the peace treaty resulting from the battle. While the inscriptions portray the usual boastful bragging common to such ancient world descriptions of battles, the terms of the treaty indicate a much more balanced stalemate. Indeed, the text of a letter from Ramesses II to the Hittite king Hattusili III also exists, in which the Pharaoh responds to Hattusili's scoffing about the Egyptian depictions of victory. The Kadesh inscriptions can perhaps therefore be characterized as one of the earliest incidences of fake news in recorded history. Insofar that the inscriptions functioned as a method for the Egyptian elite, and specifically the Pharaoh, to communicate to the populace, this propaganda attempt sought to recast the events of the battle as a glorious victory, a depiction so demonstrably inaccurate, as the treaty terms indicate, that it provoked scorn from the Hittites.

This hubristic mode of exaggerating military achievements in public is far from uncommon in the ancient or modern worlds. Of a slightly more subtle nature is the propaganda war launched by Octavian in 33 BCE, as the Second Triumvirate fell apart in acrimony. As Marcus Antonius laid claim to much of the Eastern part of Rome's territories from his base in Egypt, Octavian was aware that he needed to sway the Senate against his former ally. He therefore read what was claimed to be Marcus Antonius's will and testament aloud to the Senate, and persuaded them to post it in public in the forum by decree. The content of the will detailed a series of components designed to infuriate patriotic Romans. Large tracts of land were to be bequeathed to Marcus Antonius's half-Egyptian offspring, and there was a declaration that he wished to be buried in a mausoleum in Egypt. Though the veracity of this document remains in dispute, Octavian's use of it to sway the Roman Senate against his rival was highly successful. Marcus Antonius was stripped of his legions and effectively became an enemy of the state. Rome then declared war on Antonius's lover, the Egyptian queen Cleopatra, and in the resulting battle in 31 BCE, Octavian's forces won, leaving the path to becoming Rome's sole ruler clear for the future Emperor Augustus.

Octavian's use of smear tactics has remained a fundamental part of politics ever since. Whether the will was real or not, his ability to place the negatively perceived information directly into the hands of the populace, via publication in the forum, was crucial to ensure that he would be able to control the narrative and direct Rome towards the Imperium which he later led.

Where once there was a forum, as Jürgen Habermas has noted, later there was a public sphere, with information evolving from text on walls to publications. The development of a professional media, a slow process enabled by Gutenberg's invention of the printing press and codified over a series of centuries culminating in the emergence of the modern newspaper in the Grub Street era of the early 18th century CE, created a class of information gatekeepers beyond the reach of rulers or the state. This "fourth estate," as Thomas Carlyle described it, emerged with the legitimizing principle that it would function as a watchdog on the other loci of power—politicians, the military and the church authorities.

However, before this patina of legitimacy had been applied to the nascent discipline of journalism, it had already built up a significant history of sensationalist and inaccurate reporting. From the time of the earliest proto-newspapers and pamphlets, writers found that sensationalist stories garnered an audience and an income. Stories of monsters being born in far-off climes were a staple of the English press long before Grub Street popularized new forms of reporting inclined towards sensationalism, such as gallows-side confessions from condemned criminals. Equally, the partisan and often highly inaccurate reportage of the *Mercurii*, partisan news sheets during the English Civil War, functioned as an updated variant of Ramesses's boastful account of victory at Kadesh, as both sides attempted to spin news of victories for their supporters. So as the modern media began to take shape, various forms of fake news which functioned in a number of ways emerged alongside. Some fake news functioned as spin, or partisan and unbalanced reportage, while other forms of fake news were published solely because of their sensationalist appeal to readers.

The Church authorities quickly learnt the dangers of the press when their monopoly on revelatory knowledge was challenged by Martin Luther and his deft command of the pamphlet form. Media historian Andrew Pettegree is only one of many scholars who have examined how Luther conjoined with profit-driven printers to disseminate his heretical religious ideas. In their attempt to suppress Luther's Protestant revolution, Church authorities summoned him to the Diet of Worms where he was condemned for heretical ideas. In a previous era, this mode was sufficient to suppress such ideas, as John Wycliffe and Jan Hus had discovered. However, Luther was able to propagate his ideas quickly and in a manner which became impossible for the Church to eradicate, an activity which not only revolutionized Christianity but also preserved his own life. In his study *Brand Luther*, Pettegree notes how "Luther's best chance of survival lay in ensuring his cause remained in the public eye. The oxygen of publicity was, quite literally, a matter of life and death."[10]

It would be dangerous to overextend any comparison between Martin Luther and Donald Trump as societal reformers. However, their respective disruptions of established information flows were crucial to the success of both. Trump managed to circumvent the media's gatekeeping role by leveraging the disruptive communication technology of social media, using microblogging site Twitter to place his polemical positions directly before the populace, just as Luther had leveraged the emerging printing press technology five centuries earlier to evade the Catholic Church's control of doctrine and religious practice, again appealing directly to his audience. For both, this ability to evade the critique and constrictions of established (and establishment) information flow was essential not only for the success of their reforming agendas, but also for their own survival. While the media has posed no existential threat to Trump akin to that which the Church posed to Luther, Trump's burgeoning political career quickly became existentially dependent upon his capacity to appeal directly to the U.S. electorate in provocative and often inflammatory ways.

The Catholic Church was intent to learn from their information war with Luther however, as the pamphlet wars of the counter-reformation indicate. Certainly, by the time of the Lisbon earthquake in 1755, which almost totally destroyed the Portuguese capital and killed tens of thousands of people, the Church had learned the value of taking quick control of the narrative. In the aftermath, a pamphlet form quickly emerged, the *relações de sucessos*, which piously attributed survivor accounts to an apparition of the Virgin Mary. Voltaire was in turn incensed by this and railed repeatedly against attempts to explain natural events via the medium of revelation and religion. Though Voltaire remains a pillar of the Enlightenment, his efforts have not prevented the tendency for some people, including authority figures, to insist on revelatory rather than empirical explanations for events. This is especially prevalent, among developed countries, in the United States which, according to the Public Religion Research Institute, boasted as of 2017 a population which claimed to be 70 percent Christian.[11] By comparison, less than half of the British population claim to be religious at all. Though Trump's inflammatory rhetoric has generally fallen short of, for example, blaming Hurricane Katrina on gay people, a position which was espoused by Christian evangelical preachers, Orthodox rabbis and Muslim leaders, nevertheless his ability to communicate positions that appear to contradict empirical causation echoes and emulates the persistence of religious explanation for natural events.

This comparison helps to explain why the fad for fact-checking Trump's statements has not particularly affected him. Despite Secretary Hilary Clinton's constant refrain that the media and public should fact-check Trump's statements during the presidential election campaign, a call answered not only by the press but also by the emergence into political prominence of dedicated fact-checking organs such as Snopes, Trump generally remained unharmed by such critique from empiricism. Just as Voltaire's critique of revelatory explanations for survivors in Lisbon did not persuade the pious that miracles had not occurred, similarly those inclined to support Trump's positions, whether they were on matters as substantial as climate change or as insignificant as the inauguration attendance, were disinclined to be persuaded by even the most rigorous fact-checking conducted by the media or professional fact-checking bodies.

It therefore matters little, at least in terms of the efficacy of the "#resistance" to Trump, to assiduously correct the exaggerations, half-truths, outright falsehoods and complete inventions which emerged from the Trump presidency during its first two years, just as it was fruitless to do so during his presidential election campaign. It matters not that the term "fake news" dates back at least as far as the late 19th century (and potentially to the 1820s according to Google's Ngram viewer), and hence could not be the invention of a man living over 120 years later. Many historians, both academic and amateur, have seized on the sudden popularity of the term to remind their respective audiences that both the term and the concept did not originate with Trump, either as coiner or as perpetrator. Frederick Burr Opper's 1894 cartoon of Yellow journalism reporters scurrying to print carrying "Fake News" has been reprinted repeatedly, and the *New York Sun* story of the Great Moon Hoax of 1835 has been reprised over and again. To highlight that not only the media but also politicians have been responsible historically for faking news, many narratives have noted, *inter alia*, Benjamin Franklin's famous propaganda stories about "scalping" Indians working in league with British forces, or the politically driven propaganda on all sides during World War I and World War II.

Some of these fake news anecdotes of yore are educational. We can learn, for example, that though the *Clarksburg Daily Telegram* deliberately published a fake story in order to expose their rival publication the *Clarksburg Daily News* as guilty of content theft (complete with a non-existent protagonist whose name, when read backwards, spelled out "we fake news"), this did not actually lead to the closure of the guilty publication.[12] Though the *Daily Telegraph* overtly accused the Nazi leadership of falsifying reports of the war as early as May 1940, this neither dissuaded Josef Goebbels from his propaganda efforts nor indeed prevented the British authorities and media from reciprocating.[13] What we can learn from the history of fake news is not merely that it is a power play and an attempt to direct and control the narratives populating the public sphere, but also that its exposure tends to have little or no effect on curbing its existence.

Somehow, this lengthy history of the media faking stories for profit, from the *New York Sun*'s Great Moon Hoax of 1835 via the Yellow journalism of Hearst and Pulitzer to the *Weekly World News*'s outlandish sensationalism did little to no damage to the media's gatekeeper role of information provider to the public. However, the disruption of the digital revolution, especially Web 2.0 with its democratization of information flow, has facilitated an evolution in what was previously an issue of trust between publication and readership.

Obviously, the erosion of the media's former monopoly on information provision has led to the for-profit clickbait fake news mills to be found online today. But the public sphere itself has also been irreparably damaged in the "alternative facts" era. There are precedented attempts to squeeze the information genie back into the bottle, such as announcements by the British and French governments that they intend to legislate against fake news. However, these initiatives are doomed to failure, given that the popularity of governments in both countries is little higher than the trustworthiness of the media as assessed by the public in both countries in regular polls. This paradigm of plummeting trust in the media coinciding with plummeting support for the government may also be found in Trump's America, needless to say.

However, we are also in an unprecedented new paradigm which was arguably initiated in Russia. Not Stalin's Russia, as suggested by Republican senator Jeff Flake,[14] but Vladimir Putin's Russia. It is one created by his former chief ideologist Vladislav Surkov. During Surkov's time as first deputy chief of the Russian presidential administration (a role similar to White House chief of staff) from 1999 to 2011, Surkov is credited by many, including BBC documentarist Adam Curtis, for having created a wholly new form of political strategy. Putin opponents Pavel Khodorkovsky and Peter Pomerantsev have termed this development "postmodernist dictatorship."[15] Surkov's training as an absurdist theatre director prior to his switch to politics is credited by Curtis in particular for some of the more baffling actions of the Putin regime. The seemingly random switches in policy and the inexplicable support for political extremists or even apparent opponents, has, according to Pomerantsev, left the populace beleaguered and continuously confused, unsure of what to believe. Reality itself, according to Pomerantsev, is at stake, as Surkov's "fusion of despotism and postmodernism," a simultaneously totalitarian and relativist approach to reality itself, was overtly conducted upon the Russian public sphere as if it were a theatre stage:

> In contemporary Russia, unlike the old USSR or present-day North Korea, the stage is constantly changing: the country is a dictatorship in the morning, a democracy at lunch, an oligarchy by suppertime, while, backstage, oil companies are expropriated, journalists killed, billions siphoned away. Surkov is at the centre of the show, sponsoring nationalist skinheads one moment, backing human rights groups the next. It's a strategy of power based on keeping any opposition there may be constantly confused, a ceaseless shape-shifting that is unstoppable because it's indefinable.[16]

At the center of Surkov's efforts to date, and he remains a close advisor of Putin at the time of writing, has been the achievement of placing his master at the center of all events, positive or negative, so that in the whirlwind of information and misinformation, news and fake news, facts and alternative facts, the eye of the storm, the one unmoving object which can be relied upon for good or ill, is Putin himself.

Trump has adapted this methodology and refined it for the American public sphere, building on his own extensive experience of the popular media as well as his longstanding public image as a boorish braggart. Surrounded by an ever-changing cast of supporters, allies, semi-allies and Republican Party apparatchiks, Trump has functioned as his *own* Surkov. Trump's tweets, and the concomitant explanations, press statements, denials, and obfuscations which invariably follow, just as counter-arguments invariably follow from his fact-checkers in the Democrats, the media and professional fact-checking organizations, all serve to keep him at the eye of the storm. As a result of the postmodernist and relativist politics of the Trump presidency and the preceding presidential campaign, Americans are now forced either to spend impossible amounts of time investigating and researching all the news they encounter, or increasingly to give up and rely on the sources they have come to trust as they go about their daily lives. The risk here obviously is that Americans are retreating into echo chamber political arenas, only encountering political opinions or information with which they already agree.

For many Americans, the media does still remain the source of information they trust. However, levels of public trust in the media have been falling for some time, as previously noted. Equally, for many *other* Americans, the source of information they have come to trust has become Trump himself, just as Russians are often reluctantly obliged to acknowledge that in their damaged and relativist public sphere, Putin is the one reliable component, for good or ill. In such a political environment, where increasingly Americans are retreating into ever more distant camps on either side of a burgeoning culture war, it is no exaggeration to suggest that Kellyanne Conway's slip of the tongue may have been prophetic.

Different groups of Americans now consume and accept directly contradictory facts as their realities. In the Surkovist politics of Trump's America, one can now choose the reality one prefers. Empiricism is increasingly becoming an ideal rather than a benchmark of information, or worse, something both sides claim at the expense of their opponents. We can no longer "disprove" anything in the manner in which Ramesses's propagandist architecture can be disproven by the existence of the peace treaty with the Hittites, or the manner in which the *New York Sun's* schlocky story about life on the moon could be disproven.

America's public sphere is devolving into perceptual realities that intersect but in many areas do not co-exist. Core descriptors like "American" or "president" or "journalist" have now become polysemous, with different sectors of society espousing contradictory understandings of what they mean, creating a curious double vision for those attempting to view from the outside, as if two sets of shadows were being projected onto Plato's wall at once. This has gone far beyond rival political groupings attempting to control the narrative. There are now multiple narratives, indeed, multiple realities. In Trump's America, if you don't like the facts, there are now alternatives. Two Americas now uneasily co-exist. In one America is the legacy media, struggling to provide factual reportage in an era of falling resources as they seek a funding model in the post-digital age, facing an openly hostile administration. In the other, they are traitors to the state, deserving of lynching. In both Americas, the media is losing Trump's war on journalism.

NOTES

1. Brandy Zadrozny, "The Man Behind 'Journalist. Rope. Tree,'" *The Daily Beast,* November 8, 2016, https://www.thedailybeast.com/the-man-behind-journalist-rope-tree (28 Feb. 2018).

2. Zadrozny, "The Man Behind 'Journalist. Rope. Tree.'"

3. Elle Hunt, "Trump's Inauguration Crowd: Sean Spicer's Claims Versus the Evidence," *The Guardian,* January 27, 2017, https://www.theguardian.com/us-news/2017/jan/22/trump-inauguration-crowd-sean-spicers-claims-versus-the-evidence (28 Feb. 2018).

4. Mahita Gajanan, "Kellyanne Conway defends White House's Falsehoods as 'Alternative Facts,'" *Time,* January 22, 2017, http://time.com/4642689/kellyanne-conway-sean-spicer-donald-trump-alternative-facts/ (28 Feb. 2018).

5. WhiteHouse.Org., "Remarks by President Trump and Vice President Pence at CIA Headquarters," *Whitehouse.org.* January 3, 2018, https://www.whitehouse.gov/briefings-statements/remarks-president-trump-vice-president-pence-cia-headquarters/ (28 Feb. 2018).

6. Tim Wallace, Karen Yourish and Troy Griggs, "Trump's Inauguration vs. Obama's: Comparing the Crowds," *The New York Times,* January 20, 2017, https://www.nytimes.com/interactive/2017/01/20/us/politics/trump-inauguration-crowd.html (28 Feb. 2018).

7. Michael Wolff, *Fire and Fury: Inside the Trump White House* (London: Little, Brown, 2018), 48.

8. Michael M. Grynbaum, "Trump Strategist Stephen Bannon Says Media Should 'Keep Its Mouth Shut,'" *The New York Times,* January 26, 2017, https://www.nytimes.com/2017/01/26/business/media/stephen-bannon-trump-news-media.html (28 Feb. 2018).

9. Chris Cillizza, "Donald Trump Just Claimed He Invented 'Fake News,'" CNN.com, October 26, 2017, https://edition.cnn.com/2017/10/08/politics/trump-huckabee-fake/index.html (28 Feb. 2018).

10. Andrew Pettegree, *Brand Luther* (New York: Penguin, 2015), 89.

11. Daniel Cox and Robert Jones, "America's Changing Religious Identity," *PRII.org,* September 6, 2017, https://www.prri.org/research/american-religious-landscape-christian-religiously-unaffiliated/ (28 Feb. 2018).

12. "Caught in the Act, the Daily News Publicly Acknowledges It Steals News from the Daily Telegram," *Clarksburg Telegram,* September 25, 1903, 8.

13. H.C. Bailey, "False News Is One of Hitler's Weapons," *Daily Telegraph,* May 23, 1940, 3.

14. David Smith, "Republican Senator Jeff Flake: Trump's Attacks on Media Reminiscent of Stalin," *The Guardian,* January 17, 2018, https://www.theguardian.com/us-news/2018/jan/17/jeff-flake-donald-trump-fake-news-stalin-senate-speech (28 Feb. 2018).

15. Pavel Khodorkovsky and Peter Pomerantsev, "Russia: A Postmodern Dictatorship?" *Legatum Institute,* October 14, 2013, https://www.li.com/docs/default-source/publications/pomeransevl_russia_imr_web_final.pdf (28 Feb. 2018).

16. Peter Pomerantsev, "Putin's Rasputin," *London Review of Books* 33 no. 20 (20 October 2011): 4.

Wagging the Dog

Departing from the Truth and Alternative Realities

The Wrongful Death of Marvin Booker

Sig Langegger

Some people may dismiss the Trump administration's puerile insistence on the validity of alternative facts as the boisterous braggadocio of extremely wealthy people who are accustomed to getting around social norms, legal standards, ethical business practices, tax codes, land use regulations that obstruct them *or* that cause them problems by lying, by stretching the truth, or, simply, by changing the subject. Some might even write alternative facts off as the knee-jerk reaction of a spiteful and woefully unprepared administration to valid policy questions and professional attempts by journalists to square the administration's claims with verifiable evidence to the contrary. Some could, as many essays in this book justifiably do, raise an alarm that this administration is eroding the very foundations of a civil and democratic society: a society that is based on the rule of law and on the evidence-based enforcement of the law, a society that acknowledges the place of scientific inquiry, a modern society that depends on social norms, legal standards, and notions of ethics that are rooted in both shared ideas about justice and verifiable truths. This essay takes a different route through what has become the morass of Trump's war on truth.

Alternative facts are features of Trump's administration that could have potentially lasting impact on crucial aspects of municipal and federal governance such as policing. I argue that since at least the Nixon Administration, U.S. citizens have been experiencing two often mutually exclusive realities of policing. One reality is that police and sheriff departments are tasked to serve and protect citizens. The other reality is that police departments exist to engage in wars, like the War on Drugs and the War on Crime. The central spine of my argument is that both of these realities coexist, have long coexisted, and will likely coexist well into the future. The former reality roots in an anarchic[1] worldview that holds that human society is self-sustaining and therefore necessarily self-policing. Social trust holds this reality together. In contrast, the central component of the latter reality is fear. This reality extends Thomas Hobbs' claims that without a strong centralized government society will decay into a "war of all against all." My analysis of these realities hinges on a deadly use of force case in the City of Denver, Colorado. This essay exposes multiple attempts by the City of Denver to fabricate and destroy evidence as part of the construction of a counter-narrative about the horrific homicide of an arrestee in a detention center. This case did have a positive outcome: the essay concludes with a discussion of the ways in which Denver policymakers are currently attempting to align the alternate reality of cops at war with crime with the more civil reality of law enforcement as a public service.

On July 9, 2010, Marvin Booker, a black, homeless street preacher, was arrested on an outstanding warrant for possession of drug paraphernalia and then transported to the downtown Denver Van Cise-Simonet Detention Center. As he was directed to an isolation cell by Deputy Sergeant Flora Gomez, he veered from his path in order to retrieve his shoes. This simple misstep cost him his life. The sudden and violent death of a human being is tragic enough, but there is a more far-reaching story here, perhaps an even more terrifying one. What I share is a twisted tale of lies based on alternative facts and capped off with the construction of an entire alternate reality. I contrast different interpretations of the events that led to the death of Marvin Booker. Mr. Booker was killed in a jail facility, in front of 40 witnesses, under the surveillance of operational video cameras. None of the five deputies involved in this incident received disciplinary action of any kind. Denver's prosecuting attorney did not pursue a murder case. Blocked from a remedy in criminal court, Booker's family sued the City in civil court for the wrongful death of Marvin Booker. The Booker family won their suit. Mr. Booker's death and the resulting legal battle as in many similar excessive use of force cases involving law enforcement officers, reveals the presence of two realities: one in which law enforcement officers who routinely use excessive force in the line of duty find, spin, or manufacture justifications for their action; the other in which citizens served by such officers find such actions and justifications inexcusable.

The conceptual frame I use for my argument is the militarization of the police. To illustrate the term militarization, I survey the evolution of an alternate reality that the Founding Fathers could not have imagined ever coming to pass in the United States of America, where the adjectival form of the noun military has come to be routinely used to qualify the noun police. I then take a close look at the media coverage and court documents of the Marvin Booker trial in order to advance an argument that while alternative facts may be suspect, the alternate realities they construct are quite real.

The alternate reality of a militarized police force in the United States of America was put into words by William French, Ronald Reagan's attorney general. At his first cabinet meeting, French claimed that "[t]he Justice Department is not a domestic agency. It is the internal arm of the national defense."[2] Using the U.S. Constitution as the touchstone for legal reality, this statement must be construed in terms of alterity. This is not to say that French's statement was based in fantasy. On the contrary, it merely stems from an alternate legal reality, one more firmly grounded in the legal canon stemming from the Roman Empire than the canon of English common law upon which the U.S. Constitution is based. Although a formal review of these two legal systems is beyond the scope of this essay, in order to limn the two realities that form the basis of my argument, a brief history is in order.

In general terms the legal systems of the countries of Western Europe stem from statute law. Statute law can be understood as laws that flow down to the citizenry from the sovereign, be this Leviathan a monarch or a democratically elected government. In this system of law, the state codifies statutes that protect the state. Due mainly to the relative isolation of the British Isles from Continental Europe and the centrality of individual rights and property rights there, the British legal system evolved differently. In Britain, a system of common law developed. In cursory terms common laws arise within processes of litigation. Common laws flow from citizen disputes back to the protection of the citizenry. The Founders of the United States of America, who were all subjects of the British Empire, crafted a constitution that simultaneously uncoupled the legal system from the sovereign, as part of the separation of powers (legislative, executive and judicial) and established a system of municipal and federal courts to hammer out the continuing evolution of common law. From these different legal systems evolved distinct means of law enforcement.

During the Middle Ages feudal kingdoms on the continent were under constant threat of invasion and rebellion. In consequence, monarchs conscripted armies to thwart external threat and to expand territory. Internal order was maintained by directing these armed services toward suppressing dissent by enforcing statute laws and royal edicts. In time, the enforcement of statute laws became the responsibility of a centralized police force that emanated from and protected the sovereign. In medieval France, for example, a national police force emerged that isolated the monarchy from threat of revolt and punished crimes against the state. In continental Europe civil order was maintained by undermining civil liberties. Because of their isolation British monarchies could maintain national security and social order using separate means: one was militarized and directed outward toward the goal of national defense; the other was directed inward toward civil order. During Medieval times civil order on the British Isles was preserved by protecting lives, rights, and property from criminals. Thus, social order in medieval England was preserved by balancing civil liberties and personal accountability against the will of the sovereign.

Militarization of the Police

Although a product of both systems, police powers in the United States have historically drawn more deeply from British than Continental European legal systems. The authors of the constitution as well as each subsequent executive administration and every congress elected to uphold the constitution were keenly aware of the dangers to civil liberties posed by a standing army. To illustrate, the Boston Massacre, committed by British troops against British subjects, proved to be an organizing principle in uniting 13 very different colonies against a common enemy. This is one main reason the Founders made concerted efforts to ensure that military personnel and military tactics would be directed toward national defense, not internal security. The Third Amendment to the Bill of Rights makes this manifest by prohibiting the military from entering private civilian property during peacetime and severely curtailing the use of private property during times of war. The Founders' intent notwithstanding, the Third Amendment proves rather toothless, only expressly forbidding the quartering of troops in private homes. It took nearly a century for a clear line to be drawn between the army and police, between national defense and internal security. The Posse Comitatus Act of 1878, which effectively ended post–Civil War Reconstruction, expressly forbids the use of U.S. military in civilian law enforcement.

However, ideals have a way of tarnishing as soon as they are exposed to the glare of reality. The Posse Comitatus Act has been violated multiple times, notably by the use of federal forces against the Bonus Army[3] in 1932, and to insure school desegregation in the South during the 1950s and 1960s. In the 1980s the Posse Comitatus Act was amended five times so that military equipment and military tactics could be used in waging the War on Drugs, a war waged against U.S. citizens. Central to this state-sponsored erosion of individual liberties is the weakening of the Castle Doctrine[4] and the authentication of "stop and frisk" police protocols. Part of what has become known as Quality of Life Policing or Zero Tolerance Policing, stop and frisk protocols involve officers stopping and patting down individuals in public space. The Supreme Court has found that stop and frisk policing does not violate a person's Civil Rights, as long as law enforcement officers believe this person has committed or will soon commit a crime. This bears repeating. No other legal justification is needed outside of the frisking officer's intuition. Personal privacy disappears. The home is also no longer the ultimate refuge of personal privacy. Court decisions supporting tactics used in the War on Drugs, notably no-knock warrants,[5] have resulted in a dramatic curtailment of the efficacy of the Castle Doctrine. Importantly in both stop and frisk policing and no knock warrants, all that is required for the police to usurp rights to privacy is an officer's reasonable suspicion that a crime has been committed. The weakening of the Posse Comitatus Act and the Castle Doctrine were part and parcel of a decades-long, wide-ranging War on Drugs. This of course begs a fundamental question: Why is the United States at war against drugs? The short answer is that being tough, very tough, on crime has worked for decades to get both Democrats and Republicans elected to local and federal offices. To arrive at a more nuanced answer requires that we examine the concept of militarism.

As Kraska and Kappeler explain, since their inception, the police and the military share a fundamental founding principle—a state sanctioned use of physical force to achieve objectives, to solve problems.[6] In its most basic sense, militarism is an ideology that stresses that the use of force is the most effective and efficient way of reaching goals. Within this ideology, military hardware and martial organizational structures, along with combative tactics and techniques, are understood primarily as problem solving tools. Militarization is the implementation of militarism; that is, it is the process of organizing, arming, and training for violent conflict. Using this rough schematic we can then understand the militarization of the police as the enactment of fundamental changes to police hardware (weaponry, equipment, and technology) and police culture (uniform, language, beliefs, and core values). Although this essay concentrates on the culture of militarism in one sheriff department; in order to understand how this alternate reality sustained itself, we need to consider that this culture is pervasive in law enforcement in the United States.

Since the mid–20th century there has been a significant militarization of police forces throughout the U.S. Special Weapons and Tactics (SWAT) teams, perfected by the City of Los Angeles Police Department in the 1960s, are the most visible manifestation of how police hardware and culture has become militarized. SWAT teams now constitute a sizable portion of the police force in the United States and they consume a sizable chunk of municipal public safety budgets. Though often associated with large metropolitan areas, SWAT teams have been commonplace in small communities for at least 30 years. An essential component of these material changes are core changes to police tactics and to police culture. These changes occasionally burst into national consciousness, as the SWAT team response to the Ferguson Unrest

or the Danziger Bridge shootings in post–Katrina New Orleans help to indicate. Much of this sea change in U.S. law enforcement can be traced to a
notable propensity of U.S. policy makers to declare war on social problems.
President Johnson declared a War on Poverty; in his abbreviated term as
President, Nixon accelerated the militarization of the police by mobilizing a
War on Drugs and then a broader War on Crime. These "wars" succeeded in
dehumanizing first drug pushers then drug users, morphing them into an
enemy to be destroyed. President Bush's declaration of a potentially eternal
War on Terror shows that the tendency to default to militarism to solve complex problems appears to have become customary political practice in the
United States. This alternate reality is matter of fact; it is commonplace, normal. It gets politicians elected and keeps them in office. Because it presupposes
the existence of stark differences, it also has great potential to damage society.
This "warrior culture" amplifies socio-cultural difference as it fortifies the
boundaries between differences. To extend a common metaphor, it places *us*,
ostensibly peaceable citizens, on one side of a thin blue line while stationing
them—perpetrators of crime and chaos—on the other side. This us/them
chasm leads directly into militaristic dichotomies of victory and defeat, com-
rade and enemy.

The fundamental cultural difference between community policing and
professional policing highlights this shift in police culture. Community policing *protects* a citizenry from crime. Professional policing *combats* the dehu-
manized notion of "crime." In community policing, officers are known as
individuals. And police officers know individuals in the communities they
police—they understand local needs and have local knowledge. Community
policing ideally relies on mutually beneficial relationships between police
and citizenry. Professional policing gives rise to and normalizes the "warrior
cop."[7] The rise of this phenomenon and its social acceptance also exposes a
core element of the culture of the warrior cop, a cultural complex formed
around destroying the enemy and protecting comrades. Armored and
souped-up sophisticated weaponry is a physical manifestation of this culture.
Perhaps the most striking difference between community and professional
policing is the removal of law enforcement officers from neighborhood con-
texts. Police today often swoop in when directed by 911 dispatchers. The erasure of a daily police presence, followed by the sudden scream of sirens and
flashes of light, results in faceless cops and faceless criminals. The speed and
violence of this type of policing forces law enforcement officers to make split
second decisions. They must ascertain the motivations, character, and grievances of every single person they encounter during the single brief time they
interact with citizens, namely ticketing and arrest. To succeed in this type of
combative environment, officers are trained to make split second decisions,
in much the same way that soldiers are trained to fight belligerent enemies

of the state, by—in a different configuration from that mentioned above—protecting *us* (the other officers at the scene) and immobilizing *them* (anyone suspected of criminal activity).

As recent high profile excessive use of force cases like those involving Michael Brown, Tamir Rice, and Philando Castile have shown, these decisions are often deadly ones. The growth of professional policing has spurred another growth cycle, namely an alarming increase in the number of suspects wounded or killed by police officers. How legal teams defend the very few officers actually brought to trial for excessive use of force reveals the insidious manner by which the ideology of militarism has crept into civilian policing. The authority to take the life of a person rests solely on the intuition of the officers present at the moment deadly force is used. Put bluntly, in order to justify the use of deadly force, all an officer need do is prove is that he or she feared for her or his life. Whether this fear was founded in reality rarely matters, as the cases of a Cleveland police officer killing Tamir Rice, a 12-year-old with a toy gun. This pattern repeats itself. Michael Brown was shot six times (twice in the head) while he had his hands raised in surrender. Philando Castile was shot seven times while seated in a car during a routine traffic stop. However, most of the time police don't shoot and they don't kill. Instead, often citation leads to an arrest, detention, booking and trial.

The City of Denver, like many municipalities the United States, allocates law enforcement to its police department, and the processes of booking and detaining individuals cited with violating a law to its sheriff department. Denver's police and sheriff departments are on the front lines in the War on Crime; the City grants both departments the right to use deadly force. Loïc Wacquant exposes many contemporary relationships between the penal system and the centralized military. Aside from the sharing of sophisticated systems of restraint, weaponry, and surveillance, he points to the cross-fertilization of military terms, such as collateral damage, and military culture, like uniforms, command structures, and warrior codes.[8] Crank highlights how a culture of militarism, of using violence to solve problems, has caused a proliferation the use of military hardware, such as assault vehicles, Kevlar body armor, even grenade launchers, which are used by SWAT teams across the United States.[9] Importantly this materiel is chock full of means of protecting the soldiers on the front lines in the War on Crime. As the strange and tragic case of the Columbine Massacre thrust into view, this cultural mindset, this warrior culture has the tendency to place less importance on the protection of citizens' lives and more importance on protecting the lives of fellow officers. During the 1999 mass shooting at Columbine High School in Lakewood, Colorado, a grand total of eight hundred police officers, including three heavily armored SWAT teams, held off going inside school buildings to stop the shooters Dylan Klebold and Eric Harris as they killed 12 students and one teacher because they deemed the situation too dangerous—far too dangerous to risk an officer getting shot.

The Killing of Marvin Booker

Relying on newspaper reportage, filmed evidence, surveillance camera footage of the incident and the official use of force policies of the Denver police and sheriff departments as well as trial transcripts, the next section takes a close look at the culture of self-protection evident within the United States' increasingly militarized criminal justice system. I will deconstruct a remarkable number alternative facts the City used in its attempt to construct an alternate reality in which an exhausted Marvin Booker, a man of 56 years who weighed only 135 pounds, posed a significant enough threat to five well trained and well armed sheriff deputies to justify their killing of Booker on the spot. As is the troubling norm with use of force incidents the investigation of this incident was handled internally. After its review the Sheriff Department concluded that the use of force against Marvin Booker was justified, and therefore failed to discipline any of the deputies involved. Nor did the City file a homicide suit, perhaps because of a necessarily close relationship between law enforcement in Denver and the Denver attorney general. Also, in line with an unsettling norm in similar cases, the Booker family filed a civil rights lawsuit. In the next section I deconstruct portions of the Booker family's lawsuit and juxtapose two very different realities—one a blatant excessive use of force, the other as it was described by the defense attorneys, "Arrest Control 101."

The Denver Van Cise-Simonet Detention Center is a state-of-the-art penal facility that features a cooperative seating area for the processes of cooperative individuals charged with nonviolent crimes. After being arrested and transported to this facility, all arrestees must pass through a metal detector and submit all personal items for a search. Then they are allowed to wait to be processed in this open cooperative seating area. In this space, arrestees are allowed to move around; they have access to phones; they can watch television. After Marvin Booker was directed into this cooperative seating area, he along with many of the other arrestees present tried to get some sleep. Perhaps because Booker wore leather dress shoes that may have fit too tightly, he took off his shoes. When Deputy Faun Gomez called him up to be booked, he walked up to her desk in socked feet. When asked to take a seat, he chose to stand. However, his standing did not please Deputy Gomez, and as he did not do as he was told she decided that Mr. Booker needed to be placed in an isolation cell. She then walked around her desk toward the cells and motioned for Mr. Booker to follow her. He instead turned away from her toward the cooperative waiting area in which he had left his shoes. Within two minutes and 30 seconds he was unconscious, likely dead.

According to witnesses, Deputy Gomez began screaming, "Get in the damn cell!" at Mr. Booker, who, according to corroborated accounts, said, "Bitch, I just want to get my stuff." He then turned toward the two stairs leading down to the main waiting area, Deputy Gomez walked briskly up behind him and grabbed his arm. Obviously surprised, Mr. Booker jerked his arm away and nearly tripped and fell down this short flight of stairs. At this point Mr. Booker purportedly cursed, saying, "What the fuck?" He managed to catch his fall by grabbing the stair rail. Within four seconds two additional deputies arrived, pried his hand off the rail and tackled him to the ground. Within 10 seconds, four deputies, one using a carotid chokehold,[10] forced Mr. Booker, face-down, to the concrete floor. Immediately after that, Deputy Sharp restrained Mr. Booker's legs with an OPN.[11] Then Deputy Robinette placed his knee in the small of Mr. Booker's back while Deputy Gomez proceeded to handcuff him. These are the actual facts, all of which were captured by security cameras. Indeed, the cameras recorded a surreal scene, one marked by a disturbing contrast between absolute calm and brutal violence: four deputies forcefully tugging at a suspect's head, arms and legs, in front of obviously stunned yet completely calm bystanders, some of whom were shooed away from the immediate vicinity. All the while Deputy Grimes, while keeping Mr. Booker's neck in the carotid chokehold he used to tackle him, seems to be casually conversing with another deputy. Mr. Booker's body initially convulses with panic, and then seems to move in concert with the violent tugs, twists and pulls of the deputies. At this point, Sergeant Carrie Rodriguez uses a Taser[12] on Mr. Booker. His body goes limp. Then four deputies, each holding one of his limbs, carry his flaccid, face-down body back up the stairs and into the isolation cell Deputy Gomez initially wanted Mr. Booker to follow her toward.

Deputy Gomez's testimony, in which she explains the exact same images recorded by the surveillance cameras, reads as incredible to an extent bordering on the absurd. Struggling to justify why such extreme force was necessary to contain the threat that Mr. Booker posed, she alluded to the possibility that he was armed and dangerous. She was asked directly by the plaintiff's attorney: "So everybody is searched for weapons before they enter the cooperative seating area?" Deputy Gomez answered: "Correct." The attorney continued: "So one thing you knew is that Marvin Booker didn't have any weapons, right?" To which Deputy Gomez paradoxically answered: "No." Though this can be read as farcical, I suggest that in fact it reveals how alternative facts are produced. Alternative facts need not be based in reality; they must merely refer to a plausible interpretation of reality. Logical linkage is not necessary, only some kind of connection, no matter how tenuous.

The interpretation of reality that formed the defense argument in this case was that Mr. Booker was uncooperative and belligerent, and that his resistance increased with every escalation of force used by the deputies. This flies in the face of the sworn testimony of people present in the cooperative seating area, and directly contradicts video evidence. When Deputies Grimes and Robinnette joined Gomez, they immediately escalated a tense situation, by tackling an openly surprised man to the ground. Deputy Grimes contributed to this escalation by commencing a carotid chokehold as Mr. Booker was still standing. According to the then-relevant Denver Sheriff Department use of force policy that was read during the trial: "The application of the carotid control technique must be restricted to those situations where violent resistance is encountered or where death or serious bodily harm will be the result to the officer." Deputy Grimes commenced his engagement with Mr. Booker with a technique he was ostensibly trained to progress toward. To begin with escalated force makes sense only if we follow the trail of additional alternative facts. Deputy Gomez, in her sworn testimony stated that Mr. Booker assaulted her, claiming he struck her above her breasts. In the alternate reality presented by the defense attorneys, Mr. Booker escalated the encounter by "using his muscles" to shake off Deputy Gomez's grip while screaming obscenities at her. Following the logic underlying this alterity, disobeying an order, no matter how capricious, justifies an escalation of force, no matter the consequences.

Tackling Booker using a chokehold probably did not kill him, although Taser blasts likely did. After Deputies Gomez, Grimes and Robinette tackled Mr. Booker, he was on his stomach with Deputy Robinette's knee driving into his lower back, his arms forced behind his back, his legs restrained in the vice grip of the OPNs, his hands bound by handcuffs, and his head in Deputy Grime's carotid choke hold—a hold so intense that one witness said of it: "Honestly I thought they were going to snap his neck. It was pulled back pretty hard. This act of violence enacted upon a man quite possibly in the throes of death, seems to have been experienced by Deputy Grimes as a kind of sport." A witness recalled: "The guy that was choking him started laughing and said, 'He's a lot stronger than I thought.'" At this point, while Mr. Booker gasped for air and Deputy Grimes laughed, Deputy Gomez's view of reality was that "[h]e was still struggling. That's why each person [deputy] had escalated … their option of force."

Along with all the other defendants, she insisted that Mr. Booker was "cussing up a blue streak." They claimed he was "violently assaultive." However, multiple witnesses stated that after Mr. Booker was restrained he was neither cursing nor resisting. All witnesses testified that he was in fact writhing in pain, gasping for air, and whispering the words: "Help, I can't breathe." According to one witness, who was seated within feet of the altercation, Mr. Booker lost consciousness after he whispered, "Help." At this point this witness recalls Deputy Gomez saying to the unresponsive Mr. Booker,"If you don't stop resisting, I'm going to have to Taser you." Clearly in the thrall of an alternate reality very hastily yet expertly constructed, a second deputy said, "Let's Taser him," and a third chimed in: "Yeah, let's Taser his ass." Throughout police jurisdictions in the United States, law enforcement officers are allowed to escalate force even to the point of death, if an individual is *violently assaultive*. Neither the witness testimony nor the video evidence indicated that Mr. Booker was acting aggressively. Nonetheless in the alternative reality of the Denver Sheriff Department, Mr. Booker, unconscious and completely disabled by forceful police restraints qualified as a violently assaultive individual who could justifiably be shocked with high voltage electricity.

Conveniently for the defense of police against excess force charges, Denver's use of force policy encourages alterity. According to Sheriff Department documents relevant at this time, only the officers directly involved in a use of force incident would be capable of making the determination of whether a level of force was justifiable. This was an enormous policy loophole, within which alternative facts could easily give birth to alternative realities. In effect, the officers who would potentially be disciplined for excessive force were the only ones to determine whether escalated levels of force were justified. In the case of these five deputies, their counter-narrative was quickly taken up by their superiors. On the stand, upon being questioned on the justification of the use of a variety of escalating forms of violence on an obviously restrained arrestee, Sergeant Wilson, Deputy Gomez's supervisor, was asked, "Do you believe that Mr. Booker engaged in violent resistance with the deputies?" He replied, "Yes." On the face of it, this was a response which contradicted a verified reality. When asked how, given the recorded facts, Mr. Booker could possibly be considered a threat, he replied: "It's possible that something could happen, depending on what *other limbs* are still available" (author's emphasis). The lawyer representing the City of Denver, Thomas Rice, saw things similarly. According to him: "Everything deputies did was by the book." He argued that all of their collective actions were an excellent example of what he termed "Arrest Control 101."

Though the Taser blast may have not instantly killed Marvin instantly, it certainly rendered him unresponsive. According to a witness: "As soon as they lifted him, his head fell to the ground and saliva and drool just started coming out of his mouth." Every witness present agreed that at this point Marvin Booker posed little if any threat to the safety of the deputies. Everyone agreed on this point, everyone except the City of Denver. From the City's point of view, as Mr. Booker's flaccid body was carried away, while body fluids leaked from him, he was still using his muscles to resist, to be belligerent, to pose a menace. To illustrate, Deputy Gomez insisted that while they were carrying the body to an isolation cell, "there was resistance in him, yes. There was muscle tension," adding, "he was intentionally keeping his muscles tight." When asked to comment on the footage of the deputies carrying Mr. Booker to the isolation cell, she was asked: "Looking at the video, as he's being carried, he looks like he's just hanging there, doesn't he?" Gomez answered: "No."

As they deposited Mr. Booker's body in the isolation cell, the deputies probably knew they were not in view of security cameras. What they did, what they did not do, and what they claimed Marvin Booker did, reveals additional wrinkles in their emerging alterity. According to the sworn testimony of multiple witnesses, as soon as they set down the body, the deputies high-fived each other, while boasting, "He's strong, he's strong, he's a strong old guy here." Witnesses claim they were laughing out loud. They found the time to unwind, to laugh; however they did not do something that is required by their department in every use of force incident. They did not call immediately for medical attention. Why not? Perhaps because they themselves had come to believe that Mr. Booker was faking it. To illustrate, when they finally did call for the nurse, they asked her to bring smelling salts in order to force him to stop faking unconsciousness. Only after the nurse ascertained the gravity of Mr. Booker's condition was an ambulance called. Marvin Booker was pronounced dead upon arrival at the hospital. Perhaps there is a more sinister subtext emanating from a warrior instinct of cultural preservation. Trial transcripts certainly point to attempts to immediately conjure alternative facts. For example, according to Deputy Gomez testimony, as she was removing his handcuffs, Booker assaulted her again. In this alternate reality, while lying flat on his stomach he contorted his arms upwards and attempted to grab her.

To understand the alternative facts being used to construct the alternate reality of a violently assaultive Marvin Booker, it is instructive to pay close attention to the points at which these alternative facts are completely contradicted by verified facts. According to Deputy Gomez, Marvin Booker was uncooperative from the moment he entered the jail. All witnesses recall that he was sleeping with his shoes off. Deputy Gomez insisted that when Mr. Booker was called up to the booking desk he called her a "motherfucker," and a "bitch." No witness testimony corroborates her claim. They recall her looking impatient and that she screamed, "I told you to get in the damn cell" as Mr. Booker turned away from her. Witnesses recall Mr. Booker saying, "I'm going to get my shoes." Deputy Gomez insisted that as he turned he stated forcefully that he "wasn't going to let her take his fucking property." According to all of the deputies he never let up with the cursing, with the attitude, and with the attempts to physically harm Deputy Gomez, and that he continued to say and do these things and yell these obscenities, down the stairs, down to the floor, up to the point when the Taser was used. Then he faked unconsciousness and attempted to assault Deputy Gomez. When the evidence doesn't support one's claim, can one simply manufacture evidence? In this alternate reality, the answer is yes. The salient point here is that the alternative reality was later created to fit into the actions recorded on the security cameras, devices that did not record sound. From their position of authority, the Sheriff Department scripted a dialogue to fit their version of reality. Probably to avoid the discovery of any evidence that might unhinge an emerging counter-narrative to what everyone in the jail had just witnessed, inmates were summoned and directed to mop up Mr. Booker's saliva and any other body fluids that may have leaked from him as he was carried to the isolation cell. One witness testified that he thought: "Hey isn't this a crime scene?" What is deeply disturbing in the aftermath of this tragic and violent death, is the collective expertise of cover-up and counter-narrative exhibited by all members of the Sheriff Department. Sanitizing the scene and then delaying a call for medical assistance are both actions designed to craft a reality that fits a scenario in which an escalation of force was necessary and proper. This narrative-crafting seems to have begun as soon as Marvin Booker died, or perhaps during the incident. To recap, the defense's line was that Mr. Booker used the muscles on his small frame to not only resist control but to assault Deputy Gomez. According to two witnesses, Deputy Gomez seemed fine until police detectives came to investigate. As soon as the detectives arrived she began to limp. During his questioning at the trial, an attorney asked why one of these witnesses took note of this change in her demeanor, to which he responded: "Because I knew that they were going to try and use that as a injury … [to claim] that he tried to cause bodily harm or did cause bodily harm to a sheriff so they could find an excuse for killing him." During her cross-examination Deputy Gomez augmented this counter-narrative, stating that she was not only limping but on crutches.

The construction of this alternate reality continued for years, throughout the preparation for and during the trial. According to testimony given by the eyewitness Scott Salazar, who had an unobstructed view of Marvin Booker's death, he was contacted by a certain Michael Castro who told Salazar that he was an independent investigator looking into the Marvin Booker case. According to Salazar, during their conversation Castro implied that he was not working for the City. By the end of their talk, it was clear to Salazar that Castro was trying to get a written statement from him that Marvin Booker was assaultive and touched Deputy Gomez above her breasts. Salazar refused to sign this statement. The statement would have served well as an alternative fact central to the reality the City and County of Denver was attempting to construct. Pretending that Salazar knew all along that Castro was a police detective, the defense attorney asked directly, "When you spoke to a Denver

Police Inspector named Michael Castro, did you not say that Mr. Booker placed his hands on the deputy sheriff, touching her above her breasts and near her shoulders and pushed her back. Isn't that right?" Salazar answered, "No, that is not right. If he lied to me about giving my testimony, I don't know why he even put in that testimony. I can tell you that as many times as I've told this story, I've never once said he put his hands on the female officer." The defense countered with "So you don't believe Mr. Booker put his hands on the female officer at all," to which Salazar answered:, "He did not push her above the breast." In a final attempt to authenticate the by now obvious attempt by the Denver Police Department to fabricate evidence in order to vindicate an excessive use of force by Denver Sheriff deputies, the defense attorney asked, "And you didn't tell that to Mr. Castro when he interviewed you on January 24, 2012?" to which Salazar answered, "No."

I posit that the actions and inactions of the Denver Sheriff Department reveal a wide spread prevalence of the warrior code in U.S. law enforcement. When Deputy Gomez was asked by prosecuting attorneys, "[U]nder the circumstances that confronted Mr. Booker, where he was prone on the floor, in a carotid choke hold for a sustained period, cuffed behind his back while he was on his stomach with significant weight on his back, the OPN applied to his legs, and then Tasered, would you agree that that's a significant enough use of force to justify immediate attention to see if he's okay from a medical perspective?" she replied, "As soon as the situation is under control and safe, yes." The bar for officer safety is obviously far higher than that for the concern for the physical condition of arrested individuals. Deputy Gomez's testimony makes it abundantly clear that the overriding concern of the Denver Sheriff Department is not the public good but the good of the Denver Sheriff Department. When asked why she felt so threatened by the apparent movements of an unconscious inmate, she uses a particularly revealing phrase, saying: "If he had grabbed somebody, *we could have fallen*" (author's emphasis). In this statement Gomez reveals a central tenet of a militarized police force, that outcomes of conflict are only either absolute victory or total defeat. These are words of war, a language that corrupts, and perhaps erases, the traditional core tenet of policing, namely public service, which entails serving and protecting the public, not defeating it.

As events unfolded in the years following the death of Marvin Booker, an overarching culture of protecting fellow officers and neutralizing threat radiated upward through the chain of command in the Sheriff Department and outwards to the Police Department and the district attorney's office. The Booker family's attorneys found many indications of a possible internal cover-up. There was a mysterious gap in the video footage. The camera that would have recorded the faces of witnesses near the event seems to have been out of order during the precise time frame that the incident occurred. Evidence disappeared. Sergeant Rodriguez submitted the wrong Taser to police detectives. The one used on Mr. Booker was never recovered. If it had been, the investigators, the lawyers, and the jurors would have known the exact number and duration of each Taser blast Mr. Booker sustained. Furthermore, even though the Sheriff Department requires that deputies fill out use of force paperwork each and every time force is used, irrespective of whether they themselves used force or simply observed the use of force, this mandate was not followed. The logic given by the deputies and their supervisors for this flagrant noncompliance with department policy was that they were "under investigation by the police anyway." Moreover, even though no suspects in an ongoing investigation are allowed to meet in person or even communicate with one another, evidence shows that the five deputies under investigation met and communicated repeatedly. In fact they conferred immediately after the incident. As police detectives began their investigation and before Mr. Booker's body was taken from the Van Cise-Simonet Detention Center, the five deputies involved in this incident met outside of the facility. The day before they gave their depositions to investigators they met at a restaurant. Additionally, they repeatedly texted one another—all texts and the phones used to send and receive them conveniently disappeared before any incriminating evidence could be recovered. Only Mr. Booker's attorneys, not the Denver Police detectives investigating Booker's homicide, nor the Internal Affairs officers in either the Sheriff or Police Departments investigating this incident, and certainly no one higher up in the command chain in either of these departments, found any of these facts troubling. Why not? Perhaps they were not concerned with investigating actual facts but rather with conjuring alternative ones in practiced efforts to protect their collective. Even the judge hearing the case seemed to understand that alternative facts, or lack thereof, were completely normal within these bureaucracies. She had reason to do so. According to long-standing practice in Denver, police officers and sheriff deputies never lie, they "depart from the truth."[13] To illustrate, in pointing out unconcealed falsehoods uttered by Deputy Gomez, mistruths uttered under oath that were directly contradicted by video evidence, prosecuting attorneys used the word "lie" to describe her statements. At the use of this word, the judge interjected: "All right. Her expression is 'departing from the truth.' And asking about lying isn't going to get you anywhere. You know what she's going to say."

On October 14, 2014, the federal jury ruled in favor of the prosecution in this wrongful death lawsuit. They awarded the family of Marvin Booker a $4.65 million settlement. They also required that the City pay the Booker family attorney fees, bringing the total payout to $6 million. Two objective realities were at play—one resulting in undisciplined and uncharged deputies doing arrest and control "by the book," the other resulting in a gross violation of civil rights—emerged from the same set of circumstances. Other recent cases involving abuses of authority by law enforcement officers reveal a larger pattern. Although the police officer who fired the fatal shots at Philando Castile was acquitted of second-degree manslaughter charges, the City of Saint Anthony and Castile's mother reached a nearly $3 million settlement. The family of Michael Brown, shot dead by police in 2014, received $1.5 million from the City of Ferguson Missouri. The City of Cleveland paid $6 million to the family of Tamir Rice. The City of Baltimore paid Freddy Gray's family $6.4 million. New York City paid Eric Gardner's family $5.9 million. Obviously Denver is far from an isolated case.

Conclusion

I suggest that these settlements and the corresponding lack of criminal conviction or even departmental discipline are simply the logical outcomes of two alternate yet co-existing realities. Furthermore, such blatantly discordant responses to the same set of factual circumstances is bad for all cities whose residents continue to be policed by brutal law enforcement officers and whose budgets must be balanced with less fiscal means. The increasing prominence of alternate realities in policing parallels the chilling doublespeak, internal contradictions, alternative facts, and twitter tantrums which have become alarmingly routine in the executive branch of the federal government. Both kinds of alterity do real damage to society.

As I sketched in the foregoing pages, each reality is indeed perfectly real. One nests in democratic governance, community policing, and common law, the other in monarchial governance, centralized policing, and statute law. The former better aligns with ideals set forth in the U.S. Constitution; the latter amounts to a recipe for European style fascism. At the very least we can report that the City of Denver now recognizes and is currently working to align these realities.

This alignment has much to do with the Booker settlement and with other problems with the department. As Marvin Booker's family's lawyers argued, a culture of violence at Denver's Van Cise-Simonet Detention Center led directly to Mr. Booker's death. Every so often evidence of this culture is caught on film. This was the case in April 2013 when Deputy Roberto Roena taunted an inmate, then attacked him with taekwondo punches and kicks. Roena was suspended without pay for 90 days. This suspension may be an early sign of police culture aligning with a broader ethical context. If so, then the Jamal Hunter case dramatically refocused this alignment process. On July 31, 2011, Jamal Hunter was jailed on a misdemeanor offense and assigned to a pod in the Van Cise-Simonet Detention Center with more than 60 felons, many of whom were gang members. He was soon caught up in a jail power struggle that included both gang members and a deputy, Gaynel Rumer. Deputy Rumer allegedly compelled inmates to attack Mr. Hunter in order to protect a pod-wide pornography, liquor, and marijuana distribution ring. Consequently, Mr. Hunter was cornered in his cell, his face pummeled with fists and feet, then scalding water was poured on his genitals. While Mr. Hunter screamed, Deputy Rumer was seen on surveillance video calmly walking his rounds. As with the investigation of Marvin Booker's death, the prosecution office, the investigating police detectives and the object of the investigation, the sheriff department, colluded, this time apparently by intimidating key witnesses, all of whom were serving time in the Van Cise-Simonet Detention Center. A federal judge intervened. Noting that the investigation "smacks of a sham," U.S. District Judge John Kane requested that federal authorities investigate subversive patterns and practices of law enforcement in Denver.[14] In part to silence Mr. Hunter and keep physicians from publicly describing the permanent damage to his genitals, the City offered Mr. Hunter a $3.25 million settlement. This settlement is part of a much broader pattern. Between 2014 and April 2017 the City of Denver paid out $14.5 million to settle excessive use of force lawsuits brought against its law enforcement department. Going back to 2004, the City has paid in excess of $28 million.

The City and County of Denver, along with its taxpaying citizens, have felt the financial sting of this objective reality. Nonetheless, as in other cities, prosecuting law enforcement officers in Denver is exceedingly difficult. A code of silence prevails. In excessive use of force cases, officers simply vouchsafe for fellow officers. The department keeps the department from harm. Mirroring the SWAT team's impotent actions during the 1999 Columbine shooting, the Sheriff Department devotes massive resources to protecting itself. Standing internal policy makes this all the easier. In a system wherein the process of ascertaining and qualifying facts in an investigation flows upward through the chain of command from the deputy under investigation directly to her or his immediate supervisor, self-protection is a simple matter of aligning alternative facts and departures from the truth with a desired departmental outcome, such as justifiable force or justifiable homicide. In this way a warrior culture that relies on chokeholds and tasers to control inmates prevails over a community policing culture that would first defer to non-violent techniques in order to de-escalate potential crises.

In 2014 the Denver City Council and Mayor Michael Hancock ordered a review of police and sheriff use of force policies. Raising a considerable amount of controversy, the Denver Police Department conducted an internal review, then held public meetings, to discuss changes made to the policy. The Sheriff Department did the exact opposite in reformulating its internal policies and practices. During the next two years, the City hired a new sheriff, restructured the Sheriff Department's command staff, and, most importantly, contracted an independent consulting firm—Hillard Heintze—to help make lasting changes to the department, its policies, and its culture. Using the conceptual framework I established in the foregoing pages, the City seems to be attempting to align Sheriff Department realities with more objective realities. The Sheriff Department's updated use of force policy may be one of the most progressive in the country. Unlike the Police Department's policy, the Sheriff Department's use of force policy was not crafted internally but with the input of 44 people from a wide range of backgrounds and viewpoints, such as church pastors, citizen advocate groups, deputies, and criminal defense attorneys. It is progressive. For example, it calls for an entire new use of force incident review process. Formerly a deputy's immediate supervisor would decide whether a case should be reviewed by internal affairs. Currently a more diverse and hopefully more objective group of people will consider whether incidents require further review. Moreover, significant changes were made to the use of force policy, which differs in five noteworthy ways from its predecessor. It sets a more restrictive standard for when and how deputies use force than what is permitted under federal or state criminal and civil laws. It requires that deputies intervene when they see another deputy using inappropriate force—by trying to stop it or by notifying a supervisor. It mandates that deputies first attempt to de-escalate a situation before using force. De-escalation may involve talking calmly, listening, requesting help and even momentarily disengaging. In the event that an inmate does not cooperate or follow orders, deputies must have a planned course of action before engaging an inmate. And finally, while restraining inmates, deputies must avoid using their body weight in a way that limits an inmate's ability to breathe.

The new use of force policy is just a framework. To what degree it is implemented depends greatly on changing Denver's warrior code to a culture of protecting and serving. Susan McCampbell, President of the Center for Innovative Public Policies and a federal independent monitor for four jail systems, estimated that this culture shift could take 10 to 15 years. And we must remember that its implementation will take place in the United States of America, where not a single state complies with international laws and standards on the use of lethal force by law enforcement officers. Moreover, Colorado is especially lenient with lethal force. There it can be used on someone escaping from jail and by a private citizen who happens to be carrying out law enforcement activities, such as assisting a law enforcement officer in making an arrest.

By arguing that alternative facts are not fake, I attempted to open a dialog relevant to the political times in which we now live. Alternative facts are real. They coexist along with actual facts. Moreover, as I deconstruct in the preceding pages, alternative facts tend to create alternate realities. This production process is self-sustaining. Alternative facts protect and perpetuate alternative realities. Therefore, the alternate reality of a War on Crime will likely never fade. Politicians will continue to create self-serving realities. Put another way, there will always be work for spin doctors. Societal vigilance against the real threats of alternative facts is our only defense against them forever trumping actual facts. When we, as we eventually must, focus on the essentials, empirical facts are all that matter. Thus, our vigilance must be accompanied by renewed and reinvigorated empirical research. Many questions need to be answered. Such as, how does lying become institutionalized within power structures? Do agents within these power structures actually believe the mistruths they effortlessly manufacture? Why does society seem to accept an ever-widening rift between societal realities and political realities?

Acknowledgments

This essay would not have been possible without Wade Gardner. His provocative documentary *Marvin Booker Was Murdered* piqued my interest in this case. Conversations with him solidified my interest in crafting a scholarly argument around it. Finally he shared with me most of the documents I use as evidence supporting my argument. Helena Janes assisted me with insightful content editing and careful copyediting. Any errors are mine alone.

Notes

1. The term anarchy derives from the ancient Greek word *anarkhos*—without chief or ruler—has assumed the modern meaning of "without the state," whether oligarchic, monarchical, theological, autocratic, or democratic. However the implication of riotous and chaotic freedom from government belies the core of anarchistic theory. Anarchy is not the absence of order; rather it is order without the state.

2. Radley Balko, *Rise of the Warrior Cop: The Militarization of America's Police Forces* (New York: Public Affairs, 2013), 124.

3. The Bonus Army was assemblage upwards of 43,000 U.S. World War I veterans, their families, and affiliated groups—who gathered in Washington, D.C., in the summer of 1932 in order to publicly demand immediate redemption of their service certificates. In 1924 the U.S. government awarded World War I veterans bonuses in the form of certificates they could not redeem until 1945.

4. The Castle Doctrine, central to the notion of privacy in British common law that migrated into the U.S. legal system, establishes one's home as an ultimate refuge of personal privacy, one that a homeowner can use deadly force to protect and one that the state, barring exceptional circumstances, cannot transgress.

5. A no-knock allows law enforcement officers to enter a property without immediate prior notification of the residents, such as by knocking or ringing a doorbell. English common law has required law enforcement to knock-and-announce since the year 1604. No-knock warrants are part and parcel of the War on Drugs. In *Wilson v. Arkansas* (1995) the U.S. Supreme Court created an exception to the Castle Doctrine, which holds one's home as an ultimate bastion of privacy, in order to prevent the destruction of easily destroyed evidence such as drugs.

6. Peter Kraska and Victor Kappeler, "Militarizing American Police: The Rise and-Normilization of Paramilitary Units," *Social Problems* 44, no 1 (1997): 1–18.

7. Victor Kappeler and Peter Kraska, "Normalising Police Militarisation, Living in Denial," *Policing and Society* 25, no. 3 (2015): 268–275.

8. Loïc Wacquant, "The Curious Eclipse of Prison Ethnograhpy In the Age of Mass Incarceration," *Ethnography* 3, no. 4 (2004): 371–397.

9. John Crank, *Understanding Police Culture*, 2d ed. (New York: Routledge, 2015).

10. A carotid chokehold is a form of strangulation that compresses one or both carotid arteries and/or the jugular veins without compressing the airway. A well applied hold will lead to unconsciousness in a matter of seconds.

11. The Orcutt Police Nunchaku, or OPN, resembles the traditional Japanese martial arts weapon known as the nunchaku. However, it is not used by law enforcement officers as a weapon but for *restraint control* and *pain compliance*. OPNs are employed as vices with which to control and cause pain to the arms or legs of uncooperative suspects or inmates.

12. A Taser is an electroshock weapon. It delivers electric current that disrupts voluntary control of muscles. Someone struck by a Taser also experiences extreme pain due to an over-stimulation of sensory nerves and motor nerves, which results in strong involuntary muscle contractions. Tasers both incapacitate and cause pain compliance.

13. Christopher Osher, "Police Handcuffed by Internal Discipline," *The Denver Post*, 7 May 2016.

14. Kirk Mitchell "Judge Urges Feds to Investigate Denver Police Sheriff in Abuse Case," *The Denver Post*, 10 June 2014.

PART 2

Philosophical Observations

Sophistry Redux

Mythology and Ancient Rhetoric Reborn in the Trump Age

ANDREW GROSSMAN

The Power of Rhetoric in the Absence of Knowledge

Awash in reactionary hysteria rare even among arch-conservatives, the 2016 Republican National Convention gave the public its first taste of that propagandistic mix of misinformation and delusion we now call "alternative facts." In his acceptance speech at the convention, Donald Trump claimed that America is one of the world's "highest-taxed nations" (in fact, it's one of the lowest); that the Obama administration promoted "open borders" (in fact, Obama deported more undocumented persons than George W. Bush); that he would "restore law and order" by "appointing the best and brightest prosecutors" (in fact, presidents only appoint federal prosecutors, not the municipal personnel who prosecute most violent crimes); and, most fantastically, that "millions of Democrats will join [the Trump] movement," because he would "fix the system" (a statement not even the most rabid Trumpist could swallow).[1] These lies were only the prelude, however, to the bewildering Trumpisms that immediately followed a victory emboldened by the "alt-right." Upset that he'd lost the popular vote, Trump proclaimed that between three and five million unidentified immigrants voted illegally, some of them bused to polls by Massachusetts liberals. Unencumbered by a historical consciousness or rudimentary scholastic knowledge, Trump informed us that Andrew Jackson opposed the Civil War, which began 16 years after his death. Perhaps the most embarrassing (and now immortal) gaffe came in the early days of Trump's presidency, when he rhetorically resurrected Frederick Douglass during a Black History Month appearance, claiming that Douglass "has done an amazing job" and is now "being recognized more and more." One must applaud Douglass' ancestors for having penned a scathing editorial that ironically thanked Trump for speaking of the abolitionist in the present tense, "because his spirit and legacy are still very much alive"[2]—an especially clever takedown of temporally-challenged conservatives who long for an ignorantly idealized past.

The alternative facts of 2016 quickly became the staggering political perfidy of 2017 and 2018. Commentators right and left had foolishly assumed that Trump's wild rhetoric eventually would be curbed by conventional advisors, structural restraints, and the immovable functionaries of the deep state. Few could have imagined an administration populated by a rotation of professional sycophants, former lobbyists, white nationalists, hucksters, fraudsters, and wifebeaters. We could never have imagined, as Trump has variously claimed, that a trade war with China would be "easy to win"; that a Central American caravan packed with Arab terrorists might penetrate our vestal borders; that the Saudi-backed assassins of journalist Jamal Khashoggi were in fact of unknown origin; or that Trump devotee Cesar Sayok, a former male stripper who lived in a van, would try to assassinate the entire central leadership of the Democratic Party. It is unnecessary to rehash the many antidemocratic outrages to which we quickly became inured and which already have been recounted in Michael Wolff's *Fire and Fury*, Bob Woodward's *Fear: Trump in the White House*, James Comey's *A Higher Loyalty*, and so on. Our present concern is the debilitating effect of Trump's empty rhetoric, particularly as he exploits the propagandistic reach of a rightwing entertainment-industrial complex to further his agenda and compromise Constitutional principles.

The question is not whether Trump believes his own lies—surely, he believes a few of them and expediently peddles the rest. Beyond any single lie, the act of blinding the public with a flurry of untruths—or "alternative facts"—has become a requisite tool of rightwing politicking in the Trump age. According to *Washington Post* reporter Daniel Dale, Trump has told and/or repeated a total of 6,420 verifiable lies between the day he took office and December 24, 2018.[3] The tallied lies range from old chestnuts about crowd sizes to claims that liberal media, willing to do anything to tarnish Trump's reputation, had grossly exaggerated the number of deaths caused by Puerto Rican hurricanes in September 2017.[4] The alternativity of truth had perhaps reached its apex in December 2017, when Trump officials banned the Center for Disease Control from using the terms "evidence-based" and "science-based," suggesting instead the stock phrase "The CDC bases its recommendations on science in consideration with community standards and wishes."[5]

The scientific method was now at the mercy of undefined community *wishes* that (presumably) privilege conservative ideology over egg-headed epistemic inquiry. Apparently, the government can now *wish away* truths or least replace truth with wish-fulfillment fantasies. If these fantasies ultimately do little to advance any kind of prudent conservative agenda, it hardly matters, for Trump's followers are motivated mainly by a fantastic aesthetics of indignation. Above all, Trump engenders not so much populist outrage but a kind of impotent pleasure for the masses. As long as he infuriates liberal boogeymen and sticks his pussy-grabbing finger in the eyes of perceived elites—but not actual elites, some of whom populate his cabinet—he is fighting the good fight.

When Trump spin-doctor Kellyanne Conway first proposed the term "alternative facts"—to rationalize Trump's exaggerated claim about the size of his inauguration crowd—she likely thought the term would be an innocuous, even tactful euphemism, for the word "alternative" has the ring of anti-corporatist authenticity (e.g., alternative music, alternative cinema, etc.). But the term, reeking of reactionary denial, is clearly driven by strategy rather than style. Not only a (feeble) attempt to legitimize delusion, the word "alternative" here concedes the right's desperate attempt to find a new, softer public relations strategy, particularly as conservatives' old misinformation strategies—homophobic and antifeminist propaganda, for instance—no longer hold cultural sway. Employing what seems an ill-defined rhetoric of relativism and radical subjectivity, "alt" conservatives were now ironically invoking a kind of cut-rate social constructionism, precisely that which repulses their nationalistic and evangelical base.

If the Trumpist stew of lies and ignorance weren't wedded to egoistic power-seeking, we might write it off as a pseudo-populist backlash against the duopolistic party system that Trump pretended to upend. But power and self-aggrandizement, of course, are Trump's raison d'être. Let's return for a moment to the 2016 convention, where he shamelessly revealed his intentions. Amidst Trump's vapid braggadocio and chants of "Lock her up!" from the anti–Clinton crowd, one carefully selected applause line stood out: "Nobody knows the system better than me [*sic*], which is why I alone can fix it." Because Trump had no relevant political experience—because he was widely known as a charlatan—the rationale for his campaign hinged upon such a self-incriminating statement. After Trump delivered the line, there was a slight pause. Trump then adopted his Mussolinian pose, raised his chin, and looked heroically past the teleprompter into the distance, signaling to the throng that it was time to applaud and scream fascistically. Trump delivered the line as if he were a charismatic cleric revealing the cure for our national sickness: only a charlatan can undo a culture of charlatanism. The line was essentially a repudiation of democracy and an apologia for fascism. We do not need a politically engaged citizenry or an educated, rational electorate, but only a single-minded leader who can spearhead a cult of action, embody otherwise misdirected outrage, and (somehow) supersede Constitutional checks and balances. If fascist ideology claims that deliberative democracy is doomed to stalemates and inaction, then we logically require a leader anathematic to (or incapable of) deliberation, to rescue us from ourselves and exact a terrible revenge upon a system that has betrayed us.

It is irrelevant whether the "only I can fix it" line was written by Trump himself or by one of his salaried homunculi. The sentiment, dripping with antidemocratic hero-worship, was emblematic of the right's anxious attempt to repel neoliberalism and upset a conservative establishment that had repeatedly sold out the rank and file. Embodying the Americanist cult of the straight-shooting hero, Trump (according to his apologists) speaks "directly" to the people and is unassailably "authentic" (that is, he is an authentic liar, whereas most politicians are inauthentic liars). His coterie senses in every meddlesome fact-checker or unflattering journalist an elitist conspiracy to delegitimize his electoral victory, much as totalitarian regimes label inconvenient truths "counterrevolutionary." Given his perceived invincibility among a subset of the conservative base, Trump hasn't adherents or loyalists as much as he has fans. When journalists ask when Trump will go one lie too far and lose his base, they totally misunderstand the psychology of mass delusion. Trump fans don't care if he lies about global warming or his immigrant-repelling wall any more than they would care if their favorite actor weren't really an airborne superhero. Trump's allure is bellicosity itself, which provides to his impotent supporters the illusion that he is courageous enough to battle educated elites on their collective behalf. In a culture marked by passivity, apathy, and addiction, Trump only needs to remind his supporters that fighting is the greatest source of satisfaction. It doesn't matter that his chosen causes (e.g., the vanity wall) are the implausible fantasies of a tantrum-prone child. The blind, single-minded intensity with which he fights proves his "truth," much as, in the mind of the fundamentalist, the intensity of one's faith proves the existence of a supernatural savior.

The political (or politicized) triumph of the cultish, media-manufactured celebrity only confirms what Adorno and Horkheimer had already decried in *The Dialectic of Enlightenment*. With Trumpism, however, we've gone surreally farther than lambasting Toscanini (Adorno's favorite bourgeois target) or critiquing the alienation endemic to kitsch culture. Political life and cultural life are no longer complementary allegories or even colluding partners—they now overlap perfectly, comprising a single, unhyphenated leviathan. If the medium is indeed the message, we cannot be surprised that a game show host has turned pop culture into amateur governance and televised ubiquity into political viability. If we are honest, however, what depresses us most isn't that Washington is "Hollywood for ugly people" (an inevitable outcome of the culture industry). What really depresses us is the character of Trump's celebrity: simply, he's *the worst celebrity we have*. We can begrudgingly understand a politicized Ronald Reagan or Arnold Schwarzenegger or, in another time and place, an officeholding Charlton Heston or John Wayne. But Trump isn't a righteous cinematic hero or defender of the people. Like spiteful signs that read "English only," Trump embodies an inbred American crassness and selfishness we'd prefer to conceal from the world. As a nouveau riche capitalist, he is more self-parody than alpha male, and even his signature piece, *The Art of the Deal*, was ghost-written by journalist Tony Schwartz.

In the 1980s and 90s, long before the visibility afforded by *The Apprentice*, Manhattanites already knew Trump as an opportunistic vulgarian, a tasteless architect, and a public adulterer. Those outside New York perhaps knew him as a television pitchman for Diet Pepsi, Pizza Hut, and yes, Trump: The Game, in which card-swapping players (according to a 1989 commercial) "deal for everything they've ever wanted to own." Perhaps a few unlucky souls had witnessed his repulsive cameo in *Ghosts Can't Do it*, a 1989 sex comedy in which he flirts (sexlessly) with Bo Derek. In whatever media-manufactured guise, Trump acts like a secularized televangelist—he is a shell of self-promotion devoid of genuine content. During the 2016 campaign, leftist commentator Lawrence O'Donnell aptly called him "Lonesome Rhodes," an allusion to Andy Griffith's Janus-faced populist in *A Face in the Crowd*. But to his supporters, the sociopathic elements of his personality—the lack of empathy, the narcissism, the tactless "straight talk"—are signs of a machismo that towers above spineless globalists and decadent institutionalists. Trump's Janus-face is only another arrow in his anti-intellectual quiver. Regardless of his stagnant numbers in the polls, his obstinate supporters—disproportionately drawn from the lower classes—find succor in the luxurious power he radiates, much as movie fans live vicariously through screen stars. Trump knows that his celebrity already mediates political subjectivity—so who needs wishy-washy truth?

Trump's alleged "strength"—and we know his mind revolves around underdefined binaries of "weak" and "strong"—clearly stems from gendered assumptions, from his invasive sexism to his tone-deaf declaration that "I'm the most militaristic person there is"[6] (an attempt to distinguish his isolationism from perceived effeminacy). One need not be a strict Reichian to presume that many "ordinary" Americans voted for Trump because they preferred an authoritarian father to a flawed, untrustworthy mother. Trump's persona is defined by masculinized accoutrements of executive power, from a trophy wife to the suits and oversize ties he wears as a second skin. Even in his strained appearances on *Saturday Night Live*—orchestrated as ratings ploys by NBC—Trump insisted on sporting his business ensemble in every sketch. To witness Trump impersonate a depressive trash collector, a minimum-wage burger-flipper, or a starving ice cream man might actually have been amusing, even if the jokes would stem from the elitist notion that Trump, a hapless inheritor of wealth, is incompatible with a proletarian uniform. His suits are invested with oligarchical mystique and capitalist branding, while his giant red ties become not only enflamed phallic symbols but brazen directional signs pinpointing the organ itself. A paradoxical creature, he is an exhibitionist who fears naked transparency, a notion reflected not merely in his backpedaling and cover-ups but in the way he physically clothes his lack of content.

The cult of machismo and militaristic appearances are key to the promulgation of fascism, as Umberto Eco observes in his familiar essay "Ur-Fascism." Certainly, Trumpism shares some immediate characteristics with fascism, from the cult of personality and the rejection of intellectualism to demanding loyalty of cabinet members and demonizing "unpatriotic" mass media. His shameless admiration for Vladimir Putin and Rodrigo Duterte discloses his contempt for democracy, even if his defense of Putin against America's own intelligence agencies (at the 2018 Helsinki Summit) also hints at some still-secret element of blackmail.[7] Presently, one can only assume that Republicans are silently repulsed by Trump's love of authoritarians and inexplicable anti–American postures. Republican Congressmen were conspicuously mute when, at a September 30, 2018 rally, Trump informed adoring throngs that he and Kim Jong Un were now exchanging "love letters" and oaths of mutual admiration. One wonders how the authors of high school history textbooks will rationalize this episode, which a century from now will seem baffling, corrupt, and/or psychotic. Today, we might laugh off the episode as a sort of senile tragicomedy—but were this 1933, would Trump be trading endearing epistles with Hitler? The question may seem glib, but Trump's mix of racial animus, authoritarian posturing, nostalgic sentimentality, and willful delusion echo parts of the fascist mindset.

We must stop short, however, of the sort of simplistic equations offered by cable news pundits and journalists. Traditional fascism—as espoused by Giovanni Gentile—does have philosophical values at odds with Trumpist ones (apart from the fact that Gentile's philosophy is derived from absurd extrapolations of Hegelian monism, leavened with much Germanic nonsense about the "spirit"). Fascism is anticapitalistic and anti-individualistic; it seeks to absorb individual egos into a state apparatus that sees interminable conflict as both desirable and natural. Trump's prolonged conflicts serve not a revolutionary (or even pseudo-revolutionary) purpose but only the ego of a man who uses ambient chaos to enlarge his own singular persona. Even if Trumpism were successfully acting as a *collective* movement (rather than a personal vanity project), it would still part company with fascism ideologically. If we are to believe former Trump advisor Steve Bannon, Trumpist populism ends with the pseudo-anarchistic fantasy of devolving centralized government in the name of perceived individualism. For Gentile, the good fascist surges above the positivism of the 19th century and rejects the facile happiness promised by bourgeois individualism, which "instinctively urges him toward a life of selfish momentary pleasure."[8] Within this framework, Trumpism apparently opposes much of Gentilian fascism, which claims that, through "self-sacrifice [and] the renunciation of self-interest," the fascist man "can achieve that purely spiritual existence in which his value as a man consists."[9] Obviously, Trumpism—encompassing the man himself and his vicariously pleasured fans—is *all* about the gratification of self-interest. Trumpism further sees any self-sacrifice as "weakness," in accordance with the alt-right's highly selective reading of radical atheist Ayn Rand. Simply, we might say that Trumpism appropriates fascist tools for capitalistic ends. More philosophically, Gentile imagined fascism as a spiritual force without material image, while Trumpism, as a form of empty propaganda, rewrites fascism as a spiritless image without material force.

Can Socratic Knowledge Redeem the Visual Age?

Considering the triumph of Trump's insubstantial image, we cannot avoid examining how ocularcentrism (a topic Martin Jay has probably exhausted) dominates American political life. That Trump engineers Miss Universe pageants is apropos. Like a beauty contestant, he should dispel any illusions of aptitude or knowledge when he opens his mouth for the question-and-answer segment. Yet his image of charismatic success is so alluring that his fans interpret his neediness as vainglory and his most grammatically tortured addresses as "straight talk." Whether stumbling from halting, teleprompted speeches penned by beleaguered staffers or neurotically improvising Tweets in the dead of night, Trump abuses language like a remedial student struggling with elementary syntax. A parade of cable news pundits, psychiatrists, neurologists, linguists, and ethicists have parsed Trump's tortured grammar for signs of senility, dementia, or Constitutional incompetence. Perhaps Trump's most incoherent oratory can be found in a 2015 Hilton Head campaign rally, broadcast on C-SPAN and excerpted on an episode of John Oliver's *Last Week Tonight*:

> China isn't abiding by anything … they're buying all of our coal. We can't use coal anymore, essentially. They're buying our coal, and they're using it. Now when you talk about the planet—it's so big out there. We're here, they're there [*makes planetary hand gestures*]. It's like they're our next-door neighbor, right, in terms of the universe. Miss Universe, by the way, made a great deal when I sold that … oh, did I get rich.

That was a great deal! Oh! You know, they broke my choppers [*sic*] on that. They said, "He talks about illegal immigration, we're not going to put him on television." First of all, Univision is being sued like crazy. You wouldn't believe it. And NBC, I made a great deal with them.[10]

From a successful huckster, one expects applause lines, but not such indulgent incoherence. Revealingly, even the word "universe" leads Trump back to himself, as if every imaginable space in existence proceeds from his own ego. This infantile emotionality was revealed more dangerously in Trump's perfunctory missile attack against Syria (on April 6, 2017), an act prompted by seeing photos of Bashar al-Assad's chemical attacks on civilians. The *image* alone moved him to action, rather than the abstract, preexisting knowledge of the events, which had already been widely reported. Responding foremost to visual appeals to pathos, not logos, he is as susceptible to manipulation as are his jingoistic crowds, who replace the need for facticity with Pavlovian chanting (whether "USA, USA!" or "Lock her up!"). On occasion, he must also convince himself of the potency of his own image. During a January 2, 2019 cabinet meeting, he sprawled before him (and the assembled cameras) a Hollywood-style poster featuring the text "Sanctions Are Coming" over an image of Trump marching stern-faced through an ominous mist.[11] Trump's image-conscious infantilism might have reached its nadir on July 2, 2017, when he tweeted (to his own POTUS account) a doctored video of his 2007, publicity appearance on "Wrestlemania" that featured the CNN logo superimposed over the head of former opponent Vince McMahon. That the image perpetuated Trump's "fake news" binary, positing his pugnacious heroism against an effete liberal media, was par for the course. What is remarkable is that only two days later, on 4 July, Trumpists itching for a fight with the mainstream media perceived NPR's tweet of the Declaration of Independence as an anti–Trump diatribe. Amusingly, they misread the sentiment behind the "right of the people … to institute new government" as an attack on the Trump regime, not on King George. One could hardly impugn their logic.

Reason still makes us wonder if or when Trump fans could become disillusioned with their hero, given the limitations of his puerile rhetoric. Time and again, we have witnessed hand-wringing evangelicals support Trump as long as he packs the benches with pro-business, anti-abortion judges. Nakedly exposed, evangelicals no longer claim their hypocrisy is anything but a calculated political transaction.[12] Trump's failure to condemn Saudi Arabian agents' dismemberment of *Washington Post* journalist Jamal Khashoggi likewise failed to disillusion his ardent supporters. The assassination was but a mildly unpleasant footnote to Trump's greatest success, the installation of white, heterosexual male judges preselected by the Heritage Foundation. If Trumpists use their idol mainly as a font of Conservative pleasure or as a projection of their white grievance, his anti-establishmentarian posturing alone is sufficient. They will desert him only when he can no longer deliver the bitter delights of righteous indignation. Reason is otherwise overthrown by Trump's long-groomed image, equal parts manufactured celebrity and capitalist entitlement (i.e., inherited wealth). Nearly all critical thought since Plato has strove to demote or unmask the charismatic and/or deceptive image, which, over millennia, matured from religious totems and weeping icons into political posters and advertising montages. Tragically, our species suffers a biological predilection for ocular stimuli, for the visual cortices, occupying a disproportionate part of the brain, dispose us to see first and hear later. Without the aid of modern neurology, the Greeks, though enthralled to visual beauty, knew enough to doubt the verity of the visual. At Areopagus, the Greeks would hold their courts of justice at unlit midnight, forcing both judges and defendants to depend only on spoken logos, not deceptive appearances. Speakers before the Assembly of Athens had only their words, for which they were fully accountable. It was not for nothing that Milton famously linked Areopagus to freedom of speech itself.

At the same time, image-conscious sophists such as Gorgias and Protagoras—celebrities in their day—would charge the sons of elite families for lessons in rhetoric, the most valuable skill in a culture without lobbyists, M.B.A.s, and J.D.s. Perhaps the academic rhetorics of Gorgias and Protagoras seem quaint in an age of public relations, technocracy, and post–Orwellian doublespeak. The Greeks could never imagine the pretended objectivity of the mass-printed page or PR firms' coy layers of plausible deniability. They would be astonished by our alienating phenomenon of speechwriting, which bizarrely transplants an alien voice into one's body. Perhaps it is appropriate that our "Christian" nation, through the phenomenon of paid speechwriting, has found a capitalistic means to demonstrate Cartesian dualism.

By now, we've grown inured to watching Trump mouth speeches ghost-written by alt-right staffers—the hero is immediately exposed as a puppet with delusions of autonomy. Oddly, one wishes Trump were a hypocrite. At least a hypocrite holds actual beliefs, even though he lies about them. A prisoner of his own opportunistic ego, adjusting his opinions to the prevailing wind, Trump hasn't any core beliefs to betray. If he has no discernable beliefs, we can conclude that he is indifferent to truth-seeking. And if that is the case, we can echo the question of Plato scholar Donald J. Zeyl: "If the orator can be indifferent to truth, can he be indifferent to justice?"[13] Presumably, Trump assumes that he simultaneously can act justly and ignorantly, a proposition anathematic to Plato. Whereas Socrates sought to reduce (and yet elevate) everything to the status of knowledge, Trump sees the rejection of knowledge as the best way to insulate himself from moral responsibility. The term "alternative facts" is thus not merely a (rather unconvincing) technique of political denial; it also releases the ignorant, or those suffering a false consciousness, from the ethical mandate to know. Zeyl observes that the "Greek moral philosophers typically held that the basic alternatives for ethical choice are *alternative lives*"[14] (my emphasis) that derive from good-faith attempts at truth-finding. But if one retreats into *fallaciously* alternative—that is, *unlived*—facts, the possibility of self-transformation becomes lost to cheapest cynicism.

If Trump barely bothers to conceal his bad faith, his fans only need to overcome their conventional blindness. This, in fact, is the theme of Plato's *Ion*, a brief but pointed dialogue that critiques the empty ethos of a celebrity whose limited expertise nevertheless fools the crowd. The dialogue begins as Ion, a rhapsode and renowned expert in Homer, encounters Socrates after winning first prize in a poetry-reciting competition. At first, Socrates praises Ion's well-tailored appearance: "You have to dress in all sorts of finery and make yourself as grand as you can, to live up to your art..."[15] Socrates then examines the depth of Ion's poetic knowledge. Ion claims to be Athens' greatest rhapsode—and has the prizes to prove it—but shamelessly admits that he knows only Homer and nothing of Hesiod or other major poets. Nevertheless, Ion claims that "Homer did it better" and that "Homer is quite enough"[16] even though he has no comparative knowledge to make this claim. He presumes Homer's superiority only because the crowd says so. In turn, the crowd praises Ion for reinforcing its preconceptions. The similarities between the actor Ion and Trump—who holds a Screen Actor's Guild membership—are troubling.[17] Like Ion, Trump intentionally plays to a base willing to misperceive expertise in a single thing as broad, worldly knowledge. In Trump's case, knowledge of a publicity-driven construction enterprise and the grey areas of building codes magically translate into a deep knowledge of economics (and thus of American life). Belief in such magic translation goes hand in hand with the underlying belief that government should be "run like a business," even if conservatives who make this claim never specify what kind of business they have in mind (a brothel, perhaps?). At the end of the dialogue, Socrates argues that Ion practices a hollow skill rather than a true art. Socrates ironically suggests that Ion surely channels "divinity," for nothing else could explain how an admitted ignoramus could achieve rhetorical success. Of course, what the Greeks called divinity today's pantheists call celebrity.

Celebrity is central to two of Plato's most substantial critiques of rhetoric, *Protagoras* and *Gorgias*.[18] In each of these dialogues, Socrates, always the outsider, interrogates two renowned, revered sophists who teach the art of rhetoric in bad faith, replacing truth-seeking with power-seeking. Though Socratic dialecticism is not truth in itself, the good faith immanent in the dialectic process ideally sheds accreted layers of sophistry and stylization. Much like politicians who "pivot" to avoid truthfully answering questions, sophists engage in windy, self-satisfied monologues that sidestep good faith and pose as the final syntheses of a dialectical history that has already been tested and found true. Typical political speech is thus not so much nondi-alectical as anti-dialectical, purposefully sabotaging and defrauding poten-tially synthetic discourse. This strategy not only maintains the status quo but also pessimistically frames public dialogue as an inevitable failure or, at best, an embarrassing stalemate punctuated by nervous laughter. After witnessing enough nationally broadcast stalemates, citizens abandon the hope of dis-course or even productive action. Surrendering to corporate-sponsored pes-simism becomes the "pragmatic" response—the only response—to collective despair. To perpetuate this despair, politicians, spokespeople, and complicit journalists must continually manufacture bad faith encounters. Those who argue in good faith are usually excluded from political news cycles, which instead subsidize a rear-guard circulation of paid pundits, regime spokesmen, and political hirelings, often appearing before backgrounds that identify cor-porate or institutional affiliations. In the case of Trump, network media doubtless regretted their own protocols throughout the 2016 campaign cycle, for anti-dialectical Trump, the guru of bad faith, took advantage of their relentless coverage more ably than they could ever parry his blows.

An unprecedented triumph of bad faith, Trump's election demonstrated not only the uselessness of the Electoral College (supposedly a bulwark against stealth tyranny) but the willingness of too many voters to accept the greatest alternative fact of all—that leadership requires no particular knowl-edge. In *Protagoras*, Socrates sees the titular rhetorician as an exemplar of bad faith, for Protagoras cannot even define his own art. Protagoras' famous slogan, "Every day, day after day, you will get better and better," is bad faith made into a dictum, for eternal improvement is something no teacher can guarantee. The notion nevertheless attracted many of Athens' young elite, who believed Protagoras' rhetoric lessons could improve their social standing. It turns out, however, that Protagoras can't quite articulate the subject of his teaching, since rhetoric is ostensibly a form of communication, not a subject matter in itself. At a crucial point in the dialogue, Socrates goads Protagoras into admitting that the goal of his art really is (or should be) cultivating cit-izenship, but this admission only begs further questions. Specifically, does one fulfill civic duty through general knowledge (experience) or technical knowledge (education)? Socrates claims that a Protagorean orator cannot *convincingly* give advice on matters of technical knowledge, such as ship-building, because the sophistic replacement of content with style would go only so far. Unlike our American Founding Fathers, Socrates actually had faith in the common wisdom of citizens, and he insists that a sufficiently astute *polis* wouldn't be fooled by politicians pretending to technical knowl-edge that is obviously beyond them. If an inexpert sophist were to speak pre-tentiously on ship-building, Socrates claims, the people would "laugh at him and shout him down until he either gives up trying to speak and steps down himself, or the archer-police remove him forcibly by order of the board…"[19] Yet in *Gorgias*, written about the same time as *Protagoras*, Socrates admits that contemporary Athens knows no just, knowledgeable orators, and even rhetorical heroes such as Pericles likely stooped to pathos and rabble-rousing when speaking on subjects alien to them. Suffice it to say that an occasionally inexpert Pericles fooling Athenians is no less plausible than an eternally ignorant Trump making his base believe that he is an economic mastermind or that "he knows more than the generals."

The scenario of *Gorgias* is much like that of *Protagoras*, but the argument is ultimately more pessimistic. Socrates—here about 40 years old, perceptive but imperfect—again bursts the bubble of a powerful rhetorician, Gorgias, who claims to be the most powerful man alive. Through his dazzling oratory, Gorgias says he can not only persuade "judges … councilors … and assemblymen" but also make doctors, financial experts, and other powerholders into his "slave[s]."[20] Even generals and kings can become your slaves, Gorgias reasons, "if you've got the ability to speak and persuade the crowds."[21] The man of real power, therefore, needn't be an expert in any single discipline but only a master manipulator, one who can influence and control people of all disciplines. In a rather Trumpian move, Gorgias even balks at Socrates' accusations of empty verbosity, declaring, "There's no one who can say things more briefly than I."[22] Socrates begrudgingly admits that he is "amazed" by Gorgias' charismatic persuasiveness, which "seems … something supernatural in scope," echoing the ironic appeal to "divinity" in *Ion*.[23] But much as Socrates argued in *Protagoras* that technical knowledge is necessary, he argues here that Gorgian sophists persuade only "in a gathering," particularly "among those who don't have knowledge."[24] Socrates continues to argue—and Gorgias eventually consents—"that a non-knower will be more persuasive than a knower among non-knowers,"[25] since non-knowers are not merely unbiased by knowledge but are more likely to agree with one who shares their disposition (which explains Trump's appeal to fact-free voters convinced that "he's one of us"). By consenting to Socrates' argument, Gorgias must logically admit that sophistic oratory doesn't produce reasoned truth but only "conviction without knowing."

The orator is thus a "conviction-persuader,"[26] a term that describes the genesis of alternative facts, which replace epistemic values with intense personal conviction. Again, a religious analogy is apt: much as fundamentalists gauge the quality of one's belief by the quantitative intensity with which one holds that belief, alternative facts become actual facts when one has sufficient faith in them. In the context of Trumpism, we cannot underestimate the centrality of ignorant conviction. The acceptance of alternative facts stems from the conviction that subjective perceptions are more morally righteous and therefore "truer" than evidence proffered by scientifically-minded intellectuals. Socrates' appeal to divinity in *Ion* here becomes less and less ironic. Trump had to appease the religious extremists among the Republican base with lies precisely because they self-righteously perceive historically material facts (such as the Earth's age) as heretical. Trump may embarrass himself in the arena of transnational politics, but he knows how to exploit the mentalities of fundamentalist Christians, who are inclined to substitute feeling for fact.

In the dialogue's following section, Gorgias finally assents that empty convictions should be filled with just knowledge—but two among his gathered students, Polus and Callicles, already suspect that Gorgias is betraying his true beliefs, paying lip service to conventional values before the gathered crowd. Polus argues—correctly, in fact—that should Gorgias go out on a limb and reject conventional values of justice and knowledge, his reputation would be ruined (much as Republican voters really *would* have revolted had Trump carried out his 2018 plan to confiscate guns from potentially violent offenders[27]). Polus, ostensibly representing the views of the *polis*, then mounts an unwavering defense of Gorgias. He argues that justice is a sham and that Gorgias' original contention was correct—that rhetoricians should teach self-interested persuasion, since the natural goals of life are hedonism and accumulating power, even to the point of gross tyranny. Indignantly, Polus asks Socrates, "As if you wouldn't be envious whenever you'd see someone putting to death some person he saw fit, or confiscating his property or tying him up!"[28] (One cannot help seeing in Polus' envy Trump's own desire for the capricious power a Vladimir Putin wields.) In longing for personal power, Polus demotes justice and knowledge (for Socrates they are interchangeable) in the way that Trump glorifies outright ignorance. Believing that justice only impedes self-gratification (or what some Americans euphemistically call "freedom"), Polus declares that tyrants must be happiest of all. When Socrates retorts that such tyrants should be pitied, he invokes laughter from the onlooking crowd. Today, Socrates seems prescient rather than naïve: the pleasure-seeking Trump is undeniably a fool to be pitied, not a hero to be envied.

Polus' general claims are sustained by the hot-headed, pseudo-Nietzschean Callicles, who argues even more shamelessly for a life of self-interested hedonism. Always eager to define terms, Socrates asks Callicles to identify who, in fact, should hold this hedonistic power, if such power is indeed reserved for "the best" people. Callicles responds with what he believes is common sense. The most "intelligent in the affairs of the city" and those who are "brave ... should have a greater share than the others, the ruled."[29] Socrates responds by asking Callicles if the ruler merely rules others or whether he also is "self-controlled and master of [him]self, ruling the pleasures and appetites" of his own experience.[30] Here, Socrates invokes that particular Greek virtue of *sôphrosunê*, which denotes not only temperance but an Olympian self-mastery and self-knowledge of which moderation is only an outward sign. Callicles' response evinces a Trumpian ethos: "By the 'self-controlled,' you mean the stupid ones!"[31] Seeing *sôphrosunê* as merely a stew of social conventions meant to restrain the hoi polloi, Callicles claims that the superior man, "ought to allow his own appetites to get as large as possible and not restrain them." Furthermore, he argues, moralists "praise self-control and justice ... [only] because of the shame they feel, while they conceal their own impotence."[32] For Callicles, nothing is more shameful for "tyrants and potentates" than self-control, justice, and the merely conventional "contracts of men that go against nature."[33] In Callicles' ceaseless pursuit of pleasure and amoral desire for power, we see the ancient seed of Trump's antidemocratic ethos.

Of course, Socrates can no more condone an unchecked hedonistic calculus than he could excuse leadership that supplants knowledge with arbitrary power. For Socrates, Callicles' Trumpian appetites for wealth and pleasure only feed a life of unfulfillment. Socrates likens the never-satisfied pursuit of pleasure to futilely filling up an ever-leaking vessel (symbolic of the soul) or the act of forever scratching an itch, a dubious pleasure that quite literally bleeds into pain. Analogously, pretty Gorgian rhetoric, which Socrates likens to "cosmetics,"[34] provides temporary pleasure to listeners but results in the lasting pain of being denied unvarnished truths. Callicles is uncharacteristically evasive when Socrates asks him which pleasures the free man should enjoy. Socrates drolly wonders if the hedonistic man—exemplified by the tyrant—possesses the greatest number of shoes or enjoys the best pastries. Callicles balks at such absurd reductions, but on some level, he realizes that if he were to name any specific pleasures, they would all sound trivial and mundane, especially for a tyrant who sees himself as superhuman. The kind of pleasure experienced therefore becomes crucial. Though experiences of pleasure can resist or subvert body-controlling institutions—as cultural studies usually suggest—a negative pleasure in this case emboldens an oppressive political movement. To use Socrates' analogy, Trump fans, laboring under a false consciousness, "freely" scratch their itch into an open wound, delighting in Trump's triviality while the world collapses around them.

Judging by Trump's cheerful rallies, his success turns at least partly—I would say mostly—on the elicitation of pleasure. Even the most rabid members of his base don't expect him (or his nepotistic appointees) to reduce prescription drug prices or solve the Palestinian crisis, about which he knows nothing.[35] Trump's Twittered assaults on media personalities and a defunct Republican establishment, however, grant much-needed pleasures unthinkable from his former rivals, especially the unctuous Ted Cruz, who has technically slicker rhetoric but who is not, as Socrates puts it, "a non-knower among non-knowers." Yet Trumpian pleasure is at best a leisure-time sport of passive indignation. At worst, it springs masochistically from the impotence Nietzsche saw at the heart of *ressentiment*. But at least Trump's fans find him pleasantly useful, whereas orthodox politicians have no use-value at all.

With deadpan irony, Socrates ends his argument in *Gorgias* with a myth instead of logos. During the time of Cronus, he says, living judges determined whether men, on the days of their deaths, were just or unjust, and whether they were destined for the Isles of the Blessed or condemned to Tartarus. But because those judged were still alive and well-dressed, and because the judges were swayed by "handsome bodies, good stock, and wealth,"[36] the just were often mistakenly sent to Tartarus and the unjust to the Blessed Isles. Therefore, Socrates reasons, people must be "judged when they're stripped naked" and "when they're dead," and "the judge … should be naked … and dead, and with only his soul he should study only the soul of each person immediately upon his death, when he's isolated from all his kinsmen and has left behind on earth all adornment."[37] The Trumpian trappings of the well-tailored ego are thus dissolved.

To Callicles, as to various capitalists and libertarians today, Socrates' prescription might sound quaint or quixotic. But knee-jerk cynicism disguises more than a grain of Socratic truth. Even if we, like Callicles, balk at Socrates' pedantic virtuousness, we cannot help feel a perverse pity for Trump, whose tawdry ignorance can never be bliss. While we may be envious of Trump's wealth—or at least his ability to pay for healthcare—we feel embarrassment for his boastfully ignorant lifestyle because we know what it means to be just. His hedonism cannot overcome our pity, for we know he wastes his wealth on frivolity and trash. His money can buy neither judgment nor taste: one's mind reels at the prospect of a billionaire eating well-done steaks smothered in ketchup, as Trump is wont to do. More importantly, by equating self-knowledge with "weakness," he is unaware that he is pitiable. The next logical question is whether Trump is educable and capable of just self-correction (or even apology). Admittedly, there is little evidence that he is, particularly as he rejects dialectical good faith out of hand.[38] As of this writing (January 2019), he has fearfully retrenched himself to a heretofore unprecedented degree, partially shutting down the federal government at the behest of rightist pundits. But we should not expect a morally bankrupt septuagenarian to undergo an epiphany at our request. Rather than focusing on the transformation of a calcified individual, we should strive to transform societal values that, in turn, might change Trumpism at large. If we, as a culture, redefined masculinity to mean something other than militancy, obstinacy, and braggadocio, the Trump fan might follow Socrates' prescription to "grit his teeth and present himself [to justice] with grace and courage, as to a doctor for cauterization" of a soulful wound.[39]

Denuding the Rhetoric of the Image

By weighing Trumpism against Greek sophism, I obviously don't mean to equate Trump's dithering inarticulateness with the elegance of a Gorgias, whose ornate dependent clauses, paradoxes, and alliterations (in his *Encomium on Helen*, famously) are worlds removed from monosyllabic rabble-rousing. Speaking relatively, however, sophistic rhetoric in ancient Athens sought more or less the same effect that Trumpian rhetoric seeks in the age of visual media. Both kinds of puffery not only dazzle the masses with insubstantial flash but also empty content and reduce it to another category of style. Though a miserable orator by any standard, Trump's shuck-and-jive gives the Gorgian appearance of self-satisfied truth, and to Trump's ill-educated supporters, the appearance of conviction is indistinguishable from soothsaying. Much like Gorgias, Trump also depends on flattering, not challenging, the preconceptions of the masses. As we know, Trump constantly needs to flatter his audience of fickle, sometimes violent reactionaries, for he has only a threadbare hold on them. Because his perceived (but in fact negligible) power is a function of the masses' consent, Trump becomes the inversion of a fascist overlord, embodying the crowd as its fearful slave, not its master.

For Plato, logos must resist the ubiquitous toxin of stylization, lest it degenerate into pathetic effects. Today, however, stylization is already our degenerate politics, and sincere practitioners of logos are either shunted into academic ivory towers or dismissed as relics of pre-postmodern naiveté. In *Gorgias*, Socrates ends his lengthy disquisition on logos by telling a myth because he knows that crowds respond more to culturally shared myths than to abstract reasoning. The subtler irony is that Socrates tells a myth that holds a content of reason, parodying the sophistic use of ostensible logos as a vehicle for mythmaking. By stripping the otherwise authoritative body before its final judgment, Socrates intends in his myth to purify and de-stylize the body politic. But Socrates' myth of "naked" judgment is not merely metaphorical. Clothing constructs power just as it camouflages mortality. Like the cinematic superhero, the successful businessman and politician live through the thin fabric of their costumes. Critics of fascism frequently emphasize the cult of the uniform, at once a fetishistic accessory and a tool of deindividuation. In his essay *Ur-Fascism*, Umberto Eco observes that fascists replace philosophy with mass-manufactured markers of style, creating "a way of dressing … far more influential, with its black shirts, than Armani, Benetton, or Versace would ever be."[40] Writing in 1947, Victor Klemperer observed that clothed or uniformed appearances served much the same function in Nazi Germany. "The masked figure of the racing driver," Klemperer writes, "became a Nazi idol precisely for his quasi-militaristic crash helmet … his goggles [and] his thick gloves."[41] Though the leather-jacketed youth superficially contrasts with Trump's crumbling decadence, both share a "glassy stare which expresses a hard and thrusting determination coupled with the will to success."[42] Indeed, Trump's primary appeal drew upon the daredevil metaphor. Much as a fearless racer impossibly leaps over chasms, so will Trump, through the sheer force of his will, hurdle over the gridlock created by checks and balances and the Constitutional separation of powers.

We would not so easily believe the bellicose politician if he stood naked before us, revealing his ingrown hairs, multiple bypass scars, and sundry other mortal flaws.[43] This idea, right out of *Gorgias*, was expressed in a 2016 protest art project by the anarchist collective "INDECLINE," which erected unflattering, identical nude statues of Trump in New York, Los Angeles, San Francisco, Seattle, and Cleveland. The caricatured statues, entitled "The Emperor Has No Balls," strip away the ubiquitous, ageless business costume, negating the artificial prestige that so confused the judges of Socrates' fable. The statues present a somber Trump in his Mussolinian pose, chin outstretched, hands clasped together across a sunken chest and over a billowing gut. Cast in grotesquely pink plaster, the "Emperor" appears both sickly and newborn, yet shameless and unaware of his public nudity. No longer leader of the free world, Trump is recast as a bipedal creature bulging with mortal defect. His sagging stomach is a bag of ill-digested pleasures, his buttocks droop together in a miserable frown, and his veins bulge bluely through fattened skin. Beneath his plump pubis dangles a lonely member shrunken with disuse. Before the statues were removed by law enforcement and park officials, photo journalists captured images of astonished and bemused passersby laughing and posing. One photo featured a man crouching before the statue, hands folded in contemplation, engaged in seeming epiphany.

What's missing, as the artwork's title indicates, are Trump's balls. The titular allusion to Andersen's fable is seemingly apt. As we've said, Trump's political power, like that of Gorgias, is illusory, as it can only manifest itself in conventional, audience-flattering ways. Trump hasn't the moral courage to repudiate, for instance, the Liberty University crowd or the white supremacists within his base. But the statue's title and overall conceit get it only half right. Problematically, Trump *does* have balls—that is, he is emblematic of, and consumed by, the aggressive and self-interested values of hegemonic masculinity. Part of the masculine code is the refusal to apologize and to obstinately "stand by" one's "facts," even if those facts are fabricated. If the goal really were to humiliate Trump, the artist should have focused on presence rather than absence, granting him hideously diseased balls, or burdensome balls afflicted by crippling gigantism.

Humiliation and shame, however, are two different things. To embarrass someone as insecure as Trump is no great feat, and when humiliated, Trump does not mordantly ruminate, as Nixon did. He instead retreats shamelessly into the womb of the Twitterverse and, like a spiteful child, disseminates baseless rumors against perceived enemies. In this, he is even more ridiculously conventional than Callicles, who at least would desire less plebeian pleasures. But the moral problem with the Trump statue is that its satire, aiming only to humiliate, arises from the same ineffectual *ressentiment* that afflicts Trumpists. Rather than merely attempting to mortify Trump, might the artist—with all due irony—have redeemed him? Could the naked Trump be not a Mussolinian eunuch but a penitent kneeling before the *polis*, begging forgiveness and asking to be judged? Of course, Trump would never Socratically submit himself to justice, but I'd like to suggest that another sculptor do what I've just described. If the Socratic investigator lives an "alternative life," one that shuns convention even unto death, we can magnanimously grant Trump an alternative existence through an image of penitence he would never know—even if it is only an image.

NOTES

1. Michael D. Shear and Nick Corasaniti, "Fact-Checking the Truth That Donald Trump Promised," *The New York Times*, July 21, 2016, https://www.nytimes.com/2016/07/22/us/politics/donald-trump-fact-check.html (24 July 2017).

2. Robert J. Benz, "More and More About Frederick Douglass," *The Huffington Post*, February 10, 2017, http://www.huffingtonpost.com/entry/more-and-more-about-frederick-douglass_us_5892855fe4b01a7d8e512b13?ncid=engmodushpmg00000003 (10 Feb. 2017).

3. Interview with Dale on MSNBC, 24 December 2018. The enumerated lies include those on Trump's Twitter feed.

4. "Trump Disputes Puerto Rico Hurricane Death Toll," *BBC News*, 13 September 2018, https://www.bbc.com/news/world-us-canada-45511865 (8 Jan. 2019).

5. Lena H. Sun and Juliet Eilperin, "CDC Gets List of Forbidden Words: Fetus, Transgender, Diversity," *The Washington Post*, 15 December 2017, https://www.washingtonpost.com/national/health-science/cdc-gets-list-of-forbidden-words-fetus-transgender-diversity/2017/12/15/f503837a-e1cf-11e7-89e8-edec16379010_story.html?utm_term=.4e216c65796d (7 January 2019).

6. The statement was made at a South Carolina campaign rally in Bluffton on July 21, 2015.

7. At the Helsinki Summit, Trump told reporters that the Kremlin could not have had reason to interfere with the 2016 election, though in the same conference Putin admitted to supporting and assisting Trump (without specifying how). See, for instance, Mills Doug, "Trump-Putin Summit Is Over. The Head-Scratching? Not So Much," *The New York Times*, July 6, 2018, https://www.nytimes.com/2018/07/16/world/europe/trump-putin-summit-helsinki.html (7 July 2019).

8. Giovanni Gentile and Benito Mussolini, "The Doctrine of Fascism," *World Future Fund*, 1932, http://www.worldfuturefund.org/wffmaster/Reading/Germany/mussolini.htm (20 July 2017).

9. Gentile, "The Doctrine of Fascism."

10. A transcript of the complete Hilton Head speech can be found at http://www.whatthefolly.com/2016/01/05/transcript-donald-trumps-speech-in-hilton-head-south-carolina-part-1 (2 July 2017).

11. Michael Tackett, "A 'Game of Thrones'-Style Poster Overshadowed a Trump Cabinet Meeting. Nobody Talked About It," *The New York Times*, January 3, 2019, https://www.nytimes.com/2019/01/03/us/politics/trump-game-of-thrones-poster.html (7 Jan. 2018).

12. The most glaring hypocrisy has come from Family Research Council leader Tony Perkins, who claimed that Trump, as a non-professional politician, is entitled to a "mulligan" for his serial adulteries and sundry unbiblical behaviors. Edward-Isaac Dovere. "Tony Perkins: Trump Gets 'a Mulligan' on Life, Stormy Daniels." *Politico*, January 23, 2018, https://www.politi co.com/magazine/story/2018/01/23/tony-perkins-evangelicals-donald-trump-stormy-daniels-216498 (5 Jan. 2019).

13. Donald J. Zeyl, "Introduction," *Gorgias*, trans. Zeyl (Indianapolis: Hackett, 1987), x–xi.

14. Zeyl, *Gorgias*, ix.

15. Plato, *Ion*, trans. W.H.D. Rouse, ed. Eric H. Warmington and Philip G. Rouse (New York: Penguin, 1984), 14.

16. Rouse, *Ion*, 14–15.

17. The comparison is somewhat unfair to Ion, whose audiences are at least real. Recall that in his candidacy's earliest months, Trump hired professional actors (later recognized by their publicity headshots) to fill out his underattended rallies.

18. For the sake of space, I am setting aside Plato's much later, more doctrinaire dialogue *Sophist*.

19. Plato, *Protagoras*, trans. Stanley Lombardo and Karen Bell (Indianapolis: Hackett, 1992), 14.

20. Zeyl, *Gorgias*, 9.

21. Zeyl, *Gorgias*, 9.

22. Zeyl, *Gorgias*, 5.

23. Zeyl, *Gorgias*, 16.

24. Zeyl, *Gorgias*, 17.

25. Zeyl, *Gorgias*, 18.

26. Zeyl, *Gorgias*, 13.

27. After the 2018 school massacre in Parkland, Florida, Trump held a conference on gun control in which he said, "I like taking guns away early.... Take the guns first, go through due process second." The comments, which shocked the NRA, apparently represent the true feelings of Trump, who held moderate views on certain social issues throughout his life. Within 24 hours, Trump took back the comments, as advisors informed him that his base would not tolerate moderation on core issues. David Jackson, Deirdre Shesgreen, and Nicole Gaudiano, "Trump Says Take Guns First and Worry about 'Due Process Second' in White House Gun Meeting," *USA Today*, 28 February 2018. https://www.usatoday.com/story/news/politics/2018/02/28/trump-says-take-guns-first-and-worry-due-process-second-white-house-gun-meeting/381145002/ (1 Jan. 2019).

28. Zeyl, *Gorgias*, 31.

29. Zeyl, *Gorgias*, 64.

30. Zeyl, *Gorgias*, 64.

31. Zeyl, *Gorgias*, 64.

32. Zeyl, *Gorgias*, 64.

33. Zeyl, *Gorgias*, 65.

34. Zeyl, *Gorgias*, 23.

35. At a February 2017 joint press conference with Benjamin Netanyahu, Trump revealed his shocking ignorance about the Israeli-Palestinian conflict. He remarked that he was "looking at two-state and one-state" and would be "very happy with the one that both parties like." He continued, "But honestly, if Bibi, and if the Palestinians, if Israel and the Palestinians are happy, I'm happy with the one they like the best." Madeline Conway, "Trump Says He Can 'Live with' Either Two-State or One-State Solution for Israel," *Politico*, February 15, 2017, http://www.politico.com/story/2017/02/trump-two-state-one-state-solution-israel-235054 (24 July 2017).

36. Zeyl, *Gorgias*, 107.

37. Zeyl, *Gorgias*, 108.

38. On Christmas Day of 2018, shortly after the government shutdown began, Trump signed a bill to name a postal office after deceased army Captain Humayun Khan, whose father, Kazir Khan, had famously impugned Trump's sense of patriotism during the 2016

Democratic National Convention. Not simply a hollow gesture by a hollow man, Trump's bad-faith act reveals the pettiness of his psychology, as if the act would easily placate one of the names on his enemies list. Not by accident, Trump's great act of magnanimity involved plastering someone's name on a building.

39. Zeyl, *Gorgias*, 50.

40. Umberto Eco, "Ur-Fascism," *The New York Review of Books*, June 22, 1995, http://www.nybooks.com/articles/1995/06/22/ur-fascism/ (24 July 2017).

41. Viktor Klemperer, *The Language of the Third Reich*, trans. Martin Brady (London: Continuum, 2006), 4.

42. Klemperer, *The Language of the Third Reich*, 4. Within the context of an auto race, one thinks of Trump's endless rhetoric about "winning"—so much so that Americans will "get tired of winning," as Trump often said during the 2016 campaign.

43. In her tell-all memoir *Full Disclosure* (2018), adult film actress Stormy Daniels demeaned Trump's sexual prowess and likened his penis to a mushroom, but these attacks were short-lived, small-minded, and clearly insufficient. Trump, a man created from spectacle, can only be foiled by a much greater spectacle.

On Faith/Trust and Confidence in an Alterfactual Sense

SABATINO DIBERNARDO

Altermadness: A Parable of Two "Madmen"

A wise "madman" once said, "There are no facts, only interpretations." Such madness! In *fact*, he was quite mad—as mad, perhaps, as the Mad Hatter—and in his madness he made *Breaking News*: "God is dead." Perhaps this madness was the result of being mad at God or at the atheists (and himself) in the marketplace for this murder that had left us abandoned and tossed about vertiginously in all directions without any metaphysical foundations beneath our feet. Perhaps it was the gruesome discovery of a murder scene in which he and others stood over God's decomposing corpse ... while holding the murder weapon. What else could explain his insane behavior, walking around in the daytime with a lit lantern seeking God only to inveigh against the murderers (including himself) of God? Indeed, this diabolical act of deicide simultaneously destroyed the absolute foundation or guarantee of Truth and Meaning. *Alternatively*, this "madness" could have been just a ruse or a fabrication, since he wasn't *really*, in *fact*, "mad"—a bit of performance art, perhaps, regarding a fact of interpretation or an interpretation of facts (alternative or otherwise).

In another place and in another time that had not yet come for the wise "madman," another not-so-wise (or alternatively "wise") "madman" uttered (and incessantly tweeted) so many mad things that it's difficult to pick just one. Nevertheless, he (more than) once said live on the news, "The dishonest media is fake news (inference: 'unless they're nice to me')." Such madness! In *fact*, he was quite mad—as mad, perhaps, as a red MAGA hat-wearing Mad Hatter—and in his madness he made *Breaking News*: "Real news is dead." Perhaps this madness was the result of being mad at the news or at the reporters (and himself) for revealing some deep-seated insecurities coupled with an equally deep-seated narcissism made all the more apparent by his own mad statements. Perhaps it was due to many years as a reality television persona (*persona*: a mask—a person personifying himself), his obsessive viewing of FOX News, or his discovery of a "news" story on an alt-right website about a gruesome murder scene in which he and others stood over the news' decomposing corpse ... (they edited the part about his holding the murder weapon). Meanwhile, he desperately sought media coverage on those same "fake" news stations only to inveigh against the murders (of course, excluding himself) of "real" news. What else could explain such a self-referentially inconsistent questioning of the news covering his every word about the death of the real news? *Alternatively*, this "madness" could have been just a ruse or a fabrication, since he wasn't *really*, in *fact*, "mad"—a bit of performance art, perhaps, regarding the fictional quality of all news as a necessarily narrated selection and interpretation of linguistically constructed "facts" about the "world"... (very unlikely for this "genius" even with such a "smart brain").

This Nietzschean-inspired and doubled parable is a meditation on the linguistically mediated construction of meaning as an effect of language that is irreducible to some secure meaning by way of clear-cut binary oppositions such as fact/fiction or real/fake and the pragmatic implications of this undecidability on the truth/lie binary opposition. Thus, an essay that is ostensibly about "alternative facts" begins with a performative narrative about facts by means of an "alternative fiction."

Since it is by no means the case that our two para-fictional characters are haunted by the same madness that could be reduced to some equivalency, my suspicion is that there is an asymmetrical relationship between the two with respect to philosophical self-reflection and madness. In the case of the first "madman," there appears to be a rhetorical madness brought on by a self-reflexive complicity in the mad act of deicide and its epistemological, axiological, and existential implications. In the case of the second "madman," if there is anything approximating self-reflection, it is a narcissistic reflection of the self as an egocentric reflex. Although both "madmen" share a flair for the provocative and a questioning of facts, they are separated by an unbridgeable chasm as wide as the distance between profundity and ignorance, respectively, by virtue of their diametrically opposed motivations and ends. Each according to his own wisdom asserts in some "factual" manner something about facts in general. If, as we are reminded endlessly, one is entitled to one's opinion but not one's facts, then calling facts into question would call into question not only this truism but also the certainty of commonsensical notions regarding truth, knowledge, and meaning—an epistemological problem that has been at the heart of Western philosophy from ancient Greek philosophies to contemporary postmodern philosophies that take "incredulity toward meta-narratives"[1] as their point of departure. Simply stated, without a God's-eye-view (i.e., *sub specie aeternitatis*) or metacriterion for claims to absolute truth, knowledge, and meaning, we are situated linguistically, culturally, and historically, which is to say contextually, within the very existence that absolutistic and dogmatic claims must transcend in order to make grand metaphysical proclamations. Given this necessary condition of finitude, trust becomes the crucial element of truth utterances. Thus, the primary issue with which we will concern ourselves is the role of faith (*fides*: faith, trust) and confidence in such deliberations. In what or in whom one places one's faith/trust and confidence may precondition what one believes and thereby sees (contra "seeing is believing") when confronted with "alternative facts" (*alter*: other): as *other* facts, lies, and/or fictions. The point here is not that there is no truth but, rather, that there are so many competing claims to truth, each of which requires a level of trust, that serious thought must be given to the credibility one attributes to any source of truth in this game of confidence.

As Nietzsche well understood, the death of God was not some ontological or theological statement about deicide, it was about the death of the guarantor/guarantee of absolute truth, knowledge, and meaning (i.e., the death of a God's-eye-view, a *sub specie aeternitatis* perspective, and a metacriterion). It is no accident that he chose a certain narrative style—the religious parable—as his mode of announcing this death and with it the erasure of all foundations and direction, religious or otherwise. Since there are no guarantees in a world without such metaphysical certainties, it should come as no surprise that the highest values placed on faith/trust and confidence are also the most fragile and easily abused. When the abuse manifests itself, as with Trump's deceptive narratives that he alters as needed, the effects can be life altering on personal, social, and even global levels. Even if this period in our nation's history is described increasingly and mournfully as "post-truth" (not to be confused with philosophically informed epistemological questions regarding absolute truth), it has *not* become post-trust. Consequently, the question of *truth*, post or otherwise, has once again returned with a vengeance in popular discourse such that it may reveal its indebtedness to and the irreducibility of *trust*. Thus, from interpersonal to institutional relationships, the death of the absolute makes faith/trust and confidence all-the-more necessary, crucial, and efficacious.

It should be emphasized that these are not merely pedantic philosophical matters that the general public can do without, since it is precisely this metaphysical desire to ground the fact/fiction, real/fake, and truth/lie binary oppositions in some absolute certainty that has become "breaking news" by breaking in on itself and "making" (in both senses) the news. Thus, between the overt displays of exasperated incredulity by ostensibly neutral or objective news pundits, which after two years of a Trump presidency has given way to a certain level of desensitization, and the ridicule at the hands of comedians regarding the unabashed lies in the service of a Sheen-inspired philosophy of "winning!" perpetuated by Trump, epistemological, axiological, and ethical issues have come from the philosophical wings to take center stage for the most seriously pragmatic of political reasons.

Given the endless dissemination of disconcerting and deceptive statements made by Donald Trump & Co., it's no surprise that many of those in Trump's alterfactual orbit, due to their complicity in a host of illegal and conspiratorial activities, find themselves embroiled in legal jeopardy at the hands of Special Counsel Robert Mueller, among other investigative and prosecutorial institutions, armed not with a metaphysical but, rather, a juridical conceptualization of truth and facts. As the investigations continue, indictments, guilty pleas, prison sentences, and cooperating witnesses are starting to stack up (e.g., Michael Cohen, George Papadopoulos, Paul Manafort, Rick Gates, Michael Flynn, 13 Russian nationals, Russian agent Maria Butina, and others).[2] Judging by the increasingly anxiety-filled Trumpian tweets about "fake news" and "hoaxes" directed at the news media, the "witch hunt" attributed to the Mueller investigation, and the so-called liars or "rats" who have flipped, it would appear that Trump—notwithstanding his "smart brain"—learned nothing from Nixon's obstructionist tendencies, which he is now hiding daily in plain (tweet) sight.

In a prosecutorial strategy reminiscent of mafia trials, which flipped lower-level felons to get to the mob bosses, the Mueller investigation is making its way up the hierarchical ladder of Trump & Co.'s "cosa nostra." On December 12, 2018, Trump's longtime attorney and "fixer," Michael Cohen, was sentenced to three years in prison for his financial crimes and lying to Congress as well as his role in paying and covering up hush money payments to Stormy Daniels and Karen McDougal at the direction of then candidate Trump. Both Cohen and David Pecker, head of AMI, placed Trump in the room and at the center of a conspiracy to commit campaign finance fraud, which also implicated the top executives with check-writing abilities in The Trump Organization (viz., Donald Jr., Ivanka, and Eric; CFO Allen Weisselberg has an immunity deal). During his allocution, Cohen betrayed Trump's faith/trust and confidence and thereby turned this confidence game back on the "confidence man" himself.

Two years into Trump's presidency, the narrative of "alternative facts" (and its later *alternative*: "wrong set of facts"[3]) articulated by Kellyanne Conway early on has become the juridical site of an interrogation with serious ramifications for Trump & Co., as they must now answer for their "alternative facts" in a consistent, corroborated, and, for present purposes, *credible* manner. What is most interesting in this game of truth and lies (in both legal and moral senses) is that the courts cannot escape the question-begging nature of this reiteration of the liar's paradox, beginning with an oath to tell "the truth, the whole truth and nothing but the truth" (before God, who acts as the ultimate judge in this formulation; in the juridical world God is not and cannot be dead—for legal reasons dealing with faith/trust and confidence); namely, they must place their faith/trust and confidence in the truth-telling nature of those they have convicted of lying in order to convict others of lying; of course, without a God's-eye-view, which is admitted by the oath's reliance upon and deference to God's infinite view and absolute juridical power. Inevitably, the typical defense strategy is to highlight the liar's lies in order to impeach the liar's credibility. Prosecutors, in turn, try to provide corroborating evidence for the liar's truthful and trustworthy testimony, which it hopes will mitigate the liar's previous lies in favor of the current truth. If the courts cannot escape this problem of faith/trust and confidence in those who lack credibility, neither can Trump. Case in point, on December 11, 2018, describing what the president would like in the chief of staff replacement for General John Kelly, Kellyanne Conway stated, "somebody who will have the trust and confidence of the president."[4] Thus, it appears that the grand manipulator, too, must place his faith/trust and confidence in others while gaming the confidence of a nation. So the confidence game has come full circle from "alternative facts" to an admission that even our presidential confidence man must play by the rules of the game of interpersonal faith/trust and confidence in order to achieve his deceptive, if non-reciprocal, ends. If the lawsuits that have plagued and dissolved both Trump University and The Trump Foundation, which have deceived many, are any indication, would one expect any less from operating procedures of The Trump Organization? Indeed, would one expect any different from the Trump administration? Unfortunately, as president, he is now playing a dangerous game with democracy, the American people, and our allies. As the former Republican strategist Steve Schmidt eloquently stated on *Real Time with Bill Maher* regarding Trump: "Every day he assaults our institutions. He assaults the foundational pillars of a constitutional republic, and this is all much more fragile, I believe, than we think it is…. Democracy is lubricated by trust, faith, and belief in the system, and it has been eroded singularly by this president's constant assault on every institution that's been handed down as part of our American heritage through great sacrifice and great valor, and it is appalling."[5]

Tonight's Top Story: Fact and/or Fiction?

So how did we get here? How does one begin to make sense of nonsense, inconsistency, and unabashed deception in order to "stop the madness!"? Or, in the vernacular, who does that? Rather than focus on Trump's mental state[6] (e.g., as suffering from narcissistic personality disorder), and thereby run the risk of a dismissal in the form of an *ad hominem*, perhaps it's better to treat such "alternative facts" or deceptive assertions as a strategic deployment of a rhetoric of provocation, controversy, and manipulation in the service of a confidence game grounded in narcissism, greed, and control.[7]

With a glance back at the opening months of Trump's presidency, pundits had abandoned any positivist dreams of parsing literal or exact meanings in some realist sense regarding the truth of his utterances. Instead, they resigned themselves to a new normal for presidential rhetoric and began asking questions about faith/trust and confidence in the president—his credibility and fitness for the Office of the Presidency. This focus was usually accompanied by polls regarding faith/trust and confidence in the new president. However, it strikes one as odd given how far off the mark the polls were prior to the presidential election, that these polls themselves about faith/trust and confidence have not been consistently and rigorously subjected to a self-reflexive questioning about faith/trust and confidence in polls and polling (+/- whatever quantitative percentage arbitrarily applied to account for degrees of uncertainty), aside from an occasional *mea culpa* by some pollsters and pundits. It appears that faith/trust and confidence in quantitative analysis and necessarily selective polls have not been lost.

Nevertheless, what seems like a lifetime ago, on May 9, 2017, Conway appeared on *Anderson Cooper 360°* and instigated the viral "Cooper eyeroll." What engendered this rare sign of disgust from a usually composed Cooper was Conway's dismissal of Trump's praise of FBI Director James Comey during the presidential campaign in defense of his subsequent firing of Comey; both were based on Comey's handling of the Clinton email issue. In his exchange with Conway, who had appealed to a differentiation between *candidate* Trump and *President* Trump, Cooper calls the reality/fiction dichotomy into question: "So that person doesn't exist anymore, candidate Trump? That's a fictional character we no longer are allowed to refer to? We can now only refer to the Donald Trump who exists today?"[8] In this exchange, the reality/fiction binarism inadvertently entered media discourse as a result of a self-interested and face-saving act of flip-floppery. By exposing the contradictory belief in the praiseworthiness *and* the incompetence of Comey, Trump's real/fictional "character" in both its literary and moral senses is put into question.

Similar questions may be asked about Trump's reality TV "character" as a billionaire real estate mogul—famously known for his catch-phrase "You're fired!"—who "plays himself" on TV. This blurring of the line between the *real* Trump and a *fictional* Trump was equally blurred when a contestant from his reality TV show, *The Apprentice*, became a member of the presidential administration until her subsequent dramatic exit. Thus, the fluidity of the fact/fiction binarism that is common fare for reality TV—the fictionalization of "real life" people with which we are confronted in this "reality"—has a spill-over effect as a correlative question for and about real/fake news and "alternative facts." Questions previously reserved for the "fictional" nature of "reality" TV are now being asked about the news media and its relationship to the ostensibly self-evident existence of objective or unmediated facts raised by the lexical alternative "alternative facts." The necessarily narrated nature of the news as "stories" would lend some credence and credibility to Nietzsche's ironic assertion that "there are no facts, only interpretations" with which we began our parable.[9] In this sense, then, "alternative facts" may be read as "alternative fictions" about facts. Indeed, Russian interference in the presidential election propagated by its own self-interested "alternative fictions" via Facebook and other social media platforms revealed both its possibility and its real-life (i.e., "factual") political effects.

It should be stressed that this does *not* justify the conclusion that Trump's mad and unintentionally ironic or self-referentially inconsistent and contradictory assertions regarding "fake news" are somehow vindicated due to the absence of objective or unmediated objective facts lying around untainted by language. In *fact*, the qualifier "fake" presupposes some real news and facts, even if these are reversed in Trumpian "logic" for his own self-serving reasons. It is simply to say that such narratives of fakery and deception are a condition of possibility for the necessarily narrated representation of facts as a function of all news stories and discourse in general. Narrative is a necessary form that carries a content,[10] which, depending on the form adopted, will inflect the content by virtue of this stylistic choice. Indeed, Richard Rorty has argued that "where there are no sentences there is no truth, that sentences are elements of human languages, and that human languages are human creations"[11] and "that anything can be made to look good or bad, important or unimportant, useful or useless, by being redescribed."[12] Consequently, trying to disentangle one's subject position from some objective, mind-independent, factual reality is a complex, if not impossible, philosophical and theoretical matter. Indeed, as Rorty insists, "if one clings to the notion of self-subsistent facts, it is easy to start capitalizing the word 'truth' and treating it as something identical either with God or with the world as God's project."[13]

Nevertheless, the necessarily narrated construction of meaning is not without its real empirical effects and its accepted methods of adjudication. Moreover, as a pragmatic tool, a fact/fiction differentiation works well enough in our "language game," to use Wittgenstein's phrase, since language is both necessarily structured by binary oppositions and, yet, irreducible to any strict either/or. We tend to think digitally by virtue of the structure of language, but we can also think analogically (i.e., various positions along a spectrum rather than an either/or), which is a crucial qualifying element in this discourse. In other words, when a strict fact/fiction digital opposition is called into question, we have recourse to an analogical approach that may assist us in mapping any given narrative along a factual-fictional continuum by virtue of empirical realities, reason, and consensus in and through the necessarily narrated or constructed representation of facts. It is this humanly constructed and, yet, sufficient standard that will prove to be Trump's undoing in the courts and public opinion.

Believe Me: It's a Confidence Game

"Believe me," one of Trump's signature prefatory phrases, has become so commonplace that if it were not typically conjoined with outlandish or over-exuberant claims, one might write it off as some form of linguistic tic. However, it may just be that this habitual speech act provides us with a linguistic "tell" of sorts. (Believe me) This is the typically spoken performative speech act of any *confidence* man or woman, even as it is the unspoken condition of possibility for our speech acts in general, as Jacques Derrida noted.[14] If so, what are we to make of this explicit linguistic habit or "tell"? First, the signifying function of a "tell" in poker, and its relationship to *narrate* (*narrare*: to tell or say), indicates a typically unconscious but sometimes strategically conscious physical or linguistic manifestation that is a narration of sorts; it "tells" players something by means of an unintended disclosure of truth or an intentional strategic dissimulation. Second, the absence of any attempted epistemological justification for "alternative facts" should not be mistaken for an absence of a strategically calculated deployment of an "alternative wisdom" with intended opportunistic effects. In Trump's world, there is a consistent calculation and manipulation employed in his business, marketing, and publicity strategy—a confidence game bent on gaming our confidence. This strategy trades on credit, quite fittingly, by the self-proclaimed "king of debt" who appropriates as much credit (*credere*: to believe) as possible, even at the risk of losing all credibility and confidence (*con*—with; *fide*—faith/trust) and incurring great debt. The strategy employed in the service of his real estate and reality television businesses is now being deployed in the service of his political "business." In order to make sense and attribute some meaning (i.e., signification) to "alternative facts," it's important to see his strategic manipulation of the media and the public as a confidence game being played by the rules of ratings and "likes" with their correlative forms of cultural capital rather than the rules of epistemology regarding the metaphysics of Truth, which may simply miss or otherwise obscure the point.

There is no better paradigmatic instance of this strategic deployment of a rhetoric of provocation, controversy, and manipulation to gain media coverage and up the ante in this confidence game than Trump's hyperbolic and belligerently impetuous assertion: (Believe me) President Obama *founded* ISIS. In the following section of an interview conducted by conservative radio personality Hugh Hewitt, who attempted to "clarify" (i.e., reinterpret or redescribe) what Trump "meant" to say, Trump revealed his strategic motivation by showing his cards in a rare moment of truth:

> **HH:** I've got two more questions. Last night, you said the president was the founder of ISIS. I know what you meant. You meant that he created the vacuum, he lost the peace.
>
> **DT:** No, I meant he's the founder of ISIS. I do. He was the most valuable player. I give him the most valuable player award. I give her, too, by the way, Hillary Clinton.
>
> **HH:** But he's not sympathetic to them. He hates them. He's trying to kill them.
>
> **DT:** I don't care. He was the founder. His, the way he got out of Iraq was that that was the founding of ISIS, okay?
>
> **HH:** Well, that, you know, I have a saying, Donald Trump, the mnemonic device I use is Every Liberal Really Seems So, So Sad. E is for Egypt, L is for Libya, S is for Syria, R is for Russia reset. They screwed everything up. You don't get any argument from me. But by using the term founder, they're hitting with you on this again. Mistake?
>
> **DT:** No, it's no mistake. Everyone's liking it. I think they're liking it. I give him the most valuable player award. And I give it to him, and I give it to, I gave the co-founder to Hillary. I don't know if you heard that.
>
> **HH:** I did. I did. I played it.
>
> **DT:** I gave her the co-founder.
>
> **HH:** I know what you're arguing…
>
> **DT:** You're not, and let me ask you, do you not like that?
>
> **HH:** I don't. I think I would say they created, they lost the peace. They created the Libyan vacuum, they created the vacuum into which ISIS came, but they didn't create ISIS. That's what I would say.
>
> **DT:** Well, I disagree.
>
> **HH:** All right, that's okay.
>
> **DT:** I mean, with his bad policies, that's why ISIS came about.
>
> **HH:** That's…
>
> **DT:** If he would have done things properly, you wouldn't have had ISIS.
>
> **HH:** That's true.
>
> **DT:** Therefore, he was the founder of ISIS.
>
> **HH:** And that's, I'd just use different language to communicate it, but let me close with this, because I know I'm keeping you long, and Hope's going to kill me.
>
> **DT:** *But they wouldn't talk about your language, and they do talk about my language, right?*[15] [emphasis added].

Trump's "alternative wisdom" as a justification of his "alternative facts" is on full display here through his motivation to garner "mad" (in its multiple senses) media attention and public approval. This strategy unveils a confidence game *founded* on nothing more than a rhetoric of provocation, controversy, and manipulation. Everything turns on the semiotic significance of the signifier "founder" as either a constative declaration of fact or a performative speech act that seeks to accomplish something. When Hewitt attempted to clarify this ostensibly denotative (alternative) fact, or redescribe it in a way that might approximate some sensible interpretation, Trump trumped Hewitt's conventional hermeneutic by means of a connotative appeal to an aesthetic criterion, ironically, for a "literal" reading of "founder": "No, it's no mistake. Everyone's liking it. I think they're liking it." This was followed by an aesthetic questioning of Hewitt's self-proclaimed "understanding" of Trump's meaning: "You're not, and let me ask you, do you not like that?" Trump's rejection of Hewitt's understanding was met with one last attempt by Hewitt to ameliorate the semantic differentiation by explaining, "I'd just use different language to communicate it." Finally, the strategic motivation behind Trump's alterfactual assertion is revealed: "But they wouldn't talk about your language, and they do talk about my language, right?"

Indeed, "they" talk about Trump's madly provocative language and we, too, continue to talk and write about Trump's mad statements in a circular reinscription of this endless round of madness, which, it turns out, is not as mad as it is manipulative—a bit of performance art—not in some Kantian art-for-art's-sake aesthetic but, rather, in performing the art of deception that is less about art and more about utilizing a rhetoric of provocation, controversy, and manipulation in order to gain coverage, ratings, and "likes." From questioning President Obama's U.S. citizenship and religious identity to a host of other conspiracy (i.e., alternative) theories that Trump has peddled over the years, provocative claims are sent into the ether never to be substantiated and endlessly deferred to some future date … but always "shortly." This confidence game, however, is not all fun and games, since it happens to be playing a more serious geopolitical confidence game with much higher stakes: democracy and global stability. Indeed, Trump's unilateral decision to remove troops from Syria prompted the "no confidence" resignation of Secretary of Defense James Mattis over this move, which would create instability in the region, abandon our Kurdish allies, and provide the opportunity for Isis to fill this void (sound familiar?). In a rare moment of non-partisan critique, the typically Trump-friendly *Fox & Friends* highlighted the implications of this withdrawal during a segment with Sarah Huckabee Sanders. Co-host Brian Kilmeade pointed out the shear hypocrisy of Trump's decision to withdraw troops from Syria when he explained to Sanders that Trump "is doing exactly what he criticized President Obama for doing. He said President Obama is the founder of Isis. He just refounded Isis." And in response to Sander's dismissal of such an outlandish statement, Kilmeade replied, "leaving is helping."[16] Ironically, the "fake news"—or so it must be if it contradicts the president's narrative on this rare occasion—reported "real news" by appropriating Trump's hyperbolic "leaving is founding" semantics and using it against him.

D.C. Hold 'Em and Other "Low Culture" Games

Unfortunately, we now find ourselves at the final table of a Hold 'Em tournament with a transparent bluffer in the highest of high-stakes poker. Having speculated about Trump's motivations, what is it about our current context that brought us to this table? According to Mark C. Taylor, "In recent years, American society has undergone a disturbing crisis of confidence in many of the individuals and institutions responsible for the country's well-being. Priests, politicians, and financiers as well as the press, media, courts, and schools no longer seem trustworthy."[17] Indeed, the "change" election, which included a sizable contingent of previous Obama voters changing and placing their hopes in Trump, may confirm this erosion of faith/trust and crisis of confidence in politicians and institutions. Taylor further states, "As fundamental truths and values faded or disappeared, it no longer seemed possible to be sure what was real and what was fake.... For the past two centuries, the line separating appearance and reality, truth and illusion, the material and the immaterial, the real and the virtual has been gradually eroding."[18]

This crisis of confidence brought on by the questioning of truth, values, reality, and illusion was powerfully articulated in Nietzsche's proclamation of the "death of God" and all metaphysical foundations as so many fictions of absolute truth. This mode of critical thinking was then transposed in a postmodern register as an "incredulity toward metanarratives." It should be emphasized that the death of the metanarrative of God/Truth brought about the birth of an awareness of the fictionalization of meaning, truth, and values through "fragile fictions," as described by Ernest Becker,[19] in which we place our faith/trust and confidence. Thus, the reality/fiction binary opposition—a reified fiction about the absolute distinction between natural realities and fictional creations—discloses a culturally constructed linguistic necessity *and* permeability, which is all the more serious for its necessity and concomitant possibility of being manipulated to useful or harmful ends. Indeed, the tenuous nature of these fictions *raises* rather than *diminishes* the stakes for faith/trust and confidence in our human constructions. This is quite evident in the serious efforts made to shore up confidence in them by hiding the "fact" they are not universally natural but contingently conventional, especially when confronted with an alterity that calls our own fictions (i.e., our constructed identities) into question.

The implication of this is that our religions, national identities, politics, games, sports, among other culturally constructed institutions, are no less "real" or meaningful for being "fictional" constructions. These cultural constructions (as with more conventionally recognized "fictional" constructions, such as movies and reality TV shows) require a certain willing suspension of disbelief regarding their artificiality in order for us to believe in them as meaningful in one form or another. Since these are not fixed categories or identities, they easily elide into each other across the binary divide. This may be seen in the effacing or eliding of high/low culture distinctions in our culture's creation of images, characters, and brands by means of a confidence game that secures a confidence and faith/trust in (and desire for) images, characters, and brands toward whatever desired end (e.g., the president's "Trump" brand). Moreover, when a spectacle emanating from "low culture" invades the "pure" political other of "high culture," and the "dignified reverence" of the latter gives way to the "undignified irreverence" of the former, a certain culture shock and anger may accompany the comingling of two conventionally opposed fictions.

For example, when Trump put the "smack down" on CNN in a doctored video of his "real life" smack down of WWE's Vince McMahon (yes, Trump was a "real wrestler" for a night), this high/low comingling caused quite a bit of (self)righteous indignation. Nevertheless, it is an accurate depiction of Trump's strategic approach to business, entertainment, and politics. His professional wrestling, no-holds-barred, grudge match mentality—replete with self-aggrandizing posturing, a flair for the provocative, the hyperbolic melodrama that typifies professional wrestling's dramatically staged battle of good vs. evil—has infiltrated the presidency and politics in general. By creating a strategic "feud" between the "fake news" media and himself, Trump's professional wrestler alter ego goes to battle with CNN, and the ostensibly "dignified" space of politics is "reduced" to an "undignified" grudge match. By casting the "fake news" media as the nasty, malicious, evil "wrestler" with whom he, the valiant, populist, good "wrestler," must do battle, as his supporters cheer him on, Trump has created a villainous other for his political reality TV "show." Consequently, the news now makes the news in both senses—quite a spectacular confidence game influenced by a "fake" sport that now has "real" political effects and legal implications.

The irony of this current situation is that when we include the maddened responses of a news media culture that traffics in and, for precisely that reason, covers the mad statements of the current president, they are both drinking from the same trough, so to speak. Trump says mad things, the "fake news" media outlets cover "said" mad things, adding their own exasperated (actual and/or contrived) mad offense at "said" things that they said he said, which assists Trump in disseminating provocative statements and thereby increasing his visibility, reinforcing his desired—typically deceptive or incoherent—narrative, and ensuring free "air time," which assists "fake news" media outlets in gaining their own share of the ratings, recognition, and advertising money; all generated in a complicit "pugilistic" circle of mad(ness) reality TV/news. Conversely, Trump's "real news" ally—FOX "News"—plays the role of the sole possessor and guarantor of Truth through its "no-spin zone" narratives (see how well that worked out for Bill O'Reilly) by "unmasking" the conspiratorial, decadent liberal/progressive, and, thus, evil intentions of the "fake news" to bring down the populist savior and political messiah of the, ironically, under-represented (read: white/male/working-class American)—the stuff of television, indeed. Welcome to reality TV/news in the era of Trump.

A Concluding Bit of Madness

(Believe me) The real problem with "alternative facts" is *religious*. Seriously? Religious? Following Taylor's lead on religion and confidence games if "religion is ... most interesting where it is least obvious"[20] and "[f]aith is a confidence game,"[21] the problem, then, turns on faith/trust and confidence. In religion—among the most ancient and influential purveyors of "alternative facts"—one encounters the paradigmatic confidence game. Whatever empirical realities appear self-evident, truthful, and trustworthy, there is a realm of the Real, the *really* real, a Platonic realm of sorts that reduces empirical reality to a lesser reality, illusion, or apparent existence (depending on the "faith" tradition) to which one may gain access under the precondition of faith/trust and confidence in the ultimate "believe me." Thus, *faith* (i.e., trust) by way of a metonymic substitution for *religion* becomes a primary site for a gaming of our confidence that is replicated in places where you least expect it, and "alternative facts" are engendered by "alternative fictions" that precede them and influence "believers" to see what they believe. By gaming our faith/trust and confidence in empirical experience by means of an aftereffect of language that posits (i.e., asks us to have faith/trust in) a more real (i.e., non-evident, non-empirical) reality, the very precondition for our understanding of how to use the signifier "reality" in the first place has been systematically subverted. Consequently, even a basic differentiation between "larger" presidential inaugurations, which instigated the "alternative facts" comment in the first place, requires a distrust of our "lying eyes."

If the "believe me" associated with religion and other confidence games in the absence of some metaphysical absolute is a necessary condition for human institutions, traditions, relationships, and authorities to function, then it is not some accidental occurrence that one should hope to avoid. Rather, it appears to be a structural necessity that may be manipulated for good or ill. This has always been the not-so-holy ghost or specter haunting religion(s), which has raised faith/trust to the highest of virtues and, ironically, the questioning of (contingent) faith/trust to the most unpardonable of sins. And this is where confidence games are vulnerable to collapse upon themselves. When all the provocations, controversy, self-promotion, manipulations, and threats of hell or lawsuits no longer succeed in terms of securing faith/trust and credibility, confidence is betrayed and the faith/trust upon which it was based gives way to suspicion, distrust, and incredulity.

Notwithstanding the fluidity of binary representations, the one "fact" that should not be so easily dismissed is precisely the one that allows language and binary oppositions to function in the first place; namely, differentiation between one thing, idea, statement, signifier, etc., and its opposed other (i.e., distinguishing between what is and what is not the case) as a precondition for meaning. To deny the ability to differentiate is to deny the ability to communicate. Indeed, Nietzsche, who had a great many counterintuitive things to say about truths as forgotten illusions[22] or as "[a] mobile army of metaphors, metonyms, and anthropomorphisms"[23] highlighted the conventional linguistic rules of "truth" and the consequences one faces when contravened:

> For now that is fixed which henceforth shall be "truth"; that is, a regularly valid and obligatory designation of things is invented, and this linguistic legislation also furnishes the first laws of truth: for it is here that the contrast between truth and lie first originates. The liar uses the valid designations, the words, to make the unreal appear as real; he says, for example, "I am rich," when the word "poor" would be the correct designation of his situation. He abuses the fixed conventions by arbitrary changes or even by reversals of the names. When he does this in a self-serving way damaging to others, then society will no longer trust him but exclude him.[24]

Nietzsche's analysis regarding fixed conventions of truth/lie and the consequences for contravening this convention in society by means of a "self-serving way damaging to others" provides an appropriate diagnosis of Trump's deceitful alternative fictions as well as the consequences that are starting to appear as his potential end. Thus, as with Freud's cigar, sometimes a lie is just a lie masquerading as an "alternative fact" for one's self-serving ends, regardless of the damage it causes others.

In this context, one can only wonder if Trump has forgotten the moral of another parable, "The Boy Who Cried Wolf," which speaks to the inestimable value of faith/trust and credibility/confidence. Along similar lines of "character" or "moral" formation, in addition to his WWE wrestler character, Trump seems to have appropriated some other stereotypical characteristics from characters found in movies such as *The Godfather* and *Goodfellas*. For instance, regarding the question about getting Mexico to pay for his xenophobic wall, he came close to saying "Don['t] worry about it. They'll pay. I'll make 'em an offer they can't refuse," which, of course, has not only not come to pass but also engendered a partial government shutdown into 2019 over funds for his wall or "slats." Whether dealing with friends or foes, allies or enemies, Trump's wrestler-mafioso bravado knows no boundaries. He is more than willing to subvert the faith/trust and confidence in the very people and institutions he is supposed to defend and protect for his own selfish purposes.

However, this strategy has backfired, and he has placed himself and others in serious legal jeopardy, including the "real life" indictments of a growing list of co-conspirators and co-stars in this sad reality TV show that is threatening the faith/trust and confidence in American democracy domestically and abroad.

Unfortunately, we, too, are cast in Trump's alternative reality/fiction; one based on an updated version of *The Truman Show*—the subplot of which is borrowed from *Idiocracy*, replete with its own former professional wrestler turned president, President Camacho, and a barely cognizant, infantilized, and gullible populous. This new combination sequel, *Trum(p)an's Idiocracy*, is no less factually efficacious, as in Truman's real experience of his world for all its artificial construction. If there is little daylight between President Camacho and President Trump in terms of "character," there is one major difference between Trump's "character" and Truman's "character": Truman didn't know he was playing a character in an alterfactual reality television show for the benefit of a nation's voyeuristic desires and an entertainment industry's desire for ratings. Consequently, Trump's wrestler-mafioso bravado seems to have sent him headlong into a real—not fake—fight that we continue to watch as the news—fake, real, or somewhere in between—continues to serve the public's interests (voyeuristic and democratic).

Nevertheless, our overly confident confidence man playing his confidence game looks as though he's beginning to show signs of desperation and, perhaps, a lack of confidence in his own ability to pilot the boat away from the edge of the reality TV stage, which is getting ready to hit the legal "wall" (i.e., the empirical limit condition for this game of faith/trust and confidence). Moreover, with the Democratic Party now holding the majority in the House of Representatives, it's beginning to look like Trump's back is up against the wall on multiple fronts, each of which is starting to close in on him.

Finally, as we continue to view and participate in *Trum(p)an's Idiocracy*, we can only hope that, like Truman, we remain suspicious of the artificiality and idiocy of this bizarre "alternative reality" TV show, such that through our own critical thinking we can help steer the boat toward the edge of the stage set and put an end to this seriously dangerous confidence game—all the while wearing our own red MATA hats emblazoned with the subtitle of this book: "Make America Think Again." At least for that opportunity, we can thank Trump & Co.!

NOTES

1. Jean-François Lyotard, *The Postmodern Condition: A Report on Knowledge*, Theory and History of Literature, trans. Geoff Bennington and Brian Massumi, vol. 10 (Minneapolis: University of Minnesota Press, 1984), xxiv.

2. "Everyone Who's Been Charged as a Result of the Mueller Investigation," *The New York Times*, December 12, 2018, www.nytimes.com/interactive/2018/08/21/us/1000000060659 74.app.html.

3. Kellyanne Conway, interview by Anderson Cooper, *Anderson 360°*, May 9, 2017.

4. Kellyanne Conway, press statement, *Associated Press*, December 11. 2018. www.youtube.com/watch?v=JUxMT3vflyA.

5. Steve Schmidt, guest on *Real Time with Bill Mahr*, November 17, 2018.

6. Even former FBI director James Comey, sources say, has described him as "outside the realm of normal" and "crazy" for believing that he had been wiretapped by President Obama. Maggie Haberman, Glenn Thrush, Michael S. Schmidt, and Peter Baker, "'Enough Was Enough': How Festering Anger at Comey Ended in His Firing," *The New York Times*, May 10, 2017, www.nytimes.com/2017/05/10/us/politics/how-trump-decided-to-fire-james-comey.html.

7. See Mark C. Taylor, *Confidence Games: Money and Markets in a World Without Redemption* (Chicago: University of Chicago Press, 2004).

8. Kellyanne Conway, interview by Anderson Cooper, *Anderson 360°*, May 5, 2017. See Caitlin Gibson, "Anderson Cooper Eyerolled His Way to an Iconic GIF While Interviewing Kellyanne Conway," *The Washington Post*, 10 May 2017, https://www.washingtonpost.com/news/arts-and-entertainment/wp/2017/05/10/anderson-cooper-eyerolled-his-way-to-an-iconic-gif-while-interviewing-kellyanne-conway/?utm_term=.582b7370a5ef.

9. For a philosophical analysis of Nietzsche's statements relating to truth and theories of truth, see Maudemarie Clark, *Nietzsche: On Truth and Philosophy*, Modern European Philosophy, ed. Raymond Geuss (Cambridge: Cambridge University Press, 1990).

10. See Hayden White, *The Content of the Form: Narrative Discourse and Historical Representation* (Baltimore: Johns Hopkins University Press, 1987).

11. Richard Rorty, *Contingency, Irony, and Solidarity* (Cambridge: Cambridge University Press, 1989), 5.

12. Rorty, *Contingency, Irony, and Solidarity*, 7.

13. Rorty, *Contingency, Irony, and Solidarity*, 5.

14. On the performative act of faith/trust, truth, credit, and "believe me," see Jacques Derrida, "Faith and Knowledge: The Two Sources of 'Religion' at the Limits of Reason Alone," in *Religion*, ed. Jacques Derrida and Gianni Vattimo, Cultural Memory in the Present, ed. Mieke Bal and Hent de Vries (Stanford: Stanford University Press, 1996), 44–45.

15. Donald Trump, interview by Hugh Hewitt, *The Hugh Hewitt Show*, "Donald Trump Makes a Return Visit," transcribed by Duane Patterson, Thursday, August 11, 2016. www.hughhewitt.com/donald-trump-makes-return-visit/.

16. Brian Kilmeade's response to Sarah Huckabee Sanders on *Fox & Friends*, Fox News, December 12, 2018.

17. Taylor, *Confidence Games*, 1.

18. Taylor, *Confidence Games*, 1.

19. Ernest Becker, "The Fragile Fiction," in *The Truth About the Truth: De-Confusing and Re-Constructing the Postmodern World*, ed. Walter Truett Anderson (New York: Tarcher/Putnam, 1995), 34–35.

20. Mark C. Taylor, *About Religion: Economies of Faith in Virtual Culture* (Chicago: University of Chicago Press, 1999), 1.

21. Taylor, *About Religion*, 7.

22. Friedrich Nietzsche, "On Truth and Lie in an Extra-Moral Sense," in *The Portable Nietzsche*, ed. and trans. by Walter Kaufmann (New York: Penguin, 1976), 47.

23. Nietzsche, "On Truth and Lie," 46.

24. Nietzsche, "On Truth and Lie," 44–45.

What Is a Politician?

CHRISTOPHER W. THURLEY

What *is* a politician? The word "politics" comes from the Greek word "politika" meaning affairs of the state, which, over time, evolved into "polettiques" in Latin which, by definition, added the significance of governance into the practicing of these affairs. In the 21st century, what are the requirements of being a politician? To read laws, give opinions, collect signatures? Call constituents and ask for money? This all seems too simple when stripped down to the rudiments—these are tasks any competent college student could accomplish over a summer internship. So where is the learning, the growth? Where is the research, the struggle, the doubt, humiliation, and reflection, the criticism and constant self-evaluation that is demanded by a full, complete, and effective education? The embracing of different views is stressed in education where introspection is key to growth, but this may not be so in politics. Is a politician not just a representative edifice of a body of beliefs carried by their supporters? If so, then what a dangerous construction—a Frankenstein's creature assembled by the fragmented and, likely, ignorant views represented in the *vox populi*—an assemblage created out of boredom, a bricolage of various beliefs sewn into the anatomical likeness of a human that revels in its newfound consciousness, its praise of being lifted from the table, but ultimately, not human, not even necessarily natural (although made of natural constituent elements). These anthropomorphs lack an essential individual conscious, because it has been outsourced, since they tend to exist as a creation for the purposes of a specific party which ascribes these individuals with a set or criteria including limitations of character and thought. It is because of this necessity to adhere to Party law that these anthropomorphs do not normally, although they should—and I speak of politicians here—take their role to be necessarily growth-oriented. Instead, those in these roles act as megaphones for those they wish to excite, incite, emotionalize, and mobilize because a democracy demands a majority, so the goal must always be *more*. The goal is never *truth*, knowledge, or instruction, and if it is, politicians that use these tactics will likely not be politicians for very long. With party politics *truth* often becomes relative, or, to put it another way, it becomes lies, and the keen observer "knows that such lies rarely spring from genuine cynicism or contempt of the mob [because] a politician is wholly devoted to his party, and he has to find ways of making the worse cause seem the better. He does not want to lie, but he has to. He can evade bare-faced falsehood by gobbledygook or euphemism, by ambiguity or rede-finition."[1] This is how the word *democracy*, as George Orwell noticed, becomes used admiringly and without hesitation for any side of a political debate, but, more accurately, should instead be understood in conjunction with acts of demagoguery since "the defenders of every kind of regime claim that it is a democracy, and fear that they might have to stop using the word if it were tied down to any one meaning."[2]

It's important to keep this idea in mind through a brief detour. Medical doctors go to college for roughly ten years and then they spend another three to four years carrying out their residencies before they can be considered prepared to practice their specialty. In the United Kingdom, a doctor of philosophy achieves a degree through three to six years of academic work and research—in America, these same scholar-experts take anywhere from four to seven years. These are normally pre-career achievements, completed prior to a scholar even being considered for a position that requires this type of knowledge and ability. Upon getting a job in education, in the medical arena, or as a scientist/researcher, it is assumed that the aforementioned feats of cognitive strength, endurance, academic ability, and willpower—meaning the diligent research, fastidiousness, and hard work—will only continue, with even more enthusiasm, as an employee. Lifelong learning is at the base of higher education, so these experts do not simply stop learning and growing, but rather dedicate their lives to their areas of study. This can and does involve various forms of teaching, research, lectures, writing, fellowships, testing, review committees, publications, lab work, field studies, and conferences, not to mention an exorbitant amount of time dedicated to contemplation, read-ing, writing, revising, practicing, ruminating, and doubting, which is often incredibly frustrating when this high level of ability is coupled with, for many fields, low pay.

And then, by the grace of the erudite professors who have the same dis-tinguished titles and have gone through the same struggles to get where they are, a doctoral student becomes a fellow doctoral obtainer and all is right with the world. Endemic to the 21st century, these students are then debt-ridden, most likely poor, frequently unemployed, and, even more likely, engaged in desperate competition with other budding intelligentsia to obtain the jobs desired so that they might eat food and contribute to society as all reasoned beings hope they can do. Years of study, struggle, expectations, criticism, growth, and learning give these individuals the titles that deem them to be society's lamplighters, guiders, innovators, and leaders. Even so, the first step into these types of positions is only the beginning; only seasoned veterans of scholarship, geniuses of invention with enduring industriousness, are usually taken as the authorities in their areas of study. Professors, researchers, doctors, and pundits of their areas of expertise all research constantly to prepare for lectures, discussions, meetings, articles, curriculum activities, institutional aims, conferences, public events, et cetera ad infinitum, until this level of dedication and erudition is exuded as second nature. This makes sense and should comfort anyone who has learned from an expert, been guided by an expert, been rewarded in any way by an expert—be that in education, health, infrastructure, economy, art, or technology, in other words, the foundations of all societies. As explained in detail by Dr. Tom Nichols in his article "How America Lost Faith in Expertise" in *Foreign Affairs*, many Americans appear to lack a general understanding of the vicissitudes that accompany expertise:

> Beyond credentials lies talent, an immutable but real quality that creates differences in status even within expert communities. And beyond both lies a mindset, an acceptance of membership in a broader community of specialists devoted to ever-greater understanding of a particular subject. Experts agree to evaluation and correction by other experts. Every professional group and expert community has watchdogs, boards, accreditors, and certification authorities whose job is to police its own members and ensure that they are competent and live up to the standards of their own specialty.[3]
>
> Perhaps more importantly, Dr. Nichols adds the caveat that many non-experts fail to understand or recognize, through a kind of Dunning-Kruger effect, that "experts are often wrong, and the good ones among them are the first to admit it—because their own professional disciplines are based not on some ideal of perfect knowledge and competence but on a constant process of identifying errors and correcting them, which ultimately drives intellectual progress."[4]

This brings me to my main point. These are the experts we trust and are guided by because they possess and utilize compassion, insight, knowledge and foreknowledge. Despite the obvious flaws of human nature, these individuals and those that came before them have been scaffolding knowledge for centuries, allowing for the innovators of the 21st century and the *hoi polloi* to benefit off of and from the advancements of the work that set the foundation for this progress. There has been, historically, little reward or recognition for many of the greatest innovations, but conciliatorily, history remembers these individuals and they are held in high regard by subsequent generations. But humans are special creatures, and the common citizens of any society tend to hold many other figures of lesser ability in higher regard. These idols are more visible and tend to identify with more common traits appreciated by the populace; therefore, the average citizen looks to these figureheads as pathfinder figures for guidance and support, despite the fact that actors, pop singers, athletes, reality television stars, et cetera have little to no expertise outside of their main jobs as entertainers. If these personalities go on to enter into the realm of politics, it only makes sense then that these individuals should be critiqued, held to rigorous standards, and even more importantly, should be evaluated regarding what constitutes their assumption to enter this field. In 2016, Americans learned that the rules we *thought* governed these political positions are much more amorphous than we could have imagined, and what we *assumed* was being done to choose our leaders seems to have been achieved in the past by sheer luck. So how is it that in politics, but in no other branch of expertise or employment in general, a man with a bachelor's degree in animal science can replace a nuclear physicist as the head of the United States Department of Energy? Of the many accomplishments achieved by the previous two holders of this position, here are a few to provide some enumerated context: a Nobel Prize, degrees from America's top institutions in their field, employment at those institutions as professors, and leading positions as scholars in their fields as well as contributions to the overall discourse of their subjects. The assignment and confirmation of Rick Perry in this position remains one example of a gross breach of common sense and conduct that has extended across many of America's most esteemed leading positions in governance. This has likely occurred because the general American population, who cares even an ounce about the dangers of nuclear power, have always assumed, up until now, that logic and the rules of advancement in all Western education also applied to those that govern. In November of 2016, the majority of Americans were confronted with the fact that we have been wrong all along, therefore making it a necessity to examine the definition of a politician.

In America, if a politician never reaches the seat of the presidency, these individuals are essentially rhetoricians, honing their skills to better influence their audiences and relate to them. Suddenly, if they are lucky enough to reach the position of the president of the United States of America, they are considered sagacious experts of all matters of governance, regardless of background. This defies logic. This defies discourse and the scaffolding of human experience and knowledge. "Where are the experts?" is what any educated and intelligent personage should ask, and why are the experts, the scholars, the intellectuals not drawn to political positions of power? The paradox of politics rumbles through the annals of history, with Plato and Aristotle[5] leading the pack: "Where are we going to find a character that is simultaneously gentle and high-spirited, when gentleness and passion are opposites?"[6] No intellectuals of sound mind would willingly subject themselves to the power, scrutiny, responsibility, and loquaciousness of politics, especially since these qualities of character—and I say character intentionally because it has to be a façade—likely lead individuals down paths of different import, such as positions where connivance as a means of achieving goals is accepted and endorsed, where engaging in feats of vacuous rhetoric are applauded, and where the selling of goods becomes much more easily equated with the selling of ideas. And identity politics, political correctness, party allegiance, and *quid pro quo* exchanges only add to the corrosive effects of the political apparatus (all for different reasons). These factors crescendo into frequent usage of dichotomous language resulting in a cacophony of anger, elation, praise, censorship, confusion, and overconfidence that is bound to baffle and distort any sound perception of reality.

George Orwell saw this devolution of language, in his essay "Politics and the English Language," as taking shape in metaphors, idioms, and other empty signs and symbols distorted over time and used to fill minds incapable of original thought, to the point that this type of speech would even "think your thought for you, to a certain extent—and at need they will perform the important service of partially concealing your meaning even from yourself. It is at this point that the special connection between politics and the debasement of language becomes clear."[7] Under this estimation, one would need to be a little sick, delusional, a little vain, nay narcissistic, maybe masochistic, but ultimately sickeningly resilient, coupled with a deep—whether conscious or not—love for power and attention to be able to ascertain the position of a politician as being a good choice for a career—all qualities the average introvert, scholar, philosopher, expert, researcher, and intellectual tend to exhibit quite infrequently, if at all. In moments of shining public brilliance, the part-time extrovert and full-time scholar often reverts back into the role of an introvert, needing hours and days to recuperate from such an excursion, not to mention to reevaluate, grow, expand, and learn from errors. Even good politicians, those who seek peace and are kind, good people who strive for progressive ideals, equity, with knowledge of the past and good intentions forged out of a good education, a well-traveled life, and empathy, still must have some lingering or repressed hubristic, sinister, or utterly naive traits that should not be forgotten by their constituents simply because of what the job of a politician entails. Like a person growing up to be six-foot-five and another to only reach five-two, some of us are predestined to have idiosyncrasies and talents biologically ordained, and then decided by society as to be either useful or pointless. A politician is no different, which is an unnerving reality since we rely on them so very much. More horrifying, we generally understand and are aware of the fact that their job is essentially to use language "designed to make lies sound truthful and murder respectable, and to give an appearance of solidity to pure wind,"[8] and we sit back complacently, decade after decade, letting this apparatus run our systems and institutions.

Any goodness in the politicians who simply want to make a difference in the lives of normal people must fight valiantly, and vigilantly, to retain any semblance of character and human quality because the innate impositions of the trade require a lack of compassion due to sheer social inundation; the democratic aspect of this type of popularity requires such enthymematic, euphemistic, and arbitrary vagueness of language that can only be likened to a machine. A politician runs, by nature of the role, off of power in a democratic system, so it must strip, as Anthony Burgess's character in *The Worm and the Ring* notes, "a ruler's personality of those very attributes which it is the ambition of the civilized man to achieve [since] the gift of power is incompatible with—nay, inimical to—the greater gifts of the full life."[9] This is why a politician is essentially nothing but an incubator for tyranny, a corruptible element that is needed for the governance of human beings in society, but ultimately a decaying position with a half-life determined by the goodness of the society in which they live—a kind of litmus test for the integrity of a population. Plato was right all along in the *Republic*, but it becomes important *now*, in 2019, that we see the following patterns and attempt to save ourselves from the paths of our predecessors, so that we may stop asking the questions we have known the answers to all along:

> **Socrates**: And so tyranny naturally arises out of democracy, and the most aggravated form of tyranny and slavery out of the most extreme form of liberty?
> **Glaucon**: As we might expect.[10]

Politicians are neither experts, nor moral guides, but masters of all and nothing at the same time. A pedagogue or scholar? No, definitely not, no patience for that. A civil servant? If so, probably not for long. Some maybe, but it does not seem that the most noticeable politicians, the most effective, get into politics for those reasons. Educated? Beacons of diplomacy, intellect, economic frugality and management, advocates of democracy? Maybe, but only after years of doing other things and not by trade or tutelage from the beginning, but more like a hobby acquired over time and required by status. Philosophical idealists and pragmatic realists? Sometimes, but always behind masks of nationalistic adoration. More likely, cheap dilettantes and demagogues acting out a role characterized by previous actors, shaped by the shouts of the audience, and disgruntled with the play itself. The most dangerous, and those that are drawn magnetically to this strange position we call a politician, are the charlatans that know how to sell a gimmick, work the system to their benefit, and excite a vote from the average voter, the average human who turns back to working their job, watching their football, and not giving a damn in general—as we might expect. Whether it is despot Idi Amin in 1974 saying that he has a very good brain, meaning that he is smarter than other people and knows more, or Donald Trump repeating that very same self-characterization in 2018, half the population is allured to this type of relinquishment of responsibility to press elected officials to be honest, accurate, and genuine—instead they are apathetically credulous: he says he has a very good brain, so he must know what he talking about, right? It seems that half the population of America, whether it was in the 1980s or the 2010s, are magnetically drawn to this type of rhetoric, so that, as Marshall Berman explained in *All That Us Solid Melts Into Air*, "demagogues and demagogic movements have won power and mass adoration by relieving the peoples they rule of the burden of freedom."[11] In 1958 Aldous Huxley warned us about technology being used in Hitler's rise to extinguish the very freedoms that innovation had afforded humanity,[12] and Berman warned us in 1982 of that very same tactic from demaogogues, celebrating "modern technology, communications and techniques of mass mobilization," by using "them to crush modern freedoms"; apparently large populations of Americans can't seem to see that the loudspeaker, the television, and Twitter are one in the same, machines used to amplify and sell an idea—as we might expect.[13]

To avoid being pessimistic and deconstructive, I would also like to present an idea of how this could change for the better because we all need politicians, whether we like it or not. This is why politics surrounds all aspects of our lives and why it digs to the core of our morals and sensibilities. But our system, by the very nature of the role and what we expect from these individuals, is inherently flawed and primed for fascism, for populism, and for authoritarianism by simply adhering to the rules ordained by our sociopolitical structure (just give Sinclair Lewis's *It Can't Happen Here* for an eerie and accurate prognostication of what this could look like). So to potentially fix some of these problems, here is a starting point: First, politicians should be required to attain a higher education degree equivalent to a master's degree in policy, economics, political science, liberal arts, environmental science, and/or law before they can even be considered to run for office. The second beneficial change would consist of politicians being held accountable through critical examination periods by panels of independent bipartisan experts in order to assess policy choices—this ethics-esque committee could thereby vote to fail or pass a politician based on how well their outlooks fall in line with expert opinion. There is an important delineation to make here, that this would not be an attempt to homogenize opinion on important matters, but rather to ascertain at least whether the foundational and fundamental facts of important matters are known and understood. This alone could weed out any character who tried to argue that he doesn't *believe* evidence gathered by thousands of experts simply on the basis of "belly-feel" intuition.[14]

With some sense of optimism put into place, it is now important to ask how and why politicians, especially those on "the right" that tend to be very vocal, have now become images of their own destruction. The characters put into positions of power in the Trump administration act as detractors and dismantlers of their own positions and the purposes of the institutions they are to head. The former and current head of the Environmental Protection Agency (EPA) both want to do away with the EPA[15] and the head of the Department of Education (DE) wants to work herself out of a job.[16] Existing as they do at the moment, they are contradictive internal viruses, put into power intentionally with the purpose of dismantling the very institutions every other presidential administration in the past has sworn to protect, at varying degrees. The purpose of a politician has always been to maintain a governmental system and attempt to maintain or produce better lives for their constituents, however beneficially or selfishly, as an outward contractual agreement with the people. Beginning in 2016 with the Trump administration, these positions find themselves tasked with the opposite motives, to become the deconstructors of safety and public policy rather than the constructors of such policies that are intended to keep the population safe. Ironically, even the idea of *safety* has somehow been reduced to consist only of police, military force, and immigration enforcement while disregarding so many other types of threats that impact Americans daily, like environmental catastrophes and health issues. More unnerving is that two years into Trump's presidency many of his supporters apparently support this type of agenda and political philosophy. The acceptance of this type politically nihilistic and authoritarian philosophy is either due to his followers' hierarchy of values, or, more likely, they are still unaware of the fact, or unwilling to accept, that they have been conned through myriad acts of artifice, and/or maybe they know they've been duped but their pride will not allow them to admit it.

In pursuance of an attempt to understanding the seemingly contradictory nature of politicians during an age when we rely so heavily upon them and when they have apparently taken it upon themselves to shape into new forms completely, forms that rely on completely deviant sets of knowledge, such as "alternative facts," it may be that it is time to define the new modern era we find ourselves in since the same ubiquitous social norms and mores no longer apply, as Molly Ball explored in an article on Kellyanne Conway in *The Atlantic*: "In a universe that operates according to normal rules, that might be true—actions are supposed to have consequences; people are supposed to stop listening to you when you prove that you can't be trusted. But as Donald Trump showed again and again throughout the campaign, those rules aren't as binding as we may have once believed."[17] And the rules of the past will likely continue to be reshaped, so I would like to posit a name and an acronym, that attempts to summate the entire situation we now find ourselves in, where "reality is inside the collective skull of the Party [where] the exterior world can be ignored or shaped according to the Party's will [and] the past does not determine the present; the present modifies the past [or] the past does not exist, and so we are at liberty to create it."[18] Defining this zeitgeist, this new model of alternative reality, is integral, just as it is with defining a politician, to help understand the rules, goals, limitations, and modus operandi of the movement so as to present an opposition, or solution, toward the problems it awakens.

In order to set a foundation for this postulation, it's important to explain the background and genesis of such a shift in eras, a movement outside of and beyond a concept known as postmodernism. Inextricably linked are, for better or worse, theoretical (a priori) and empirical (a posteriori) groundings for all types of ideologies and theories that bring with them ethics, morals, and perspectives that are innately political. Paulo Freire's English translation of *Pedagogy of the Oppressed* that arrived in 1970 does a great job to help situate the problem of there existing an elected demagogue and the ignorant, oppressed populations that tend to admire and be attracted to such a leader. This emerges out of a depletion of emotional intelligence, where the oppressed only know the language of the oppressor, so that if they are ever lucky enough to rise out of their subjugation, they exert upon others the same forces pressed upon them because they know no different form of mediation, governance, or hierarchical structure. Donald Trump's rise to power in the 2016 election is a perfect example of this type of stratagem—the oppressed being drawn to the language of an oppressor in the guise of their revolutionary leader, their champion, which, of course, he is not and will not be, especially as more people figure out the deviousness of the Republican tax cut.[19] Trump's, and many prominent Republican's, rhetoric toward detractors also feeds into this narrative by attempting to bifurcate the American population, since "leaders cannot treat the oppressed as mere activists to be denied the opportunity of reflection and allowed merely the illusion of acting, whereas in fact they would continue to be manipulated—and in this case by the presumed foes of manipulation."[20] Here, the oppressed are both his detractors and supporters—those who stand to be negatively impacted the most by his proposals, and who are yet his most ardent supporters. Intellectuals and scholars saw the signs and the dangers of his populist rise early on, but this knowledge did nothing to ward off the fascination. Freire summarized this populist attraction eloquently by stating that "manipulation, sloganizing, 'depositing,' regimentation, and prescription cannot be components of revolutionary praxis, precisely because they are components of the praxis of domination."[21] Of course, the erudite have known this and have been outspoken in their opposition to these kinds of ideas most notably since the end of World War II, but the masses easily succumb to historical amnesia and forget that a person of Trump's character, by very nature of the words he uses, is antithetical to any form of positive revolution. More unnerving is how potent his messages are to those of the directly oppressed, or the optimistically oppressed as we see in America—the groups that are oppressed but refuse to accept this or acknowledge it except when it can benefit them. So they're drawn to the very language that oppresses them, just so they can fight to achieve some semblance of dominance, and this time in America it worked.

Allow me then to propose that we have now officially moved out of the postmodern era, if indeed we were ever *in* it, and into something wholly new and different, a new world order that acts as an exacerbation of previous modes of thought, where the current administration denies all information that is not immediately disseminated by them and lathers on laudation to pundits that craft "semi-plausible … counternarrative[s], so that those who don't want to look past the façade of Trump's Potemkin village don't have to."[22] This results in what I would like to call the Post-Rational Imitational Simulation Matrix (PRISM) era. Briefly, and with full autonomy in the definition that follows, I provide an explanation that should be expounded upon and adapted, with the hope being that this doesn't take full form, and that America, and the world, are able to combat any movement toward the PRISM era as often and persistently as possible. The first fight must be in figuring out, finally, what a politician is, or what we wish it to be. If we do not figure this out, there's no telling how far this type of thinking could be stretched and applied.

The PRISM era, taking shape from 2016 onward, could be defined as having a general access to all human knowledge that is either recognized or ignored, resulting in discrepancies of absolute knowledge when in fact the capability exists to achieve this type of erudition, therefore creating an artificial matrix based on patterns of reality, but which defies the reality achieved through the scaffolding of knowledge. This is different from superficial knowledge that could be defined as the spurning of facts and findings due to shallow understandings, because it couples this ignorant reticence and unwillingness with excessive confidence in one's ignorance which materializes into a kind of pseudo-reality. The PRISM state of mind and its antithesis are two dichotomies that then exist in a world exponentially expanding in human technological capacity and opportunity, therefore skewing modern and postmodern constructions of thought in order to paradoxically push both to the future and pull toward the past—the allusion to these past periods may be defined as resembling the modernist concept of new realities and growth, which is inharmoniously entwined with the postmodernist quality of resisting structures of absoluteness to subvert the very progresses of modernist innovation in order to steer toward visions of entropy rather than organizational advancements. It is this environment, the current state of affairs, which then produces characters of supreme ingenuity, compassion, intuition, and precocious wisdom (the elite scientists at NASA for instance), while also, and alternatively, creating ersatz characters and stratagems that purport to exist on the same plane and abide by the same rules, both benefiting from the advancement and working to undermine this process simultaneously (Donald Trump). The two realities are therefore existing at the same time, constructed out of the same environments and geneses, with both believing the other is a parody of some earlier version of themselves. The neo-liberal becomes the conservative, conservative idealism becomes liberal progressivism, creating a paradox or contradictory set of imitable qualities which move the nuanced human brain into two separate camps of thought: each side is to be entitled a "post-rational simulacra" projection since they believe their reality is correct and absolute, and they are perceived outwardly from the opposite side as defying all the norms figured in their separate camps of thought—the difference being that one side, although diluted, has a firm grasp of evidence-based realities. The result is that the language used to describe both sides reduces to a state of polysemy, or multiple interpretations, lacking any type of fixed denotation. This dichotomous foundation compounds into the alternative left and alternative right where visions are distorted to appear to have similar contemporary worldviews and seek similar utilitarian ends, but where each side views the problems encountered as being symptomatic of completely different issues and to be solved only by actions suited to their separate realities and the rules that govern them (these ideas also manifest into a hierarchy of values that become politicized). The left rests with science, new-age hippieness, outlandish and contradictory permissiveness, and ironic condemnations of free speech, while the right rests on mysticism, religion, neoconservatism, ill-conceived relativism, and consumerist exceptionalist idealism. Both purport to seek truth, safety, health, and prosperity only through the separate paradigms of thought that engage in rejections of past knowledge and the accumulation of it, respectively. This could be explained as being the highest form of *gaslighting*, so much so that the zeitgeist is defined, or derived, out of it and those in power implement its edifice. In summation, two realities are created, both legitimized by their respective camps of thought that utilize completely separate bodies of knowledge created out of the same human compendium. The establishment of this duality effectively moves the Western world out of the postmodern period and into the PRISMatic period of human thought. Perhaps the only thing that could shake people from this hypnotic cognitive slumber would be a catastrophic event like another world war, although war need not be the only possible catalyst because we may all soon have an extreme climate change reckoning to tangle with.

The effects of the PRISM era could be broad and deep because of its intrinsic ability to appear as a legitimate progression arising out of redacted historical narratives and former governmental approaches as well as apparently admissible alternative ways of perceiving the established order of history and advancement. But these projections, as the name and indeed the acronym lean toward, are facile propositions piled upon imitations, simulations of order and legitimacy that, ultimately, deny rational thought and facts, all in the guise of simply promoting a *new*, but neither more or less dangerous or safe, way of looking at the world and America's place in it—new for the sake of being new. It is crucial that the simulation does not reach the necessary marketability in order to achieve the status of a simulacra. Therein lies the danger of this new form of discipline, this new matrix, that reshapes what we've always known into what Michel Foucault states may be "identified neither with an institution nor with an apparatus; it is a type of power, a modality for its exercise, comprising a whole set of instruments, techniques, procedures, levels of application, targets; it is a 'physics' or an 'anatomy' of power, a technology."[23] In utilizing this alternate reality, by gaslighting essentially, this new view makes the sane and knowledgeable question their understanding of the world or even of a what a politician is and/or should be; for the more ignorant, it makes them question everything they have ever known or been taught; therefore, they begin to distrust so-called paragons of truth and education. The effect of this reaches Foucault's third criteria of his tactics of power that increases "both the docility and the utility of all the elements of the system."[24] Finally, the words of Jean Baudrillard help wrap this idea up: "By crossing into a space whose curvature is no longer that of the real, nor that of truth, the era of simulation is inaugurated by a liquidation of all referentials … that is to say of an operation of deterring every real process via its operational double [a] perfectly descriptive machine that offers all the sign of the real and short-circuits all its vicissitudes. Never again will the real have the chance to produce itself."[25] The precession of the simulacra—or truth derived from whatever evidence is available—is the simulation, and although close to half the population, as the election demonstrated, now perceives reality through the prism dictated by the proposed simulacra, it is the other half's responsibility to expose it, to define it, to situate it, and to make real the truths that we have learned through education, through progress, through experimentation, through science and discourses of all kinds once again undeniably visible. The postmodern period formed organically during a time that needed a new perspective, a vision that distrusted all views before it,[26] but it has since morphed and become something far more pernicious where "facts no longer have a specific trajectory, they are born at the intersection of models,"[27] and the model presented now is a terrifying one.

Kellyanne Conway's "alternative facts" statement was declared a mistake "a blip, a trivial error, virtually a typo," where instead she meant to say, "alternative information."[28] She went so far as to give an example of "alternative information" too, which she likely did not realize may be even more terrifying than her previous statement: "She said, giving an example: Three plus one equals four, but so does two plus two. Anyway, she contended, nobody cared about 'alternative facts' except the elite, out-of-touch intelligentsia."[29] With no stretch of hyperbole, those intelligentsia likely read this and thought, "At least she didn't say 2 + 2 = 5," but that day may yet arrive. In fact, it may already be at this point. With doctored videos now being shared by the most powerful government in the world, who knows what could be next.[30]

So asking "What is a politician?" is not enough, but it is a start, and a necessary one to combat the rise of PRISM, making it essential, as it always is, for us to look backward before we press on into this brave new alternative world.

NOTES

1. Anthony Burgess, *1985* (London: Beautiful Books, 1978, 2010), 45.

2. George Orwell, "Politics and the English Language," *Horizon*, April 1946, 5(N).

3. Tom Nichols, "How America Lost Faith in Expertise," *Foreign Affairs*, March/April 2017, https://www.foreignaffairs.com/articles/united-states/2017–02–13/how-america-lost-faith -expertise (12 Dec. 2017).

4. Nichols, "How America Lost Faith in Expertise."

5. Aristotle declared that "the end [or goal] of politics is the best of ends; and the main concern of politics is to engender a certain character in the citizens and to make them good and disposed to perform noble actions" (Clayton), and Plato added that to be a good politician, one must not be "ignorant of himself [because he] will also be ignorant of others and of political things, and, therefore, will never be an expert politician" (Korab-Karpowicz). Remember first that these were goals, not requirements, and Plato and Aristotle knew the dangers of not meeting these standards.

6. Plato, *Republic*, ed. Robin Waterfield (Oxford: Oxford University Press, 2008), 67.

7. Orwell, "Politics and the English Language," 7(N).

8. Orwell, "Politics and the English Language," 10(N).

9. Anthony Burgess, *The Worm and the Ring* (Sussex, UK: William Heinemann 1961, 1970), 252.

10. W. J. Korab-Karpowicz, "Plato: Political Philosophy," *Internet Encyclopedia of Philosophy*, ed. James Fieser and Bradley Dowden, 2017, http://www.iep.utm.edu/platopol/.

11. Marshall Berman, *All That Is Solid Melts Into Air* (New York: Penguin, 1982, 19888), 11.

12. Aldous Huxley, *Brave New World Revisited* (New York: Perennial Library, 1969), 38: "Hitler's Minister for Armaments, Albert Speer, delivered a long speech in which with remarkable acuteness, he described the Nazi tyranny and analyzed its methods. 'Hitler's dictatorship,' he said, 'differed in one fundamental point from all its predecessors in history. It was the first dictatorship in the present period of modern technical development, a dictatorship which made complete use all technical means for the domination of its own country. Through technical devices like the radio and the loud-speaker, eighty million people were deprived of independent though…. As a result of this there has arisen the new type of the uncritical recipient of order…. Many a man has been haunted by the nightmate that one day nations might be dominated by technical means.'"

13. *Ibid.*

14. "Trump on Climate Change Report: 'I don't believe it,'" *BBC News*, 26 November 2018, https://www.bbc.com/news/world-us-canada-46351940 (1 Dec. 2018).

15. Coral Davenport, "Scott Pruitt Is Seen Cutting the E.P.A. with a Scalpel, Not a Cleaver," *The New York Times*, 5 February 2017,https://www.nytimes.com/2017/02/05/us/politics/scott-pruitt-is-seen-cutting-the-epa-with-a-scalpel-not-a-cleaver.html (12 Dec. 2017); Abigail Abrams, "What to Know About Andrew Wheeler, a Former Coal Lobbyist Who Will Temporarily Replace Scott Pruitt as EPA Chief," *Time*, 6 July 2018, http://time.com/5331352/andrew-wheeler-epa/ (1 Dec. 2018).

16. Yamiche Alcindor, "Rough First Week Gives Betsy DeVos a Glimpse of the Fight

Ahead," *The New York Times*, 19 February 2017, https://www.nytimes.com/2017/02/19/us/politics/betsy-devos-education.html?_r=0 (12 Dec. 2017).

17. Molly Ball, "Kellyanne's Alternate Universe," *Atlantic Monthly*, April 2017, 49(N).

18. Burgess, *1985*, 44, 50.

19. William Gale, Hillary Gelfond, Aaron Krupkin, Mark Mazur, and Eric Toder, "Effects of the Tax Cuts and Jobs Act: A Preliminary Analysis," *Brookings Institute*, 14 June 2018, https://www.brookings.edu/research/effects-of-the-tax-cuts-and-jobs-act-a-preliminary-analysis/.

20. Paulo Freire, *Pedagogy of the Oppressed* (New York: Bloomsbury, 1970, 2016), 126.

21. Freire, *Pedagogy of the Oppressed*, 126.

22. Ball, "Kellyanne's Alternate Universe," 44(N).

23. Michel Foucault, *Discipline and Punish: The Birth of the Prison* (New York: Vintage, 1977, 1995), 215.

24. Foucault, *Discipline and Punish*, 218.

25. Jean Baudrillard, *Simulacra and Simulation* (Ann Arbor: University of Michigan Press, 1981, 2006), 2.

26. Berman, *All That Is Solid Melts Into Air*, 9: "Post-modernist social though pours scorn on all the collective hopes for moral and social progress, for personal freedom and public happiness, that were bequeathed to us by the modernists of the eighteenth-century Enlightenment."

27. Baudrillard, *Simulacra and Simulation*, 16.

28. Ball, "Kellyanne's Alternate Universe," 49(N).

29. Ball, "Kellyanne's Alternate Universe," 49(N).

30. Drew Harwell, "White House Shares a Doctored Video to Support Punishment of Journalist Jim Acosta," *The Washington Post*, 8 November 2018, https://www.washingtonpost.com/technology/2018/11/08/white-house-shares-doctored-video-support-punishment-journalist-jim-acosta/?noredirect=on&utm_term=.e96965a8fedb.

PART 3

Historical
Observations

Of Crowd Sizes and Casualties

The Ominous Similarities Between Trump-Era America and Wartime Japan in the Use of Alternative Facts

SEAN D. O'REILLY

In essence, "alternative facts" is just another name for Hitler's infamous "big lie." Hitler crowed in *Mein Kampf* that "the broad masses of a nation are always more easily corrupted in the deeper strata of their emotional nature than consciously or voluntarily; and thus in the primitive simplicity of their minds they more readily fall victims to the big lie than the small lie."[1] Like the proverbial "emperor's new clothes," big lies and alternative facts must involve an outrageous and often quite obvious falsehood, anything from the misinformation campaign about former President Barack Obama's birth certificate or religious beliefs to the size of inaugural crowds in January 2017 to the scale of alleged voter fraud in the 2016 election (allegations which were also made in the November 2018 election); if one repeats the lie often enough, one's supporters can be relied upon to continue believing it.[2] All one must do is present an appealing, if not necessarily plausible, counter-narrative to one's supporters, who are already emotionally predisposed to support whatever one says. If anything, comfortingly appealing stories enjoy an easy victory over truth or (non-alternative) facts. As Republican political strategist Frank Luntz once stated, "A compelling story, even if factually inaccurate, can be more emotionally compelling than a dry recitation of the truth."[3]

It might be surprising to some that this "big lie" tactic works at all, and many critics of the current U.S. administration might jump to the conclusion that only the gullible are susceptible to this sort of manipulation. In fact, almost everyone is potentially vulnerable to these tactics due to the disconfirmation bias, documented by Stanford researchers and many others. Adherents of a given belief require an enormous preponderance of evidence against a particular belief to start questioning it, and are highly motivated to find weaknesses in any such evidence; but if presented with "facts" that seem to support what one already believes, most people will accept these facts readily, without subjecting this comforting evidence to anything close to the same level of intellectual scrutiny. In other words, people long for confirmation of what they already believe (or want to believe), but will furiously resist attempts to disprove those beliefs.

Rarely if ever has an American administration so openly used this "big lie" tactic, but other nations throughout history have experimented with similar strategies, and the results of these experiments can offer valuable lessons to those seeking to make sense of the current era in the United States. A particularly close, if naturally imperfect, analogy can be drawn to the "alternative facts" used by the wartime Japanese administration from 1942 to 1945. At that time, there was a mounting body of evidence that the Americans were steadily advancing towards the Japanese homeland, so looked at dispassionately, any Japanese subject with a map could easily have verified that the government's pronouncements about the war were fabrications; once the B-29 bombing campaign of the homeland began, it would have been even harder for people to deny Japan was heading towards defeat. And yet essentially no anti-war or anti-propaganda protest emerged in war-torn Japan. How, in Japan's case, did the alternative facts become the only facts—and could such a thing happen in the United States today? Moreover, are ordinary Japanese subjects' reactions, once these alternative facts were decisively exposed as lies, a potentially accurate predictor of Americans' likely response to any such future unmasking of alternative facts as what they are—lies? These questions are the focus of this essay.

I will compare early 1940s Japan with Trump-era America in order to argue that once regimes begin to promote alternative facts, and succeed in convincing or cowing a sizable proportion of the populace into accepting them as well, three tragic stages tend to occur in succession. Firstly, contrary to the opinions of most skeptics, who tend to assume that secretly, at least, officials spouting alternative facts surely do not believe such lies themselves and will not jeopardize their country to maintain them, unfortunately the opposite has often been the case. Representatives of an "alternative facts" regime, despite being well-informed and thus surely knowing intellectually these "facts" are nothing but lies, are inexorably compelled to support, and in some cases voluntarily accept, the official version of events, even to the point of squandering precious resources to protect these facts from harsh scrutiny. Secondly, regime representatives and the believing populace feed each other's belief in, or commitment to, these alternative facts, binding these two groups together in a web of complicity from which there is no easy exit.

And thirdly, once the edifice of lies comes tumbling down—and it will—it is likely to trigger, among the heretofore supportive populace, either true-believer syndrome on the one hand, or righteous indignation against the demagogues running the regime on the other. Either way, there is not much chance it will trigger self-examination or admission of responsibility among "regular" people, and little hope that most once-believing members of the public will be any less vulnerable to the big lie/alternative facts tactics in the future. In other words, many former backers of alternative facts regimes like the ones controlling wartime Japan or Trump-era America will remain ready, even after the disintegration of the regime they supported, to be activated by the next alternative facts-peddling demagogue who comes along.

Stage One: Even Well-Informed Leaders Start Sacrificing Resources to Maintain the Big Lie

By November 1944, the Imperial Japanese Navy had already been devastated by repeated battles with numerically and, increasingly, technologically superior U.S. forces. In particular, nearly all of Japan's aircraft carriers had already been sunk. But Japan possessed one secret weapon, the enormous *Shinano*, a Yamato-class super-battleship that had been laboriously converted into a supercarrier. It set sail in mid–November 1944, with a captain, Toshio Abe, who as a soon-to-be rear admiral was privy to accurate information on Japan's dire situation, and on U.S. offensive capabilities. Nonetheless, the official position of the government and the military was that Japan was involved in an "advance by turning"; using the term "strategic retreat" was quite out of the question, as no less an authority than journalist and expert on the navy Masanori Ito learned when he dared to use such a term in public.[4] Press releases continued to sing the praises of Japanese ships and weapons while denigrating or downplaying the enemy's.

Unfortunately for the many hundreds on board when the supercarrier *Shinano* set sail, Abe had apparently "drunk the Kool-Aid," despite knowing it was poison. He was so confident in this mighty ship's capabilities, having remarked out loud that he believed it was in fact "unsinkable," and so publicly contemptuous of the enemy's, that even after his ship was hit, almost immediately after leaving on its inaugural voyage, by four U.S. torpedoes, Abe ordered the ship to proceed full-speed ahead, rather than diverting to a nearby port for repairs.[5] This decision led to the ship sinking quite rapidly in deep water, with the loss of many hundreds of its crew, a disaster that could have easily been avoided had Abe chosen to act according to the real, rather than the alternative, facts. The question is, why did Abe fail to do so? Had he truly come to believe the propaganda, despite the accurate information to which he was privy? Or was he simply forced to *act as though he believed* what his military and administration were claiming? After all, this huge ship was, to the inventors of alternative facts, a game-changing weapon (though by late 1944, those like Abe with access to accurate information knew that nothing, and certainly not a single aircraft carrier, however big, could stem the U.S. advance), and it would be exceedingly bad publicity if it were ever revealed, not only that the ship was attacked so close to its original port, but its captain had assumed the worst and retreated to the nearest friendly port. Thus it is possible that Abe sacrificed hundreds of lives, and the enormous material investment of this ship, three years in the making, because of fears it would call the alternative facts narrative of the war into question.

In fact, the entire Imperial Japanese Navy was trapped in much the same way as individuals like Abe. Having projected confidence for years over the outcome of a war with the United States and Great Britain, Navy representatives found themselves imprisoned by their own rhetoric and thus unable to protest when the Imperial Japanese Army continued to demand half of all materiel allocations (even for items and materials far more critical to shipbuilding, etc., than to the army), a state of affairs which further degraded the IJN's fighting ability.[6] In other words, having once supported a highly exaggerated "alternative facts" version of the war, the IJN chose to make do with what they had, and expose the nation to further damage, rather than risk exposing the big lie by admitting the war situation was dire. In such a climate, defeat was already certain and all Japan's planners intellectually knew it; Navy Minister Yonai privately admitted that "after Midway, I was certain there was no chance of success."[7] But no one dared publicly float the idea that Japan might lose, and begin planning accordingly, even though this more pragmatic approach could have saved many lives.[8] Alternative facts had, in the end, become more important than national security.

So it was that Abe let his ship sink rather than expose the alternative facts of the wartime Japanese regime as lies. But this adherence to alternative facts doomed not only his ship but his own life, as he elected to go down with his ship. One widely repeated tenet of naval combat for the Japanese was that it is best for a captain not to survive the loss of his ship (in partial atonement for having failed to prevent the ship's sinking). From a utilitarian standpoint, of course, this viewpoint is wasteful in the extreme: often ships sink for reasons having little or nothing to do with the (in)competence of their captains. Worse yet, only seasoned, veteran officers would ever be put in charge of a ship, especially a "last best hope" such as the *Shinano*, and having all the accumulated experience of these senior officers be lost in a futile symbolic gesture is surely detrimental to the country's ability to wage war.

Some of the officers who ultimately decided to go down with their ships must have realized the wastefulness of this policy. Why then did they feel unable to choose any other option? Partly it is due to the precedent of many other captains having chosen this fate—no one presumably wanted to be known as the "coward captain" who chose life when all his predecessors had chosen a purportedly noble death—but it is also due to the rhetoric of press releases by the Japanese government and parroted in the mass media celebrating the glorious sacrifice of those who opted for suicide rather than dishonor.

This rhetoric had been building for many years, and accelerated into high gear after the infamous "three human bombs" incident in Shanghai in early 1932. Three Japanese soldiers died while setting a bomb to destroy a barbed-wire fence protecting Shanghai from the Japanese assault. But the Japanese army concluded that the usefulness of this incident would be much increased (and potential embarrassment to the army much diminished!) if, instead of admitting that the three had died because of incompetence—their officer had made the fuse too short—this snafu was covered up, and their deaths re-characterized as a noble sacrifice, an intentional suicide charge to take down the fence.[9]

The "alternative fact" version of the incident cannot have fooled any rational listener with knowledge of the Japanese military's capabilities. The army was certainly capable of setting bombs off only once its own soldiers were out of harm's way—and given this, why volunteer to blow oneself up, reducing the army's strength needlessly, if one can destroy obstacles safely from a distance?[10] But instead of reacting with skepticism, much of the Japanese populace began celebrating these three as national heroes. As to the question of responsibility for this falsehood, however, who is ultimately to blame: the propagandists, for making this up, or the "regular" people, for accepting it hook, line and sinker, and continuing to patronize the many retellings of the story in popular culture?

The same logic of rhetoric versus reality can be usefully applied to the popular cultural celebration of kamikaze pilots both in and after World War II in Japan. Here, too, the evidence of Japan's looming defeat by late 1944 was clear "to anyone who bothered to study a map" (since the "victories" being reported in the Japanese press kept drawing closer and closer to the home islands), and yet even after defeat was written on the wall, the press and the public at large seized on this alternative fact of Japan's supposedly greater spiritual commitment to the war effort.[11] Consciously contrasting Japan's alleged spiritual superiority with the American technological and numerical advantage, both press and public continued to praise kamikaze suicide attackers *as though their attacks could actually affect the outcome of the war*, something that was patently false. This was especially clear after the war was brought home in a terrifying way starting in November 1944, when B-29 bombers came within easy operational range of Japan's home islands; once the bombings of urban centers started, no one could seriously believe the war was going well anymore. Yet even after this point, the Japanese public continued to toe the party line on the war.

Some readers might object at this point, since obviously Trump-era America and wartime Japan are quite different. It must seem unlikely that the sort of wholesale fabrication of facts occurring in the latter, up to and including the actual banning of books which recount a different version of official facts, could also potentially occur in the former. And it is true that these two regimes have many differences, foremost among them being the Trump administration's relatively short tenure (compared to the years-long wartime Japanese regime, in any case). We might say that the United States under Trump is at an earlier stage of deploying alternative facts. And besides, the initial goal of an alternative facts regime is not necessarily to go so far as to ban contradictory accounts, but rather to provide a plausible narrative to please those emotionally predisposed to support the regime—to give them a leg to stand on, as it were.

However, this is not to say that wartime Japan holds no warnings for those observing the current situation in the United States. For one thing, the sense of national unity that emerged in Japan was largely due to the total war situation, and such a sense of unity, in which some civil liberties are suspended or denied to certain groups and principled opposition against the regime in control becomes very costly indeed, actually happened during World War II in the United States, as the example of the Japanese internment shows. Nor is the Trump administration blind to the connection between the deeply problematic internment of Japanese-Americans on the one hand, and their own attempts at travel bans and anti–Muslim discrimination on the other. Some high-profile Trump supporters have gone so far as to cite the Japanese internment—one of the worst stains against American ideals of civil liberty and equality in the nation's history—approvingly, as *precedent!*[12] In any case, a public sphere severely muted by nationalist fervor and a sense of unity is certainly within the realm of possibility should the United States in the near future once again enter into a major war. But what are the practical steps by which such a weakened public sphere could be created?

The first step in bringing an alternative facts-based narrative into the mainstream is in wielding economic pressure on, and against, news outlets willing to criticize the emerging narrative or its regime, demonizing them as puppets of foreign regimes, unpatriotic, and so forth. In Japan's case, as the war worsened, the government was able to exert total control over the paper supply, exercising de facto veto power over every publication (since any criticism of the regime could expect no more paper to print anything). So it is easy to point the finger of blame at the regime in charge. But doesn't ultimate responsibility lie, once again, with the consumers of the alternative facts-based narrative? It was they who gave even left-wing publications a motive to publish patriotic pro-regime propaganda in Japan, and it is they who might encourage the same development in the United States. Just because the process takes some time does not mean journalists or "regular" people can afford to rest on their laurels: the only thing that can reverse this alternative facts-fueled poisoning of the mass media is active, principled journalist and consumer resistance.

Stage Two: Both the Regime and Its Supporters Continue Mutually to Prop up the Big Lie, and Neither the Regime Nor the Public Can Extricate Themselves from It

The Japanese wartime government's control over the mass media—and thus, the information being fed to the public—was never even close to total. The government's system of influencing media reportage used suggestive and unofficial "consultations" rather than openly repressive tactics.[13] In such a system, it was still possible, if potentially costly in economic terms, to publish veiled criticisms of government policy, and this occasionally happened. But generally speaking, over time, the regime and the media formed, if not an alliance per se, at least a détente, accelerating a mutually reinforcing campaign to shore up the alternate reality that Japan was headed to ultimate victory. For the media, this was due to the twin motivators of higher sales for more patriotic, reassuring pro-war reportage on the one hand, and self-preservation on the other; after compromising on the truth once, and publishing or broadcasting "alternative facts" (i.e., lies), the only options left to a media outlet were coming clean, a high-risk move with little promise of reward given the patriotic public, or doubling down. At this point, the big lie had become so fundamental to the identity of the wartime regime and so frequently "fed" by the reports of the mass media that coming clean was out of the question.

This collusion between the press and the regime did not appear overnight. In fact, it took a period of several years to reach its mature form. The initial step by both regime and the (majority) pro-war faction of the public was to reward favorable coverage, with more lenient oversight by the government and higher consumption by the public. This economic pressure on would-be sources of resistance among the mass media meant other newspapers and media outlets had a powerful incentive to fall in line, and faced more and more serious economic consequences if they refused. That is how the big lie spreads, after all: once endorsed, maintaining it becomes fundamental to the continued survival of both government and media.

It is fairly easy to map this story of the deterioration of wartime Japan's mass media onto Trump-era America. The news sources most favorable to the Trump administration (Fox News, etc.) face the same cost-benefit analysis and have drawn the same logical conclusion as those Japanese media outlets who, in the mid–1930s, began parroting the official governmental line and thus earning the praise of both the regime and much of the public. At this point, with the entire machinery of the news reportage devoted to defending the regime's alternative facts, and more importantly, with a sizable proportion of the populace continuing to respond favorably to this approach, it goes without saying that (like the right-leaning newspaper Yomiuri shinbun in wartime Japan) Fox News has a powerful economic disincentive against breaking with the administration.

Similarly, the regime and its backers can be expected to do whatever they can to increase their influence over a wider and wider swathe of the mass media. This is true whether by forced consolidation (in wartime Japan) or through attempts by Trump supporters to buy the remaining hostile media sources and begin to exert a transformative influence from within.[14] While the public at large remains responsible, at least partly, for all the actions of the demagogues they support, regimes that successfully prevent dissenting voices from being heard and thus gaining traction can and do reduce the chance that segments of the populace will be able to move from silent, private dismay to a more organized, public and vociferous form of protest.

The demagoguery of, say, Cleon of Athens is bad enough if all he were guilty of was exaggerating his state's strength and actively hamstringing peace efforts abroad. But if it could be proven that he had also systematically destroyed the careers of those who spoke against him, then we could reasonably say such a demagogue, by stifling opposing voices and thereby preventing doubt from developing among his supporters, has more responsibility than the public for what he does while in power. But which kind of demagogue is Trump? Is his administration actually able to crush organized opposition in the media, such that its supporters could reasonably cry foul and feel no guilt about bringing his regime to power?

Stage Three: Even After the Big Lie Unravels, Regime Backers Won't Respond with Contrition or Feel Any Guilt about Their Demagogue's Actions ... and May Never Cease Support

In the 1970s, M. Lamar Keene famously analyzed what is now known as "true-believer syndrome." He was flabbergasted to find, even after he himself presented sufficient evidence to demonstrate incontrovertibly that his "psychic" abilities were fraudulent, that he was simply unable to convince some of the people who had chosen to believe in his allegedly supernatural powers no matter what evidence he showed them.[15] This phenomenon often appears when predictions about the end of the world are made and become an article of faith for a particular group, yet subsequently come and go without incident: to resolve the cognitive dissonance such a situation creates, adherents can either make the costly choice of disavowing the entire edifice of belief that now underlies their identity, or double down on their faith and find a plausible-sounding explanation or reinterpretation to banish the inconvenient facts confronting them.

By mid–1945, after enduring the destruction of nearly every urban area, the Japanese populace all over the country had been exposed to the certainty of Japan's imminent defeat. But there is an astonishing story here: during the U.S. Occupation, just after the war ended, SCAP conducted surveys of ordinary Japanese intended to investigate morale in the final months of the war. More than two-thirds reported themselves convinced by mid–1945 that the war was utterly lost.[16] Yet even at this stage, when a strong majority of the population was now bitterly opposed to the war, concerted opposition to the government, or public protests against the war, failed to materialize. If almost seven out of ten adults in Japan wanted their government to sue for peace, why did they remain silent? Moreover, is it appropriate for them to consider themselves blameless for the war simply because—at the very end—they had privately changed their minds and felt they could now say they had been "duped" by the militarists?

Yet at the same time, what of the nearly three in 10 who, even when confronted by incontrovertible evidence of Japan's looming defeat, and the intellectual certainty that further resistance was futile, vowed to fight on to the bitter end? It is difficult to identify which of these figures, the 68 percent who became "pacifists in name only" and protested their innocence loudly in the postwar period, or the 28 percent with what might be called a form of true believer syndrome and continued their commitment to Japan's disastrous war, is more disturbing.

Conclusion

In this essay, I have argued that the parallels between wartime Japan and Trump-era America are potentially quite strong, with some predictive value. If America under Trump follows the same degenerative pattern as wartime Japan in its use of alternative facts, we can expect to see, in stage one, Trump supporters begin to sacrifice national security to protect their alternative facts version of the country and the world (for example, by colluding with hostile foreign governments, etc.), followed by a second stage involving greater and greater mutual reinforcement between the regime and its supporters, aided and abetted by pro-regime media sources. But it is the third stage that is perhaps most distressing to contemplate: once the Trump regime falls, either to impeachment or, more likely, to electoral defeat, what can we expect from the millions of erstwhile Trump supporters? If they turn on their demagogue, will they simply blame him for everything and deny any responsibility themselves? Moreover, is it possible some supporters, in the grip of true believer syndrome, will never abandon their leader, no matter how problematic his conduct, and never reject the Hitler-esque big lie?

Godwin's Law notwithstanding, when it comes to the Trump administration, unfortunately the probability of a rapid reductio ad Hitlerum result in any discussion is very high, because the same manipulative tactics are being used. What is truly ominous, however, is that unlike postwar West Germans, characterized by a largely sincere and concerted effort to atone for the crimes a willing populace enabled a demagogue to commit, it seems that many of Trump's supporters, if and when they finally do grow disillusioned with their demagogue, might prefer the exculpatory path followed by most Japanese imperial subjects starting in late 1945.

This "we were duped" path would simply re-channel their anger away from the targets Trump had chosen for them and onto Trump himself, thereby excusing them for any responsibility for their demagogue's actions. But a demagogue is only as strong as his or her supporters, and thus supporters (and to a lesser extent, those who chose not to oppose such a demagogue) must bear some share of responsibility for whatever reckless actions their chosen leaders undertake. There were plenty of warning signs about Trump before and during the election, but like the Japanese subjects in the early 1940s who preferred to hold onto the comforting lie of Japanese "victories," Trump supporters chose to turn a blind eye to Trump's many faults. It is my sincere hope that, when the disillusionment with Trump does come, it will extend to personal soul-searching for at least some of those ultimately responsible for Trump's actions: the voters who elected him. But the analogy with wartime Japan, where the silent majority did nothing to prevent or end the policies they later claimed to oppose, and a vocal minority simply continued to double down on their support for the regime and has shown no sign of contrition at any point, gives little reason for optimism.

NOTES

1. *Mein Kampf*, vol. 1, ch. 10, n.p.
2. Indeed, thanks to the psychological concept of the "illusory truth effect," Hitler was right: repeating the same thing over and over again wears down listeners' skepticism. Emily Dreyfuss, "Want to Make a Lie Sound True? Say It Again. And Again. And Again." *Wired*,

February 11, 2017, https://www.wired.com/2017/02/dont-believe-lies-just-people-repeat/ (14 Jan. 2018).

3. As quoted in Michael D'Antonio, *A Consequential President* (New York: St. Martin's, 2016), 127.

4. Ito Masanori, in a lecture at Kobe University in early 1943, refused to use the non-sensical term "advance by turning" (since the "turn" was to the north, towards Japan!) and called the withdrawal from Guadalcanal what it was—a retreat—but was browbeaten by the police for this transgression and coerced into using the alternative facts-style term thereafter. Ito Masanori, *The End of the Imperial Japanese Navy* (New York: MacFadden, 1965, orig. pub. 1956), 68.

5. Ito, *The End of the Imperial Japanese Navy*, 22.

6. The Army continued to make these demands for materiel. Ito, *The End of the Imperial Japanese Navy*, 75.

7. Admiral Ugaki and others continued to speak only of victory, trapped by their own optimistic rhetoric: "The main thing is to win, and we surely will win." Meanwhile, Yonai was privately admitting defeat was certain. Richard Overy, *Why the Allies Won* (New York: Pimlico, 2006, orig. pub. 1995), 40, 51.

8. For example, very little effort was made to prepare an adequate air defense against aerial attack of the Japanese homeland, despite this being certain to occur once Japan came within bombing range: it was presumably judged too dangerous to the alternative facts version of the war to make obvious and visible preparations, even if such lack of preparation risked—and indeed cost—hundreds of thousands of lives to the B-29s, which, thanks to this failure to develop an effective air defense system, could fly at a mere 7000 feet. Overy, *Why the Allies Won*, 153–154.

9. Louise Young, *Japan's Total Empire* (Berkeley: University of California Press, 1998), 77.

10. In fact, there was evidence contradicting the romanticized view of this story available from day one, since the unit sent to blow up the fence was actually a squad of six, and the other three came back safely. Obviously the unit had no intention of blowing themselves up or, presumably, all six would have done so. Written accounts contradicting the official, heroic version were banned, but no ban can completely prevent those wishing to investigate from doing so; it seems few were interested in debunking alternative facts in Japan. Young, *Japan's Total Empire*, 77.

11. Ito, *The End of the Imperial Japanese Navy*, 68.

12. E.g., Carl Higbie, while being interviewed on November 16, 2016, for Fox News, used the internment as a precedent for a "Muslim registry": http://www.businessinsider.com/megyn-kelly-muslim-registry-2016-11 (14 Jan. 2018).

13. Gregory Kasza, *The State and the Mass Media in Japan, 1918–1945* (Berkeley: University of California Press, 1993), 169.

14. For example, in December of 2017, it was reported that the financiers behind the recent buy-out of Time, Inc., were none other than the arch-conservative Koch brothers, who despite their public contempt for Trump have still rallied support for the more straight-forwardly conservative elements of Trump's agenda, notably tax reform. Bess Levin, "The Koch Brothers Found One Thing They Hate More Than Donald Trump," *Vanity Fair*, https://theintercept.com/2017/12/01/time-magazine-koch-brothers-meredith-corp/ (14 Jan. 2018).

15. See, e.g., M. Lamar Keene, *The Psychic Mafia* (New York: Prometheus Books, 1976), 150.

16. Overy, *Why the Allies Won*, 371.

Wild Irishmen, Alternative Facts and the Construction of America's First "Wall"

DEBRA REDDIN VAN TUYLL

Once upon a time, a young nation named America elected a leader who was revered by some and despised by others. Those who revered the president believed he would adopt wise policies and lead the republic to its rightful place in the world. They believed all that was needed was for the people to listen to the president's wise counsel and do as he said. For those who despised the president, the thought of listening to him, much less following his policies, was a lot like being forced to eat glass. So they gathered in mass meetings, they signed petitions, they demonstrated in the streets. And the president pronounced them misguided fanatics who did not understand the proper place of the people in a republic.

That story may sound familiar. It may sound so familiar that anyone reading this might be tempted to think it is referring to American political culture during the Trump administration.

They would be wrong, however. The election described above was held in 1796, and the newly elected president was Federalist John Adams. The people taking to the streets were Thomas Jefferson's Democratic-Republicans, whom today's Democrats claim as their legacy party. Adams won with 71 (26 percent) votes in the electoral college to Jefferson's 68 votes (25 percent).[1]

Donald Trump, then, is neither the first president to squeak by in the Electoral College nor to polarize the American people. Nor are he and his staff the first Americans to resort to using alternative facts to win approval for their policies and perspectives.

The issues that prompted American leaders to resort to alternative facts have varied—inaugural crowd size for Trump, and his perceived need for a physical wall to bar illegal immigrants from entering the United States; critical aliens and a pesky opposition party for Adams; Trump's fears foreign terrorists will perpetuate another 9/11 or London- or Paris-style attacks in America; Adams fears that Irish immigrants would become internal agitators and would conspire with the French to stage an invasion of the United States.[2] Both presidents used alternative facts to make silly, unsupported arguments and to try to claim greater presidential powers over immigration and to silence critics.[3] And both, ultimately, failed to have a permanent wall, legal or physical, built to keep out immigrants. Trump, however, midway through his presidency, took a step to force Congress to fund his wall: he and his Republican supporters forced a government shutdown when he could not get the $5 billion he wanted for his wall. The shutdown is playing out even as this is being written, thus the outcome in unknown. Likely, Trump will fail, as did Adams; once Congress reconvenes after the 2018 Christmas break, the new Democratic majority in the House of Representatives intends to push through a bill that will reopen the government. As the shutdown loomed in the run-up to the Christmas holiday, however, White House Press Secretary Sarah Sanders could have been channeling John Adams when she accused Democrats of choosing to protect illegal immigrants rather than Americans.[4]

Immigration has been an issue through much of American history, and Americans have long had a love-hate relationship with immigrants. In the 1850s, a political party, the Know Nothing (American) party arose, founded on an anti-immigration, anti–Catholic platform following the wave of Irish emigrants fleeing the Great Famine. Today, Americans debate extending protections to youths covered by the Deferred Action for Childhood Arrivals (DACA) program. President Trump has laid blame for protecting the DACA children at the feet of Congressional Democrats. Congressional Democrats have responded that the president "either lying" or "completely delusional."[5] At the same time, and on into the late 19th century, American railroads employed alternative facts to recruit immigrants west, particularly. In 1882, Congress passed the Chinese Exclusion Act, the first law in American history to prohibit immigration by a specific ethnic group amidst a flurry of alternative facts, including accusations of fraudulent activities by the Chinese Embassy; that Chinese immigrants were "coolie slaves" who were filthy, diseased heathens. That law would not be repealed until the 20th century. On the occasion of the Chinese Exclusion Act in 2017, the ACLU marked its similarity to Trump's proposed ban on persons from certain Muslim countries in an article on its website. More recently, during World War II, American interned thousands of Japanese Americans and, even more recently, the country has been dealing with President Donald Trump's threat to ban temporarily immigrants from primarily Muslim countries. These measures have all been grounded in fear, and the arguments in support of them have often employed alternative facts.[6]

Americans also have never quibbled too much about using alternative facts to win political debates. Starting with the 27 grievances in the Declaration of Independence, many of which laid at King George III's feet every political annoyance Americans could think of. For example, Americans argued they were being taxed without representation in Parliament. They were calling for direct representation. The British perspective, though, was grounded in virtual representation, or the idea that every member of Parliament represented every subject of the British empire. Further, American grievances dealt with issues that fell more within Parliament's responsibilities than the king's.

Because it came so early in the history of America, the Adams presidency is a good place to begin a discussion of "alternative facts" and their role in American political culture because that is when alternative facts arrived on the American political scene in a big way. And they have never left, as even the mainstream media is beginning to realize.[7] Further, alternative facts have become a defining trait of American political culture, and, one suspects, they always will be.

This is also a good place to begin considering American immigration policy and the construction of walls to keep out unwanted aliens, for during the Adams administration, the first such wall was constructed. Only, Adams and his administration constructed a legal, rather than a physical wall. Adams's legal wall consisted of four laws intended to: keep out new foreigners, particularly Irish refugees fleeing the 1798 United Irishman rising; make it more difficulty for aliens to achieve naturalization; disenfranchise immigrants who sided with the opposition party; and silence aliens who spoke out against Adams' administration policies and officials.[8]

The United Irishman rising is key to the debate over these four new laws and the alternative fact-based propaganda war they spawned. Their short-lived-but-exceedingly bloody rising was a response to the American and French revolutions and the inspiration they provided for the Irish to attempt to overthrow British rule and establish a republic of their own. After only four months, the British crushed the rebellion. Thousands fled Ireland, and many came to America. While it seems overly romantic to write that these Irish immigrants brought with them their ideals of democracy and republicanism, the truth of the matter is, they did. They saw themselves as exiles from their home country who had been forced out by a foreign power that denied them their political autonomy and religious freedom.[9]

This late 1790s wave of immigration happened at exactly the same moment America was embroiled in an undeclared war with France over a diplomatic incident triggered in part by a treaty that favored Britain over France. Given the Irish alliance with France, perhaps the Adams administration had a good reason to be wary of the influx of Irish. The arrival of presumed Irish radicals was frightening to many of Adams's party because their attitudes and political expectations preconditioned them to support the opposing Democratic-Republican party championed by Thomas Jefferson and James Madison.[10] The outcome was a propaganda war in which alternative facts flew fast and furiously as Americans debated the extent of the danger posed by the "hoards of wild Irishmen" who were flocking to America.[11]

This essay will examine the role of alternative facts in constructing the American political culture that has persisted throughout most of the country's history. It will examine how politicians and the partisan press used alternative facts to build a legal wall to keep out unwanted immigrants. The essay will focus on the fear-mongering rhetoric Adams and his fellow Federalists employed to gain support for the Alien and Sedition Acts. The work will be grounded in the use of "alternative facts" found in letters and other materials written by Adams's cabinet members, government ministers, and Congressmen as well as materials published in Federalist party newspapers, particularly the *Gazette of the United States*, which was the leading party organ.

The Background: Wild Irishmen in America

Certain Americans watched uneasily as tides of Irishmen, particularly those with ties to the United Irishmen, swarmed to their shores in the late 1790s. Not only were these refugees reputed to be rapists, robbers, murders, and worse (the same type of misinformation used against unwanted immigrant groups throughout American history), many espoused questionable political principles such as republicanism and democracy. Further, these newcomers came from a nation with close ties to France. In the eyes of the Federalist party-dominated government, that made these men and women dangerous. A threat to national security, even, as they might side with France if that country invaded America. Also, they were adding even greater numbers to the 250,000 of their countrymen already in America. The numbers alone were not the problem—the problem was that these immigrants leaned toward the opposing Democratic-Republican party.[12]

It only made sense that the Federalist administration of President John Adams would perceive the tide of Irish immigrants as almost as great a threat to American security as the French themselves.[13] Congressman Harrison Gray Otis of Massachusetts grumbled common Federalist sentiment in a letter to his wife: "If some means are not adopted to prevent the indiscriminate admission of wild Irishmen & others to the right of suffrage, there will soon be an end to liberty and property." In Congress, Otis elaborated on this theme, stating that he did "not wish to invite hordes of wild Irishmen, nor the turbulent and disorderly of all parts of the world to come here with a view to disturb our tranquility, after having succeeded in the over throw of their own Governments."[14]

As governments will when faced with threats to domestic security, Federalists sought a means of stemming the threat these "wild Irishmen" posed. They needed to stop in the influx of aliens and disenfranchise those who were already in the United States.[15] Their solution, passage of the Alien and Sedition Acts, was intended "to address the presence of enemy and friendly aliens in the country if war occurred with France," and to prevent "what the Federalists considered slanderous and seditious actions designed to bring the Adams administration into disrepute." Federalists viewed criticism of government and government officials as equivalent to insurrection. The objective, then, in pursuing the Alien and Sedition Acts was to silence the opposition, both foreign and domestic, to ensure that the barriers to citizenship were high enough that aliens had little hope of scaling them, and to make it more difficulty for aliens to achieve the franchise to vote.[16]

If this scenario sounds familiar, it should. The Alien and Naturalization Acts gave President Adams the powers over foreigners that Donald Trump sought early in his presidency: the power to keep out foreigners and the power to ban and deport aliens with no due process—no judge, no jury, no trial. The Alien and Naturalization Acts allowed non-citizens to be deported simply at the word of the president and also placed a tax on every immigrant a ship brought to America. These acts were aimed specifically at Irish and French immigrants, but primarily targeted at the Irish because there were so many more of them. The final act in the set of four, the Sedition Act, allowed dissenting voices to be silenced. Irish-born journalists were the most frequent target. The law afforded punishment for anyone who criticized the president or Congress. Interestingly, the vice president, Democratic-Republican Thomas Jefferson, was not covered by the law.[17] In concert, the four acts built a wall—temporarily at least—intended to keep aliens out, or, if they had already gotten in, to disenfranchise and to silence them if they disagreed with the government. The Federalist-controlled Congress was, without a doubt, addressing national security concerns with these laws, but they also, conveniently, had the potential to decimate the Democratic-Republican party's political base.

The debates over the four laws were inflammatory, but only the Sedition Act was truly successful (from the Federalist perspective). Sources vary over how many people were prosecuted under the Sedition Act, but at the very least 17 people, most of whom were foreign-born editors of Democratic-Republican newspapers, were arrested for publications that criticized the president or Congress.[18] Ultimately, at least for their two year duration, these laws produced an effective legal barrier—a legal wall—to immigration into the United States. And the arguments both for and against the laws were built on what might well be considered the 18th century's version of alternative facts.

Defining Alternative Facts

The term "alternative facts" has been thrown around a lot since presidential aide Kellyanne Conway used it in defending Sean Spicer's erroneous claim that Trump's inauguration was graced with the largest number of attendees ever. Chuck Todd, the *Meet the Press* host who was interviewing Conway when she used the term, understood the phrase as nothing more than a euphemism for lying. "Alternative facts are not facts," he told Conway. "They're falsehoods." Provable falsehoods.[19] In the Conway-Spicer matter, Todd was right. Conway's "alternative facts" was a euphemism she resorted to, hoping to deflect Spicer's overestimate. The phrase, though, in not quite so black-and-white; it has had other meanings attributed to it.

Donald Trump himself, or, rather, the ghost writer of his 1987 book *Trump: The Art of the Deal,* used a similar phrase to mean essentially the same as Kelleyanne Conway's "alternative facts." Ghost writer Tony Schwartz used "truthful hyperbole," with Trump's approval, to refer to innocent exaggeration that is effective in promotion. Schwartz has since stated that he rejects the idea that deceit can ever be innocent.[20]

For the more linguistically inclined, StackExchange, a series websites that offers expert-generated content, offers a site that deals with etymology of words and phrases. According to StackExchange, the phrase "alternative facts" has been in the American lexicon for at least 100 years. What it means depends on context, according to the website. For example, when preparing for court testimony, forensic scientists have been advised that "alternative facts" are simply competing facts.[21] In the physical sciences, the web site maintains, alternative facts are true but seemingly contradictory.[22]

Intent is perhaps the most important attribute of an alternative fact, according to StackExchange. The website's authors interpret Kellyanne Conway's usage to imply that alternative facts arise when individuals engage in a discussion with different facts but arrive at different conclusions. The site's authors illustrate their interpretation with the classic example of several blind men who are asked to describe an elephant but who are then given only one part of the animal to examine—the ears, the trunk, the tail, the legs, the torso. Each blind man presents correct facts about the part of the elephant they touched, but their descriptions do not capture the "truth" of the animal because none of them possess all the facts. Likewise, StackExchange writers suggest that "Conway was conceding that the media had started from factual information, but she believed that their information was leading them to incorrect *conclusions*. She meant that Spicer's facts were equally correct, but that his conclusion was better."[23]

Ultimately, two conflicting definitions of alternative facts exist. One focuses on "fact," the other on an "alternative." In the former, logical positivists such as Todd's focus on the fact part of the phrase. They consider a fact to be undisputable truth. The idea of an "alternative" fact is either nonsensical or noxious to such people. In the latter, Conway's more modern, relativistic approach focuses on the "alternative" component and reflects the contemporary post-truth attitude common among those whose thinking has been shaped by philosophers such as Foucault and Derrida. For those who think like Conway, everyone's truth is equal. A "fact" is mutable, for it is grounded emotion and personal belief. Todd is working from an older understanding of the nature of facts as an either-or. Conway has moved on to the modern conception of the truth of facts as being of secondary importance.

Conway's understanding of the nature of facts and truth in politics is actually not new, despite all the commentary about "post-truth" and "post-truth politics" over the past three decades.[24] Jennifer Hochschild of Harvard University has argued that the rise of post-truth/post-fact politics is actually a return to the politics and media practices of early America. Her evidence is the pamphlet and newspaper wars that hallmarked America's inseparable political and journalistic cultures of the 18th and 19th centuries.[25] In those periods politics and the press were virtual Siamese twins, bound inextricably together by financial and political interests. Another scholar, the Harvard-educated Jeffrey L. Pasley, now at the University of Missouri, has postulated that the press served as the central institution of early American political life in the late 18th century and first half of the 19th century. From the 1790s through the 1860s, at least, newspapers served as "the 'lynchpin' of … party politics." He argues that newspapers were the foundation of late 18th- and 19th-century political parties.[26]

Pasley dates this symbiotic relationship between the press and politics from the 1790s because that is when the first American political parties, the Federalists and the Democratic-Republicans, arose. Parties were not provided for in the Constitution; they were born of conflicts that arose during George Washington's presidency. The 1795 Jay Treaty was a particular point of dissention with the pro–British Federalists supporting it and the pro–French Democratic-Republicans opposing it.[27] Washington himself had qualms about the treaty, but those reservations did not keep him from lying to the public about the treaty. The president with so great a reputation for truth-telling that a mythology grew up about his inability to lie went to the American public and exhorted them to support a treaty even though he was uncertain it was a good idea. He encouraged his subordinates to do the same thing.[28] In Todd's parlance, Washington lied. In Conway's he presented alternative facts. In either case, Washington's decision to put expedience ahead of truthfulness shows just how long alternative facts have been a part of American political culture.

The 1796 election fanned the already-smoldering party embers. This election, perhaps more than any other event in American history, established the basic political culture that persists in the United States to this day: "the basic ideological dynamic of a democratic, rights-spreading American 'left' arrayed against a conservative, social order-protecting 'right.'" Choosing from a slate of four candidates in 1796, Americans elected a president and a vice president with two widely divergent visions of what America should be. John Adams, the "conservative, social order-protecting" right-winger would serve as president, and his chief opponent, the "democratic, rights-spreading" left-winger would serve as vice-president.[29] Adams won by three electoral college votes.[30] The nascent political parties that had formed during Washington's presidency blossomed during this contentious election.[31] And while Stephen Skowronek has argued that American presidents have always been "battering rams" and "blunt, disruptive force[s]," they never could have had such impact without the assistance of partisan newspapers.[32]

Alternative Facts in American Political and Journalistic History

Donald Trump and his minions were hardly the first American politicians or political operatives to resort to alternative facts as a means of saving face or winning a debate. Former President Bill Clinton used alternative facts masterfully during his grand jury testimony. Deputy Independent Counsel Solomon Wisenberg point blank accused the president's attorney Robert Bennett of lying when he claimed there was no sexual relationship between Clinton and White House intern Monica Lewinsky. President Clinton replied, "It depends on what the meaning of the word "is" is." Clinton was arguing that meanings are fluid and dependent on circumstances—different circumstances allow for different (alternative) interpretations of a fact set.[33]

Political truth, facts, or alternative facts would have little impact, either today or in the Early Republic, without the press as its accomplice. Today's media landscape has more and different kinds of channels than were available to politicians in the Early Republic, and many of those channels afford direct access to voters (think President Trump's incessant tweets). Further, many of today's channels are much more accessible and far more pervasive (social media, for example), than the media that existed in early America. Further, contemporary news practices and procedures, coupled with a decline in professionalism, create an environment in which alternative facts can flourish virtually unchecked.[34] For example, the breaking news division of the dominant newspaper in one large southern city in America finds its stories not through the legwork of being out and about in the community but by sitting in an office monitoring social media feeds. In terms of media practice, apparently little changed since the 1790s. Then, editors sat in their offices and waited for news to arrive in the form of letters or newspapers from other places. The influence of the press in contemporary times is harder to gauge. In earlier periods, the influence was clearer. One writer, Pierre Dupont de Nemours, observed that many Americans in the Early National period read the Bible, but everyone read newspapers. "The fathers read the newspaper aloud to their children while the mothers are preparing breakfast," he wrote.[35]

In the Early Republic, the party press served as a direct conduit from party or politician to the people just as social media and websites do today. They also acted as the glue "that held parties together between elections and conventions."[36] These party newspapers did not profess, did not even attempt, impartiality or objectivity. They avowedly existed to support primarily political principles and the politicians who espoused them. In a very real sense, one could refer to the Early Republic as the pre-truth era—the functional equivalent of the post-truth era that came prior to America's brief 20th-century flirtation with objectivity and facts in both politics and journalism. It, like the current post-truth period, was hallmarked by highly polarized politics and by political rhetoric grounded in emotion rather than reason. Alternative facts were commonplace, as illustrated by the example of the debates over whether Irish immigration constituted a threat to the nation.

As might be expected in an age of pre-truth politics and journalism, editors and politicians, with great abandon, accused the opposition (political or journalistic) of lying and deceit, just as they do in the current post-truth period. In an argument that sounds ominously like President Trump's allegation that the press (his actual words were "the Fake News Media," which would be any media outlet that did not support his policies or presidency) is "the true enemy of the people," William Cobbett, editor of Philadelphia's leading Federalist newspaper in 1795, charged that American newspapers had done more harm to the country than its enemies could ever dream of by "mislead[ing] the people at home and misrepresent[ing] them abroad." He complained that Americans read newspapers by the thousands, and those who read newspapers read little else. "To suppress them is impossible; they will vomit forth their poison; it is a privilege of their natures that no law can abridge," he complained. The only alternative was to publish as an antidote to the "gall and untruth" published by the Democratic-Republican press.[37]

Likewise, the New York *Evening Post* published a little ditty in its first issue that accused those who viewed public issues differently of being liars. It specifically targeted the leading Democratic-Republican editor, William

Duane of the *Aurora*, and one of his colleagues, James Cheetham of the New York *American Citizen*. The poem read:

> Lie on Duane, lie on for pay,
> And Cheetham, lie thou, too;
> More against truth you cannot say
> Than truth can say 'gainst you.[38]

Echoing the "outside agitators" rhetoric Southerners would use against Civil Rights activists in the 1950s and 1960s, after losing the 1800 presidential election to Thomas Jefferson, John Adams wrote that he had been defeated by "a group of foreign liars, encouraged by a few ambitious native gentlemen." Adams specifically named the liars he had in mind: American-born Democratic-Republican editor Philip Freneau, plus three foreign journalists (one Irish, one Scottish, and one English) and one Irish-born congressman who resorted to journalism to defend himself against a sedition charge in 1799.[39]

The Federalists were not the only ones who complained about the opposition manipulating the American people. In 1798, as debate over the Sedition Act heated up in Congress, Thomas Jefferson wrote that, once "the reign of witches" was over and "their spells dissolve," government would get on the right path again on. In that same letter, Jefferson also referred to politics as a game, albeit a game where important principles were at stake.[40] Seemingly, he saw more clearly than Adams that competition between political ideologies was less black-and-white and more a matter of how one describes the elephant. Later in the letter, Jefferson sagely observed that "in every free & deliberating society there must, from the nature of man, be opposite parties & violent dissensions & discords; and one of these, for the most part, must prevail over the other for a longer or shorter time. Perhaps this party division is necessary to induce each to watch & delegate to the people the proceedings of the other."[41] He concluded the letter with a postscript that showed he understood the nature of alternative facts in political culture. He reminded the recipient, John Taylor, not to let anything he had written get out to the public. "A single sentence, got hold of by the Porcupines,[42] will suffice to abuse & persecute me in their papers for months."[43] The "Porcupines" and the "foreign liars" were instrumental not only in constructing and maintaining political parties, they were also heavily involved in building support for and against public issues and government policies. Perhaps the most heated debate in the Early Republic, and one that touched newspapers in multiple ways, was over the Alien and Sedition Acts.[44]

John Adams and his administration inherited a delicate problem from George Washington. When war broke out in Europe in 1792, Washington had declared America to be a neutral state. This declaration violated an existing treaty with France, nor did it stop Great Britain, America's largest trading partner, from seizing American merchant ships that were carrying goods to the French West Indies.[45] Americans were outraged, and some demanded a declaration of war. Congress settled for an embargo and negotiations with Great Britain.[46] The conflict was resolved by the Jay Treaty, which built a stronger Anglo-American alliance but angered the French. This was the problem Adams inherited and that he attempted to solve in 1797 by sending a diplomatic mission to France. French officials, however, were not particularly interested in negotiating with a weak country such as the United States, and they demanded bribes before they would agree to negotiations. The mission failed and resulted in the undeclared Quasi-War.[47]

Meanwhile, England was dealing with Ireland's most recent bid for independence. Led by a group known as the Society of United Irishmen and ideologically premised on the American and French Rebellions, the United Irishmen wanted to establish a democratic republic in Ireland, patterned after that of France. The United Irishmen rebellion sought and received French aid, but the British effectively put down the rising in only a few months.[48]

America was drawn into the fray in the aftermath of the rising when Britain proposed to deport several leaders of the rebellion to the United States. American Minister to Great Britain Rufus King stridently objected; he feared that the importation of Irish rebels with French sympathies could only end badly. King predicted in a letter to Alexander Hamilton that "France will pursue with us the Plan that she has elsewhere found successful. She will endeavor to overthrow us by the Divisions among ourselves which she will excite and support by all the means of which she is mistress."[49]

The divisions of which King spoke were the party divisions that had arisen out of conflicting views among Washington's cabinet regarding the nature of America and the relationship between the government and the people.[50] Washington, Hamilton, and Adams formed the core of the Federalist party, which believed the government should speak for the people. Jefferson and Madison led the Democratic party, which believed the people should speak for themselves. Federalists were wary of too much democracy and averse to populism. They wanted a strong central government whose foreign policies would protect commercial interests and encourage economic development. The Democratic-Republicans preferred a weak federal government, strong state governments, foreign policies that favored other republics, and citizen involvement in decision-making.[51]

Adams's Federalist administration was fearful of Irish immigrants because most sided with the republicanism of the Democratic-Republican party and also because of the United Irishmen alignment with the French. King wrote to Secretary of State Timothy Pickering that he could not see how the Irish malcontents who were emigrating to America could ever be useful

American citizens. He also fretted that no one was vetting Irish émigrés. At least the Scots coming to America brought with them certificates from their churches that attested to "their honesty, sobriety and generally good character."[52]

Perhaps the Federalists had reason to be fearful. The Irish did constitute the largest immigrant community in America at the time. Through the 1790s, some 60,000 Irish emigrated to America. Some 250,000 to 400,000 were already residents who had come prior to the American Revolution. America's population in 1790 was 3.9 million, hence close to a tenth of the population was Irish or Irish American. Second, America was at war with the French, and the French were allies of the Irish. There was every chance, Federalists believed, that if France decided to invade, the American Irish would serve boots on the ground, so to speak, for the French, a sort of precursor of the argument from the Cold War period that members of the American Communist Party were poised to aid Soviet Communists in attacking America. In both cases, the arguments were grounded in fear-mongering rather than actual facts.[53]

The *New Hampshire Gazette* claimed the United Irishmen in America were in league with the French and could have nothing good in mind for the United States. The paper claimed that the society had invited the French to their country and would do the same in America if given the chance. "Whatever may be the certain objects of the Institution [the United Irishmen] it cannot be salutary to us. The main branch of the family in Ireland corresponds with the French –and have invited them into their country," the paper's editors claimed. "If we are not complaisant [*sic*] to these Foreigners, they may give the same invitation for our country."[54] The *Gazette of the United States* concurred. That paper argued the United Irishmen in Ireland and those in America adhered to the same principles and were in constant contact with one another. "Thus, it is evident, the gang in America is altogether subordinate to that of Ireland." The group's aim, the paper claimed, was to foment revolution in America.[55]

Alternative facts dominated the partisan debates in the late 1790s over the nature of American political culture and the threat the Irish posed to it. The chief purveyor of alternative facts was the budding partisan press. These newspapers served as the handmaidens of parties by marshaling and broadcasting arguments that supported party positions, and they excelled at invective and vitriol, much of which was counterfactual—such as the Federalist argument that the Irish in America would side with the French in case of an invasion during the Quasi War.

Cobbett was as suspicious of the Irish in America as were his party's leaders. He wrote in the *Gazette of the United States*, "It is evident the gang in America is altogether subordinate to that of Ireland; its views, its appeals are equally so." His evidence to support his contention was the creation of a new all-Irish militia unit in Baltimore. The unit had been named the Republican Company, and its uniforms were, in his opinion, strikingly similar to those of the French.[56] It would have been difficulty for the new company's uniform not to have resembled that of the French; military uniforms of the day generally consisted of breeches, boots, waist coats, and jackets, and they usually came in some combination of red, blue and white (at least for America, Great Britain, and France). It would have been difficulty to have found a uniform significantly different from that of the French, though the 1798 Irish rebels wore green frock coats or their regular peasant clothing with a green scarf around their necks.[57] Further, the most common indicator of one's political leanings was not clothing so much as hat decoration. For example, should one which to express one's support for the Federalist party, one would wear a black cockade on one's hat. From a Federalist perspective, to do otherwise could be interpreted as declaring anti–American sentiments—another alternative Federalist fact.[58]

Other Federalists saw even broader conspiracies at play. A correspondent who signed his letter "Observatory" claimed there was a seven-year-old global conspiracy involving the Illuminati, the object of which was to arm the people of Ulster and to achieve the overthrow of Great Britain. Observatory further claimed that the Illuminati was the force behind the Franco-Hibernian alliance and that they were, of course, working with the United Irishmen, and that the Irish in America were secretly working with the French to overthrow America as well.[59] The *New Hampshire Gazette* seconded Observatory's claims by noting that, whatever their intentions might be, nothing the United Irishmen had in mind for America could be good. Because of their alliance with the French, the paper's editors encouraged keeping an eye on the Irish in America lest they ally with France against their new homeland.[60]

By the same token, the Franco-Hibernian alliance that put Federalists like Cobbett in such a tizzy involved Ireland and the Irish who had remained at home, not those who had emigrated to the United States. True, Irish immigration stepped-up as a result of the United Irishmen rebellion, but that alone was no evidence the Irish in America would aid a French invasion of their new home.

Some Federalists simply engaged in fear-mongering by making unsubstantiated accusations against the American Irish. Writing for Cobbett's *Gazette of the United States,* correspondent "S" reported that on a recent trip to Montgomery County, Pennsylvania, he had become more convinced than ever of the need to keep a keen eye on the United Irishmen living in that district. He found them to be virulently pro–French and anti–American, and he also believed the United States admitted too many "outcasts from the French and Irish nations; but particularly … the latter." His evidence was an encounter with a Captain John whom "S" labeled a "champion of sedition."[61]

"A Gentleman of Respectability in Frederick County, Virginia," wrote to a Massachusetts paper that he suspected the French would capitalize on the lack of patriotism in America to wage a take-over by propaganda rather than a physical invasion. He believed that the French would "excite sedition and rebellion under pretense of oppression in Ireland, and when they have inspired a portion of the people with a hatred of their own government, then they will kindly offer their aid."[62]

Another correspondent, "Anglo Americanus," writing for the Wooster *Massachusetts Spy* claimed to have come across and English statute book that referred to a 1422 act of Parliament that ordered the deportation of all Irish living in England because they were murders, rapists, robbers and felons, caused riots, and committed other offenses. It is apparently true that Parliament did pass an act in in 1422 to deport some Irish—those who were unemployed. The law was apparently intended to deal with a gang of men from Hampshire but of Irish ancestry who were enormously successful thieves. "Anglo Americanus" used alterative facts to spice up his story a bit to make it more sensational and to back up the Federalist view of the Irish as criminals and agitators.[63]

Other newspapers defended the United Irishmen and Irish American immigrants by disputing published alternative facts. *Greenleaf's New York Journal and Patriotic Register* defended the United Irishmen's aims as being rather similar to those of America two decades previously. In a jab against the Anglophile Federalists, the paper's editor wrote, "It is said that the United Irishmen are traitors—How long have the United States resigned their independence, and become with Britain one and indivisible?" The editor continued, " The United Irishmen state precisely in the same odious circumstances with relation to England that John Adams stood 20 years ago—they consider George III, an intolerable tyrant now, as we did then."[64]

Greenleaf's New York Journal also offered reasons for why the Irish might wish to escape their country, reasons that, though they were favorable to the Irish, also carried the taint of alternative facts. The paper reported that murders in Ireland were common. According to recently received Dublin papers, a women was "stabbed in a thousand places for singing a song; and … a beautiful young girl was shot through the heart for wearing earrings."[65]

Conclusion: 'Lie on Duane' … and Cheetham and Cobbett and Conway and…

A scribbler's doggerel on journalists/political pundits and truth seems to apply across the board, whether to those of contemporary vintage Kellyanne Conway and Sean Spicer, or those of the Early Republic, William Duane, James Cheetham, or William Cobbett,

> More against truth you cannot say
> Than truth can say 'gainst you.[66]

But this rhyme overlooks one very important reality of American political culture: ours is a system built on debate and, in more rational times, compromise across partisan views. Today, as in much of America's history, those views have been disseminated, even amplified, by a partisan media. Likely, Duane, Cheetham, and Cobbett would each have identified himself professional as a printer, not a journalist; that distinction between the artisan who physically created the newspaper and the scribe who scribbled the content had not yet been made. However, all three would certainly have agreed that they were spokesmen for particular political ideas, and probably for particular politicians or parties as well.

American politics and American political journalism have almost always been contact sports punctuated by short periods of bi-partisan political life and non-partisan journalism. It is hardly surprising that in the country's earliest days alternative facts would flying fast and furious across the pages of America's newspapers on just about any topic, immigration included. This would especially be true when America was engaged in an undeclared war that had a lot in common with the contemporary war against terror and the Middle Eastern conflicts. Crackdowns on immigration, setting immigrants up as straw-man enemies of the people, they are both born of fear of destabilization. Fred Siebert's classic study of when governments are most likely to crack down on free speech extends to other civil liberties. When governments are destabilized, when politicians' hold on power is threatened, crackdown on liberties occur. That is not just an American phenomenon, it is a global phenomenon, but one that has special meaning in a country whose cornerstone value is, after all, liberty of the people.

Adams feared Irish collusion with a French invasion of American shores. Trump, more than any other president who has held office since the first Gulf war, seems to be sensitive to Americans' fears, real or imagined, that are the by-product of 9/11. Aliens, particularly those of particular ethnicities and religions, are viewed suspiciously by a large segment of American society. Trump has tapped into that fear—evidence suggests he probably even shares it—to get elected president of the United States, something unimaginable to many who live in the blue state zones but that is eminently logical and even predictable to those who live in the red states where the Tea Party and other ultra-conservative groups thrive. Sociological theory postulates, and lived experience demonstrates, that when people are afraid, they develop in-group biases against anyone foreign to them. Trump's physical wall and Adams' legal wall are and were tangible evidence of that bias.[67]

Nor is it surprising to find history repeating itself when both American political culture and journalistic culture have returned to older models where media function as extensions of politics. The opposition press, in such a political culture, functions as an adversary to the party in power, which is likely to portray its opponents as threats to the Republic and its citizens, hence Trump's comment about the press being the enemy of the people. From his perspective and that of his supporters, it is. In such a political culture, there cannot be such a thing as a loyal opposition. Partisanism, particularly the extreme partisanism that has hallmarked both the Early Republic and contemporary America, renders debate even more shrill. The debaters earnestly believe the country's future is at stake, and they must do or say whatever is necessary to the bring the opposition press to heel and Americans to their senses. If that means exaggerating a bit—perhaps even stepping over the line into an untruth, well, so be it. The ends justify the means.

Political scientists seem to agree that partisanism is, indeed, the defining characteristic of American political culture and that the bipartisanism of the post–World War II period was an anomaly. But it was a period in which bipartisanism made sense. The country had, in the previous 30 years, successfully survived the Great Depression and a second world war. The country and the people were prospering. Americans thought of their country as a force for good in the world. Then, too, Americans in the 1950s, 1960s and 1970s, were very conscious, thanks to Joseph McCarthy, of the havoc ideologues could wreck. Add to that the fact that the religious-right was not yet involved in politics, the divisive Civil Rights, women's, student, pro-life/pro-choice movements were at best nascent if not non-existent, and the Fairness Doctrine still existed (thus requiring non-partisan broadcast news coverage), and that period's bi-partisanism begins to make sense.[68]

Perhaps it is fair to conclude that Americans have always had a tendency to build walls whose foundations are constructed with alternative viewpoints, alterative facts, particularly where immigration is concerned, and the media has always been an accomplice in the wall-building, albeit at times an unwitting accomplice. The Brookings Institute, for example, maintains that the press has hindered immigration policy-making "for decades."[69] The walls have not generally been physical ones—and as often as not, they have been walls that have dealt with domestic, rather than foreign, political matters. It is the press, of course, that sets the agenda for debate on immigration, provides facts—alternative or otherwise—and information Americans use to for opinion about immigration in general and about particular groups of immigrants. Irish immigration and the consequent passage of the Alien and Sedition Acts of 1798 may well have been the origin of this tendency in American political culture. Certainly, the American Federalist party's campaign for and administration of this set of four anti-immigration/anti-immigrant laws seems to fit the pattern of wall-building grounded upon alternative facts.

Truthful hyperbole—deceit, in plain terms—may not always be innocent, but whether it is always harmful is another question entirely.

The debate over who should be allowed into the United States and who should not has a long history in America. President Trump's controversial comment regarding admission of people from "shithole" countries echoed the debate over excluding "coolie slaves" in 1882 when the Chinese Exclusion Act was enacted. Ambassadors, members of Congress, news commentators, and ordinary Americans accused the president of being a racist and making a shameful comment when he questioned why the current lottery system for immigrants—adopted in1990—should not be ended and a merit-based system instituted. Some, including Congresswoman Mia Love, R–Utah, the daughter of Haitian immigrants, argued that President Trump's language was "unkind, divisive, and elitist," and that his proposal flies "in the face of our national values." President Trump's language was crude at best, but his thinking about immigration was really not different from John Adams's. Some émigrés—those most like the Americans already here—are more desirable than others.[70] Adams wanted immigrants who would share Federalist values, and he and his administration were willing to resort to alternative facts about those they deemed undesirable. Trump's comment was grounded in the same sort of clichés and stereotypes and Adams's. While most Irish who came to American during the Adams administration did tend to favor the Democratic-Republican party, and many were fleeing the United Irishman rising, there is little evidence any wanted to facilitate a French invasion of America. Why would they? America represented the kind of society with the sort of political culture they were seeking. Fear motivated Adams. Frustration seems to have been Trump's primary motivation. Both resorted to exaggeration, hyperbole, and, yes, even the use of alternative facts to press their cases with the American public. In the end, almost always, American will end up erring on the side of civil liberty—though there may be egregious violations of civil liberties along the way. President Trump's 2018 asked for $18 billion across two years to build his border wall. As debate over the budget intensifies, even congressional Republicans do not seem inclined to appropriate that much money to the project.[71]

Only recently, the (Sydney, New South Wales) *Australian* newspaper's Tony Makin observed that alternative facts and fake news are not synonymous. He wrote, "bringing to light alternative facts that are true can help balance a story."[72] As divisive as they may be, debates over the facts of any given situation—immigration or other—are a hallmark of American political culture. They are the stock-and-trade of the way Americans conduct their public life, and that is because such debates are good for democracy. They allow Americans to air their differences and come to compromises—when they can overcome their partisanship.

NOTES

1. *Annals of Congress*, February 1797, 2096, https://memory.loc.gov/cgi-bin/ampage?collId=llac&fileName=006/llac006.db&recNum=290 (2 March 2018).
2. White House Office of the Press Secretary, "Executive Order: Enhancing Public Safety in the Interior of the United States," 25 January 2017, Executive order full text available from https://www.whitehouse.gov/the-press-office/2017/01/25/presidential-executive-order-enhancing-public-safety-interior-united (26 June 2017); White House Office of the Press Secretary, "Executive Order: Border Security and Immigration Enforcement Improvements," 25 January 2017, Executive order full text available from https://www.whitehouse.gov/the-press-office/2017/01/25/executive-order-border-security-and-immigration-enforcement-improvements (26 June 2017); "Executive Order: Protecting the Nation from Foreign Terrorist Entry Into the United States," 27 January 2017, Executive Order full text available from https://www.whitehouse.gov/the-press-office/2017/01/27/executive-order-protecting-nation-foreign-terrorist-entry-united-states (26 June 2017).
3. Marco Sioli, "Repression in the Early Republic: John Adams, the Alien and Sedition Acts, and the Politics of Exclusion," *Rivista di Studi Americani* (*Review of American Studies*) 19 (2008), 158.
4. Ashley Killough, "Government Shutdown Looks Set to Drag on to 2019 After House and Senate Adjourn Until Next Week," *CNN*, https://www.cnn.com/2018/12/27/politics/shutdown-update-thursday/index.html (28 Dec. 2018).
5. Eli Watkins, "Kaine: Trump 'Lying' or 'Delusional' on DACA," *CNN Politics*, 25 March 2018, https://www.cnn.com/2018/03/25/politics/tim-kaine-daca-cnntv/index.html/ (27 March 2018).
6. Theodore C. Blegen, "The Competition of the Northwestern States for Immigrants," *Wisconsin Magazine of History* 3, no. 1 (1919), 3–29; "An Act to Execute Certain Treaty Stipulations Relating to Chinese," Primary Documents in American History, Library of Congress, https://www.loc.gov/rr/program/bib/ourdocs/chinese.html (24 July 2017); *San Francisco Evening Bulletin*, May 13, 1882; Sang Hea Kil, "Fearing Yellow, Imagining White: Media Analysis of the Chinese Exclusion Act of 1883," *Social Identities* 18, no. 6 (2012): 667.
7. Harry Bruinius, "Why Journalism Is Shifting Away from 'Objectivity,'" *Christian Science Monitor*, 6 July 2017, https://www.csmonitor.com/USA/Politics/2017/0706/Why-journalism-is-shifting-away-from-objectivity (10 July 2017); Abdi Soltani, "Repeating the Mistakes of the Past: Anniversary of the Chinese Exclusion Act," ACLU Northern California, 5 May 2017, www.aclunc.org/blog/repeating-mistakes-past-anniversary-chinese-exclusion-act (3 March 2018).
8. "Alien and Sedition Acts," Primary Documents in American History, the Library of Congress, https://www.loc.gov/rr/program/bib/ourdocs/Alien.html (5 June 2017).
9. Kerby A. Miller, *Emigrants and Exiles: Ireland and the Irish Exodus to North America* (Oxford: Oxford University Press, 1985), 4–7.
10. Richard Brookhiser, "The Politics of Immigration: Clashing Impulses," *American History* (10 May 2017): 17.
11. Samuel Eliot Morison, *The Life and Letters of Harrison Gray Otis, Federalist, 1765–1848*, vol. 1 (Boston: Houghton and Mifflin, 1913), 107, 108.
12. . Teri Diane Halperin, *The Alien and Sedition Acts of 1798: Testing the Constitution* (Baltimore: Johns Hopkins University Press, 2016), 38; Wendel Bird, *Press and Speech Under Assault: The Early Supreme Court Justices, The Sedition Act of 1798, and the Campaign Against Dissent* (New York: Oxford University Press, 2016), 277; David A. Wilson, *United Irishmen, United States: Immigrant Radicals in the Early Republic* (Ithaca: Cornell University Press, 1998), 1–3; Michael Durey, "Thomas Paine's Apostles: Radical Émigrés and the Triumph of Jeffersonian Republicanism," *William and Mary Quarterly* 44, no. 4 (October 1987): 661–688.
13. Halperin, *The Alien and Sedition Acts of 1798*, 5.
14. Morison, *The Life and Letters of Harrison Gray Otis*, 107, 108
15. Sioli, "Repression in the Early Republic," 157; Edward C. Carter, II, "A 'Wild Irishman' Under Every Federalist's Bed: Naturalization in Philadelphia," *Pennsylvania Magazine*

of History and Biography 94, no. 3 (July 1970): 333; Fred Siebert, *Freedom of the Press in England, 1476–1776: The Rise and Decline of Government Controls* (Urbana: University of Illinois Press, 1952), 10.

16. Arthur H. Garrison, "The Internal Security Acts of 1798: The Founding Generation and the Judiciary During America's First National Security Crisis," *Journal of Supreme Court History* 34, no. 1 (2009): 5.

17. For the full text of these four laws, see the *Statutes at Large of the United States of America* (Boston: Charles C. Little and James Brown, 1845), 566, 570, 577, 596.

18. Bird, *Press and Speech Under Assault*, xxii–xxiii; Sioli, 158.

19. Aaron Blake, "Kellyanne Conway Says Donald Trump's Team Has 'Alternative Facts,' Which Pretty Much Says It All," The *Washington Post*, 22 January 2017, https://www.washingtonpost.com/news/the-fix/wp/2017/01/22/kellyanne-conway-says-donald-trumps-team-has-alternate-facts-which-pretty-much-says-it-all/?utm_term=.ffc1cf10e0d3 (11 May 2017).

20. Jane Mayer, "Donald Trump's Ghostwriter Tells All," *The New Yorker*, 25 July 2016, http://www.newyorker.com/magazine/2016/07/25/donald-trumps-ghostwriter-tells-all (11 May 2017).

21. Bill Nelson, Amelia Phillips, and Christopher Steuart, *Guide to Computer Forensics and Investigations*, 5th ed. (Boston: Centage Learning, 2016), 515.

22. "What Is an Alternative Fact?" English Language and Usage, https://english.stackexchange.com/questions/369628/what-is-an-alternative-fact (11 May 2017).

23. "What Is an Alternative Fact?"

24. Steve Tesich, "A Government of Lies," *The Nation* (6 January 1992), 12; Richard Kreitner, "Post-Truth and Its Consequences: What a 25-Year-Old Essay Tells Us about the Current Moment," *The Nation* (30 Nov. 2016), https://www.thenation.com/article/post-truth-and-its-consequences-what-a-25-year-old-essay-tells-us-about-the-current-moment/ (6 June 2017); Ralph Keys, *The Post-Truth Era: Dishonesty and Deception in Contemporary Life* (New York: St. Martin's Press, 2004).

25. Christina Pazzanese, " Politics In a 'Post-Truth Age," *Harvard Gazette* (14 July 2016), http://news.harvard.edu/gazette/story/2016/07/politics-in-a-post-truth-age/ (28 June 2017).

26. Jeffrey L. Pasley, *"Tyranny of Printers": Newspaper Politics in the Early American Republic* (Charlottesville: University of Virginia Press, 2001), 1, 3; Jeffrey L. Pasley, "Two National Gazettes: Newspapers and the Embodiment of American Political Parties," *Early American Literature* (1 January 2000): 51; Joel L. Sibley, *The American Political Nation, 1838–1893* (Stanford: Stanford University Press, 1991), 54.

27. Norman K. Risjord, *Jefferson's America, 1794–1800*, 2d ed. (Lanham, MD: Rowman & Littlefield, 2002), 283.

28. George Washington to Alexander Hamilton, 29 July 1795, *Founders on Line, National Archives (https://founders.archives.gov/documents/Hamilton/01-18-02-0318)*, accessed 11 May 2017; Joseph J. Ellis, *His Excellency, George Washington* (New York: Vintage, 2004), x–xii, 147.

29. Jeffrey L. Pasley, *The First Presidential Contest: 1796 and the Founding of American Democracy* (Lawrence: University of Kansas, 2013), 10.

30. "Electoral College Box Scores, 1789–1996," U.S. Electoral College, National Archives and Records Administration, https://www.archives.gov/federal-register/electoral-college/scores.html#1796 (27 June 2017).

31. Donald E. Heidenreich, "Conspiracy Politics in the Election of 1796," *New York History* 92, no. 3 (Summer 2011): 151–165; Arthur Scheer, "The Significance of Thomas Pinckney's Candidacy in the Election of 1796," *South Carolina Historical Magazine* 76, no. 2 (April 1975): 51–59.

32. Stephen Skowronek, *The Politics Presidents Make* (Cambridge: Harvard University Belknap Press, 1997), 27, 28, 30; Mel Laracey, "The Presidential Newspaper as an Engine of Early American Political Development: The Case of Thomas Jefferson and the Election of 1800," *Rhetoric and Public Affairs* 11, no. 1 (2008): 8.

33. "Clinton's Grand Jury Testimony, Part 4," Clinton Accused, washingtonpost.com Special Report: Documents from the Starr Referral, http://www.washingtonpost.com/wp-srv/politics/special/clinton/stories/bctest092198_4.htm (27 July 2017).

34. Marju Himma-Kadakas, "Alternative Facts and Fake News Entering Journalist Content Production Cycle," *Cosmopolitian Civil Societies: An Interdisciplinary Journal* 9, no. 2 (2017): 25–27.

35. Quoted in Louis Edward Inglehart, *Press Freedoms: A Descriptive Calendar of Concepts, Events, and Court Actions from 4000 B.C. to the Present* (New York: Greenwood Press, 1987), 178.

36. Pasley, "Two National Gazettes," 52.

37. William Cobbett, "Proposals for Publishing a News-Paper to be Entitled, Porcupine's Gazette and Daily Advertiser," Evans Early American Imprint Collection, http://quod.lib.umich.edu/e/evans/N22884.0001.001/1:13?rgn=div1;view=fulltext (27 June 2017); Donald Henderson Stewart, *The Opposition Press of the Federalist Period* (Albany: State University of New York Press, 1969), 635; Donald J. Trump, Tweet from @realDonaldTrump, 7:03 a.m., October 29, 2018, https://twitter.com/realDonaldTrump?ref_src=twsrc%5Etfw%7Ctwcamp%5Etweetembed%7Ctwterm%5E1056879122348195841&ref_url=https%3A%2F%2Fwww.vox.com%2Fpolicy-and-politics%2F2018%2F10%2F29%2F18037894%2Fdonald-trump-twitter-media-enemy-pittsburgh (28 Dec. 2018).

38. Reprinted in Allan C. Clark, "William Duane," *Records of the Columbia Historical Society* 9 (106): 4. Attributed to *The New York Evening Post*, 16 November 1801.

39. John Adams to Benjamin Stoddert, 31 March 1801, *The Works of John Adams, Second President of the United States*, vol. 9 (Boston: Little, Brown, 1854), 582.

40. Thomas Jefferson to John Taylor, 4 June 1798, the Founders Online, National Archives and Records Administration, https://founders.archives.gov/?q=reign%20of%20witches&s=1111311111&sa=&r=7&sr (2 June 2017).

41. Jefferson to Taylor, 4 June 1798.

42. A reference to William Cobbett and other Federalist editors.

43. Jefferson to Taylor, 4 June 1798.

44. Matthew Rainbow Hale, "'Many Who Wandered in Darkness': The Contest Over American National Identity, 1795–1798," *Early American Studies: An Interdisciplinary Journal* 1, no. 1 (2003): 128, 130; William Stinchcombe, "The Diplomacy of the WXYZ Affair," *William and Mary Quarterly* 34, no. 4 (1977), 590; Card Ludwig Lokke, "The Trumbull Episode: A Prelude to the 'X Y Z' Affair," *New England Quarterly* 7, no. 1 (1934): 100–114; Halperin, *The Alien and Sedition Acts of 1798*, 14.

45. Garrison, "The Internal Security Acts of 1798," 2.

46. Jerald A. Combs, *The Jay Treaty: Political Battleground of the Founding Fathers* (Berkley: University of California Press, 1970), 121.

47. Sioli, "Repression in the Early Republic," 157.

48. Jon Latimer, "French Farce at Fishguard," *Military History* 13, no. 7 (March 1997): 38.

49. Rufus Kind to Alexander Hamilton, 2 July 1798, Founders Online (https://founders.archives.gov/documents/Hamilton/01-21-02-0298; accessed 16 May 2017).

50. Halperin, *The Alien and Sedition Acts of 1798*, 120, 128–129.

51. Halperin, *The Alien and Sedition Acts of 1798*, 4, 5.

52. Rufus King to Timothy Pickering, 19 July 1798, ed. Charles R. King, M.D., *The Life and Correspondence of Rufus Kind, Comprising His Letters, Private and Official, His Public Documents and His Speeches* (New York: G. Putnam's Sons, 1895), 637.

53. Halperin, *The Alien and Sedition Acts of 1798*, 30, 25, 27; Kerby A. Miller, *Emigrants and Exiles: Ireland and the Irish Exodus to America* (Oxford: Oxford University Press, 1988), 137; POP culture: 1790 U.S. Census Bureau, https://www.census.gov/history/www/through_the_decades/fast_facts/1790_fast_facts.html (16 May 2017).

54. Pourtsmouth *New Hampshire Gazette*, 16 January 1799, 3.

55. "*Nomenque erit indelebile vestrum*," *Gazette of the United States*, 18 December 1798, 3.

56. "*Nomenque erit indelebile vestrum*," 3.

57. Based on exhibits at the 1798 Center, Enniscorthy, Ireland.

58. *Greenfield* (Connecticutt) *Gazette,* 6 August 1798, 2; Richard N. Rosen, *American Aurora: A Democratic Republican Returns* (New York: St. Martin's Press, 1997), 3; Sioli, 157.

59. "From the Gazette of the United States," *New York Commercial Advertiser*, 1 November 1798, 2.

60. *"Nomenque erit indelebile vestrum,"* 3.

61. "Communication," *Gazette of the United States and Philadelphia Daily Advertiser*, 29 January 1799, 2.

62. "Communication," Brookfield, Massachusetts, *Political Repository*, 23 April 1799, 2.

63. "Miscellany," *Courier of New Hampshire*, 18 May 1799, 4. Reprinted from the Wooster *Massachusetts Spy*; Ralph A. Griffiths, *King and Country: England and Wales in the Fifteenth Century* (London: Hambledon Press, 1991), 229.

64. *Greenleaf's New York Journal and Patriotic Register*, 2 January 1799, 2.

65. *Greenleaf's New York Journal and Patriotic Register*, 2 January 1799, 2.

66. Reprinted in Allan C. Clark, "William Duane," *Records of the Columbia Historical Society* 9 (106): 4. Attributed to *The New York Evening Post*, 16 November 1801.

67. J. C. Turner and K. J. Reynolds, "An Integrative Theory of Intergroup Convlict," in W. G. Austin and S. Worchel, *The Social Psychology of Intergroup Relations* (Monterey: Brooks/Cole, 1979), 33–47; J. C. Turner and K. J. Reynolds, "The Story of Social Identity," in *Rediscovering Social Identity: Core Sources*, ed. T. Postmes and N. Branscombe (New York: Psychology Press, 2010).

68. Hahrie Han and David W. Brady, "A Delayed Return to Historical Norms: Congressional Party Polarization after the Second World War," *British Journal of Political Science* 37, no. 3 (July 2007): 506, 507, 512; Nicholas T. Davis and Johanna L. Dunaway, "Party Polarization, Media Choice, and Mass Partisan-Ideological Sorting," *Public Opinion Quarterly* 80, Special issue (2016): 272, 273.

69. A Report on the Media and the Immigration Debate, Brookings Institution, vi, https://www.brookings.edu/wp-content/uploads/2012/04/0925_immigration_dionne.pdf (3 March 2018).

70. Ali Vitali, Kasie Hunt, and Frank Thorp, V, "Trump Referred to Haiti and African Nations as 'Shithole' Countries," *NBC News*, 12 January 2018, https://www.nbcnews.com/politics/white-house/trump-referred-haiti-african-countries-shithole-nations-n836946 (3 March 2018).

71. Kevin Liptak, "Trump Budget Proposal Still Seeking Wall Funding," *CNN Politics*, https://www.cnn.com/2018/02/12/politics/budget-white-house/index.html (12 March, 2018).

72. Tony Makin, "Here Are Some Alternative Facts—Not Fake News, but Quite Bad," *The Australian* (Sydney, New South Wales), 9 June 2017, http://webcache.googleusercontent.com/search?q=cache:50Y0Hpv2aFEJ:www.theaustralian.com.au/opinion/here-are-some-alternative-facts-not-fake-news-but-quite-bad/news-story/99e7b7bdbf24b6d1d0d90cb51adc279b+&cd=1&hl=en&ct=clnk&gl=ie (5 July 2017).

The Alternative Electorate: Mapping Trumped-Up Claims of Voter Fraud in the 2016 Election

The Alternative Electorate

Mapping Trumped-Up Claims of Voter Fraud in the 2016 Election

Jacopo della Quercia

Much has been said and written on Donald Trump's repeated—and baseless—claims of widespread voter fraud in the 2016 election, but few attempts have been made to visualize how such a scenario might have appeared on the electoral map. After all, what benefit could such an exercise into the counterfactual offer researchers? Trump lost the popular vote to former secretary of state Hillary Clinton in 2016 by more than 2.8 million votes. End of story. Any attempt to illustrate the contrary would be as much a work of fantasy as *Game of Thrones*. However, this should not deter the academic community, voting rights groups, or *Game of Thrones* fans from confronting the danger that Trump's false narrative on the 2016 electorate could pose to democracy in the United States.

Any argument that three to five million "illegal ballots" cost Trump the popular vote in 2016 is completely without merit.[1] The allegation has been thoroughly debunked by a consensus of independent studies, statewide audits, government officials, academics, journalists, and even by the president's own attorneys. In their objection to Green Party candidate Dr. Jill Stein's petition for a recount in Michigan, then President-elect Trump's lawyers filed that "all available evidence suggests that the 2016 general election was not tainted by fraud or mistake."[2] A May 2017 study by the Brennan Center for Justice similarly found that noncitizen voting in the 2016 election was "exceedingly rare," occurring at a rate of roughly 0.0001 percent—or 30 suspected instances—out of 23.5 million votes across 12 states.[3] In California, Virginia and New Hampshire, states Trump specifically named on Twitter as sites of "serious voter fraud," the Brennan study noted that "no official we spoke with identified an incident of noncitizen voting in 2016."[4] Simply put, widespread voter fraud did *not* occur during the 2016 election, regardless of whatever Donald Trump says or tweets.

Nevertheless, when a sitting president of the United States tells Congressional leaders that three to five million "illegal ballots cost him the popular vote," members of Congress, the news media, and the voting public tend to listen.[5] When that same president signs an order to stomp out non-existent voter fraud across the country, it becomes a threat to the voting rights of three to five million Americans who legally voted for his political opponent.[6] And even after his administration's investigation into non-existent voter fraud was forced to cease its efforts, the president remained defiant to reality, adding that the committee disbanded "despite substantial evidence of voter fraud."[7] Such wonton disregard for facts presents a twisted view of an antidemocratic, authoritarian United States less akin to the precepts of U.S. Constitution and more befitting the writings of George Orwell: one where "who controls the past controls the future; who controls the present controls the past."[8] In short, by attempting to rewrite the history of the 2016 election to the extent they have, the Trump administration has become the single biggest domestic threat to democracy in America.

What would such a map of the 2016 election have looked like? Ironically, one that shows how even the most modest adjustment to the U.S. electorate could make any notion of fair elections a fantasy in the United States.

The Electorate

The official count of the 2016 U.S. presidential election came to 304 electoral votes for Donald Trump, 227 for Hillary Clinton, and 7 for other candidates by means of faithless electors.[9] Despite receiving a larger share of the Electoral College than any Republican presidential candidate since George H. W. Bush, Trump failed to win the popular vote, receiving only 62,984,825 votes (46.09 percent) to Secretary Clinton's 65,853,516 (48.18 percent).[10] This 2.8 million vote margin between the two candidates should provide some insight into why Trump settled upon three to five million "illegal ballots"— and with no evidence—as a focus of his post-election animosity. If one merely erased those three to five million votes from Secretary Clinton's totals, Trump would have found himself in better company than John Quincy Adams, Rutherford B. Hayes, Benjamin Harrison, and George W. Bush, who similarly lost the popular vote in elections that resulted in historically unpopular presidencies.

So why did it come to this? Why did Trump and his administration resort to such outright lies about the popular vote in the 2016 election? Was Trump trying to manufacture a mandate for his presidency? Is his administration actively trying to disenfranchise Democratic-leaning voters throughout the country? Is this all a smokescreen to distract the public from the clandestine—and possibly illegal—role Russia might have played in his campaign?[11] Or is Trump just in denial about losing a popularity contest to Hillary Clinton, or to a Democrat, or to a woman—or perhaps all three? As of this writing, we simply don't know all the answers to all the questions surrounding Donald Trump's disregard for the electoral process. All that can be said for certain is that, as president, Trump has repeatedly refused to accept the legitimacy of his popular vote loss to Secretary Clinton, and the consequences of this could lead to the most comprehensive purge of voters from the U.S. electorate in history.

The "Alternative" Electorate

So what should the 2016 election have looked like according to Donald Trump? To find out, we have to take Trump for his word and deduct three to five million votes from Secretary Clinton's totals, and from the overall popular vote. After all, when Trump says three to five million "illegal" ballots cost him the popular vote, it is safe to assume that he is not talking about Gary Johnson or Jill Stein voters. (Especially since deducting five million votes from third-party candidates in 2016 would have resulted in Secretary Clinton winning a 50.01 percent of the popular vote to Donald Trump's 47.84 percent.)

If we deduct three million Clinton voters from the 2016 electorate, the 2016 election takes on a wholly different narrative. Trump would have won the popular vote in a squeaker: 62,984,825 votes (47.12 percent) to Secretary Clinton's 62,853,516 (47.02 percent) out of a total 133,669,237 votes. His popular vote margin of 131,309 votes would have likely drawn comparisons to John F. Kennedy's 112, 827-vote margin over Richard Nixon in 1960, or maybe even Trump-favorite Andrew Jackson's 140,839-vote margin over John Quincy Adams in 1828.[12] It is also likely that several states Secretary Clinton won would have been carried by Trump in this scenario. How many? Let's put it this way: Secretary Clinton won New Hampshire by only 2,736 votes out of a total 744,296, and less than one month into his administration, Trump claimed "thousands" of voters were "brought in on buses" from Massachusetts to vote "illegally" in New Hampshire in 2016. As per usual, President Trump did not offer any evidence to substantiate his accusation.[13]

Out of the 20 states Secretary Clinton carried in 2016, all but five could have flipped to Trump by a total of less than 3 million votes: New

Hampshire (2,736 votes), Maine, both at-large and in its 1st Congressional District (22,142 and 58,390 respectively), Nevada (27,202), Minnesota (44,765), Delaware (50,476), New Mexico (65,567), Rhode Island (71,982), Vermont (83,204), Colorado (136,386), Hawaii (138,044), Virginia (212,030), Oregon (219,703), Connecticut (224,357), Washington (520,971) and New Jersey (546,345) as well as the District of Columbia (311,268).[14] Trump could have ended his evening with more than 400 electoral votes in his column— more than any candidate since George H. W. Bush in 1988. It would have been what any impartial political observer could have described as "a massive landslide."

A deduction of 1 million more votes from Secretary Clinton's total would have been enough to add Maryland (734,759), Massachusetts (904,303), or even President Barack Obama's home state of Illinois (944,714) to Trump's spoils.[15] Secretary Clinton would have carried only four states, fewer than any presidential candidate, Republican or Democrat, since Walter Mondale in 1984. However, unlike Ronald Reagan's 16.9 million popular vote margin over to Mondale, Trump's margin over Secretary Clinton's would have been much smaller: only 1,131,309 votes (0.85 percent) out of a total 132,669,237. Percentagewise, this outcome would have been the seventh closest presidential election in U.S. history.[16]

Lastly, if five million votes were deducted from Secretary Clinton's total popular vote in 2016, it would have been enough paint the entire map Republican with the exception of California, New York, and the District of Columbia. The 2016 election would have ended in a way no serious political scientist on the planet would have considered mathematically possible.

Simply put, Trump's claim that as many as five million ballots were cast illegally during the 2016 election could have resulted in him winning a lot more than the popular vote against Hillary Clinton. If spread across enough of the country, Trump could have carried as many as 451 electoral votes across 48 states (all but California, New York, and the District of Columbia), with only 47.84 percent of the popular vote: a number smaller than George W. Bush's 47.87 percent share of the popular vote in 2000.

Of course, such discrepancies between the electoral and popular votes have always been an aspect to how the United States elects its presidents. Either candidate could have secured the necessary 270 electoral votes to win the U.S. presidency by carrying as few as 11 states: California (55 electoral), Texas (38), New York (29), Florida (29), Pennsylvania (20), Illinois (20), Ohio (18), Michigan (16), Georgia (16), North Carolina (15), and New Jersey (14). Conversely, one could win a majority of the popular vote but still be denied the presidency, as Samuel J. Tilden was during the 1876 election. Until the Constitution is amended, the Electoral College is the decisive arbitrator to who wins the presidency, the popular vote be damned.

Conclusion

Scenarios such as the "alternative" interpretations of the 2016 election above should be taken as a warning to the threat that Donald Trump's repeatedly false claims of voter fraud pose to voting rights across the United States. When James Madison famously observed in *Federalist* No. 51 that government would not be necessary "if men were angels," he apparently failed to anticipate how few Americans today would be like Madison.[17] The 2016 election took place amid a perfect storm of partisan paralysis, voter discrimination, and foreign interference the likes of which our founders neither anticipated nor provided the necessary tools to quickly fix. How could the Founding Fathers have imagined an invention like Twitter when defining "speech"? What protection does the Constitution offer from Russia hackers penetrating U.S. voter systems?[18] When does voter protection become voter intimidation? And at what point is democracy in America no longer representative of democracy?

These are important questions that will hopefully be answered in the near future. Until then, Americans may want to take a long, hard look at their country and ask themselves where they would rather live: in the United States as it is, or in the United States of Donald Trump.

NOTES

1. Abby Phillip and Mike DeBonis, "Without Evidence, Trump Tells Lawmakers 3 Million to 5 Million Illegal Ballots Cost Him the Popular Vote," WashingtonPost.com, 23 January 2017, https://www.washingtonpost.com/news/post-politics/wp/2017/01/23/at-white-house-trump-tells-congressional-leaders-3-5-million-illegal-ballots-cost-him-the-popular-vote (21 July 2017).

2. Donald J. Trump and Donald J. Trump for President, Inc.'s Objections to Dr. Jill Stein's Recount Petition at 2, In re *Petition for Recount for the Office of President of the United States of America* (State of Michigan Board of State Canvassers, filed Dec. 1, 2016).

3. Christopher Famighetti, Douglas Keith, and Myrna Pérez, "Noncitizen Voting: The Missing Millions," *Brennan Center for Justice*, 5 May 2017, https://www.brennancenter.org/publication/noncitizen-voting-missing-millions (21 July 2017).

4. Donald Trump, Twitter post, November 27, 2016, 7:31 p.m., http://twitter.com/realDonaldTrump (21 July 2017).

5. Phillip and DeBonis, "Without Evidence."

6. Louis Nelson, "Trump Signs Executive Order Creating Voter Fraud Commission," Politico.com, 11 May 2017, www.politico.com/story/2017/05/11/trump-voter-fraud-commission-238263 (21 July 2017).

7. Michael Tackett and Michael Wines, "Trump Disbands Commission on Voter Fraud," NYTimes.com, 3 January 2018, https://www.nytimes.com/2018/01/03/us/politics/trump-voter-fraud-commission.html (10 Feb. 2018).

8. George Orwell, *1984* (New York: Signet, 1941) 248.

9. United States, Federal Elections Commission, "Official 2016 Presidential General Election Results," 30 January 2017, https://transition.fec.gov/pubrec/fe2016/2016presgeresults.pdf (21 July 2017).

10. United States, Federal Elections Commission, "Official 2016 Presidential General Election Results."

11. Jo Becker, Matt Apuzzo, and Adam Goldman, "Trump's Son Met with Russian Lawyer After Being Promised Damaging Information on Clinton," NYTimes.com, 9 July

2017, https://www.nytimes.com/2017/07/09/us/politics/trump-russia-kushner-manafort.html (21 July 2017).

12. David Leip, "Dave Leip's Atlas of U.S. Presidential Elections," http://uselection atlas.org/RESULTS (21 July 2017).

13. Eli Stokols, "Trump Brings up Vote Fraud Again, This Time in Meeting with Senators," Politico.com, 10 February 2017, www.politico.com/story/2017/02/trump-voter-fraud-senators-meeting-234909 (21 July 2017).

14. Federal Elections Commission, "Official 2016 Presidential General Election Results."

15. Leip, "Dave Leip's Atlas of U.S. Presidential Elections."

16. Leip, "Dave Leip's Atlas of U.S. Presidential Elections."

17. James Madison, The Federalist No. 51, in The Federalist Papers (New York: Dover, 2014), 254.

18. Cynthia McFadden, William M. Arkin, and Kevin Monahan, "Russians Penetrated U.S. Voter Systems, Top U.S. Official Says," NBCNews.com, 8 February 2018, https://www.nbc-news.com/politics/elections/russians-penetrated-u-s-voter-systems-says-top-u-s-n845721 (10 Feb. 2018).

PART 4

Pop Cultural Observations

Speaking Post-Truth to Power

Comedy as Alternative Facts
in Saturday Night Live

Melanie Piper

The scene is the first presidential debate between Donald Trump and Hillary Clinton. The candidates stand at their podiums under the glare of television lights with the declaration of independence emblazoned in powder blue behind them. The assembled audience, in the room and at home, wait to see how this anticipated event plays out. They don't have to wait long. Trump jumps in on Clinton's first answer, claims victory simply for staying calm, and bids goodnight to the Hofstra audience.

"There's still 88 minutes left," moderator Lester Holt reminds the Republican candidate. "It's a 90-minute debate."

Trump turns back to the podium, mouth agape, ready to continue his stream of consciousness speech. Only now, the words will not come. His broad shoulders slump a little, a crack in the façade. He is caught out. For one brief moment, it is clear that he is not the gilded voice of the people that tells it like it is.

Then, the machine starts again. Trump leans forward.

"My microphone is broken."

The words come without him having to think as the audience roars their approval.

"She broke it. With Obama, she and Obama stole it, they took it to Kenya. They took my microphone to Kenya and broke it and now it's broken."

Donald Trump is back on track, saved by his own version of the truth.

This scene is, of course, not what happened at the first Trump versus Clinton debate on September 27, 2016. Rather, it is a moment from the satirical restaging of the event for *Saturday Night Live*'s (*SNL*) October 1 cold open sketch.[1] With Alec Baldwin in the role of Trump and Kate McKinnon as Clinton, so began *SNL's* approach to Donald Trump as the Republican nominee for president, and, eventually, president-elect and commander in chief. In this essay, I examine *SNL's* approach to the Trump administration as a public offering of alternative facts to Trump's self-image. By using comedy and satire as its own kind of alternative facts, *SNL's* parody highlights the administration's breaks with the norms of presidential politics, not only within the sketches themselves but also the much-talked about extratext of Trump's repeated public responses to Baldwin's impersonation.

To begin, it is useful to unpack the origin of the term "alternative facts" in order to consider how it can potentially be applied to satire in the Trump era. When questioned about Sean Spicer's first press briefing and his claims that Trump's inauguration garnered "the largest audience to ever witness an inauguration, period," Kellyanne Conway claimed that Spicer gave "alternative facts" to the idea that his claim was a "falsehood."[2] This constructs the concept of alternative facts as being information that reinforces or supports an existing opinion, ideological viewpoint, desire, or feeling. The "facts" that Spicer offered were claims that were not based on objective evidence, and which served to further the administration's desired narrative. This narrative (that Trump's inauguration audience was the largest in history) was contrary to widely circulated evidence such as photographs of the event and ridership numbers provided by DC Metro for January 20.[3] Conway's claim that these are "alternative facts" suggests that an alternative fact constitutes a subjective creation of evidence, either through complete fabrication, or selective reframing. With alternative facts, fact becomes nothing more than a statement of how one wishes the world to be, or how they see the world in ways that are evidently unseeable to those who, they believe, are unwilling to see them. In the case of the Trump administration, the reluctant seers constitute what Trump has repeatedly declared to be their number one political enemy: the "fake news" mainstream press.

This conceptualisation of alternative facts could also be applied to the impersonation of a celebrity in sketch comedy, like those featured on *Saturday Night Live*. Both require appropriating reality, filtering it through a subjective point of view, bending and shaping it to suit a specific purpose, and producing something new and not-quite-real that tries to persuade the listener or viewer to see the world the same way as the creator of this new reality does. Here I propose the idea that this approach to "alternative facts" and "fake news" is not entirely the domain of the political right in the era of Trump. Fake Twitter accounts and invented Facebook stories have been produced to appeal to the desires of progressives,[4] and widely circulated memes like Texts from Hillary and Biden Bro have been described as a kind of alternate reality of "liberal fan fiction."[5] In the era of Trump, the re-imagining of actuality can serve the purpose of "wish-fulfilment and catharsis,"[6] and *SNL*'s performance of the Trump administration functions in a similar way.

Through the way satirical impersonations use the material of the real to construct an alternative take on reality, sketches like *SNL*'s political content be considered as operating in the mode of "docucomedy."[7] Much like the mode of docudrama, which structures meaning in film and television forms and genres such as the biopic or the historical miniseries, docucomedy re-creates or re-purposes elements of the real to ground itself "within the actuality it represents."[8] Through this grounding in reality, the mode of docucomedy structures the impersonation sketch's satirical critique. The sketch is therefore able to argue for its take on the impersonated subject as a truthful and valid critique of the reality it represents. In this way, the political satire of the impersonation sketch offers a "counternarrative," a means of making sense of things to those whose lives "do not reflect their culture's common ideals."[9] Given the divisive nature of the Trump administration, and Trump's consistently sub-50 percent approval rating,[10] it would perhaps be a stretch to label their ideological viewpoint as the common ideals of American culture. However, those opposed to the administration's worldview are nevertheless faced with the reality that Trump was elected to power, the ideals of the Trump administration have been culturally endorsed by a significant segment of the American population and the narratives of the administration have become the dominant guiding factor of public discourse. Trumpism is undoubtedly a firmly entrenched worldview and power structure that necessitates counternarrativisation as part of the meaning-making process for those who do not subscribe to its ideology. In approaching *Saturday Night Live*'s treatment of Trump and his administration as political satire that operates in the mode of docucomedy, drawing on the material of the real to offer a counternarrative of that same reality, we can begin to see how *SNL*'s take on the Trump administration can be considered a kind of alternative fact. In this case, however, satire has become an alternative *to* alternative facts, representing a subjective view of Trump that is in direct conflict with Trump's publicly presented view of himself. These comedic alternative-alternative facts about the Trump administration present the material of the actual world through the subjective filter of the way "the other side" understands it to be, reflecting a collective desire for the way things *should* be.

At its most fundamental level, comedy is about breaking rules. This may involve breaking the accepted rules of the everyday, such as language, logic, or contextually acceptable behavior.[11] Given that this could also describe Trump's actual, everyday behaviour outside of any comedic framework, the question becomes how exactly does *Saturday Night Live* construct a version of Trump that provides a satirical counternarrative, when much of its past political impersonations are based in this comedic principle of disruption?

Before I move on to considering Alec Baldwin's impersonation of Donald Trump, it is worth looking at the tradition of political impersonation on *SNL* in order to fully examine just how the sketch version of Trump highlights his disruptive, norm-breaking nature.

Jeffrey P. Jones, in his examination of satirical representations of past presidents, writes that *Saturday Night Live* has often been at the forefront of determining how the president is filtered through the lens of popular culture. However, Jones argues that in general, the show's sketch caricatures are "typically missing any form of meaningful political critique," and, rather, derive their comedy from the performer's mimetic impersonation that merely replicates rather than criticizes "personal mannerisms and political style." The humour derived from the impersonation, therefore, does not usually engage with any sustained critique of policy, the substance of politics, or political persona.[12] In the early years of the show, when *SNL* was positioned as countercultural, presidential impersonations like Chevy Chase's Gerald Ford and Dan Aykroyd's Richard Nixon and Jimmy Carter were not mimetic and made no attempt to look or sound like the subject of the impersonation. The comedian's claim they were the president for the purposes of the sketch was enough for the show's hip approach to comedy, thus allowing leeway for critical humour that was not derived from the impersonation's pleasures of mimetic recognition.[13] Jones argues that as *Saturday Night Live* moved away from its countercultural origins and became mainstream, attaining the status of a flagship late-night show on a major broadcast network, its political impersonations took on a more inoffensive, lowest-common-denominator type of humor. This approach worked to portray the "human foibles" of politicians, rather than engaging in a satirical critique of the president's or candidate's capabilities as a leader.[14]

The role that self-performance and political persona plays in the branding of politicians has evolved and grown exponentially into the early 21st century, and shifted the viability of this satirical approach. Graeme Turner argues that the proliferation of information in contemporary media needs to be understood through the lens of entertainment. With so much information available to consumers, media producers are continually vying for a piece of an increasingly fragmented audience, resulting in "the rise of entertainment and its ascendancy over information as the most marketable regime of content."[15] This dominance of entertainment over information has shaped the performance and representation of politics through the conventions of entertainment media, to capture audience interest in otherwise boring or complex issues.[16] The intrusion of entertainment discourse into the realm of the political has led to a focus on the politician as persona, with individual politicians and their narratives serving as shortcuts for constituents to make political judgements. This increased focus on individual personas viewed through the lens of entertainment discourse over the substance of issues has contributed to the celebrification of politics. Donald Trump, as a former reality television star and internationally known name brand, is, of course, the most obvious example of this, and perhaps (for the foreseeable future) the apex of this evolution of the role of the public persona in politics.

As the focus on individual personalities has evolved, so too has *Saturday Night Live*'s treatment of politicians shifted. As Jones notes in later writing on Will Ferrell's impersonation of George W. Bush during the 2000 presidential campaign and Tina Fey's impersonation of Sarah Palin throughout the 2008 campaign, the representation of the "outlandish personal tics of the candidates" in these cases "was exactly where the satiric critique belonged."[17] Here, I will briefly consider *Saturday Night Live*'s approach to Sarah Palin in 2008 in more depth. Tina Fey's Palin is the most recent example of a political impersonation that has captured the cultural zeitgeist in a manner similar to Baldwin's Trump. Therefore, the Palin sketches offer a salient comparison to illustrate how *Saturday Night Live*'s approach to Trump's particular disregard for the norms of national political performance highlight his disruptive nature, and how *SNL*'s Trump provides a counternarrative of the actual Trump.

Sarah Palin can be considered to have disrupted political norms regarding her lack of national experience or the apparent lack of vetting conducted by the McCain campaign prior to her nomination. Even so, her *SNL* representation was constructed in a way that generated humour by disrupting norms within the comedic context of each sketch. Take, for example, the vice presidential debate sketch,[18] which parodies the debate between Palin and Joe Biden (played by Jason Sudeikis). The sketch re-creates the public frame of the political debate through its resemblance to the actual event in terms of its set and staging. We can think about the debate stage using sociological theorist Erving Goffman's ideas of front and back regions. Goffman defines a region as "any place that is bounded by some degree to barriers of perception."[19] In its staging for public view, the front region of the political debate is bound by expectations of particular behaviours within that region. By mimicking the front region of the debate stage, the sketch conjures those expectations in the viewer's mind. Fey's Palin, as a character in sketch comedy, frequently disrupts this front region frame by revealing the preparation that has gone into her debate performance. These disruptive utterances constitute a revelation of the "back region," where "the impression fostered by the performance is knowingly contradicted."[20] Revealing back region aspects of the political machine behind Palin, or Palin's interior thoughts about her performance as a politician not only highlights and satirically critiques the actual Palin's inexperience and lack of knowledge but generates laughter through the incongruity of such a revealing utterance within the context of a televised debate.

For example, a run of jokes in the sketch about Palin's question dodging tactics illustrate how a back region utterance disrupts the expectations of the debate region. When moderator Gwen Ifill (played by Queen Latifah) first poses a question to Palin about the economy, Fey's Palin does not immediately acknowledge the question and instead responds with a backwards compliment to Joe Biden's hair plugs. The comedic effect of Palin's question dodging is heightened as the sketch plays out by becoming more obvious with each repetition. When asked if she would like to respond to comments Biden has made about her running mate, John McCain, Palin responds, "No, thank you. But I would like to talk about bein' an outsider." Next, when asked about climate change, Palin first answers that she is unsure if this "climate change hoozie-what's-it is manmade, or just a natural part of the End of Days." She then plainly states her desire to change topics: "But I'm not gonna talk about that. I'm gonna talk about taxes." In the third repetition of the joke, Ifill asks Palin a direct question about healthcare. In this final escalation of the Palin-dodging-questions pattern, her response is at its most blunt and obvious, clearly fracturing the pretence of what is appropriate for a debate. She cheerfully responds, "I'm gonna ignore that question and instead, talk about Israel." Rather than the somewhat subtle approach that the actual Palin took to dodging questions in the debate, here *SNL*'s Palin is constructed to disrupt the norms and expectations of the debate frame. This disruption generates humour with the incongruity of her behavior that is inappropriate for the debate context. Additionally, this disruption makes a satiric critique about Palin's unpreparedness by focusing on both a specific instance of Palin's shortfalls as a candidate and the aspects of her persona, such as charm and folksiness, that she uses to try to mask her shortcomings. The point here is that she is limited to speaking on the topics she has rehearsed answers for, rather than addressing questions as they come, and her pathway out of that is to skate by on her charming, folksy persona.[21]

This technique of stating the presumed subtext of the actual event within the comedic text of the sketch can be thought of as "refracting political realities," where the "impersonation parody can articulate the hidden subtext of a political situation in a unique way, borrowing from and reinventing a political figure's own behaviour."[22] In the run of question-dodging jokes from the Palin debate sketch, the material of the real—the re-creation of the debate stage, the mimicry of the political figures through Fey's and Sudeikis's performances, the fact that Palin did dodge questions on numerous occasions in the actual debate—is reconfigured to reveal the comedic subtext of the actual moment. Here, the subtext is Palin's lack of knowledge that is covered by rehearsed, scripted answers. The subtext is articulated as the comedic text, and, thus, the satiric critique of the sketch, through the way Fey's Palin openly reveals the political machination behind her actions: she does not want to talk about one particular topic, so here is one for which she has a rehearsed answer.

This brief example of how *SNL* constructed Sarah Palin as a sketch character that disrupted norms with back region revelations within the context of the sketch raises a question about how this approach can work when it comes to satirically impersonating Donald Trump. The actual Trump can easily be compared to Fey's characterization of Palin in many ways: seemingly ignorant of or uninterested in the normal expectations of political performance, and freely stating his desires to not conform to those expectations. Jon Greenaway writes that Trump's political performance during the Republican primaries was successful because "he expresses what the other candidates not just won't, but cannot—the dark, twisted, and unacceptable elements of right-wing political discourse that can, in the mainstream, no longer be said."[23] As the first two years of his presidency have shown, Trump has continued to operate in this manner in his rallies, interviews, Tweets, and press conferences, and maintaining solid support from his core base because of it. So if the actual Donald Trump is flagrantly breaking—and completely changing—accepted political norms in reality, how can *Saturday Night Live* approach him within a comedic framework? How can they take the material of the real and use it to illuminate the subtext of the moment? How can they pull the curtain back on the political machine to show what is happening behind the scenes, if the target of the satire himself often refuses to engage with the norms of what happens in front of the curtain?

Alec Baldwin's impersonation of Donald Trump takes many cues from *Saturday Night Live*'s traditional approach to presidential impersonation. There is a focus on personal style, mannerisms, and patterns of speech. In Baldwin's first appearance as Trump, the debate sketch described at the opening of this essay, we see Trump's puckered and pouting facial expression that Baldwin has heightened to the point of a resembling grotesque toddler. This expression is not only a mimetic reference to the parodied subject, but itself a commentary on Trump's demeanour in the way Baldwin scrunches his face and sulkily pouts at both his opponents and his supporters. There are the references to Trump's particular patterns of speech, his accent, the requisite repetition of "yuge" and odd pronunciation of "China" which makes it sound more like a part of the female anatomy. Trump's bragging and hyperbole are there, heightened along with his other recognisable characteristics to the point of absurdity. To see these characteristics replicated and twisted just enough to serve the comedic framework is funny because they are recognisable and because, in the context of the Candidate Trump sketches, the idea of a reality television celebrity becoming President of the United States is given permission to be as absurd as it sounds at first hearing. The idea is temporarily granted some freedom from the reality it represents.

However, rather than comedically breaking the frame of political performance, *Saturday Night Live*'s Trump becomes incongruently funny when
it is the frame of his own persona and self-image that is broken. As such,
Sketch Trump is often more self-aware than the actual Trump. In the first
debate sketch, at the moment that Lester Holt (Michael Che) calls Trump
back to the podium when Trump freezes for a second of gaping silence, this
is a Trump who knows that he is in over his head. The expectations of Trump's
persona are broken, and it is incongruously funny to see Trump acknowledge
that he does not belong on the political stage and that he lacks the knowledge,
the experience, or the interest required of the position. It is incongruously
funny to see a version of Trump that acknowledges his status as an entertainer,
rather than simply running on that status as his political platform. These
moments of revealing an incongruously self-aware Trump crop up in many
of Baldwin's Trump sketches, particularly when establishing the character
during the campaign and following the election. In the third debate sketch,
Trump gets stuck in an incoherent ramble about his plan to defeat ISIS (in
between sniffing into the microphone) and is finally stopped by debate moderator Chris Wallace (Tom Hanks). Baldwin's Trump drops his head in relief,
and gasps, "Oh, thank God. I don't know if you could tell, but I was really
spinning out of control there."[24] In the first post-election Trump sketch, we
see him taking his first meetings as president-elect and frantically Googling
"what is ISIS?" when his 30-day play to defeat them is brought up. He greets
Mike Pence (Beck Bennett) as "the reason I'm never going to get impeached"
and asks for reassurance that Pence will be doing everything.[25] In *SNL*-
Trump's first press conference as president-elect, he opens "by answering the
question that's on everyone's mind: yes, this is real life, it's really happening,"
before claiming that he will be replaced as president by Mike Pence in two
months. Later in the sketch, among all the golden shower puns and references
to the existence of "the Pee Pee Tape" prompted by the then-recent news of
the Steele Dossier, we see a Trump who acknowledges Russia's involvement
in influencing the election. Not only that, but this Trump acknowledges his
submission to Russia as he allows himself to be easily blackmailed by Vladimir
Putin (Beck Bennett) into switching his story that China and/or Canada is
behind the hack.[26]

Rather than the approach taken to Sarah Palin, where disruptions to the
machinations of political performance were largely manufactured within the
sketch, the Trump sketches show his break with normal political performance
by instead targeting Trump's persona as the institution to be satirised. This
version of Trump comedically disrupts expectations about the actuala Trump's
persona with back region revelations that the persona is a sham, that "alternative facts" are nothing but lies, and that Donald Trump's all-important ego
and sense of self can be broken apart for the purposes of ridicule. In the

laughter generated by the comedic transgression of what is expected of Trump, the expectations are simultaneously acknowledged and dismissed by the principles of comedic rule-breaking. Through this laughter, communal bonds form among the audience and with the joke-teller to the exclusion of the butt of the joke.[27] The communal effects of laughter in conjunction with wide-spread dissatisfaction with Trump and a desire to see him purposefully rendered as an object of ridicule can account for the cultural relevance and success of *SNL* (and other political satire) early in the Trump era. By February of 2017, *Saturday Night Live*'s overall season ratings were the highest they had been in 22 years, up 22 percent from the previous season.[28] The role that *SNL*'s counternarrativised Trump played in making sense of his election in the cultural zeitgeist waned somewhat as the Trump administration became a fact of everyday life. *Vanity Fair*'s Joanna Robinson reported that the 2017–2018 season saw a ratings dip from the high of an average 11 million weekly viewers to 9.4 million, crediting Trump fatigue as a contributing factor.[29]

Another possibility for the dip in *SNL*'s later ratings could be that Trump himself has largely disengaged from regularly criticising the show on Twitter as he did during his campaign and shortly after the election. The exclusion effect that comedic discourse has on the butt of the joke was clearly evident in Trump's early response to *SNL*'s representation. Trump tweeted about *SNL* and Alec Baldwin's impersonation four times in a relatively short period: once as candidate on October 16, 2016,[30] as president-elect on November 20[31] and December 3, 2016,[32] and again on January 15, 2017,[33] just five days before his inauguration. Although not as much of a regular occurrence, Trump still tweeted about *SNL* well into his presidency. A tweet criticizing Baldwin (first referred to as "Alex Baldwin" in an error-ridden early morning message that was quickly deleted, revised, and re-posted)[34] appeared on March 2, 2018,[35] Kanye West's MAGA hat wearing appearance was tweeted about on September 30, 2018,[36] and a claim that *SNL* was part of the "unfair news coverage" that should be "tested in courts" went out on December 16, 2018.[37]

Trump's response to *Saturday Night Live* offers a further example of how the sketches highlight his break with political norms and engagement with the discourse of alternative facts. However, a politician responding to their comedic impersonation is not, in itself, something new. Josh Compton has examined references to *Saturday Night Live* parodies in presidential rhetoric and found that, for the most part, the responses have been positive or, at the very least given the sense that the President is good-humoured and can take a joke. Compton found that Gerald Ford responded to Chevy Chase's bumbling, klutzy impersonation of him with a self-deprecation that "both dismissed and embraced his *SNL* parody"[38]; that George H. W. Bush also played along with the joke, frequently mentioning, and sometimes praising, Dana Carvey's impersonation of him in public remarks[39]; and that Bill Clinton mentioned impersonations of him by Phil Hartman and Darrell Hammond, again with self-deprecating humour and "a mild, humorous rebuke" of Hammond's impersonation.[40] George W. Bush did not ever mention Will Ferrell, the first actor to impersonate him on *SNL*, by name, but threw a light jab his way when asked whose impersonator was better: his or his father's. Bush Jr. answered Dana Carvey.[41] Vice President Dick Cheney, however, responded to *SNL* sketches about him in similar ways to past presidents that gave the sense that he was "embracing the humor, that he [was] in on the jokes."[42] It perhaps speaks volumes about Donald Trump that even Dick Cheney was willing to give the impression, at least in public, that he had a sense of humour about himself. In addition to the presidential references to *Saturday Night Live* impersonations Compton writes of, there are also the appearances that presidential or vice presidential candidates have made on the show. Cameos by recent candidates like Hillary Clinton, Barack Obama, John McCain, and Sarah Palin have had similar effects of endowing their political personas with a sense of good-humored sociability and the idea they can take a joke. Before Baldwin's impersonation, Donald Trump himself made an appearance on *Saturday Night Live* while running for the Republican nomination, hosting the November 5, 2015, episode. At that time, Trump was more than willing to tweet about *SNL*'s ratings success.[43]

While candidates and sitting presidents responding to their *SNL* parodies is not unusual, it is the form of Trump's response that has broken political norms. In his tweets, Trump described the show as a boring, unfunny hit job and "the worst of NBC"[44]; claimed that Baldwin's portrayal of him "stinks," and "just can't get any worse"[45]; and declared the show to be biased, one-sided, and evidence of the "media rigging [the] election"[46] that "can't be legal"[47] It is not only the open hostility Trump shows towards *SNL* and Baldwin's impersonation in these tweets that breaks with the norms established by previous presidential engagement with *SNL*, but his framing of *SNL* as something other than a comedy show. By invoking the idea of bias, or that the Trump team should receive "equal time" in response (as he did in his November 20 tweet, after he had already won the election), it suggests that a satirical sketch comedy show should be held to a standard of objectivity that is inherently impossible within its form. Satire is, by its very nature, "aggressive and critical."[48] While satirical humor has the primary intention of generating laughter, it is through that laughter that audience and satirist engage with a communal understanding and agreement about their target: that something is not right, that there is a gap between the way things are and the way things should be. It is this element of criticism that Trump responds to in his tweets, attempting to regain some of his power over *Saturday Night Live*'s characterisation of him. He claims the show to be something that it is not (by imbuing it with a duty to be fair and objective, or speaking about it in the same context as NBC's news division), while simultaneously diminishing what it is trying to be (by labelling the show as "unfunny"). His claims that the show is "unwatchable" and "the worst of NBC" are in themselves evidence of the Trump era alternative facts rhetoric. Although Trump frequently measures success in terms of television ratings, such as during his National Prayer Breakfast mocking of Arnold Schwarzenegger's job hosting *The Apprentice*[49] or his claim that his appearance on *Face the Nation* garnered the highest ratings since 9/11,[50] his criticisms of *SNL* are not in line with popular response in terms of the show's early post–Trump ratings spike.

By generating counternarratives to dominant ideological points of view, or bringing to light gaps between the way societal institutions are and the way they should be, political satire "might inspire individuals to reappraise normative experience, to question the foundations of society's dominant stories and, thus, to challenge power."[51] The response to Alec Baldwin's impersonation of Donald Trump on *Saturday Night Live* suggests that the role of political satire in the Trump era is to help make sense of political norm-breaking and the redrawn boundaries of public discourse, It is not only *Saturday Night Live* that has offered a popular counternarrative of Trump. *The Late Show with Stephen Colbert* saw a similar post–Trump ratings bump as its politically focused comedy resonated with audiences in ways that late night competitors Jimmy Fallon and Jimmy Kimmel did not.[52] New series have also presented alternative Trumps: Comedy Central's *The President Show* features Anthony Atamanuik's impersonation of Trump in an Oval Office-turned talk show set, and Showtime's *Our Cartoon President* (a spinoff of a recurring Colbert segment) puts an animated version of Trump, his administration, and his family, into a pseudo-sitcom format.

In the world of Trump, comedy and satire have become their own kind of alternative facts. These are the alternative facts that are being offered up as counterclaims to Trump's falsehoods, alternative facts to Trump's perception of himself and the empty catchphrases of his persona. Just as *SNL*'s alternative-Trump captured a sense of the cultural zeitgeist, it also captured the attention of the President himself. Evidence suggests that having been presented with *Saturday Night Live*'s alternative facts about Donald Trump, Donald Trump continues to reject the reality shared by a public united by political satire, a reality viewed through an ideologically divergent subjective interpretation of objective facts.

NOTES

1. "Donald Trump vs. Hillary Clinton Debate Cold Open," *Saturday Night Live*, season 42, episode 1, aired October 1, 2016, on NBC, https://www.youtube.com/watch?v=-nQG-BZQrtT0 (24 Jan. 2018).

2. Kellyanne Conway interviewed by Chuck Todd, *Meet the Press*, aired January 22, 2017, on NBC, https://www.youtube.com/watch?v=VSrEEDQgFc8 (24 Jan. 2018).

3. Max Kutner, "Inauguration and Women's March by the Numbers," *Newsweek* 2017, http://www.newsweek.com/trump-inauguration-numbers-how-many-attended-545467 (24 Jan. 2018).

4. Robinson Meyer, "The Rise of Progressive 'Fake News,'" *The Atlantic*, 3 February 2017, https://www.theatlantic.com/technology/archive/2017/02/viva-la-resistance-content/515532/ (30 Nov. 2018).

5. Ezekiel Kweku, "Liberal Fan Fiction," *MTV News*, 7 February 2017, http://www.mtv.com/news/2979835/liberal-fan-fiction/ (30 Nov. 2018).

6. Kweku, "Liberal Fan Fiction."

7. Melanie Piper, "Docucharacters: Public Persona as Character in Film, Television, and Fandom" (PhD diss., University of Queensland, 2017), 113, doi:10.14264/uql.2018.54.

8. Steven N. Lipkin, *Docudrama Performs the Past: Arenas of Argument in Films Based on True Stories* (Newcastle upon Tyne: Cambridge Scholars, 2011), 3.

9. Megan Hill, "Developing a Normative Approach to Political Satire," *International Journal of Communication* 7 (2013): 328.

10. "How Popular Is Donald Trump?" *FiveThirtyEight* 2018, https://projects.fivethirtyeight.com/trump-approval-ratings (30 Nov. 2018).

11. Susan Purdie, *Comedy: The Mastery of Discourse* (Toronto: University of Toronto Press, 1993), 5.

12. Jeffrey P. Jones, "With All Due Respect: Satirizing Presidents from *Saturday Night Live* to *Lil' Bush*," in *Satire TV: Politics and Comedy in the Post-Network Era*, ed. Jonathan Gray, Jeffrey P. Jones, and Ethan Thompson (New York: New York University Press, 2008), 38.

13. Jones, "With All Due Respect," 39–41.

14. Jones, "With All Due Respect," 43.

15. Graeme Turner, *Re-Inventing the Media* (London: Routledge, 2016), 49.

16. Liesbet Van Zoonen, *Entertaining the Citizen: When Politics and Popular Culture Converge* (Lanham, MD: Rowman & Littlefield, 2005), 69.

17. Jeffrey P. Jones, "Politics and the Brand: *Saturday Night Live*'s Campaign Season Humor," in *Saturday Night Live and American TV*, ed. Nick Marx, Matt Sienkiewicz, and Ron Becker (Bloomington: Indiana University Press, 2013), 81.

18. "VP Debate Open: Palin/Biden," *Saturday Night Live*, season 34, episode 4, aired October 4, 2008, on NBC, https://www.youtube.com/watch?v=_iyIbbxVzrU (24 Jan. 2018).

19. Erving Goffman, *The Presentation of Self in Everyday Life* (London: Penguin, 1990), 109.

20. Goffman, *The Presentation of Self*, 115.

21. For a more in-depth analysis of Sarah Palin as a sketch character on *Saturday Night Live*, see Piper, "Docucharacters," 94–112.

22. Jason T. Peifer, "Palin, *Saturday Night Live*, and Framing: Examining the Dynamics of Political Parody," *The Communication Review* 16, no. 3 (2013): 170.

23. Jon Greenaway, "Donald Trump: The Id of Republican Politics," *JSTOR Daily* 2015, https://daily.jstor.org/donald-trump-the-id-of-republican-politics/ (24 Jan. 2018).

24. "Donald Trump vs. Hillary Clinton Third Debate Cold Open," *Saturday Night Live*, season 42, episode 4, aired October 22, 2016, on NBC, https://www.youtube.com/watch?v=kjyltrKZSY (24 Jan. 2018).

25. "Donald Trump Prepares Cold Open," *Saturday Night Live*, season 42, episode 7, aired November 19, 2016, on NBC, https://www.youtube.com/watch?v=JUWSLlz0Fdo (24 Jan. 2018).

26. "Donald Trump Press Conference Cold Open," *Saturday Night Live*, season 42, episode 11, aired January 14, 2017, on NBC, https://www.youtube.com/watch?v=4_Gf0mGJfP8 (24 Jan. 2018).

27. Purdie, *Comedy*, 5.

28. Cynthia Littleton, "*Saturday Night Live* Flexes Post-Election Ratings Muscle," *Variety*, 5 February 2017, http://variety.com/2017/tv/news/saturday-night-live-ratings-18–49-demo-melissa-mccarthy-1201978637/ (24 Jan. 2018).

29. Joanne Robinson. "*SNL* Struggles to Find Its Identity in the Era of Trump Fatigue,"

Vanity Fair, 17 May 2018, https://www.vanityfair.com/hollywood/2018/05/saturday-night-live-season-review-trump-fatigue-ratings (30 Nov. 2018).

30. Donald Trump (@realdonaldtrump), "Watched Saturday Night Live hit job on me. Time to retire the boring and unfunny show. Alec Baldwin portrayal stinks. Media rigging election!" Twitter, 16 October 2016, 4:14 a.m., https://twitter.com/realdonaldtrump/status/787612552654155776 (7 Feb. 2018).

31. Donald Trump (@realdonaldtrump), "I watched parts of @nbcsnl Saturday Night Live last night. It is a totally one-sided, biased show—nothing funny at all. Equal time for us?" Twitter, 20 November 2016, 5:26 a.m., https://twitter.com/realdonaldtrump/status/800329364986626048 (7 Feb. 2018).

32. Donald Trump (@realdonaldtrump), "Just tried watching Saturday Night Live—unwatchable! Totally biased, not funny and the Baldwin impersonation just can't get any worse. Sad" Twitter, 3 December 2016, 9:13 p.m. https://twitter.com/realdonaldtrump/status/805278955150471168 (7 Feb. 2018).

33. Donald Trump (@realdonaldtrump), "@NBCNews is bad but Saturday Night Live is the worst of NBC. Not funny, cast is terrible, always a complete hit job. Really bad television!" Twitter, 15 January 2017, 2:46 p.m., https://twitter.com/realdonaldtrump/status/820764134857969666 (7 Feb. 2018).

34. Mark Osborne, "Donald Trump Attacks 'Alex' Baldwin on Twitter Over Impersonation," *ABC News*, 2 March 2018, http://abcnews.go.com/Politics/donald-trump-attacks-alex-baldwin-twitter-impersonation/story?id=53459224 (18 Mar. 2018).

35. Donald Trump (@realdonaldtrump), "Alec Baldwin, whose dying mediocre career was saved by his terrible impersonation of me on SNL, now says playing me was agony. Alec, it was agony for those who were forced to watch. Bring back Darrell Hammond, funnier and a far greater talent!" Twitter, 2 March 2018, 6:07 a.m., https://twitter.com/realdonaldtrump/status/969529668234829825 (18 Mar. 2018).

36. Donald Trump (@realdonaldtrump), "Like many, I don't watch Saturday Night Live (even though I past hosted it)—no longer funny, no talent or charm. It is just a political ad for the Dems. Word is that Kanye West, who put on a MAGA hat after the show (despite being told "no"), was great. He's leading the charge!" Twitter, 30 September, 2018, 9:57 a.m., https://twitter.com/realdonaldtrump/status/1046443996074127361 (2 Jan. 2019).

37. Donald Trump (@realdonaldtrump), "A REAL scandal is the one sided coverage, hour by hour, of networks like NBC & Democrat spin machines like Saturday Night Live. It is all nothing less than unfair news coverage and Dem commercials. Should be tested in courts, can't be legal? Only defame & belittle! Collusion?" Twitter, 16 December, 2018, 5:58 a.m., https://twitter.com/realdonaldtrump/status/1074302851906707457 (2 Jan. 2019).

38. Josh Compton, "Live from DC: *Saturday Night Live* Political Parody References in Presidential Rhetoric," *Comedy Studies* 7, no. 1 (2016): 65.

39. Compton, "Live from DC," 65–66.

40. Compton, "Live from DC," 66–67.

41. Compton, "Live from DC," 67.

42. Compton, "Live from DC," 70.

43. Donald Trump (@realdonaldtrump), "Thank you to all of those who gave me such wonderful reviews for my performance on @nbcsnl Saturday Night Live. Best ratings in 4 years!" Twitter, 8 November 2015, 4:47 p.m., https://twitter.com/realdonaldtrump/status/663518286915702784 (24 Jan. 2018).

44. Trump, "@NBCNews is bad"; Trump, "Watched Saturday Night Live."

45. Trump, "Just tried watching"; Trump, "Watched Saturday Night Live."

46. Trump, "Just tried watching"; Trump, "I watched"; Trump, "Watched Saturday Night Live."

47. Trump, "A REAL scandal."

48. Peifer, "Palin, *Saturday Night Live*, and Framing," 158.

49. Seth Kelley, "President Trump Slams Arnold Schwarzenegger for Exiting *The Apprentice*: 'He Was Fired,'" *Variety*, 4 March 2017, http://variety.com/2017/biz/news/president-trump-arnold-schwarzenegger-apprentice-fired-1202002170 (24 Jan. 2018).

50. Jack Moore, "President Trump Bragged That His TV Ratings Are the Highest Since

September 11," *GQ*, 24 April 2017, http://www.gq.com/story/donald-trump-911-ratings (24 Jan. 2018).

51. Hill, "Developing a Normative Approach," 329.

52. Josef Adalien, "Late-Night Ratings: Stephen Colbert's Lead Over Jimmy Fallon Is Bigger Than Ever," *Vulture*, 16 April 2018, https://www.vulture.com/2018/04/late-night-ratings-early-2018-colbert-fallon.html (30 Nov. 2018).

The Oven That Cooked Up Pizzagate

4chan's Politically Incorrect *Board* and *Alt-Right Conspiracy Culture*[1]

JEFFREY J. HALL

On the afternoon of December 4, 2016, Edgar Maddison, armed with a rifle and a handgun, walked into Comet Ping Pong, a popular Washington, D.C., pizza restaurant. Maddison was there in response to Internet conspiracy theorists who believed the restaurant to be the center of a child sex trafficking ring involving prominent members of America's Democratic Party, including Hillary Clinton. Convinced he was conducting an investigation into the deviant activities taking place within the backrooms of Comet Ping Pong, Maddison was prepared for a violent confrontation with criminals. Instead, Maddison found himself inside a normal pizza restaurant. After forcing panicked customers and employees out of the restaurant, Maddison spent 20 minutes searching its premises, desperately trying to find hidden rooms and tunnels. Despite attempts to shoot his way through locked doors, Maddison found nothing. No one was hurt in the incident, but Maddison was arrested and convicted of felony assault.[2]

Maddison later claimed that he had "just wanted to do some good," and after discovering no children at the restaurant, he realized that "the intel on this wasn't 100 percent."[3] In fact, the "intel" was *fake news*—the Internet conspiracy theory about Comet Ping Pong's sex trafficking ring, known afterward as "Pizzagate," had been thoroughly and repeatedly debunked by mainstream news media after it had gained popularity through online social media in November 2016. These debunkings had little affect on Maddison, who believed that powerful forces were covering-up the truth about Pizzagate.

Like thousands of others, he placed more trust in information from alternative news sources on the Internet, such as conspiracy theory blogs and YouTube videos. Although he later apologized and admitted he was wrong, the Pizzagate theory survives. The incident was incorporated into the theory as a "false flag," meant to help demonize and discredit Pizzagate believers. As of the time this essay was submitted for publication in early 2019, there were still Pizzagate-related forum posts, blog posts, and YouTube videos being created daily. Websites such as http://pizzgate.wiki continue to add new "evidence" to a flourishing conspiracy theory.

The origins of Pizzagate can be traced back to posts on 4chan, one of the Internet's most popular bulletin boards. The posts were found on a subsection of the site—the *Politically Incorrect* bulletin board (also known as "/pol/"),[4] an online gathering place for thousands of supporters of Donald Trump's presidential campaign. Like almost all posts on 4chan, its authors were completely anonymous and will likely never be known. The initial post, created at in the early evening of November 2, 2016, contained only a few sentences claiming that a photo of children eating pizza discovered in a Clinton staffer's email attachment was proof that they were "shopping off" children to potential pedophiles.[5] Over the course several hours, other anonymous users replied to the initial post, concluding that emails related to pizza must have something to do with pedophilia. Searching through thousands of emails in a database released by Wikileaks, they conducted research to back up the initial claim. By the end of the day, several threads, composed of hundreds of replies, had been created. On November 3, an elaborate conspiracy theory had taken form, and discussion threads from that morning began to refer to the perceived cover-up as "Pizzagate." The Pizzagate conspiracy theory quickly spread to other social media platforms, reaching millions of people across Reddit, Twitter, YouTube and Facebook.

Pizzagate became one of the most infamous and bizarre examples of "fake news" stories that were said to have influenced voters during the 2016 election. Most journalistic and academic sources that have attempted to explain its emergence have generally credited 4chan as its source, but have only offered limited analysis of the cultural processes that led to its creation. As an anonymous bulletin board with a very odd structure,[6] 4chan is notoriously difficult for outsiders to understand.[7] In this essay, I offer my own insights, drawn from over one year of online ethnographic observation of 4chan's /pol/ board.[8] Through the course of my research, I witnessed the rise in popularity of Pizzagate. I argue that Pizzagate is a special kind of alternative truth/conspiracy theory—one that was created in a meme-like fashion through anonymous processes of trial-and-error that are part and parcel to 4chan's culture of meme creation. The anti–Clinton conspiracy theory of Pizzagate supported Donald Trump—a presidential candidate who embraced and encouraged conspiracy theorists. With the help of 4chan's large user base, the Pizzagate theory spread with rapid speed in the crucial final days leading up to the presidential election.

4chan's /pol/: Home of the Anonymous Alt-Right

Pizzagate began as one of the final volleys in a campaign of online activism carried out by 4chan's pro–Trump users in the year leading up to the 2016 presidential election. From the early days of the Republican primary campaign, 4chan's /pol/ board gravitated towards support for Trump. Gaining attention for the creation of memes; the spreading of news stories; and the organizing of online harassment of anti–Trump journalists, 4chan became known as a center for the so-called "Alt-Right" (alternative right), a "loosely organized far-right movement that shares a contempt for both liberal multiculturalism and mainstream conservativism: a belief that some people are inherently superior to others; a strong Internet presence and embrace of certain elements of online culture; and a self-presentation as being new, hip, and irreverent."[9]

4chan started in 2003 as a bulletin board that allowed users to post text and images anonymously. Although it initially focused on fandom of Japanese pop culture, it has expanded to appeal to a wide range of discussion topics, and recently reported traffic of over 20 million users each day.[10] As of June 2017, 4chan had over 66 topical discussion boards, with popular sections including Japanese animation, video games, firearms, sports, pornography, and the Random board.[11]

Among 4chan's many boards, /pol/ was the most active in late 2016.[12] The message at the top of the /pol/ board introduces it as a place "for the discussion of news, world events, political issues, and other related topics," but that is not an entirely accurate description. According to users of the site, 4chan's administrators created /pol/ in 2011 as a place to "quarantine" racist and offensive political discussion.[13] Until then the users of other boards had complained about racist and offensive posts, but due to a policy of preserving a certain degree of free expression, users with extreme viewpoints were directed to a new board, rather than having their views completely banned from the site. Instead of withering away in isolation, /pol/ gradually grew to become 4chan's most active board. Due to /pol/'s popularity and the supremacist ideology expressed in some of its posts, many of its users like to claim that the rest of 4chan's boards are the actual "quarantine" boards, and /pol/ is the true center of 4chan.

There are two features of 4chan that set it apart from other popular English language web forums: its anonymity and its ephemerality. Borrowing concepts from Japanese bulletin board culture, it allows users to post anonymously. While it does allow users the option to identify themselves via pseudonyms, this practice is discouraged and the vast majority of posts on the site are made under one name: "Anonymous" (shortened to "Anon" in user conversations). In contrast to social media sites that maintain a record of user postings, all content on 4chan is ephemeral in nature. As new discussion threads are posted, older and less active discussion threads are automatically deleted. Research on *Random* (/b/), which was traditionally 4chan's most active board, found that the majority of discussion threads had very short lifespans—averaging about six minutes each.[14] A few popular threads had lifespans of up to six hours, a long time on 4chan, but "near-instantaneous when compared to the forever-archived nature of most other websites."[15] My own observations of activity on /pol/ found similarly short lifespan for many threads. Although there are certain third-party websites that save and archive old 4chan posts, 4chan has no official archive. Users cannot browse threads that have been deleted. Under such constraints, it may seem unlikely that users could create a cohesive community. However, as Mannivan has observed, this community has been maintained through the efforts of active users who save and share images and texts created by other users:

> Within this discourse community, users who disseminate institutional memory and translate information into cultural capital are considered valuable. These users, like the rest of 4chan's population, are anonymous and fluctuating but were present at key moments in 4chan's history. To become a valuable user, Anons must maintain a consistent presence, peruse vast amounts of content, and develop a discerning eye for valuable cultural capital representative of 4chan's history, politics of duplicity, and implicit social rules. Where relevant information is lacking, 4channers must seek out paratextual evidence, link to other boards, or delve into their personal archives to make information institutionally significant.[16]

The more replies a thread receives, the longer it survives. Images and texts that are included in the first few posts of a popular thread have a greater chance of being seen, saved, and shared again by other users. If these texts or images go on to be reposted by many other users, they can become *memes*, or "contagious patterns of 'cultural information' that get passed from mind to mind and directly generate and shape the mindsets and significant forms of behavior and actions of a social group."[17] The popularity of memes helps them rise to the top of the sea of posts on 4chan, acting as a "locus of memory" that can overcome anonymity and ephemerality.[18] Or, to put it another way, memes "constantly return to act as the pillar of familiarity, standing against the stream of posts and responses."[19] Memes can undergo many transformations as users create and share their own alterations to the original meme. The most popular memes have countless variations, and 4chan users often maintain categorized folders that allow for the quick sharing of a certain type of meme.

4chan has become famous as a "meme factory" and many memes born on its boards have spread to other areas of the Internet. For example, LOL-Cats, a meme that combines images of cute cats with deliberately misspelled and grammatically incorrect English, first emerged on 4chan and spurned the creation of *I Can Has Cheezburger,*[20] a multi-million-dollar website devoted to the sharing of LOLCat images.[21] Another example are Advice Animals—which combined photos of certain animals with humorous personality traits.[22]

Memes are not limited, however to funny and cute images of animals; they can also be highly serious and even political. During the 2016 presidential campaign, /pol/ users referred to their activities as a "Meme War" against Hillary Clinton and her supporters. Through the creation and dissemination of pro–Trump memes, they believed themselves to be building support for Donald Trump and weakening the Clinton campaign. In addition, /pol/ users frequently wrote posts expressing a belief that the Clinton campaign was using paid operatives to engage in online memetic warfare against Donald Trump.

Within this context, 4chan became a factory for "weaponized memes." As a ruthlessly ephemeral board in which only the fittest memes survive for future dissemination, it would manufacture appealing political content capable of popularity on wider social media platforms. Like any other cultural product that emerged from 4chan, if one conceptualizes the Pizzagate conspiracy theory as a meme, it is easier to understand how it became so popular and how a platform like 4chan proved to be an influential source of Alt-Right "alternative facts."

Cooking Up Pizzagate

The users of 4chan's /pol/ board acted as an anonymous collective attempting to cook up the perfect conspiracy theory. These users had a wide variety of information at their disposal. In this case, /pol/ users drew upon a Wikileaks database of thousands emails, gained through cyberattacks on the Democratic National Committee's and former Clinton campaign chief John Podesta's email accounts. The initial post outlining a possible pedophile ring was a basic suggestion, drawing upon a single photo in one email attachment and pre-existing conspiracy theories that the Clintons had ties to sex trafficker Jeffrey Epstein. The photo, as some users replying to the initial posts pointed out, was an image of journalists Laura Ling and Euna Lee eating pizza with Lee's daughter after Bill Clinton had successfully arranged their release from a North Korean prison. However, one user who acknowledged the error summed up the mood in the thread by writing, "the pedo stuff still is out there."[23] Thus, despite having been born of a pizza photo that was easily proven to be unrelated to pedophile rings, 4chan's anonymous users continued to work on the premise that a Clinton-backed pedophile ring existed and proof of it was somewhere within the database of leaked emails. The fact that some of 4chan's own users had shown the pizza photo to be unrelated did not stop others from centering their investigative activities around other emails that mentioned pizza.

Through a process of trial and error, the anonymous authors worked together to flesh out the first Pizzagate claims, progressively creating an incredibly elaborate conspiracy theory involving Comet Ping Pong and other pizza restaurants. Every few hours, a discussion thread would become too long, prompting dedicated users to create a new thread on the same topic. Whenever this happened, the first post in the new discussion thread would summarize the latest version of the conspiracy theory. The older threads, along with the unpopular ideas that were not copied and reposted into the new threads would disappear. In this manner the Pizzagate theory developed like meme—there were countless variations of it created by countless anonymous users, but only those that gained the attention and appreciation of their peers would see their creations live on in new threads.

Because the process was entirely anonymous, no user risked embarrassment if he/she suggested a change that the other users found too ridiculous or unpalatable. If other anonymous users ignored or attacked a suggested addition to the Pizzagate theory, that addition's author did not suffer any reduction in his or her reputation. Future suggested additions by the same user in new discussion threads would appear as anonymous postings, with other 4chan users having no way of knowing who was making the suggestion. This meant that a user who repeatedly suggested radical and strange changes to the pizza theory could keep suggesting changes, and the other anonymous chefs would at least be willing to give the changes the same attention that they gave to other suggestions made by anonymous users. A user with enough dedication could repeatedly make the same suggestions in new threads, and, if lucky, an idea that had initially failed to gain acceptance could be incorporated into some accepted variations of the meme.

Outside of the anonymous corners of the Internet, the initial creation of a falsehood, rumor, or conspiracy theory generally requires that one or more individuals place their personal reputation on the line when making an extraordinary claim. The gathering of evidence to support a theory also takes a considerable amount of time, and in the case of a Pizzagate, which developed over a period of just a few days, required cooperation of many people who were willing to sift through archival data and find information supporting the initial claim. To reach a larger audience, publishing companies, radio show hosts, or other media outlets were necessary to spread that claim to a wider audience. Even if something started through rumors which could not be traced back to a single source, to quickly spread to a mass audience, it would need the approval of some media gatekeepers. Claims from completely anonymous sources would rarely be treated as credible under such circumstances.

However, Pizzagate was born in a very different way. As something that started and grew through completely anonymous 4chan posts, its many authors were engaging in a risk-free collective enterprise with essentially no rules. All participants were part of a community that valued anonymity, so claims from anonymous sources were the norm. A user could make any claim imaginable without the danger of being outed to people they knew in the offline world. Hundreds, or even thousands of anonymous 4chan users could mobilize behind the theory and use Reddit or Twitter pseudonyms to add to its proliferation. With the cloak of anonymity, they were largely safe from ever being held accountable for the consequences of their online actions.

As a meme, the Pizzagate conspiracy theory did not have any one single accepted version. 4chan posted many variations of the theory, but the most popular versions of Pizzagate tended to have some of the same ingredients. Through a complicated and convoluted stringing together of bits of information found in emails, pizza restaurant websites, and social media accounts, it became generally accepted among Pizzagate believers that Comet Ping Pong was a central part of the pedophile ring, containing secret rooms that housed child sex slaves, and that John Podesta and other people tied to the Clinton campaign used code words in their emails to refer to their victims. Examples include "pizza" referring to little girls, "pasta" referring to little boys, and "ice cream" as a code word for male prostitutes.[24] Seemingly innocent emails about food took on a new character as evidence of depraved sex crimes. Users also cited emails and social media posts about performance art shows to argue that the Pizzagate pedophile ring was practicing bizarre satanic rituals.[25]

The creation of the Pizzagate theory was complicated by the presence of numerous users who were likely more interested in creating a ridiculous conspiracy theory. They reveled in 4chan's culture of trolling, duplicity, and causing offense. For them, the more extreme that Pizzagate became, the more amusing it would be to unleash it on the general public. However, given the anonymous nature of their community, no one could be sure who was acting in good faith to make Pizzagate a credible theory. Some users undoubtedly contributed suggestions that were meant to swing Pizzagate towards the outlandishly implausible. As early as the first few Pizzagate discussion threads, one could find users who were apparently getting a sense of glee out of how strange the theory was becoming, such as one who wrote, "this is some solid tinfoil nuttery. Keep up the good work, boys!"[26] Users who questioned the value of Pizzagate and dismissed it as nonsense were almost always denounced as "shills" of the Clinton campaign, and users constantly reminded each other that Clinton's Internet operatives were in their midst, trying to throw them off the trial of the pedophile ring.[27] On an anonymous board, claims of shilling can be neither proven or disproven, yet the ability of users to draw upon the shared idea that shills were among them helped Pizzagate's anonymous creators gain a sense of solidarity against anyone who dared to question them.

Evan Malmgren has observed that the alt-right is a movement that is "really a product of an older Internet culture that revels in the political nihilism that online anonymity permits."[28] Noting that there were numerous political and ideological contradictions in online posts by members of alt-right Internet communities, Malmgren believes that some users were not motivated by any real political goals and were "simply amused at the fact that they are taken seriously at all."[29] My own experiences on /pol/ found this nihilism to be ever-present. Although Pizzagate discussion threads contained many posts from users who seemed clearly motivated by the desire to help expose a pedophile ring, there were many others who took joy in the fact that their outlandish posts were being taken seriously by people outside of 4chan. One user summed up such a feeling in a post the day after the December 2016 gunman incident at Comet Ping Pong, writing: "even if Pizzagate turns out to be complete bullshit, I take solace in knowing that 4chan managed to meme a guy into firing an automatic weapon in a pizza shop over satanic pedophiles and make national headlines because of it."[30] Many Pizzagate discussion threads often referred to participants as "larpers" or people who were "larping," suggesting that some users were treating Pizzagate as a form of live-action roleplaying—only pretending that they actually believed in the theories they were crafting.[31]

The Appeal of Pizzagate and Its Political Convenience

Whether or not those who crafted Pizzagate were true believers, the incident eventually had a special resonance with thousands of people. What made it so appealing? When 4chan users constructed a conspiracy theory involving bizarre occult rituals and sexual abuse, they were drawing upon themes that had long-existed within the fringes of American society.

Psychologist Jim Kline has argued that the Pizzagate theory draws upon powerful archetypal elements and societal taboos, noting that there are many historical examples of popular conspiracy theories involving a sinister elite engaging in anti-human acts such as ritual murder, rape, and perverse sexual acts.[32] Kline mentions specific conspiracy theories, such as the anti–Semitic "blood libel" theory involving ritual Jewish sacrifice of gentile children and the witch hunts of Colonial America, both of which have some similarities with Pizzagate.

It was especially apt to apply such theories to Hillary Clinton, as there were already several popular conspiracy theories involving the Clintons. Since Bill Clinton's Presidency, tabloid newspapers and conservative talk radio had speculated about the Clintons' involvement in a variety of sinister deeds, including sexual assault and murder.

The Pizzagate conspiracy theory was born before Kellyanne Conway's January 2017 statements in support of using "alternative facts," but it became popular during a political campaign by a man who has a history of endorsing conspiracy theories when convenient. During the early years of Barack Obama's presidency, Trump was one of the most prominent supporters of a conspiracy theory claiming that Obama had been born outside of the United States. During his campaign for the presidency, Donald Trump embraced these old Clinton conspiracy theories and the fringe that believed them, pledging to "lock up" Hillary Clinton for her crimes.[33] Trump also appeared on Alex Jones' Infowars program in late 2015, a media outlet that is known for advancing conspiracy theories that the 9/11 terror attacks and Sandy Hook school shooting were orchestrated by the U.S. government. Trump told viewers of the program that Jones had an "amazing" reputation and sought their support in his presidential race.[34]

Alex Jones' Infowars stands out as one of the few larger media outlets that actually devoted positive media coverage to the Pizzagate theory. As Pizzagate began to spread from 4chan to other online social media, Jones and other Infowars reporters devoted coverage to it as if it were a real news story, encouraging viewers to carry out their own investigations of Comet Pizza. It is unclear whether or not Edgar Maddison was one of Alex Jones' listeners, but after the shooting incident Jones began to distance himself from the theory, eventually apologizing to Comet Pizza's owners for his role in spreading a false narrative.[35]

For some believers in the other Clinton conspiracies espoused by talk radio hosts such as Alex Jones, it did not seem like a huge leap to believe that Pizzagate was real. While Donald Trump never endorsed the Pizzagate theory, and fired an aide who shared a pro–Pizzagate Twitter link,[36] the Trump campaign and Trump administration did not fully disassociate themselves with others who had supported the Pizzagate theory. Rather than distance itself from conspiracy theorists, the White House has gone as far as granting temporary press credentials to Infowars and citing an Infowars article in a press release about climate change protests.[37] A lawsuit filed in July 2017 claimed that the Trump administration successfully convinced conservative media outlets to provide coverage to a conspiracy theory alleging that the Democratic party and the Clintons may have been involved in the death of DNC staffer Seth Rich.[38] (The lawsuit was later dismissed, but the judge's ruling acknowledged that conservative media had helped perpetuate "a politically motivated story not having any basis in fact.")[39] Conspiracy theories have the potential to be a convenient distraction from unfavorable press coverage. Within the context of a campaign and a presidency that have encouraged trust of the alternative facts peddled by conspiracy theorists while discouraging trust of traditional media outlets, it is no surprise that some people were ready to accept Pizzagate's claims.

While the Pizzagate theory had wider cultural resonance, it needed people to make it known beyond the confines of 4chan. The 4chan community achieved this by mobilizing and spreading its message across the Internet. During my research, I observed almost daily attempts by 4chan users to collectively mobilize to either share a particular news story or to harass, or even threaten ideological enemies. Most users seemed to have one or more accounts under pseudonyms on social media sites such as Reddit, Twitter, Facebook and YouTube. It can be difficult to measure the influence of any given website, especially one that is populated almost exclusively by anonymous users making ephemeral posts. However, my observations of 4chan users claiming success in the spreading of Pizzagate and other news stories to outside social media platforms are supported by recent quantitative research on 4chan's influence. Using several months of data from 4chan, Reddit, and Twitter, Zannetou et al. suggests that alternative news dissemination begins on fringe web communities such as 4chan's /pol/ and Reddit's The_Donald.[40] Notably, one particular pattern emerged in their data about 4chan: whereas stories that spread from Twitter or Reddit tend to spread at a very rapid pace, "when a story becomes popular after a day or two, it is usually the case it was posted on 4chan first."[41] Another group of researchers used a database of over eight million /pol/ posts to prove the existence of "raids" in which 4chan users would flood the comment sections of selected YouTube videos with negative and hateful comments.[42] I observed such patterns during the creation of Pizzagate, which took a few days to spread from 4chan to the wider Internet and involved users "raiding" other social media to harass people they believed were part of the conspiracy or its cover-up.

Conclusion

Pizzagate stands as a powerful example of how 4chan's anonymous bulletin board culture can create and spread influential conspiracy theories. Its *Politically Incorrect* board, populated by thousands of users who believe variations of extreme right-wing ideology along with the nihilistic desire to create and revel in chaos, was able to collectively construct an elaborate "fake news" story and spread it to millions of Internet users. In addition to potentially influencing voters in the 2016 Presidential Election, the Pizzagate conspiracy theory prompted harassment of innocent restaurant owners, and could have caused a mass shooting. After the 2016 Presidential Election, many of 4chan's users celebrated Donald Trump's victory and continued to wage a "Meme War" against Trump's political opponents and the mainstream media.

In the two years following President Trump's inauguration, the Pizzagate conspiracy theory continued to thrive on social media. One variation of it, known as "Frazzledrip," alleged that "Hillary Clinton and her longtime aide Huma Abedin had sexually assaulted a girl and drank her blood."[43] Frazzledrip was often presented alongside the claims of QAnon, a pro–Trump conspiracy theory that, like Pizzagate, involved sensational claims of pedophilia rings and originated on 4chan's /pol/ board. The QAnon theory became so popular that its believers, sporting t-shirts and banners emblazoned with the letter "Q," became a noteworthy presence at President Trump's political rallies throughout 2018.[44]

My observations of the /pol/ community lead me to believe that in America's current social and political climate, in which the Trump administration has sought to actively promote the alternative facts of fringe media over that of traditional media outlets, it is not unreasonable to expect that conspiracy theories and political propaganda created by 4chan's anonymous meme-makers could continue to influence politics in the United States.

NOTES

1. This work was supported by JSPS KAKENHI Grant Number 10757420.

2. Merrit Kennedy, "'Pizzagate'Gunman Sentenced to 4 Years in Prison," *NPR*, 22 June 2017, www.npr.org/sections/thetwo-way/2017/06/22/533941689/pizzagate-gunman-sentenced-to-4-years-in-prison (30 June 2017).

3. Adam Goldman, "The Comet Ping Pong Gunman Answers Our Reporter's Questions," *The New York Times*, 7 December 2016, www.nytimes.com/2016/12/07/us/edgar-welch-comet-pizza-fake-news.html (13 June 2017).

4. It can be found at http://boards.4chan.org/pol/.

5. Anonymous, comment on "Thread No. 95752720: PODESTA IS A FUCKING PEDO," *4chan Politically Incorrect—/pol/* 6 November 2016, archive.4plebs.org/pol/thread/95752720 (1 June 2017).

6. 4chan boards are organized into anonymous discussion "threads" containing up to hundreds of anonymous "posts" in reply other anonymous posts within the thread. Recently active threads are most visible on the main page of each section of the site, but all threads disappear from the site within several hours of being posted.

7. It can be very difficult for an uninitiated observer to make sense of anonymous discussion threads in which conversations are built on a shared understanding of various memes, in-jokes, and a memory of previous postings that have long-since disappeared from the site. Hostility towards outsiders is a common feature of 4chan's culture, and new arrivals to the community are expected to spend several months to a year quietly observing board culture before posting.

8. This method of research is also known as "Netnography"—a form of non-participant observation of online culture. My research was conducted between December 2015 and January 2017, and involved daily observation of /pol/ threads during peak usage times. The research has also been supplemented by third-party archives of 4chan discussion threads.

9. Matthew Lyons, "An Antifascist Report on the Alternative Right," in *Ctrl-Alt-Delete* (Montreal: Kersplebedeb Publishing, 2017), 1.

10. David Reid, "Google Ups Its Social Media Game by Hiring 4Chan's Poole," *NBC News*, 8 March 2016, www.nbcnews.com/tech/tech-news/google-ups-its-social-media-game-hiring-4chan-s-poole-n533881 (10 June 2017).

11. The Random board is a forum in which users can post about topics that do not fall within the categories covered by other boards.

12. Anonymous, comment on "Thread No. 98416902," *4chan Politically Incorrect—/pol/* 14 November 2016, archive.4plebs.org/pol/thread/98416902 (10 June 2017).

13. Anonymous, comment on "Thread No. 348108: On Containment Boards," *4chan Discussion—/q/* 8 December 2012, 4chandata.org/q/On-containment-boards-a292226 (15 June 2017).

14. Michael S. Bernstein, Andrés Monroy-Hernández, Drew Harry, Paul André, Katrina Panovich and Greg Vargas, "4chan And/b: An Analysis of Anonymity and Ephemerality in a Large Online Community," in *Proceedings of the Fifth Annual International Conference on Weblogs and Social Media, Barcelona, Spain, 17–21 July 2011*, 51–58 (Menlo Park, CA: The AAAI Press, 2011).

15. Bernstein, Monroy-Hernández, Harry, André, Panovich and Greg Vargas, "4chan And/b."

16. Vyshali Manivannan, "Attaining the Ninth Square: Cybertextuality, Gamification, and Institutional Memory on 4chan," *Enculturation* 15 (November 2012): enculturation.camden.rutgers.edu/attaining-the-ninth-square.

17. Michele Knobel and Colin Lankshear, "Online Memes, Affinities, and Cultural Production," in *A New Literacies Sampler* (New York: Peter Lang, 2007), 199.

18. Gabriella Coleman, "Net Wars Over Free Speech, Freedom, and Secrecy or How to Understand the Hacker and Lulz Battle against the Church of Scientology" (lecture, the Next Hope, New York, 17 July 2010).

19. Lee Knuttila, "User Unknown: 4chan, Anonymity and Contingency," *First Monday* 16, no. 10 (3 October 2011): doi:10.5210/fm.v16i10.3665.

20. It can be found at http://icanhas.cheezburger.com/.

21. Jed R. Brubaker, "Wants Moar: Visual Media's Use of Text in LOLcats and Silent Film," *Gnovis Journal* 8, no. 2 (2008): www.gnovisjournal.org/2008/05/13/wants-moar-visual-medias-use-of-text-in-lolcats-and-silent-film/.

22. Marta Dynel, "'I Has Seen Image Macros!' Advice Animals Memes as Visual-Verbal Jokes," *International Journal of Communication* 10 (2016): ijoc.org/index.php/ijoc/article/view/4101/1556.

23. Anonymous, comment on "Thread No. 95752720: PODESTA IS A FUCKING PEDO," *4chan Politically Incorrect—/pol/* 6 November 2016, archive.4plebs.org/pol/thread/95752720 (1 June 2017).

24. Sean Adl-Tabatabai, "WikiLeaks: Pedophile 'Code Words' Found in Podesta Emails," *Your News Wire*, 1 December 2016, yournewswire.com/wikileaks-pedophile-code-words-podesta/ (17 July 2017).

25. Comment on "Thread No. 96390054: EWO," *4chan Politically Incorrect—/pol/* 6 November 2016, archive.4plebs.org/pol/thread/96390054 (15 June 2017).

26. Anonymous, comment on "Thread No. 95769324: PODESTA IS A FUCKING PEDO GENERAL: IT'S LITERALLY NOTHING GOYS EDITION," *4chan Politically Incorrect—/pol/* 3 November 2016, archive.4plebs.org/pol/thread/95769324 (9 June 2017).

27. Anonymous, comment on "Thread No. 98378974: EYES WIDE OPEN /EWO/ "FIGHT OFF THE SHILLS"EDITION," *4chan Politically Incorrect—/pol/* 14 November 2016, archive.4plebs.org/pol/thread/98378974 (7 June 2017).

28. Evan Malmgren, "Don't Feed the Trolls," *Dissent* 64, no. 2 (Spring 2017): 9–12.

29. Malmgren, "Don't Feed the Trolls," 9–12.

30. Anonymous, comment on "Thread No. 101715031: Eyes Wide Open /EWO/ True DeKEKtive Edition," *4chan Politically Incorrect—/pol/* 6 December 2016, archive.4plebs. org/pol/thread/101715031 (8 June 2017).

31. Anonymous, comment on "Thread No. 96791858: THEY ARE ALL CANNIBALS. PODESTA, DAVID BROCK, ETC EAT THE CHILDREN THEY RAPE," *4chan Politically Incorrect—/pol/* 8 November 2016, archive.4plebs.org/pol/thread/96791858/ (9 June 2017).

32. Jim Kline, "C. G. Jung and Norman Cohn Explain Pizzagate: The Archetypal Dimension of a Conspiracy Theory," *Psychological Perspectives* 60, no. 2 (2017): 186–195.

33. Eric Boehlert, "Embracing the 'Clinton Crazies,' Trump Becomes AM Talk Radio's Nominee for President," *Huffington Post*, 25 May 2016, www.huffingtonpost.com/eric-boehlert/embracing-the-clinton-cra_b_10129482.html (11 June 2017).

34. "Donald Trump Tells All on the Alex Jones Show," *Infowars*, 2 December 2015, www.infowars.com/donald-trump-tells-all-on-the-alex-jones-show/ (9 June 2017).

35. Paul Farhi, "Conspiracy Theorist Alex Jones Backs off 'Pizzagate' Claims," *The Washington Post*, 24 March 2017, www.washingtonpost.com/lifestyle/style/conspiracy-theorist-alex-jones-backs-off-pizzagate-claims/2017/03/24/6f0246fe-10cd-11e7-ab07-07d9f521f6b5_story.html.

36. BBC Staff Writer, "Trump Aide Michael Flynn Jnr Out After 'Pizzagate' Tweets," *BBC News*, 7 December 2016, www.bbc.com/news/world-us-canada-38231532 (1 Aug. 2017).

37. Josh Katzowitz, "Donald Trump Links Himself to InfoWars Once Again," *Daily Dot*, 15 June 2017, www.dailydot.com/layer8/donald-trump-infowars-link/ (1 Aug. 2017).

38. David Folkenflik, "Behind Fox News' Baseless Seth Rich Story: The Untold Tale," *NPR*, 1 August 2017, www.npr.org/2017/08/01/540783715/lawsuit-alleges-fox-news-and-trump-supporter-created-fake-news-story (1 Aug. 2017).

39. Alan Feuer, "Judge Dismisses Two Lawsuits Against Fox News Over Retracted Seth Rich Story," *The New York Times*, 2 August 2018, www.nytimes.com/2018/08/02/nyregion/seth-rich-fox-news-lawsuits.html (20 Dec. 2018).

40. Savvas Zannettou, Tristan Caulfield, Emiliano De Cristofaro, Nicolas Kourtellis, Ilias Leontiadis, Michael Sirivianos, Gianluca Stringhini, and Jeremy Blackburn, "The Web Centipede: Understanding How Web Communities Influence Each Other Through the Lens of Mainstream and Alternative News Sources," *ArXiv Preprint ArXiv:1705.06947*, 19 May 2017, https://arxiv.org/abs/1705.06947 (1 June 2017).

41. Savvas Zannettou, Tristan Caulfield, Emiliano De Cristofaro, Nicolas Kourtellis, Ilias Leontiadis, Michael Sirivianos, Gianluca Stringhini, and Jeremy Blackburn, "The Web Centipede" (1 June 2017).

42. Gabriel Emile Hine, Jeremiah Onaolapo, Emiliano De Cristofaro, Nicolas Kourtellis, Illias Leontiadis, Riginos Samaras, Gianluca Stringhini, and Jeremy Blackburn, "Kek, Cucks, and God Emperor Trump: A Measurement Study of 4chan's Politically Incorrect Forum and Its Effects on the Web," *Proceedings of the Eleventh International AAAI Conference on Web and Social Media (ICWSM 2017): Montreal, 15–18 May 2017*, aaai.org/ocs/index.php/ICWSM/ICWSM17/paper/download/15670/14790.

43. Craig Timberg, Elizabeth Dwoskin, Tony Romm and Andrew Ba Tran, "Two Years After #Pizzagate Showed the Dangers of Hateful Conspiracies, They're Still Rampant on YouTube," *The Washington Post*, 10 December 2018, www.washingtonpost.com/business/technology/hateful-conspiracies-thrive-on-youtube-despite-pledge-to-clean-up-problematic-videos/2018/12/10/625730a8-f3f8-11e8-9240-e8028a62c722_story.html (20 Dec. 2018)

44. Brandy Zadrozny and Ben Collins, "How Three Conspiracy Theorists Took 'Q' and Sparked Qanon," *NBC News*, 15 August 2018, www.nbcnews.com/tech/tech-news/how-three-conspiracy-theorists-took-q-sparked-qanon-n900531 (20 Dec. 2018).

From Mary Tyler Moore to Kellyanne Conway

Constructing a Synthetic Media Environment

TERRI TOLES PATKIN

Mary Tyler Moore created Kellyanne Conway. The notion seems ridiculous: Mary Tyler Moore was a determined young woman and talented actor who faced discrimination on multiple fronts; yet she persisted, and became a beloved cultural icon. How could she have been the genesis for Kellyanne Conway, who blandly looks into the cameras and doubles down on completely fictionalized alternative facts? And yet Moore's contribution to the television environment of the middle to late 20th century set the stage for the contemporary surreal political masquerade where style trumps substance, "reality" is followed by "show," and truthiness passes for news. There are three avenues by which Moore might have influenced Conway: the individual, the collective, and the institutional.

The route of individual influence is largely speculative. Did Conway, born in 1967, watch *The Mary Tyler Moore Show*? It's conceivable: the program's 168 episodes first began airing in 1970 and the show remained on the air until 1977, after which it went into syndication. It won 29 Emmy Awards, including outstanding comedy series consecutively from 1975 to 1977, and spin-offs of the program continued to air until 1980.[1] In an age when families sat down to view the limited selection of programming together, it's not implausible that her family watched the popular program on Saturday nights. Conway (née Fitzpatrick) was raised by four women—her mother, two aunts, and grandmother—following her parents' divorce when she was three; they may well have been drawn to the stories of strong women like Mary, Rhoda, and Phyllis on television. And as it turns out, Conway has acknowledged that she idolized Moore's character as a child,[2] admiring her composed and stylish presentation on her weekly program. Moore's big smile trumped her feminism and reporting skills for Conway, who dismisses the feminist movement as peripheral in her pantheon of values.[3] But to posit that Conway's performance as a media spokesperson mirrors or even was shaped by Moore's talents projects the argument onto untenable ground.

Rather, Moore's influence might more realistically be framed as part of the collective experience of Conway's generation as they consumed the popular culture offerings of the day, including Moore's show. Mary Tyler Moore (1936–2017) was certainly a role model in many ways during the 1960s and 1970s. Her television roles challenged gender stereotypes; her portrayal of housewife Laura Petrie on *The Dick Van Dyke Show* and especially her role as spunky television producer Mary Richards on *The Mary Tyler Moore Show* paved the way for women in the workplace in general, and women in media in particular. On camera, Moore often played the straight lines, allowing her male colleagues to be perceived as the funny ones, even when the success of the scene was due to her delivery. Her work legitimated the competent and powerful female, and in that way may have opened doors for a woman to serve as top advisor to the President. Moore's characters evolved in tandem with the nation's embrace of feminism; her struggles at home and in the workplace resonated with an audience facing similar dilemmas.[4]

Conway's generation grew up in an era where there were a handful of television channels available and core elements of popular culture were widely shared. Collectively, the audience responded to what was on offer, and Moore's program, like many others of the time, addressed rapidly-changing social mores in their plot lines. A full third of the writers on the show were women,[5] an unprecedented number, and their portrayal of Mary as a single, working woman both mirrored and shaped social change. Even the theme song changed, reflecting the character's increasing self-assurance and independence, the lyric evolving from "how will you make it on your own" to the hopeful "you might just make it after all" to the still more confident "you're gonna make it after all."[6]

But even if Kellyanne Conway personally never watched these specific television programs, their influence on the television business was significant. The behind-the-scenes institutional framework constructed by Moore's efforts, among others, facilitated the contemporary media environment so amenable to alternative facts, and this is where the true line of influence may be discovered. Indeed, as the success of the *Mary Tyler Moore Show* increased, appearing as a guest star on the program became something of a status symbol in Hollywood. Moore and her husband Grant Tinker used the show's popularity to spin off a family of sitcoms via their MTM Corporation, which became one of the most powerful corporations in the television business. Indeed, MTM dominated the airwaves for a number of years, producing over 45 dramas and sitcoms, ranging from *WKRP in Cincinnati* and *The Bob Newhart Show* to *Hill Street Blues*, *St. Elsewhere*, and *Remington Steele*,[7] to name just a few. Over the years, MTM launched many shows, mostly successful, using the same formula: a central character backed by a zany cast of supporting actors located in a specific geographic place (New York, Vermont, or Minneapolis, as opposed to the ambiguous suburban locale of most other sitcoms of the day) tackled a variety of everyday problems with wit and fundamental decency.[8] MTM's shows and their counterparts blanketed the airwaves. Every night, a nation divided by Vietnam, Watergate, and social change came together to consume the offerings of the three major networks (ABC, CBS, NBC) that formed the oligarchy of prime-time broadcasting. Through the lens of television programming, Americans learned the lessons of shared community and shared history.

Although Moore's role in the company was largely symbolic, she was the face of the company, and it was her company that shaped the half-century of television programming which ultimately constructed an environment that nurtured the era of reality television, 24/7 news cycles, and alternative facts. Conway came of age as that media environment reached its peak. Even if her family didn't even own a television set, young Kellyanne Fitzpatrick would still have been exposed to the media environment that Moore and Tinker created through her friends, school, church, and community. Television was part of American culture, part of history, part of the stories people told. Conway's childhood as audience member positioned her well to move to the other side of the camera as an adult, and today, the former beauty pageant winner, pollster, and the first female campaign manager for a Presidential campaign continues to serve in an ambiguously-defined role as a top advisor to President Trump.[9] Conway's framing of the notion of alternative facts in the political arena simultaneously privileges specific narratives within the Trump worldview and contextualizes political discourse in the framework of a media environment that has become even more formidable since the days when Mary Tyler Moore ruled the airwaves.

Just three days before Moore's death, Kellyanne Conway introduced the concept of alternative facts into the popular lexicon during her appearance on NBC's *Meet the Press*. Defending President Trump's generous assessment of crowd size during the inauguration, she stated, "You're saying it's a falsehood. And they're giving—Sean Spicer, our press secretary—gave alternative facts."[10]

But the media environment that nurtured the growth of alternative facts was being cultivated for well over a generation before Kellyanne Conway popularized the term. Rose K. Goldsen's critical evaluation of what she called the Consciousness Industry identified the systemic effects of television technology on the psychological and sociological underpinnings of American—eventually global—culture in the late-middle 20th century.[11] Television distilled an increasingly complex world into neat half-hour segments punctuated by commercials and problems resolved by the time the credits rolled. Television came to join "[l]iterature and art, drama and music, song and story, ballads and rhymes and chants, tales and play and games, myth and history"[12] in our struggle to balance authentic texts that help us understand the human condition with inauthentic ones that "muddle thought, drop a veil between us and our fellow human beings, disguise our own social realities."[13] It created first its own alternate reality, and then constructed a hybrid world of so-called reality television.

Clearly, Mr. Trump's background in reality television has shaped his approach to politics, particularly his stint hosting *The Apprentice*.[14] He teases upcoming appearances and events. He conflates the quotidian—a particularly delicious piece of chocolate cake—with the extraordinary—launching a deadly missile strike in Syria.[15] And we, the audience, have been conditioned to enjoy the contrived challenges, the elimination rituals, the false sense of community shared through vicarious experience. Chanting "lock her up" together erects a wall around our own beliefs. It helps us reconstruct a feeling of community (Gemeinschaft) while continuing to enjoy the anonymity of urban society (Gesellschaft). We create, in short, a pseudo-Gemeinschaft which looks superficially like community but whose roots do not go as deep.[16] Just as one program represents only the tip of the iceberg of the reality show mindset, so too does Moore's influence on Conway personify the development of the media industry over the past decades.

Mediated entertainment shapes identity, both that of participant and of audience member. At its most basic level, identity tells us who we are and where we are placed in time and space. Identity is fluid, constantly being balanced between cultural production and consumption, continually being regulated and changing. Its symbolic marking simultaneously denotes difference and emphasizes shared characteristics.[17] The narrative develops day after day: James Comey morphs from hero to villain to victim to hero again depending on the needs of the narrative and the narrator as the audience sits back to watch events unfold with increased passivity. "Lordy, [we] hope there are tapes,"[18] because that means the show will return for a second season. Ratings rule the day.

Optics stand in for authenticity; negative content is dismissed as phony. Digital media have accelerated the effect of the electronic media on news, shifting control of the narrative from news-makers (politicians) to news-traders (media personalities). The constant stream of nearly real-time data creates a situation in which political figures, rather than selecting the information to be released to the public, now primarily are in the business of shaping and spinning information already in the public eye. The transformation of data (facts) into information (news) opens the door to accusations of "fake news" when the interpretation of the facts doesn't fit the worldview of a powerful actor.

The delicate balance of appearing open and transparent while simultaneously attempting to control information flow has marked political life for the past generation.[19] This is not a new rhetorical strategy for Mr. Trump. In 1989, he purchased a full-page advertisement in *The* (apparently not-yet-failing) *New York Times* calling for increased law enforcement and stronger penalties for crime following the attack on the Central Park jogger, a move identified as part of his attempt to rebrand himself as a civic hero with political aspirations rather than simply a celebrity.[20] The growing dependence of the media on pseudo-events, where the camera focuses our attention on a preferred narrative, concentrates power in the hands of those who create such events.[21] Conway dismisses the evidence of words and images captured on tape, arguing that the audience is inappropriately focused on objective data instead of truly understanding the lovable curmudgeon hidden beneath the surface. During an appearance on MSNBC, she lamented, "Why is everything taken at face value? You can't give him the benefit of the doubt on this and he's telling you what was in his heart, you always want to go with what's come out of his mouth rather than look at what's in his heart."[22]

Almost every family has that one quirky relative, the one without a filter, who makes inappropriate jokes at the holiday dinner or whose stories are just plain embarrassing. President Trump fills that role on a national scale; say what you will about him, he's not boring. A sort of "television uncle," he fits himself into our daily routines. Early critics of television identified the set itself as a presence in the household, a family member that demands attention and joins the family as it goes about the activities of the day. "Like any other new family member, it alters traffic patterns, changes the rhythms of the day, the very atmosphere of the homes it enters, introducing its own views of the world, its own interpretations of reality, its own images and symbolic forms."[23] Television's bias is toward the affective and emotional over the cognitive and reasoned; fact-checking isn't nearly as captivating as watching the drama unfold on live TV. And the set is now joined by a panoply of digital platforms such as Twitter that direct our attention towards specific narratives, and perhaps more significant, away from other ones. Talking points poll well, and the narrative of terror provides a time-honored vessel for influence. Conway's attempts to combine that predisposition with the administration's emerging anti-media narrative, however, can stray well beyond the realm of alternative facts. In an interview with Chris Matthews, she refers to a fictitious terror plot as she attempts to simultaneously support Trump's proposed travel ban and challenge the objectivity of media reporting. "Two Iraqis came here to this country, were radicalized and they were the masterminds behind the Bowling Green massacre…. It didn't get covered."[24]

Had the Bowling Green Massacre actually occurred, it would have been easy to cover, because it would have fallen neatly into the storytelling packaging favored by television. Historically, television was constrained by the technical limitations of videography: small screens and over-the-air distribution contributed to the construction of images that did not allow for the subtleties of film. Half-hour or one-hour program formats broken up by commercials every few minutes limited the complexity of the plot. Programs featured easy-to-understand black-and-white dichotomies, good guys and bad guys. Cowboys and (what were then called) Indians. Cops and robbers. Doctors and diseases.

The predicable formula of crime shows blanketing the country every night featured "wrongs … righted, victims avenged, and victimizers awarded their just desserts."[25] There was a comfort in the routine; everyone knew what to expect. That the good guys were mainly older white males and the victims were women or people of color, elderly or poor or otherwise marginalized only began to raise eyebrows as that narrative began to be questioned by the civil rights and feminist movements of the 1960s and 1970s. But even as the demographic composition of television's fictional victims slowly began to change, the underlying theme remained constant. "Against the ever-present danger that continually threatens ever-beleaguered victims, stand the forces of the State. 'The State is your Protector, America,' is the implicit subtitle."[26]

That predisposition suits the so-called war on terror well. Terrorists are Bad Guys, and even if all citizens of certain countries aren't terrorists, the Good Guys need to watch out for them. Immigrants may come to America and somehow become radicalized right under our noses, unless there's a sheriff in town who is on the lookout, ready with a travel ban and a wall to protect the country. The spy and police dramas so popular on television fabricated a cultural understanding that, first, there are evil people out there, enemies of the state, and second, they are so clever that we must fabricate complex and intricate means to defeat them.[27] "Our mission, should we choose to accept it," is the legitimation of the media worldview through our passive acceptance of the narrative. Reinforcing this predisposition through a generation of entertainment programming set the stage for our acceptance of a parallel narrative in news programming. The trinity of victim, victimizer, and protector became so standardized and predictable a story line that it reduced the intensity of our response via imaginal desensitization; we discern no need for serious concern when the same narrative takes over the news.[28]

But the primary function of the television media environment was and is marketing. Ultimately, the audience is the product, not the consumer, of television. The entertainment business is simply a means of delivering viewers to advertisers; selling attention, selling products, selling ideas. We don't like to admit this, pretending that commercials stand outside the rest of the show, identified by noticeable breaks. "Now the whole show becomes a commercial for itself, its stars, even its own props. It's the spectacle of the pitchman working the most glamorous midway of all times, coast to coast and worldwide."[29] And that ethos has now spread to the White House, where it's no alternative fact to note that Trump brands and Trump properties form an ever-present back beat to the business of politics.[30] Conway understands that.

She even made an ill-considered attempt to use her platform as White House spokesperson to promote the family's products as the *Fox & Friends* hosts looked on in astonishment. "Go buy Ivanka's stuff is what I would say.... I'm going to give a free commercial here: Go buy it today, everybody; you can find it online."[31] In addition to the ethical breach, Conway's statement punctures the media industry's own alternative fact, the myth that the media exists for the benefit of the audience, not vice versa. Not only are television shows structured to hold attention until the commercial comes along—using editing, video, and story techniques to build attention to a climax just before cutting to the commercial—but they condition the audience to expect—even demand—more of the same. Entertainment programming is deliberately produced to avoid offending the audience or creating strong emotional responses, in order to avoid hampering the response to the commercial message. Indeed, television programming presents a generally business-supportive image, avoiding any content that might counteract the message of the advertisers.[32]

In the days before the remote control, we learned to watch with divided attention, paying more conscious attention to the program and diminishing our attention during the ads. It is an emotional roller coaster, and our imaginations are safely strapped in for the ride.

Television programs face a continuing dilemma. To hold an audience, they must evoke human feelings, stir human emotions, engage human passions. Yet as soon as viewers find their intellectual curiosity awakened, as soon as they allow themselves to be gripped by fear or anxiety, love or hate, terror or revulsion or rage, as soon as they are on the way to being overcome by laughter or engulfed by tears, the program delivers them to the commercials. Reactions that have been engaged are disengaged. Under an avalanche of repetition and a constant barrage of interruptions, emotions the programs might have called into being simply have no chance to develop.[33]

Psychologists call this use of divided attention reciprocal inhibition. A form of conditioning, it is often utilized in clinical settings as a way to desensitize people and relieve agitation about certain stimuli (e.g. fear of flying or of large dogs) by using electric shock or images to build positive or negative associations. This behavior modification process, called imaginal desensitization, extinguishes emotional response and allows the person to remain relaxed as he encounters anxiety-provoking stimuli in real life. And the broadcasters soon learned that the familiar dramatic formulas of ritualized violence and sexual imagery needed to become increasingly explicit over time in order to hold the audience's attention. Our emotional ties reattach to new, alternative images.[34] We eagerly await the next tweet, the next pronouncement, the next meme, the next comedic parody.

We are so focused on the content of the media that we have missed the fundamental point that the television environment—now a wider media environment—shapes not only what we communicate and the ways in which we communicate it, but the very foundation of how we perceive the world that we are communicating about. The narcotization of the audience via popular culture, desensitization and information overload, and the false transparency of the surveillance society have led to the co-mingling of medium and message; we have become characters in our own cultural drama. As Conway points to the power of the "Internet of things," she fails to take into account that she represents the very institution whose potential surveillance of the audience causes concern, explaining, "There was an article this week that talked about how you can surveil someone through their phones, certainly through their television sets, any number of different ways. And microwaves that turn into cameras, et cetera. So we know that that is just a fact of modern life."[35]

Even without a nosy microwave, the reality of the always-on all-encompassing media environment encourages not just surveillance but taking the results out of context. The triumph of imagery, dating back at least to the Daisy Girl commercial in 1964 or the Nixon-Kennedy debates in 1960, has become miles more sophisticated in today's unrelenting media environment. There is no privacy any more, and some of that is at our own hand. As Conway knelt on a sofa in the Oval Office, knees separated, busily using her cell phone during a meeting with leaders of historically black colleges and universities, the Internet discovered etiquette.[36] Despite evidence that she was taking a photo of the group, her apparently casual approach invited criticism; the surveillor became the surveilled. As the figurehead for the Trump brand—in some ways paralleling Moore's function at MTM—she becomes both purveyor and quarry of the media environment she was instrumental in creating.

That environment is constructed through cinematic techniques used across media platforms to tell stories, and these have the side effect of shaping audience perception. These methods construct a comfortable and familiar synthetic experience through the continual use of editing techniques including altered speeds of movement, either slow or fast motion; reenactments of the same action (instant replay); instantaneous cutting from one scene to another; excerpting fragments of events; juxtaposing events widely separated by time or space; shifting points of view, via moving cameras, zoom lenses, or multiple cameras; combined sight from one source and sound from another (e.g., background music, sound effects, dubbed dialogue); merging, altering, or distorting visual images, particularly through computer graphics techniques and multiple-exposure processing; manufacturing "events" through animation or computer graphics.[37]

As audience members, we have come to expect these techniques as a routine part of effective visual storytelling, which makes them transparent to us. Synthetic experience is fundamentally different from real experience, yet synthetic experience has become increasingly the mode by which both real and synthetic events are presented to media audiences. Alternative facts rely on the plasticity of the synthetic world rather than the rigidity of shared primary interaction; we are asked to privilege the vision of the camera lens above that of our own eyes.

At the same time, the magic of contemporary media is that the audience feels as if we are hidden in Goffman's backstage region, privy to the secret lives of celebrities and politicians.[38] Media create a false sense of intimacy by turning public and private inside out, integrating the real with the synthetic, offering us vicarious intimacy in an increasingly isolated world.[39] We hyper-analyze Melania's hand swats and the Pope's facial expressions, we revel in details that compare Obama's nightly snack of seven almonds[40] with Trump's double scoop of ice cream for dessert,[41] we speculate on what could have caused a word like "covfefe" to be released into the twittersphere. Because it forms a dialogic connection between the interpersonal and the mass, between the narrative of the individual and that of the social order, media technology permits us to create parasocial relationships with media characters. Meyrowitz identifies the process by which television separated social place from physical place, blurring boundaries across demographic categories (childhood and adulthood, masculine and feminine), status (high and low), and personal domains (public and private).[42] The intimacy of the television lens penetrates what used to be intimate space, and unmasks the politician's carefully-constructed media image, revealing formerly private backstage behaviors and interactions. The distinction between public and private has eroded to the point where a hesitation of even a few seconds takes on monumental significance. Media capture the idiosyncratic particulars of the President's behavior and preserve them for future generations; our leaders must constantly be "on," projecting an image. Their spokespeople struggle to keep up; some alternative facts may be released into the atmosphere simply as by-products of the fast-paced demands of the news cycle. If a fact looks real and sounds real, perhaps it can pass as real?

Boorstin identified the characteristics of the pseudo-event: it is a planned occurrence, established primarily for the purpose of being recorded, with an ambiguous relationship to the underlying reality of the situation. The proportion of pseudo-events masquerading as news has increased exponentially since Boorstin's coining of the term, due in no small part to the dominance of the visual media.[43] The construction of synthetic images relies on the believability of the representation; it is not truth that matters, but rather credibility. Looking directly into the camera and sincerely making comments is interpreted as authentic. We respond to emotion as divorced from logic as Trump is from Marla Maples. It feels sincere to the speaker; it feels sincere to the audience. Maybe this is why no one seems to care when contradictory video or tweets from the past are unearthed by eager journalists or comedians. That was a different "season"; what matters most is the present. Conway clearly delineates ethical accountability from legal jurisdiction; objectivity falls outside her job description, as she states, "I'm not Inspector Gadget. I don't believe people are using their microwaves to spy on the Trump campaign. However, I'm not in the job of having evidence. That's what investigations are for."[44]

Indeed, "having evidence" appears to be of little concern in a Trumpian world. The size of crowds, hands, or election results all depends on the emotional response of a president rather than some objective measurement. And when one deals in emotion, fact-checking takes a back seat. Sean Spicer can get so carried away with the anti–Syria narrative that he can totally reconstruct history. Frederick Douglass is still alive. Ever heard of Susan B Anthony? No Jews mentioned on Holocaust Remembrance Day.[45]

These narratives don't cause meaningful outrage because they are situated in a medium that operates in the present tense. Democracy requires the overlay of both the past and future on the present. We are increasingly governed by way of mass media, making the populace governable through the acceptance of ideas and symbols in the pathways of imagination.[46] "If a demagogue can take over the mass media, he can use the techniques of mass persuasion like those allegedly now employed by media advertisers to persuade individuals to accept dictatorship."[47] It does not require Big Brother. Indeed, we surveil ourselves through social media: Facebook posts, Instagram photos of our meals, our Twitter addictions. Reality has become interpreted through mediation; the phrase "photos or it didn't happen" is the motto of an era where an event doesn't truly matter if no photographs were uploaded onto social media. And besides, one can delete a post if a better alternative version comes along later. Fake news leads to fake reality, or as Conway puts it, "You can turn on the TV and people literally say things that just aren't true."[48]

Apparently unaware of the irony, Conway's astonishment at the elasticity of truth cuts to the heart of the matter. Truth, objective and shared, becomes truths, subjective and multiple. Whichever alternative truth resonates best on camera becomes the preferred narrative. "The power to dominate a culture's symbol-producing apparatus is the power to create the ambience that forms consciousness itself. It is a power we see exercised daily by the television business as it penetrates virtually every home with the most massive continuing spectacle human history has ever known."[49]

That power relies on the difference between a denotative photograph, one that indexes consensual reality, and a connotative one, which contains symbolic, generalized, and universal meanings extending well beyond the specific image recorded. Objective and documentary photos, which Zelizer refers to as *as is* photographs, contrast with *as if* ones, which are contingent or imaginative.[50] Trumpworld is filled with *as if* moments. As an experienced showman, Trump is well-known for saying or implying things with little or no documentation of fact. From Muslims celebrating on rooftops in New Jersey after September 11 to Ted Cruz's father having ties to the Kennedy assassination to rising inner city crime rates to a 42 percent unemployment rate, his casual approach to fact-checking is well documented. And that's not counting his tendency to exaggerate, especially about his opponents.[51] The distinction between representation and reality is reduced in today's media-intense postmodern world, where audience awareness of both the media's simulation and their own consumption of signification conflates the phony and the real. News/documentation is set in opposition to art/expression, and in a post-truth era, we have come to trust the authenticity of images less and less. As Baudrillard proposed, the copy becomes just as real as the original, a process hastened by the widespread use of technologies of reproduction.[52] We rely increasingly on what Stephen Colbert has called truthiness, that evoked subjective feeling of authenticity that exists regardless of accuracy.[53]

The quest for genuineness within the realm of digital iconography intersects with cultural memory. By photographing something, we symbolically take possession of the thing being photographed, in much the same way that some tribespeople once interpreted photography as imprisoning the soul.[54] Communication of meaning through published images constructs a relationship among three participants: subject, photographer, and audience, all the more so when the image (as opposed to the word) becomes charged with historical significance when placed in presidential context.[55] As Barthes notes, the photographic reference is the undeniably tangible thing placed before the lens; it unequivocally states *what has been,* but the digital media environment invites us to explore the alternatives of *what might have been* and *what could be* as co-equal truths that shape memory.[56]

Our memories of public events, especially emotionally-charged or significant ones (e.g., the September 11 attacks) are long-lasting and consistent, and they are formed from a montage of images from our own experiences and from the media. The placement of images in constructing collective memory intertwines individual affective memory with cultural cognitive memory in a kaleidoscopic retelling that layers subjective meanings onto the ground of consensual reality to form the social imagination. The personal intersects with the public, both cognitively and affectively.[57] This cognitive ground has shaped consciousness in ways that will sound strangely familiar to those familiar with Donald Trump's political career. Funkhouser and Shaw[58] identify five tendencies linked to the prevalence of synthetic experience:

- low tolerance for boredom or inactivity;
- heightened expectations of perfection and of high-level performance;
- expectations of quick, effective, neat resolution of problems;
- misperceptions of certain classes of physical and social events; and
- limited contact with, and a superficial view of, one's own inhabited environment.

The media, especially television, have created a 24/7 communication environment that shapes our cultural disposition toward unreality. Donald J. Trump is the embodiment of that environment. Whether it is the blurring distinction between the real and the constructed image, or the deliberated denial and distortion of reality, this pseudo-reality delivers an oversimplified simulation that emphasizes entertainment over information. "The fundamental purpose of all forms of unreality is to provide an illusion of control. If men cannot control the realities with which they are faced, then they will invent unrealities over which they can maintain the illusion of control."[59] Once one enters the realm of illusion, alternative facts are the only ones that matter. Truth becomes intersubjective and fungible, a strategic weapon in the service of hegemony, even as Conway insists, "We have a very high respect for the truth."[60]

The media environment has complicated the distinction between public and private, and created additional variations on those categories, where media coverage carries events beyond a particular frame in space and time, making them accessible to a global audience.[61] The result is that we tend to conflate events in the real world with mediated events; we have a "critical human tendency to confuse what is real with what only *seems* to be real,"[62] leading to tagging anything that doesn't fit neatly as fake news.

Truth is defined on the fly, and the difference between actor and action is blurred. Trump's tweets are clearly "presidential," argues Conway, because after all, he's the president.[63] The effect is augmented the more technologies that are included. The assault on truth appears to be moving from the verbal to the physical these days, as reporters are arrested and assaulted for simply doing their jobs.[64] It is easy to attribute these actions to recent rhetoric about fake news and alternative facts, and certainly that atmosphere hasn't been helpful. But focusing on the optics of what's on the screen is like being pick-pocketed while you watch a street magician play the shell game. We're so focused on where we think the problem is that we're missing the big con, which is that for two generations now as a society we have allowed the construction of a media environment that shapes our consciousness and our culture. Like one of those "choose your own adventure" books where the reader can select from a variety of plot lines and endings, today's media environment constructs a wonderland of choices that expand our imagination. "Media" lives in the present tense, focused on the scoop, the news cycle, the viral video, the hashtag. "The press" connects the present to past and future; it provides context and collective memory. Assaults on the media—and media people—represent more than just an attempt to control the narrative; they mark the success of the consciousness industry in shaping our social reality.

Mary Tyler Moore's influence on Kellyanne Conway can certainly be distinguished on an individual level in Conway's confident on-air demeanor, and her fierce loyalty to her boss. In person, she is apparently as likeable as the fictional Mary Richards, charming and funny and social.[65] Whether Conway is speaking to an audience of one, as some have proposed, or to a global village, she can turn the world on with her smile. But even more influential has been the influence of the media environment constructed by Moore and others on a cultural level, which through both content and structure, created a virtual world that facilitated the rise of Donald J. Trump as reality show president and his loyal, if sometimes misguided, sidekick, and her basket of alternative facts. Whether the on-camera talking head is Kellyanne Conway or Sean Spicer or Sarah Huckabee Sanders, they're following a script that's been written over a generation of television history. The constructed synthetic reality that Moore and MTM deliberately created in the pursuit of profit over the course of a generation cultivated a media environment that extends well beyond a single program or even a single medium; it set the stage for an era where fake news and alternative facts thrive. Moore made it possible not just for Kellyanne Conway to "make it after all" but also to construct an approach to the truth that is as flexible as the digital environment, to "make it up after all." As sociologist Rose K. Goldsen warned, "It is still possible to turn off the television set. It is no longer possible to turn off the television environment."[66]

Notes

1. "Mary Tyler Moore," Internet Movie Database, http://www.imdb.com/title/tt0065314/ (10 Jan. 2018).

2. Olivia Nuzzi, "Kellyanne Conway Is a Star," *New York Magazine*, March 18, 2017, http://nymag.com/daily/intelligencer/2017/03/kellyanne-conway-trumps-first-lady.html (10 Jan. 2018).

3. Nuzzi, "Kellyanne Conway Is a Star."

4. Jason Bonderoff, *Mary Tyler Moore* (New York: St. Martin's Press, 1986).

5. Reese, Hope, "The Real Feminist Impact of *The Mary Tyler Moore Show* Was Behind the Scenes," *The Atlantic*, May 16, 2013.

6. Randall Roberts, "The Story of How 'Love Is All Around' Became the Theme to 'The Mary Tyler Moore Show,'" *Los Angeles Times*, January 26, 2017, http://beta.latimes.com/entertainment/music/la-et-ms-mary-tyler-moore-sonny-curtis-theme-20170126-story.html (15 Jan. 2018).

7. Mary Tyler Moore, *After All* (New York: G.P. Putnam's Sons, 1995).

8. Bonderoff, *Mary Tyler Moore.*

9. "Kellyanne Conway Biography," Biography.com, February 24, 2017, http://www.biography.com/people/kellyanne-conway-022217 (10 Jan. 2018).

10. Eric Bradner, "Conway: Trump White House Offered 'Alternative Facts' on Crowd Size," *CNN*, January 22, 2017, http://www.cnn.com/2017/01/22/politics/kellyanne-conway-alternative-facts/_(10 Jan. 2018).

11. Rose K. Goldsen, *The Show and Tell Machine: How Television Works and Works You Over* (New York: Dial Press, 1977).

12. Goldsen, *The Show and Tell Machine*, 280.

13. Goldsen, *The Show and Tell Machine*, 280.

14. "The Apprentice," Internet Movie Database, http://www.imdb.com/title/tt0364782/ (10 Jan. 2018).

15. Dan Merica, "Trump, Xi Talked Syria Strike Over 'Beautiful' Chocolate Cake," *CNN*, April 12, 2017, http://www.cnn.com/2017/04/12/politics/donald-trump-xi-jingping-syria-chocolate-cake/(10 Jan. 2018).

16. Ferdinand Tonnies, *Community and Association* (London: Routledge and Kegan Paul, 1955).

17. Kathryn Woodward, *Concepts of Identity and Difference* (London: Sage, 1997).

18. Andrew Rosenthal, "'Lordy, I Hope There Are Tapes,'" *The New York Times*, June 8, 2017, https://www.nytimes.com/2017/06/08/opinion/lordy-i-hope-there-are-tapes.html (10 Jan. 2018).

19. Joshua Meyrowitz, *No Sense of Place: The Impact of Electronic Media on Social Behavior* (Oxford: Oxford University Press, 1985).

20. Brenda Cooper, David Descutner, and Sandra Alspach, "From Celebrity Entrepreneur to Civic Hero: Donald Trump's Campaign of Self-Transformation," in *American Heroes in a Media Age*, ed. Susan J. Drucker and Robert S. Cathcart (Cresskill, NJ: Hampton Press, 1994), 188–202.

21. Erik Barnouw, *The Sponsor: Notes on a Modern Potentate* (Oxford: Oxford University Press, 1978).

22. Benen, Steve. "Conway: Look at Trump's Heart, Not What's Come Out of His Mouth." *MSNBC.* January 9, 2017, http://www.msnbc.com/rachel-maddow-show/conway-look-trumps-heart-not-whats-come-out-his-mouth (10 Jan. 2018).

23. Goldsen, *The Show and Tell Machine*, 2.

24. MSNBC, *Hardball with Chris Matthews.* MSNBC video, 05:41, February 2, 2017, http://www.msnbc.com/hardball/watch/matthews-pushes-conway-on-use-of-executive-power-868952643695 (10 Jan. 2018).

25. Goldsen, *The Show and Tell Machine*, 233.

26. Goldsen, *The Show and Tell Machine*, 233.

27. Barnouw, *The Sponsor.*

28. Goldsen, *The Show and Tell Machine.*

29. Goldsen, *The Show and Tell Machine*, 266.

30. Karen Yourish and Troy Griggs, "Tracking the President's Visits to Trump Properties," *The New York Times*, June 25, 2017, https://www.nytimes.com/interactive/2017/04/05/us/politics/tracking-trumps-visits-to-his-branded-properties.html (10 Jan. 2018).

31. Richard Perez-Pena and Rachel Abrams, "Kellyanne Conway Promotes Ivanka Trump Brand, Raising Ethics Concerns," *The New York Times*, February 9, 2017, https://www.nytimes.com/2017/02/09/us/politics/kellyanne-conway-ivanka-trump-ethics.html?_r=0_(10 Jan. 2018).

32. Barnouw, *The Sponsor.*

33. Goldsen, *The Show and Tell Machine*, 7–8.

34. Goldsen, *The Show and Tell Machine*, 7–8.

35. Michael A. Memoli, "Kellyanne Conway on Surveillance: We Have 'Microwaves That Turn into Cameras,'" *Los Angeles Times*, March 13, 2017, http://www.latimes.com/politics/washington/la-na-essential-washington-updates-more-than-just-spying-microwaves-why-1489416182-htmlstory.html (10 Jan. 2018).

36. Theresa Avila, "Kellyanne Conway Has an Interesting Way of Sitting on the White House Sofa," *The Cut*, February 28, 2017, http://nymag.com/thecut/2017/02/kellyanne-conway-sits-awkwardly-in-oval-office-photo.html (10 Jan. 2018).

37. G. Ray Funkhouser and Eugene F. Shaw, "How Synthetic Experience Shapes Social Reality," *Journal of Communication* 40, no. 2 (1990): 77.

38. Erving Goffman, *The Presentation of Self in Everyday Life* (Garden City, NY: Doubleday Anchor, 1959).

39. Karen A. Cerulo, Janet M. Ruane, and Mary Chayko, "Technological Ties That Bind: Media-Generated Primary Groups," *Communication Research* 19, no. 1 (1992): 109–129.

40. Michael D. Shear, "Obama Sets the Record Straight on His 7-Almond Habit," *The New York Times*, July 28, 2017, https://www.nytimes.com/2016/07/29/us/politics/obama-sets-the-record-straight-on-his-7-almond-habit.html (10 Jan. 2018).

41. Frank Bruni, "Donald Trump à la Mode," *The New York Times*, May 13, 2017, https://www.nytimes.com/2017/05/13/opinion/sunday/donald-trump-a-la-mode.html?_r=0 (10 Jan. 2018).

42. Meyrowitz, *No Sense of Place*.

43. Daniel Boorstin, *The Image: A Guide to Pseudo-Events in America* (New York: Harper Colophon, 1961).

44. Peter Walker, "Kellyanne Conway Says She Is 'Not Inspector Gadget' or 'in Job of Having Evidence' After Microwave Comments," *Independent*, March 13, 2017, http://www.independent.co.uk/news/world/americas/kellyanne-conway-microwave-comments-not-inspector-gadget-job-having-evidence-response-a7627441.html (10 Jan. 2018).

45. Ryan Bort, "A Brief Tour Through Donald Trump's Questionable Understanding of American History," *Newsweek*, March 30, 2017, http://www.newsweek.com/donald-trump-brief-tour-american-history-576866 (10 Jan. 2018).

46. Goldsen, *The Show and Tell Machine*.

47. Herbert Gans, *Popular Culture and High Culture*, rev. ed. (New York: Basic Books, 1999), 58.

48. Ted Johnson, "Kellyanne Conway Criticizes 'Presumptively Negative' Media Coverage of Trump," *Variety*, April 12, 2017, http://variety.com/2017/biz/news/kellyanne-conway-criticizes-trump-media-coverage-1202029112/ (10 Jan. 2018).

49. Goldsen, *The Show and Tell Machine*, 14.

50. Barbie Zelizer, *About to Die: How News Images Move the Public* (Oxford: Oxford University Press, 2010).

51. Chris Cillizza, "President Trump Just Keeps Saying Things That Aren't True," *CNN*, April 12, 2017, http://www.cnn.com/2017/04/12/politics/donald-trump-sean-spicer-truth/ (10 Jan. 2018).

52. Jean Baudrillard, *Simulacra and Simulation*, trans. S. F. Glaser (Ann Arbor: University of Michigan Press, 1994).

53. Stephen Colbert, "The Word—Truthiness," *The Colbert Report*, October 17, 2017, http://www.cc.com/video-clips/63ite2/the-colbert-report-the-word-truthiness (10 Jan. 2018).

54. Sontag, Susan, *On Photography* (New York: Farrar, Straus and Giroux, 1977).

55. Julianne H. Newton, *The Burden of Visual Truth: The Role of Photojournalism in Mediating Reality* (Mahwah, NJ: Lawrence Erlbaum, 2001).

56. Roland Barthes, *Camera Lucida: Reflections on Photography* (New York: Hill and Wang, 1981).

57. William Hirst, et al., "A Ten-Year Follow-Up on a Study of Memory for the Attack of September 11, 2001: Flashbulb Memories and Memories for Flashbulb Events," *Journal of Experimental Psychology: General* 144, no. 3 (2015): 604–623.

58. Funkhouser and Shaw, "How Synthetic Experience Shapes Social Reality," 85–86.

59. Mitroff, Ian and Warren Bennis, *The Unreality Industry: The Deliberate Manufacture of Falsehood and What it is Doing to our Lives* (New York: Oxford University Press, 1989), 6.

60. Lisette Rodriguez, "Kellyanne Conway Defends White House's Credibility: We Have 'High Regard' for Facts," *ABC News*, February 7, 2017, http://abcnews.go.com/Politics/kellyanne-conway-defends-white-houses-credibility-high-regard/story?id=45334577 (10 Jan. 2018).

61. Meyrowitz, *No Sense of Place*.

62. Byron Reeves and Clifford Nass, *The Media Equation: How People Treat Computers, Television, and New Media Like Real People and Places* (Cambridge: Cambridge University Press, 1996), 11.

63. Margaret Sullivan, "The Post-Truth World of the Trump Administration Is Scarier Than You Think," *The Washington Post*, December 4, 2016, https://www.washingtonpost.com/lifestyle/style/the-post-truth-world-of-the-trump-administration-is-scarier-than-you-think/2016/12/02/ebda952a-b897–11e6-b994-f45a208f7a73_story.html?utm_term=.3fedc5a8c5e8 (10 Jan. 2018).

64. Fred Barbash, "Fox News Crew 'Watched in Disbelief' as Montana's Greg Gianforte 'Slammed' and 'Began Punching' Reporter," *The Washington Post*, May 25, 2017, https://www.washingtonpost.com/news/morning-mix/wp/2017/05/25/fox-news-crew-watched-in-disbelief-as-gianforte-slammed-and-punched-reporter/?utm_term=.9c34f03723f3 (10 Jan. 2018).

65. Nuzzi, "Kellyanne Conway Is a Star."

66. Goldsen, *The Show and Tell Machine*, xi.

About the Contributors

Robin **Blom** is the graduate director and an assistant professor of journalism at Ball State University, where he teaches media theory, media law and ethics, media analytics, and data journalism. His research examines reasons for why people believe things that are false and do not believe things that are true, in particular the believability of news reports.

Jim **Clarke** is a senior lecturer and course director of English and journalism at Coventry University. He was previously a national investigative newspaper reporter and political correspondent in Ireland for two decades, having written for *The Guardian, The Daily Telegraph, The Irish Independent, The Evening Herald* and *The Irish Sunday Mirror.* He is the author of *The Aesthetics of Anthony Burgess* (Palgrave, 2017) and *Catholicism and Science Fiction* (Gylphi, 2018).

Jacopo **della Quercia** is a scholar with Humanities New York. His work has been featured in the *New York Times* bestseller *You Might Be a Zombie and Other Bad News* (Plume, 2011), *Game of Thrones versus History* (Wiley-Blackwell, 2017), *Business Insider*, the *Huffington Post*, the *New York Observer, Reader's Digest, RealClearPolitics*, and *Slate*, among others.

Sabatino **DiBernardo** is an associate lecturer in religion, philosophy, and humanities at the University of Central Florida in the Department of Philosophy. His teaching areas include the philosophy of religion, popular music and culture. His courses engage in a poststructuralist interrogation of religious language and functions in and through various popular media. His research interests focus on the deconstructive role of irony in philosophy, religion, popular music and culture.

Justin D. **García** is an assistant professor of anthropology at Millersville University of Pennsylvania. Other publications include "Latin Lords of the Ring" in *Wrestling with Identity* (McFarland, 2018) and "Hispanic/Latino Identity as Racial Misnomer" in *Race in America* (Praeger, 2017).

Andrew **Grossman** is a regular contributor to *Bright Lights Film Journal* and *Popmatters*, and a contributor to the *New Dictionary of the History of Ideas*. He has contributed to numerous critical anthologies, including *Film and Literary Modernism, Movies in the Age of Obama, Asexualities, Transnational Chinese Cinema,* and *Hong Kong Horror Cinema*.

Jeffrey J. **Hall** is a junior researcher at the Waseda University Organization for Regional and Inter-Regional Studies in Tokyo. He also teaches American history and international relations at Hosei University. His research focuses on war memory, civil-military relations, Internet media, and conservative activism in contemporary Japanese and American society.

Sig **Langegger** is an associate professor at Akita International University in Japan. The context of his research is public space—he is interested in how public spaces are planned and designed, how they are regulated and policed, and how they impact manifold trajectories of health and well-being within marginalized communities. The primary foci of his research interests are gentrification and the criminalization of homelessness.

Salvador Jiménez **Murguía** is a professor of sociology at Akita International University in Japan. Murguía's work appears in dozens edited volumes and academic journals. He is author of *Epic Fails* (Rowman & Littlefield, 2018) and *Food as a Mechanism of Control and Resistance in Jails and Prisons* (Lexington, 2018). His research interests include deviant behavior, race and racism, popular culture, and new religious movements.

Sean D. **O'Reilly** is an assistant professor of Japan studies at Akita International University, he teaches a wide range of courses on Japanese history, cinema and popular culture, including two traveling seminar courses. His research, which began with a Fulbright Scholarship to Japan in 2012, concerns the strong connections in Japan between history and popular culture, specifically the many cinematic depictions of key figures from Japan's past and what they signify for viewers without historical training.

Melanie **Piper** teaches in film, television, and media studies at the University of Queensland in Australia. Her research has focused on the adaptation of public personas to fictionalized characters in a variety of screen media, from the biopic to sketch comedy to real person fan fiction. She has published several articles based on this research, including in journals such as *Persona Studies* and *Transformative Works and Cultures*.

Christopher W. **Thurley** is an English instructor and the coordinator of the Writing Center at Gaston College. A doctoral candidate at Manchester Metropolitan University, he is researching Anthony Burgess' time in America and the impact it had on his life and work.

Terri **Toles Patkin** is a professor of communication at Eastern Connecticut State University. Her research focuses on freedom of expression, popular culture, and the intersection of interpersonal and mediated communication, and spans time frames from prehistoric cave art to social media memes.

Debra Reddin **van Tuyll** is a professor of communication at Augusta University. She is the author or editor of six books, including *The Confederate Press in the Crucible of the American Civil War* (Peter Lang, 2012). Her research focuses on the earliest Irish American newspapers (published prior to the wave of Great Famine-related immigration) and the effect of the Civil War on the press in the western and midwestern United States.

Bibliography

Abadi, Mark, and Maxwell Tani. "Megyn Kelly Shut Down a Trump Supporter Who Said Japanese Internment Camps Were Precedent for a Muslim Registry." *Business Insider.* 16 November 2016. http://www.businessinsider.com/megyn-kelly-muslim-registry-2016-11 (14 Jan. 2018).

"An Act to Execute Certain Treaty Stipulations Relating to Chinese." *Primary Documents in American History.* Library of Congress. https://www.loc.gov/rr/program/bib/ourdocs/chinese.html.

Adams, John, to Benjamin Stoddert, 31 March 1801. *The Works of John Adams, Second President of the United States,* vol. 9. Boston: Little, Brown, 1854.

Adelson, Eric. "How President Donald Trump Led to a Wrestler Becoming the Most Reviled Man in Mexico." *Yahoo Sports.* 15 June 2017. https://sports.yahoo.com/president-donald-trump-led-wrestler-becoming-reviled-man-mexico-191510838.html (21 July 2017).

Adl-Tabatabai, Sean. "WikiLeaks: Pedophile 'Code Words' Found in Podesta Emails." *Your News Wire.* 1 December 2016. yournewswire.com/wikileaks-pedophile-code-words-podesta/ (17 July 2017).

Agren, David. "'Bad Hombres': Reports Claim Trump Spoke of Sending Troops to Mexico." TheGuardian.com. 1 February 2017. https://www.theguardian.com/us-news/2017/feb/02/bad-hombres-reports-claim-trump-threatened-to-send-troops-to-mexico (21 July 2017).

Alcindor, Yamiche. "Rough First Week Gives Betsy DeVos a Glimpse of the Fight Ahead." *New York Times.* 19 February 2017. https://www.nytimes.com/2017/02/19/us/politics/betsy-devos-education.html?_r=0 (12 Dec. 2017).

"Alien and Sedition Acts." *Primary Documents in American History.* The Library of Congress. https://www.loc.gov/rr/program/bib/ourdocs/Alien.html.

Annals of Congress. February 1797 (2096). https://memory.loc.gov/cgibin/ampage?collId=llac&fileName=006/llac006.db&recNum=290.

Austin, J. L. *How to Do Things with Words.* Cambridge: Harvard University Press, 1975

Avila, Theresa. "Kellyanne Conway Has an Interesting Way of Sitting on the White House Sofa." *The Cut.* February 28, 2017. https://www.thecut.com/2017/02/kellyanne-conway-%09sits-awkwardly-in-oval-office-photo.html (10 Jan. 2018).

Bailey, H.C. "False News Is One of Hitler's Weapons." *Daily Telegraph.* May 23, 1940.

Balko, Radley. *Rise of the Warrior Cop: The Militarization of America's Police Forces.* New York: Public Affairs, 2013.

Ball, Molly. "Kellyanne's Alternate Universe." *Atlantic Monthly,* April 2017.

Baudrillard, Jean. *Simulacra and Simulation.* Ann Arbor: University of Michigan Press, 2006.

Baum, Matthew A. "Sex, Lies, and War: How Soft News Brings Foreign Policy to the Inattentive Public." *The American Political Science Review* 96, no. 1 (2000): 91–109.

Barbash, Fred. "Fox News Crew 'Watched in Disbelief' as Montana's Greg Gianforte 'Slammed' and 'Began Punching' Reporter." *The Washington Post.* 25 May 2017. https://www.washingtonpost.com/news/morning-mix/wp/2017/05/25/fox-news-crew-watched-in-disbelief-as-gianforte-slammed-and-punched-reporter/?utm_term=.9c34f03723f3 (10 Jan. 2018).

Barnouw, Erik. *The Sponsor: Notes on a Modern Potentate*. Oxford: Oxford University Press, 1978.

Barthes, Roland. *Camera Lucida: Reflections on Photography*. New York: Hill and Wang, 1981.

Baudrillard, Jean. *Simulacra and Simulation*. Trans. S. F. Glaser. Ann Arbor: University of Michigan Press, 1994.

BBC Staff Writer. "Trump Aide Michael Flynn Jnr Out After 'Pizzagate' Tweets." *BBC News*. 7 December 2016. www.bbc.com/news/world-us-canada-38231532 (1 Aug. 2017).

Beck, Julie. "This Article Won't Change Your Mind." *The Atlantic*. 13 March 2017. https://www.theatlantic.com/science/archive/2017/03/this-article-wont-change-your-mind/519093/ (21 July 2017).

Becker, Ernest. "The Fragile Fiction." *The Truth About the Truth: De-Confusing and Re-Constructing the Postmodern World*, 34–35,edited by Walter Truett Anderson. New York: Tarcher/Putnam, 1995.

Becker, Jo, Matt Apuzzo, and Adam Goldman. "Trump's Son Met with Russian Lawyer After Being Promised Damaging Information on Clinton." NYTimes.com. 9 July 2017. https://www.nytimes.com/2017/07/09/us/politics/trump-russia-kushner-manafort.html (21 July 2017).

Benen, Steve. "Conway: Look at Trump's Heart, Not 'what's come out of his mouth." *MSNBC*. January 9, 2017. http://www.msnbc.com/rachel-maddow-show/conway-look-trumps-%09heart-not-whats-come-out-his-mouth (10 Jan. 2018).

Benz, Robert J. "More and More About Frederick Douglass." *The Huffington Post*. 1 February 2017, https://www.huffingtonpost.com/entry/more-and-more-about-frederick-douglass_us_5892855fe4b01a7d8e512b13?ncid=engmodushpmg00000003 (21 Dec. 2017).

Bernstein, Michael S., Andrés Monroy-Hernández, Drew Harry, Paul André, Katrina Panovich, and Gregory G. Vargas. "4chan and/b: An Analysis of Anonymity and Ephemerality in a Large Online Community." In *Proceedings of the Fifth Annual International Conference on Weblogs and Social Media, Barcelona, Spain, 17–21 July 2011*, 51–58. Menlo Park, CA: The AAAI Press.

Bialik, Kristen. "Key Facts About Race and Marriage, 50 Years After Loving v. Virginia." *PewResearch.org*. 12 June 2017. http://www.pewresearch.org/fact-tank/2017/06/12/key-facts-about-race-and-marriage-50-years-after-loving-v-virginia/ (21 July 2017).

Bier, David. "A Wall Is an Impractical, Expensive, and Ineffective Border Plan." *Cato.org*. 28 November 2016. https://www.cato.org/blog/border-wall-impractical-expensive-ineffective-plan (21 July 2017).

Biography.com. "Kellyanne Conway Biography." Biography.com. February 24, 2017. http://www.biography.com/people/kellyanne-conway-022217 (10 Jan. 2018).

Bird, Wendel. *Press and Speech Under Assault: The Early Supreme Court Justices, The Sedition Act of 1798, and the Campaign Against Dissent*. New York: Oxford University Press, 2016.

Blake, Aaron. "Kellyanne Conway Says Donald Trump's Team Has 'Alternative Facts,' Which Pretty Much Says It All." *The Washington Post*. 22 January 2017. https://www.washingtonpost.com/news/the-fix/wp/2017/01/22/kellyanne-conway-says-donald-trumps-team-has-alternate-facts-which-pretty-much-says-it-all/?utm_term=.ffc1cf10e0d3 (25 Jan. 2017).

Blegen, Theodore C. "The Competition of the Northwestern States for Immigrants." *Wisconsin Magazine of History* 3, no. 1 (1919): 3–29.

Boehlert, Eric. "Embracing the 'Clinton Crazies,' Trump Becomes AM Talk Radio's Nominee for President." *Huffington Post*. 25 May 2016. www.huffingtonpost.com/eric-boehlert/embracing-the-clinton-cra_b_10129482.html (11 June 2017).

Bonderoff, Jason. *Mary Tyler Moore*. New York: St. Martin's Press, 1986.

Boorstin, Daniel. *The Image: A Guide to Pseudo-Events in America*. New York: Harper Colophon, 1961.

Bort, Ryan. "A Brief Tour Through Donald Trump's Questionable Understanding of American History." *Newsweek*. March 30, 2017. http://www.newsweek.com/donald-trump-brief-tour-american-history-576866 (10 Jan. 2018).

"Boston Men Jailed for Turmp-Inspired Hate Crime Attack." Reuters.com. 16 May 2016.

Accessed July 21, 2017. http://www.reuters.com/article/us-usa-mexico-beating-idUSK CN0Y805K (21 July 2017).

Bradner, Eric. "Conway: Trump White House Offered 'Alternative Facts' on Crowd Size." *CNN.* January 22, 2017. http://edition.cnn.com/2017/01/22/politics/kellyanne-conway-alternative-%09facts/ (10 Jan. 2018).

Brand, Anna. "Trump Puts a Price on His Wall: It Would Cost Mexico $8 Billion." MSNBC.com. 9 February 2016. http://www.msnbc.com/msnbc/donald-trump-says-his-wall-would-cost-8-billion (21 July 2017).

Brookhiser, Richard. "The Politics of Immigration: Clashing Impulses." *American History* (10 May 2017): 17–18.

Brubaker, Jed R. "Wants Moar: Visual Media's Use of Text in LOLcats and Silent Film." *Gnovis Journal* 8, no. 2 (2008): 117–24.

Bruni, Frank. "Donald Trump à la Mode." *New York Times.* 13 May 2017. https://www.nytimes.com/2017/05/13/opinion/sunday/donald-trump-a-la-mode.html?_r=0 (10 Jan. 2018).

Brunius, Harry. "Why Journalism Is Shifting Away from 'Objectivity.'" *Christian Science Monitor.* 6 July 2017. https://www.csmonitor.com/USA/Politics/2017/0706/Why-journalism-is-shifting-away-from-objectivity (25 July. 2017).

Bump, Philip. "Donald Trump's Mexico Border Wall Will Be as High as 55 Feet, According to Donald Trump." *The Washington Post.* 26 February 2016. https://www.washington post.com/news/the-fix/wp/2016/02/26/so-how-high-will-donald-trumps-wall-be-an-investigation/?utm_term=.85d19d0dd0eb (21 July 2017).

_____. "The Initial Estimate Is Here: Trump's Wall Will Cost More Than a Year of the Space Program." *The Washington Post.* 10 February 2017. https://www.washingtonpost.com/news/politics/wp/2017/02/10/the-initial-estimate-is-here-trumps-wall-will-cost-more-than-a-year-of-the-space-program/?utm_term=.4e38c32693f4 (21 July 2017).

Burgess, Anthony. *1985.* London: Beautiful Books, 2010.

_____. *The Worm and the Ring.* Sussex: William Heinemann, 1961, 1970.

Carter, Edward C. "A 'Wild Irishman' Under Every Federalist's Bed: Naturalization in Philadelphia." *Pennsylvania Magazine of History and Biography* 94, no. 3 (July 1970): 331–346.

Cassidy, John. "The Facts About Immigration." *The New Yorker.* 31 March 2017. http://www.newyorker.com/news/john-cassidy/the-facts-about-immigration (21 July 2017).

"Caught in the Act, the Daily News Publicly Acknowledges It Steals News from the Daily Telegram." *Clarksburg Telegram,* September 25, 1903.

Cerulo, Karen A., Janet M. Ruane, and Mary Chayko. "Technological Ties That Bind: Media-Generated Primary Groups." *Communication Research* 19, no. 1 (1992): 109–129.

Chavez, Leo R. *The Latino Threat: Constructing Immigrants, Citizens, and the Nation.* Stanford: Stanford University Press, 2008.

_____. *Shadowed Lives: Undocumented Immigrants in American Society,* 2d ed. Orlando: Harcourt Brace, 1998.

Cillizza, Chris. "Donald Trump Just Claimed He Invented 'Fake News.'" CNN.com. 26 October 2017. http://edition.cnn.com/2017/10/08/politics/trump-huckabee-fake/index.html (2 Jan. 2018).

_____. "President Trump Just Keeps Saying Things That Aren't True." *CNN.* April 12, 2017. http://www.cnn.com/2017/04/12/politics/donald-trump-sean-spicer-truth/ (10 Jan. 2018).

_____. "Sean Spicer Held a Press Conference. He Didn't Take Questions. Or Tell the Whole Truth." *The Washington Post.* 21 January 2017. https://www.washingtonpost.com/news/the-fix/wp/2017/01/21/sean-spicer-held-a-press-conference-he-didnt-take-questions-or-tell-the-whole-truth/?utm_term=.40981c3b6c0b (7 Feb. 2018).

_____. "Why Pro Wrestling Is the Perfect Metaphor for Donald Trump's Presidency." CNN.com. 2 July 2017. http://www.cnn.com/2017/07/02/politics/trump-wrestling-tweet/index.html (21 July 2017).

Clark, Allan C. "William Duane." *Records of the Columbia Historical Society* 9, no. 106, 4. Attributed to *The New York Evening Post,* 16 November 1801.

Clark, Maudemarie. *Nietzsche: On Truth and Philosophy.* Modern European Philosophy, edited by Raymond Geuss. Cambridge: Cambridge University Press, 1990.

Clayton, Edward. "Aristotle: Politics." *Internet Encyclopedia of Philosophy*, edited by James Fieser and Bradley Dowden, 2017. http://www.iep.utm.edu/aris-pol/.

"Clinton's Grand Jury Testimony, Part 4." Special Report: Documents from the Starr Referral. Washingtonpost.com. 1998. http://www.washingtonpost.com/wpsrv/politics/special/clinton/stories/bctest092198_4.html (12 Jan. 2017).

Cobbett, William. "Proposals for Publishing a News-Paper to be Entitled, Porcupine's Gazette and Daily Advertiser." Evans Early American Imprint Collection. http://quod.lib.umich.edu/e/evans/N22884.0001.001/1:13?rgn=div1;view=fulltext (12 Jan. 2017).

Cohen, Stephen. "KOMO Attacks 'Biased and False News' in Sinclair-Written Promos." *The Seattle Post-Intelligencer.* 3 April 2018. https://www.seattlepi.com/seattlenews/article/KOMO-fake-news-Sinclair-promos-12792032.php (21 April 2018).

Colbert, Stephen. "The Word—Truthiness." *The Colbert Report.* October 17, 2017. http://www.cc.com/video-clips/63ite2/the-colbert-report-the-word-truthiness (10 Jan. 2018).

Coleman, Gabriella. "Net Wars Over Free Speech, Freedom, and Secrecy or How to Understand the Hacker and Lulz Battle Against the Church of Scientology." Lecture, the Next Hope, New York, 17 July 2010.

Combs, Jerald A. *The Jay Treaty: Political Battleground of the Founding Fathers.* Berkley: University of California Press, 1970.

Compton, Josh. "Live from DC: *Saturday Night Live* Political Parody References in Presidential Rhetoric." *Comedy Studies* 7, no. 1 (January 2016): 62–78.

Constable, Pamela. "For Illegal Immigrants with Babies, the Anchor Pulls in Many Directions." *The Washington Post.* 20 September 2015. https://www.washingtonpost.com/local/social-issues/for-illegal-immigrants-with-babies-the-anchor-pulls-in-many-directions/2015/09/20/d5d7a2f0-570d-11e5-b8c9-944725fcd3b9_story.html?utm_term=.a52e4689e6ad (21 July 2017).

Contorno, Steve, and Louis Jacobson. "Fact-Checking Kellyanne Conway on the 'Bowling Green Massacre.'" *Politifact.com.* 3 February 2017. http://www.politifact.com/truth-o-meter/statements/2017/feb/03/kellyanne-conway/fact-checking-kellyanne-conways-bowling-green-mass/ (10 Feb. 2017).

Conway, Kellyanne. Interview by Chuck Todd. *Meet the Press.* Aired 22 January 2017, on NBC. https://www.youtube.com/watch?v=VSrEEDQgFc8.

____. Interview by Anderson Cooper. *Anderson Cooper 360.°* Aired 5 May 2017 on CNN.

Cooper, Brenda, David Descutner, and Sandra Alspach. "From Celebrity Entrepreneur to Civic Hero: Donald Trump's Campaign of Self-Transformation." *American Heroes in a Media Age*, 188–202, edited by Drucker, Susan J. and Robert S. Cathcart. Cresskill, NJ: Hampton Press, 1994.

Corasaniti, Nick. "Donald Trump Releases Plan to Combat Illegal Immigration." *New York Times.* 16 August 2015. https://www.nytimes.com/2015/08/17/us/politics/trump-releases-plan-to-combat-illegal-immigration.html?mcubz=1 (21 July 2017).

Coulter, Ann. *¡Adios, America! The Left's Plan to Turn Our Country into a Third World Hellhole.* Washington, D.C.: Regnery Publishing, 2015.

Cox, Daniel and Robert Jones. "America's Changing Religious Identity." *PRRI.org.* 6 September 2017. https://www.prri.org/research/american-religious-landscape-christian-religiously-unaffiliated/ (30 Dec. 2017).

Crank, John. *Understanding Police Culture*, 2d ed. New York: Routledge, 2015.

D'Antonio, Michael. *A Consequential President.* New York: St. Martin's, 2016.

Davis, Nicholas T., and Johanna L. Dunaway. "Party Polarization, Media Choice, and Mass Partisan-Ideological Sorting." *Public Opinion Quarterly* 80 (special issue 2016): 272–297.

Davenport, Coral. "Scott Pruitt Is Seen Cutting the E.P.A. with a Scalpel, Not a Cleaver." *New York Times.* 5 February 2017. https://www.nytimes.com/2017/02/05/us/politics/scott-pruitt-is-seen-cutting-the-epa-with-a-scalpel-not-a-cleaver.html (12 Dec. 2017).

Derrida, Jacques. "Faith and Knowledge: The Two Sources of 'Religion' at the Limits of Reason Alone." *Religion*, edited by Jacques Derrida and Gianni Vattimo. *Cultural Memory in the Present*, edited by Mieke Bal and Hent de Vries. Stanford: Stanford University Press, 1996.

Diamond, Jason. "WWE's Linda McMahon Approved to Lead Small Business Administration."

RollingStone.com. 14 February 2017. http://www.rollingstone.com/sports/news/wwe-linda-mcmahon-joins-trump-administration-small-business-w466987 (21 July 2017).

Diaz, Daniella. "Pence to Kaine: 'You whipped out that Mexican thing again.'" CNN.com. 5 October 5 2016. http://www.cnn.com/2016/10/05/politics/mike-pence-mexican-thing-time-kaine-vp-debate/index.html (21 July 2017).

Doherty, Carroll. "5 Facts About Trump Supporters' Views of Immigration." *PewResearch.org*. 25 August 2016. http://www.pewresearch.org/fact-tank/2016/08/25/5-facts-about-trump-supporters-views-of-immigration/ (21 July 2017).

Donald J. Trump and Donald J. Trump for President, Inc.'s Objections to Dr. Jill Stein's Recount Petition at 2, *In Re Petition for Recount for the Office of President of the United States of America*. State of Michigan Board of State Canvassers. 1 December 2016. Available at http://www.michigan.gov/documents/sos/Objection_to_Recount_Petition_544089_7.pdf (21 July 2017).

Dreyfuss, Emily. "Want to Make a Lie Sound True? Say It Again. And Again. And Again." *Wired*. 11 February 2017. https://www.wired.com/2017/02/dont-believe-lies-just-people-repeat/ (14 Jan. 2018).

Durey, Michael. "Thomas Paine's Apostles: Radical Émigrés and the Triumph of Jeffersonian Republicanism." *William and Mary Quarterly* 44, no. 4 (October 1987): 661–688.

Dynel, Marta. "'I Has Seen Image Macros!' Advice Animals Memes as Visual-Verbal Jokes." *International Journal of Communication* 10 (2016): 660–88. ijoc.org/index.php/ijoc/article/view/4101/1556.

Eco, Umberto. "Ur-Fascism." *The New York Review of Books*. 22 June 1995. http://www.nybooks.com/articles/1995/06/22/ur-fascism/ (30 July 2017).

"Electoral College Box Scores, 1789–1996." U.S. Electoral College, National Archives and Records Administration https://www.archives.gov/federal-register/electoral-college/scores.html#1796.

Ellis, Joseph J. *His Excellency, George Washington*. New York: Vintage Books, 2004.

Factcheck.Org. "Remarks by President Trump and Vice President Pence at CIA Headquarters." *Factcheck.org*. https://transcripts.factcheck.org/remarks-president-trump-vice-president-pence-cia-headquarters (3 Jan. 2018).

Fahrenthold, David A. "Trump Driving Migrant Debate Among GOP Field." *The Washington Post*. 17 August 2015. https://www.washingtonpost.com/politics/with-trumps-rise-hard-line-immigration-ideas-take-hold-in-gop/2015/08/17/85dbbf3e-4506-11e5-846d-02792f854297_story.html (21 July 2017).

Famighetti, Christopher, Douglas Keith, and Myrna Pérez. "Noncitizen Voting: The Missing Millions." *Brennan Center for Justice*. 5 May 2017. https://www.brennancenter.org/publication/noncitizen-voting-missing-millions (21 July 2017).

Farhi, Paul. "Conspiracy Theorist Alex Jones Backs Off 'Pizzagate' Claims." *The Washington Post*. 24 March 2017. www.washingtonpost.com/lifestyle/style/conspiracy-theorist-alex-jones-backs-off-pizzagate-claims/2017/03/24/6f0246fe-10cd-11e7-ab07-07d9f521f6b5_story.html (1 Aug. 2017).

Flores, Reena. "Donald Trump: 'Anchor Babies' Aren't American Citizens." CBSNews.com. 19 August 2015. https://www.cbsnews.com/news/donald-trump-anchor-babies-arent-american-citizens/ (21 July 2017).

Folkenflik, David. "Behind Fox News' Baseless Seth Rich Story: The Untold Tale." *NPR*. 1 August 2017. www.npr.org/2017/08/01/540783715/lawsuit-alleges-fox-news-and-trump-supporter-created-fake-news-story (1 Aug. 2017).

Foucault, Michel. *Discipline and Punish: The Birth of the Prison*. New York: Vintage Books, 1995.

Freire, Paulo. *Pedagogy of the Oppressed*. New York: Bloomsbury, 2016.

Funkhouser, G. Ray, and Eugene F. Shaw. "How Synthetic Experience Shapes Social Reality." *Journal of Communication* 40, no. 2 (1990): 75–87.

Gajanan, Mahita. "Kellyanne Conway Defends White House's Falsehoods as 'Alternative Facts.'" Time.com. 22 January 2017. http://time.com/4642689/kellyanne-conway-sean-spicer-donald-trump-alternative-facts/ (5 Jan. 2018).

Gans, Herbert. *Popular Culture and High Culture*, rev. ed. New York: Basic Books, 1999.

Garrison, Arthur H. "The Internal Security Acts of 1798: The Founding Generation and the Judiciary During America's First National Security Crisis." *Journal of Supreme Court History* 34 no, 1 (2009): 1–27.

Gentile, Giovanni, and Mussolini, Benito. "The Doctrine of Fascism." *The World Future Fund* 1932. http://www.worldfuturefund.org/wffmaster/Reading/Germany/mussolini.htm (25 July 2017).

Gibson, Caitlin. "Anderson Cooper Eyerolled His Way to an Iconic GIF While Interviewing Kellyanne Conway." *The Washington Post*. 10 May 2017. www.washingtonpost.com/news/arts-and-entertainment/wp/2017/05/10/anderson-cooper-eyerolled-his-way-to-an-iconic-gif-while-interviewing-kellyanne-conway/?utm_term=.582b7370a5ef (10 May 2017).

Goddard, Taegan. "2016 Republicans Are Completely Ignoring the Lessons of Their 2012 'Autopsy.'" TheWeek.com. 1 June 2015. http://theweek.com/articles/557753/2016-republicans-are-completely-ignoring-lessons-2012-autopsy (21 July 2017).

Goffman, Erving. *The Presentation of Self in Everyday Life*. London: Penguin, 1990.

Goldman, Adam. "The Comet Ping Pong Gunman Answers Our Reporter's Questions." *New York Times*. 7 December 2016. https://www.nytimes.com/2016/12/07/us/edgar-welch-comet-pizza-fake-news.html (1 Aug. 2017).

Goldsen, Rose K. *The Show and Tell Machine: How Television Works and Works You Over*. New York: Dial Press, 1977.

Gonzalez-Barrera, Ana. "Apprehensions of Mexican Migrants at U.S. Borders Reaches Near-Historic Low." *PewResearch.org*. 14 April 2016. http://www.pewresearch.org/fact-tank/2016/04/14/mexico-us-border-apprehensions/ (21 July 2017).

____. "More Mexicans Leaving than Coming to the U.S." *PewHispanic.org*. 19 November 2015. http://www.pewhispanic.org/2015/11/19/more-mexicans-leaving-than-coming-to-the-u-s/ (21 July 2017).

Gramlich, John. "Trump Voters Want to Build the Wall, But Are More Divided on Other Immigration Questions." *PewResearch.org*. 29 November 2016. http://www.pewresearch.org/fact-tank/2016/11/29/trump-voters-want-to-build-the-wall-but-are-more-divided-on-other-immigration-questions/ (21 July 2017).

Gray, Rosie. "Trump Defends White Nationalist Protesters." *The Atlantic*. 15 August 2017. https://www.theatlantic.com/politics/archive/2017/08/trump-defends-white-nationalist-protesters-some-very-fine-people-on-both-sides/537012/ (18 Aug. 2017).

Greenaway, Jon. "Donald Trump: The Id of Republican Politics." *JSTOR Daily*. 17 August 2015. https://daily.jstor.org/donald-trump-the-id-of-republican-politics/ (7 Feb. 2018).

Griffiths, Ralph A. *King and Country: England and Wales in the Fifteenth Century*. London: Hambledon Press, 1991.

Grynbaum, Michael M. "Trump Strategist Stephen Bannon Says Media Should 'Keep its mouth shut.'" *New York Times*. 26 January 2017. https://www.nytimes.com/2017/01/26/business/media/stephen-bannon-trump-news-media.html (1 Jan. 2018).

Haberman, Maggie, Glenn Thrush, Michael S. Schmidt, and Peter Baker. "'Enough was enough': How Festering Anger at Comey Ended in His Firing." *New York Times*. 10 May 2017. www.nytimes.com/2017/05/10/us/politics/how-trump-decided-to-fire-james-comey.html (10 May 2017).

Haddon, Heather. "Donald Trump Says Immigrant Deportations to Be Done in Two Years." *Wall Street Journal*. 11 September 2015. https://blogs.wsj.com/washwire/2015/09/11/donald-trump-says-immigrant-deportations-done-in-two-years/ (21 July 2017).

Hale, Matthew Rainbow. "'Many Who Wandered in Darkness': The Contest Over American National Identity, 1795–1798." *Early American Studies: An Interdisciplinary Journal* 1, no.1 (2003): 127–175.

Halperin, Teri Diane. *The Alien and Sedition Acts of 1798: Testing the Constitution*. Baltimore: Johns Hopkins University Press, 2016.

Han, Hahrie, and David W. Brady. "A Delayed Return to Historical Norms: Congressional Party Polarization After the Second World War." *British Journal of Political Science* 37, no. 3 (July 2007): 505–531.

Heidenreich, Donald E. "Conspiracy Politics in the Election of 1796." *New York History* 92, no. 3 (Summer 2011): 151–165.

Henderson, Stewart Donald. *The Opposition Press of the Federalist Period.* Albany: State University of New York Press, 1969.

Hill, Megan. "Developing a Normative Approach to Political Satire." *International Journal of Communication* 7 (2013): 324–337. http://ijoc.org/index.php/ijoc/article/view/1934/856.

Himma-Kadakas, Marju. "Alternative Facts and Fake News Entering Journalist Content Production Cycle." *Cosmopolitan Civil Societies: An Interdisciplinary Journal* 9, no. 2 (2017): 25–41.

Hine, Gabriel Emile, Jeremiah Onaolapo, Emiliano De Cristofaro, Nicolas Kourtellis, Illias Leontiadis, Riginos Samaras, Gianluca Stringhini, and Jeremy Blackburn. "Kek, Cucks, and God Emperor Trump: A Measurement Study of 4chan's Politically Incorrect Forum and Its Effects on the Web." *Proceedings of the Eleventh International AAAI Conference on Web and Social Media (ICWSM 2017): Montreal, 15–18 May 2017*, 92–101. aaai.org/ocs/index.php/ICWSM/ICWSM17/paper/download/15670/14790.

Hirst, William, et al. "A Ten-Year Follow-Up on a Study of Memory for the Attack of September 11, 2001: Flashbulb Memories and Memories for Flashbulb Events." *Journal of Experimental Psychology: General* 144, no. 3 (2015): 604–623.

Hunt, Elle. "Trump's Inauguration Crowd: Sean Spicer's Claims Versus the Evidence." *The Guardian.* 27 January 2017. https://www.theguardian.com/us-news/2017/jan/22/trump-inauguration-crowd-sean-spicers-claims-versus-the-evidence (4 Jan. 2018).

Huntington, Samuel P. *Who Are We? The Challenges to America's National Identity.* New York: Simon & Schuster Paperbacks, 2004.

Inglehart, Louis Edward. *Press Freedoms: A Descriptive Calendar of Concepts, Events, and Court Actions from 4000 B.C. to the Present.* New York: Greenwood Press, 1987.

Internet Movie Database. "Mary Tyler Moore." *IMDb.* http://www.imdb.com/title/tt0065314/ (10 Jan. 2018).

_____. "The Apprentice." *IMDb.* http://www.imdb.com/title/tt0364782/ (10 Jan. 2018).

Ito, Masanori. *The End of the Imperial Japanese Navy.* New York: MacFadden, 1965 (orig. pub. 1956).

Jaffe, Alexandra. "Kellyanne Conway: WH Spokesman Gave 'Alternative Facts' on Inauguration Crowd." NBCNews.com. 22 January 2017. https://www.nbcnews.com/meet-the-press/wh-spokesman-gave-alternative-facts-inauguration-crowd-n710466 (21 July 2017).

Jefferson, Thomas to John Taylor, 4 June 1798, The Founders Online, National Archives and Records Administration. https://founders.archives.gov/?q=reign%20of%20witches&s=1111311111&sa=&r=7&sr= (12 Jan. 2017).

Johnson, Ted. "Kellyanne Conway Criticizes 'Presumptively Negative' Media Coverage of Trump." *Variety.* 12 April 2017. http://variety.com/2017/biz/news/kellyanne-conway-criticizes-trump-media-coverage-1202029112/ (10 Jan. 2018).

Jones, Alex. "Donald Trump Tells All on the Alex Jones Show." *Infowars.* 2 December 2015. www.infowars.com/donald-trump-tells-all-on-the-alex-jones-show/ (9 June 2017).

Jones, Jeffrey P. "Politics and the Brand: *Saturday Night Live's* Campaign Season Humor." *Saturday Night Live and American TV,* 77–91, edited by Nick Marx, Matt Sienkiewicz, and Ron Becker. Bloomington: Indiana University Press, 2013.

_____. "With All Due Respect: Satirizing Presidents from *Saturday Night Live* to *Lil' Bush.*" 37–63 in *Satire TV: Politics and Comedy in the Post-Network Era,* edited by Jonathan Gray, Jeffrey P. Jones, and Ethan Thompson. New York: New York University Press, 2008.

Kadetsky, Elizabeth. "Bashing Illegals in California." *The Nation* (17 October 1994): 416–422.

Kaplan, Rebecca. "Bobby Jindal: Immigration Without Assimilation Is Invasion." CBSNews.com, 30 August 30 2015. http://www.cbsnews.com/news/bobby-jindal-immigration-without-assimilation-is-invasion/ (21 July 2017).

Kappeler, Victor, and Peter Kraska. "Normalising Police Militarisation, Living in Denial." *Policing and Society* 25, no. 3 (2015): 268–275.

Kasza, Gregory. *The State and the Mass Media in Japan, 1918–1945.* Berkeley: University of California Press, 1993.

Katzowitz, Josh. "Donald Trump Links Himself to InfoWars Once Again." *Daily Dot.* 15 June 2017. www.dailydot.com/layer8/donald-trump-infowars-link/ (1 Aug. 2017).

Keene, M. Lamar. *The Psychic Mafia.* New York: Prometheus Books, 1976.

Kelley, Seth. "President Trump Slams Arnold Schwarzenegger for Exiting *The Apprentice*: 'He was fired.'" *Variety*. 4 March 2017. http://variety.com/2017/biz/news/president-trump-arnold-schwarzenegger-apprentice-fired-1202002170 (7 Feb. 2018).

Kennedy, Merrit. "'Pizzagate' Gunman Sentenced to 4 Years in Prison." *NPR*, 22 June 2017. www.npr.org/sections/thetwo-way/2017/06/22/533941689/pizzagate-gunman-sentenced-to-4-years-in-prison (30 June 2017).

Kessler Glenn, Salvador Rizzo, and Meg Kelly. "President Trump Has Made 3,001 False or Misleading Claims So Far." *The Washington Post*. 1 May 2018. https://www.washingtonpost.com/news/fact-checker/wp/2018/05/01/president-trump-has-made-3001-false-or-misleading-claims-so-far/?utm_term=.7e6bea98db31 (05 May 2018).

Keys, Ralph. *The Post-Truth Era: Dishonesty and Deception in Contemporary Life*. New York: St. Martin's Press, 2004.

Khodorkovsky, Pavel, and Peter Pomerantsev. "Russia: A Postmodern Dictatorship?" *Legatum Institute*. 14 October 2013. https://www.youtube.com/watch?v=qMIHmzgzVBU (22 Dec. 2017).

Kil, Sang Hea. "Fearing Yellow, Imagining White: Media Analysis of the Chinese Exclusion Act of 1883." *Social Identities* 18, no. 6 (2012): 663–667.

King, Rufus King, to Alexander Hamilton, 2 July 1798. Founders Online (https://founders.archives.gov/documents/Hamilton/01-21-02-0298).

_____. to Timothy Pickering, 19 July 1798. *The Life and Correspondence of Rufus Kind, Comprising His Letters, Private and Official, His Public Documents and His Speeches*, edited by Charles R. King, M.D. New York: G. P. Putnam's Sons, 1895.

Klemperer, Viktor. *The Language of the Third Reich*. Trans. Martin Brady. London: Continuum Books, 2006.

Kline, Jim. "C. G. Jung and Norman Cohn Explain Pizzagate: The Archetypal Dimension of a Conspiracy Theory." *Psychological Perspectives* 60, no. 2 (2017): 186–94.

Knobel, Michele, and Colin Lankshear. "Online Memes, Affinities, and Cultural Production." *A New Literacies Sampler*, 199–227. New York: Peter Lang, 2007.

Knuttila, Lee. "User Unknown: 4chan, Anonymity and Contingency." *First Monday* 16, no. 10 (October 3, 2011): doi:10.5210/fm.v16i10.3665.

Kraska, Peter and Victor Kappeler. "Militarizing American Police: The Rise and Normilization of Paramilitary Units." *Social Problems* 44, no. 1 (1997): 1–18.

Kreitner, Richard. "Post-Truth and Its Consequences: What a 25-Year-Old Essay Tells Us About the Current Moment." *The Nation*. 30 November 2016. https://www.thenation.com/article/post-truth-and-its-consequences-what-a-25-year-old-essay-tells-us-about-the-current-moment/ (12 Jan. 2017).

Korab-Karpowicz, W. J. "Plato: Political Philosophy." *Internet Encyclopedia of Philosophy*, edited by James Fieser and Bradley Dowden, 2017. http://www.iep.utm.edu/platopol/.

Kutner, Max. "Inauguration and Women's March, by the Numbers." *Newsweek*. 21 January 2017. http://www.newsweek.com/trump-inauguration-numbers-how-many-attended-545467 (7 Feb. 2018).

Laracey, Mel. "The Presidential Newspaper as an Engine of Early American Political Development: The Case of Thomas Jefferson and the Election of 1800." *Rhetoric and Public Affairs* 11, no. 1 (2008): 7–46.

Latimer, Jon. "French Farce at Fishguard." *Military History* 13, no. 7 (March 1997): 38.

Lee, Michelle Ye Hee. "Donald Trump's False Comments Connecting Mexican Immigrants and Crime." WashingtonPost.com. 8 July 2015. https://www.washingtonpost.com/news/fact-checker/wp/2015/07/08/donald-trumps-false-comments-connecting-mexican-immigrants-and-crime/ (21 July 2015).

Leip, David. "1880 Presidential General Election Results," "1884 Presidential General Election Results," "1888 Presidential General Election Results," "1960 Presidential General Election Results," "1968 Presidential General Election Results," "2000 Presidential General Election Results," and "2016 Presidential General Election Results." *Dave Leip's Atlas of U.S. Presidential Elections*. http://uselectionatlas.org/RESULTS (21 July 2017).

Levi, Heather. *The World of Lucha Libre: Secrets, Revelations, and Mexican National Identity*. Durham: Duke University Press, 2008.

Levin, Beth. "The Koch Brothers Found One Thing They Hate More Than Donald Trump," *Vanity Fair.* May 18, 2017. https://theintercept.com/2017/12/01/time-magazine-koch-brothers-meredith-corp/ (14 Jan. 2018).

Lind, Dara. "Donald Trump Perfectly Explains His Entire Campaign Strategy, in One Bizarre Tweet." *Vox.com.* 20 July 2016. https://www.vox.com/2016/7/20/12237172/donald-trump-tweet-melania (12 June 2017).

Lipkin, Steven N. *Docudrama Performs the Past: Arenas of Argument in Films Based on True Stories.* Newcastle Upon Tyne: Cambridge Scholars, 2011.

Littleton, Cynthia. "*Saturday Night Live* Flexes Post-Election Ratings Muscle." *Variety.* 5 February 2017. http://variety.com/2017/tv/news/saturday-night-live-ratings-18–49-demo-melissa-mccarthy-1201978637/ (7 Feb. 2018).

LoBianco, Tom. "Donald Trump Promises 'Deportation Force' to Remove 11 Million." *CNN.com.* 12 November 2015. http://www.cnn.com/2015/11/11/politics/donald-trump-deportation-force-debate-immigration/index.html (21 July 2015).

Lokke, Card Ludwig. "The Trumbull Episode: A Prelude to the 'X Y Z' Affair." *New England Quarterly* 7, no. 1 (1934): 100–114.

Lyons, Matthew. "An Antifascist Report on the Alternative Right." *Ctrl-Alt-Delete*, 1–18. Montreal: Kersplebedeb Publishing, 2017.

Lyotard, Jean-François. *The Postmodern Condition: A Report on Knowledge.* Translated by Geoff Bennington and Brian Massumi. Theory and History of Literature, vol. 10. Minneapolis: University of Minnesota Press, 1984.

Madison, James. "The Federalist No. 51." *The Federalist Papers*, 254. New York: Dover, 2014.

Makin, Tony. "Here Are Some Alternative Facts—Not Fake News, but Quite Bad." *The Australian,* 9 June 2017. http://webcache.googleusercontent.com/search?q=cache:50Y0Hpv2aFEJ:www.theaustralian.com.au/opinion/here-are-some-alternative-facts-not-fake-news-but-quite-bad/news story/99e7b7bdbf24b6d1d0d90cb51adc279b+&cd=1&hl=en&ct=clnk&gl=ie (12 Jan. 2017).

Malmgren, Evan. "Don't Feed the Trolls." *Dissent* 64, no. 2 (Spring 2017): 9–12. doi:10.13 53/dss.2017.0042.

Manivannan, Vyshali. "Attaining the Ninth Square: Cybertextuality, Gamification, and Institutional Memory on 4chan." *Enculturation* 15 (November 2012): enculturation.camden.rutgers.edu/attaining-the-ninth-square.

Marquardt, Alex. "Exclusive: Bornstein Claims Trump Dictated the Glowing Health Letter." *CNN.com.* 2 May 2018. https://edition.cnn.com/2018/05/01/politics/harold-bornstein-trump-letter/index.html (2 May 2018).

"Massey Study Shows Rapid Loss of Spanish Among Mexican Immigrants in the United States." *Princeton.edu.* 13 September 2006. http://www.princeton.edu/main/news/archive/S15/81/82E45/index.xml?section=topstories (21 July 2017).

Mayer, Jane. "Donald Trump's Ghostwriter Tells All." *The New Yorker.* July 25, 2016 http://www.newyorker.com/magazine/2016/07/25/donald-trumps-ghostwriter-tells-all (12 Jan. 2017).

McFadden, Cynthia, William M. Arkin, and Kevin Monahan. "Russians Penetrated U.S. Voter Systems, Top U.S. Official Says." NBCNews.com. 8 February 2018. https://www.nbcnews.com/politics/elections/russians-penetrated-u-s-voter-systems-says-top-u-s-n845721 (10 Feb. 2018).

Memoli, Michael A. "Kellyanne Conway on Surveillance: We Have 'Microwaves that turn into cameras.'" *Los Angeles Times.* 13 March 2017. http://www.latimes.com/politics/washington/la-na-essential-washington-updates-more-%09than-just-spying-microwaves-why-1489416182-htmlstory.html (10 Jan. 2018).

Merica, Dan. "Trump, Xi Talked Syria Strike Over 'Beautiful' Chocolate Cake." *CNN.* 12 April 2017. http://edition.cnn.com/2017/04/12/politics/donald-trump-xi-jingping-syria-%09 chocolate-cake/ (10 Jan. 2018).

Meyrowitz, Joshua. *No Sense of Place: The Impact of Electronic Media on Social Behavior.* Oxford: Oxford University Press, 1985.

Miller, Kerby A. *Emigrants and Exiles: Ireland and the Irish Exodus to North America.* Oxford: Oxford University Press, 1985.

Mitchell, Kirk. "Judge Urges Feds to Investigate Denver Police Sheriff in Abuse Case." *The Denver Post*, 10 June 2014.

Mitroff, Ian, and Warren Bennis. *The Unreality Industry: The Deliberate Manufacture of Falsehood and What It Is Doing to Our Lives*. New York: Oxford University Press, 1989.

Mixter, David, and Edward R. Henry. "Introduction to Webs of Memory, Frames of Power: Collective Remembering in the Archaeological Record." *Journal of Archaeological Method and Theory* 24 (2017): 1–9.

Moore, Jack. "President Trump Bragged That His TV Ratings Are the Highest Since September 11." *GQ*. 24 April 2017. http://www.gq.com/story/donald-trump-911-ratings (7 Feb. 2018).

Moore, Mary Tyler. *After All*. New York: G.P. Putnam's Sons, 1995.

MSNBC. *Hardball with Chris Matthews*. MSNBC. February 2, 2017. http://www.msnbc.com/hardball/watch/matthews-pushes-conway-on-use-of-executive- (10 Jan. 2018).

Morison, Samuel Eliot. *The Life and Letters of Harrison Gray Otis, Federalist, 1765–1848*, vol. 1. Boston: Houghton and Mifflin, 1913.

Mulligan, Kenneth. "The Implications of Fictional Media for Political Beliefs." *Working Papers*, Paper 8 (2012): 1–34.

Nelson, Bill, Amelia Phillips, and Christopher Steuart. *Guide to Computer Forensics and Investigations*, 5th Boston: Centage Learning, 2016.

Nelson, Louis. "Trump Signs Executive Order Creating Voter Fraud Commission." Politico.com. 11 May 2017. www.politico.com/story/2017/05/11/trump-voter-fraud-commission-238263 (21 July 2017).

Newton, Julianne H. *The Burden of Visual Truth: The Role of Photojournalism in Mediating Reality*. Mahwah, NJ: Lawrence Erlbaum, 2001.

Nichols, Tom. "How America Lost Faith in Expertise." *Foreign Affairs*, March/April 2017. https://www.foreignaffairs.com/articles/united-states/2017-02-13/how-america-lost-faith-expertise (12 Dec. 2017).

Nietzsche, Friedrich. "On Truth and Lie in an Extra-Moral Sense." *The Portable Nietzsche*. Edited and translated by Walter Kaufmann. New York: Penguin, 1976.

Newman, Rick. "5 Trump Myths About Illegal Immigration." Yahoo.com. 23 February 2017. https://finance.yahoo.com/news/5-trump-myths-about-illegal-immigration-193622157.html (21 July 2017).

Nixon, Ron. "Border Wall Could Cost 3 Times Estimates, Senate Democrats' Report Says." *New York Times*. 18 April 2017. https://www.nytimes.com/2017/04/18/us/politics/senate-democrats-border-wall-cost-trump.html?mcubz=1 (21 July 2017).

_____. "Job One at Homeland Security Under Trump: Immigration." *New York Times*. 13 July 2017. https://www.nytimes.com/2017/07/13/us/politics/dhs-immigration-trump.html (21 July 2017).

Nuzzi, Olivia. "Kellyanne Conway Is a Star." *New York Magazine*. March 18, 2017. http://nymag.com/daily/intelligencer/2017/03/kellyanne-conway-trumps-first-lady.html (18 Jan. 2018).

Orwell, George. *1984*. New York: Signet, 1941.

_____. "Politics and the English Language." *Horizon*, April 1946.

Osborne, Mark. "Donald Trump Attacks 'Alex' Baldwin on Twitter Over Impersonation." *ABC News*. 2 March 2018. http://abcnews.go.com/Politics/donald-trump-attacks-alex-baldwin-twitter-impersonation/story?id=53459224 (18 March 2018).

Osher, Christopher. "Police Handcuffed by Internal Discipline." *The Denver Post*, 7 May 2016.

Oster, Aaron. "Donald Trump and WWE: How the Road to the White House Began at 'Wrestlemania.'" RollingStone.com. 1 February 2016. http://www.rollingstone.com/sports/features/donald-trump-and-wwe-how-the-road-to-the-white-house-began-at-wrestlemania-20160201 (21 July 2017).

Overy, Richard. *Why the Allies Won*. New York: Pimlico, 2006 (orig. pub. 1995).

Papenfuss, Mary. "'Pray for Sweden,' Twitter Uses Giggle After Trump's Latest Stumble." *HuffingtonPost.com*. 20 February 2017. https://www.huffingtonpost.com/entry/trump-sweden-twitter_us_58aa36f6e4b037d17d291bea (22 Feb. 2017).

Parker, Ashley. "Donald Trump's 'Taco Bowl' Message: I Love Hispanics.'" *New York Times*. 5 May 2016. https://www.nytimes.com/politics/first-draft/2016/05/05/donald-trump-taco-bowl/ (21 July 2017).

Pasley, Jeffrey L. *The First Presidential Contest: 1796 and the Founding of American Democracy.* Lawrence: University of Kansas, 2013.

_____. "Two National Gazettes: Newspapers and the Embodiment of American Political Parties." *Early American Literature* (1 January 2000): 51–86.

_____. *"Tyranny of Printers": Newspaper Politics in the Early American Republic.* Charlottesville: University of Virginia Press, 2001.

Passel, Jeffrey S., and D'Vera Cohn. "Number of Babies Born in U.S. to Unauthorized Immigrants Declines." *PewResearch.org.* 11 September 2017. http://www.pewresearch.org/fact-tank/2015/09/11/number-of-babies-born-in-u-s-to-unauthorized-immigrants-declines/ (21 July 2017).

_____. "Overall Number of U.S. Unauthorized Immigrants Holds Steady Since 2009." *PewHispanic.org.* 20 September 2016. http://www.pewhispanic.org/2016/09/20/overall-number-of-u-s-unauthorized-immigrants-holds-steady-since-2009/ (21 July 2017).

Pazzanese, Christina. " Politics in a 'Post-truth age." *Harvard Gazette.* 14 July 2016 http://news.harvard.edu/gazette/story/2016/07/politics-in-a-post-truth-age/ (12 Jan. 2017).

Peifer, Jason T. "Palin, *Saturday Night Live,* and Framing: Examining the Dynamics of Political Parody." *The Communication Review* 16, no. 3 (July 2013): 155–177.

Perez-Pena, Richard, and Rachel Abrams. "Kellyanne Conway Promotes Ivanka Trump Brand, Raising Ethics Concerns." *New York Times.* 9 February 2017. https://www.nytimes.com/2017/02/09/us/politics/kellyanne-conway-ivanka-trump-ethics.html?_r=0 (10 Jan. 2018).

Pettegree, Andrew. *Brand Luther.* New York: Penguin, 2015.

Phillip, Abby, and DeBonis, Mike. "Without Evidence, Trump Tells Lawmakers 3 Million to 5 Million Illegal Ballots Cost Him the Popular Vote." WashingtonPost.com. 23 January 2017. https://www.washingtonpost.com/news/post-politics/wp/2017/01/23/at-white-house-trump-tells-congressional-leaders-3-5-million-illegal-ballots-cost-him-the-popular-vote (21 July 2017).

Piper, Melanie. "Docucharacters: Public Persona as Character in Film, Television, and Fandom." Ph.D. diss., University of Queensland, 2017. doi: 10.14264/uql.2018.54.

Plato. *Gorgias.* Translated by Donald J. Zeyl. Indianapolis: Hackett, 1987.

_____. *Ion.* Translated by W.H.D. Rouse, edited by Eric H. Warmington and Philip G. Rouse. New York: Penguin, 1984.

_____. *Protagoras.* Translated by Stanley Lombardo and Karen Bell. Indianapolis: Hackett, 1992.

_____. *Republic.* Edited by Robin Waterfield. Oxford: Oxford University Press, 2008.

_____. *The Republic—Book VIII.* Translated by Benjamin Jowett. The Internet Classics Archive by Daniel C. Stevenson, 2000. http://classics.mit.edu/Plato/republic.mb.txt.

Politi, Daniel. "Donald Trump in Phoenix: Mexicans Are 'Taking our jobs' and 'Killing us.'" Slate.com. 12 July 2015. http://www.slate.com/blogs/the_slatest/2015/07/12/donald_trump_in_phoenix_mexicans_are_taking_our_jobs_and_killing_us.html (21 July 2017).

Pomerantsev, Peter. "Putin's Rasputin." *London Review of Books* 33, no. 20 (20 October 2011): 3–6.

POP Culture: 1790 U.S. Census Bureau https://www.census.gov/history/www/through_the_decades/fast_facts/1790_fast_facts.html (16 May 2017).

Purdie, Susan. *Comedy: The Mastery of Discourse.* Toronto: University of Toronto Press, 1993.

Rademacher, Virginia Newhall. "Trump and the Resurgence of American Noir." *Persona Studies* 2, no. 2 (2016): 90–103.

"Real Time with Bill Maher: Ann Coulter on Immigration (HBO)." YouTube.com. 19 June 2015. https://www.youtube.com/watch?v=tW0GowO_MaM (21 July 2017).

"Real Time with Bill Maher: Overtime—June 19, 2015 (HBO)." YouTube.com. 19 June 2015. https://www.youtube.com/watch?v=0–2uSG1xUEg (21 July 2017).

Reese, Hope. "The Real Feminist Impact of *The Mary Tyler Moore Show* Was Behind the Scenes." *The Atlantic.* May 16, 2013. https://www.theatlantic.com/sexes/archive/2013/05/the-real-feminist-impact-of-i-the-mary-tyler-moore-show-i-was-behind-the-scenes/275875/ (15 Jan. 2018)

Reeves, Byron, and Clifford Nass. *The Media Equation: How People Treat Computers, Television, and New Media Like Real People and Places.* Cambridge: Cambridge University Press, 1996.

Reid, David. "Google Ups Its Social Media Game by Hiring 4Chan's Poole." *NBC News.* 8 March 2016. www.nbcnews.com/tech/tech-news/google-ups-its-social-media-game-hiring-4chan-s-poole-n533881 (10 June 2017).

Reid, Gregory. "The Republican Party's White Strategy." *The Atlantic.* July/August 2016. https://www.theatlantic.com/magazine/archive/2016/07/the-white-strategy/485612/ (21 July 2017).

"A Report on the Media and the Immigration Debate." Brookings Institution. https://www.brookings.edu/wpcontent/uploads/2012/04/0925_immigration_dionne.pdf (12 Jan. 2017).

Rhodan, Maya. "Donald Trump Raises Eyebrows with 'Bad Hombres' Line." Time.com. 19 October 2016. http://time.com/4537847/donald-trump-bad-hombres/ (21 July 2017).

Risjord, Norman K. *Jefferson's America, 1794–1800,* 2d ed. Lanham: Rowman & Littlefield, 2002.

Roberts, Randall. "The Story of How 'Love Is All Around' Became the Theme Song for 'The Mary Tyler Moore Show.'" *Los Angeles Times.* 26 January 2017. http://beta.latimes.com/entertainment/music/la-et-ms-mary-tyler-moore-sonny-curtis-theme-20170126-story.html (15 Jan. 2018).

Rodriguez, Lisette. "Kellyanne Conway Defends White House's Credibility: We Have 'High Regard' for Facts." *ABC News.* February 7, 2017. http://abcnews.go.com/Politics/kellyanne-conway-defends-white-houses-credibility-high-regard/story?id=45334577 (10 Jan. 2018).

Rorty, Richard. *Contingency, Irony, and Solidarity.* Cambridge: Cambridge University Press, 1989.

Rosen, Richard N. *American Aurora: A Democratic Republican Returns.* New York: St. Martin's Press, 1997.

Rosenthal, Andrew. "'Lordy, I Hope There Are Tapes.'" *New York Times.* 8 June 2017. https://www.nytimes.com/2017/06/08/opinion/lordy-i-hope-there-are-tapes.html (10 Jan. 2018).

Ross, Janell. "The Myth of the 'Anchor Baby' Deportation Defense." *The Washington Post.* 20 August 2015. https://www.washingtonpost.com/news/the-fix/wp/2015/08/20/the-myth-of-the-anchor-baby-deportation-defense/ (21 July 2017).

Salisbury, Ian. "The Insane Numbers Behind Trump's Deportation Plan." Time.com. 14 November 2016. http://time.com/money/4566401/trumps-deportation-immigration-plan-numbers/ (21 July 2017).

Saturday Night Live. Season 34, episode 4, "VP Debate: Sarah Palin and Joe Biden." Aired 4 October 2008, on NBC. http://www.nbc.com/saturday-night-live/video/vp-debate-open-palin—biden/n12319?snl=1.

_____. Season 42, episode 1, "Donald Trump vs. Hillary Clinton Debate Cold Open." Aired 1 October 2016, on NBC. https://www.youtube.com/watch?v=-nQGBZQrtT0.

_____. Season 42, episode 4, "Donald Trump vs. Hillary Clinton Third Debate Cold Open." Aired 22 October 2016, on NBC. https://www.youtube.com/watch?v=-kjyltrKZSY.

_____. Season 42, episode 7, "Donald Trump Prepares Cold Open." Aired 19 November 2016, on NBC. https://www.youtube.com/watch?v=JUWSLlz0Fdo.

_____. Season 42, episode 11, "Donald Trump Press Conference Cold Open." Aired 14 January 2017, on NBC. https://www.youtube.com/watch?v=4_Gf0mGJfP8.

Scala, Dante J., and Andrew E. Smith. "Does the Tail Wag the Dog? Early Presidential Nomination Polling in New Hampshire and the United States." *The American Review of Politics* 28 (2007/2008): 401–424.

Scheer, Arthur. "The Significance of Thomas Pinckney's Candidacy in the Election of 1796." *South Carolina Historical Magazine.* 76, no. 2 (April 1975): 51–59.

Schleifer, Theodore. "Trump Defends Criticism of Judge with Mexican Heritage." CNN.com. 5 June 2016. http://www.cnn.com/2016/06/03/politics/donald-trump-tapper-lead/index.html (21 July 2017).

Schwartz, Tony, "I Wrote 'The Art of the Deal' with Trump: His Self-Sabotage Is Rooted in His Past." *The Washington Post.* 16 May 2017.

Shear, Michael D. "Obama Sets the Record Straight on His 7-Almond Habit." *New York Times.* 28 July 2017. https://www.nytimes.com/2016/07/29/us/politics/obama-sets-the-record-straight-on-his-7-almond-habit.html (10 Jan. 2018).

Shear, Michael D., and Corasaniti, Nick. "Fact-Checking the Truth That Donald Trump Promised." *New York Times.* 21 July 2016. https://www.nytimes.com/2016/07/22/us/politics/donald-trump-fact-check.html (24 July 2017).

Sibley, Joel L. *The American Political Nation, 1838–1893.* Palo Alto: Stanford University Press, 1991.

Siebert, Fred. *Freedom of the Press in England, 1476–1776: The Rise and Decline of Government Controls.* Urbana: University of Illinois Press, 1952.

Sinderbrand, Rebecca. "How Kellyanne Conway Ushered in the Era of Alternative Facts." *The Washington Post.* 22 January 2017. https://www.washingtonpost.com/news/the-fix/wp/2017/01/22/how-kellyanne-conway-ushered-in-the-era-of-alternative-facts/?utm_term=.f2a7c490ee21 (25 Jan. 2017).

Sioli, Marco. "Repression in the Early Republic: John Adams, the Alien and Sedition Acts, and the Politics of Exclusion." *Rivista di Studi Americani* (*Review of American Studies*) 19 (2008): 151–172.

Skowronek, Stephen. *The Politics Presidents Make.* Cambridge: Harvard University Belknap Press, 1997.

Smith, David. "Republican Senator Jeff Flake: Trump's Attacks on Media Reminiscent of Stalin." *The Guardian* 17 January 2018. https://www.theguardian.com/us-news/2018/jan/17/jeff-flake-donald-trump-fake-news-stalin-senate-speech (19 Jan. 2018).

Soltani, Abdi. "Repeating the Mistakes of the Past: Anniversary of the Chinese Exclusion Act." *ACLU Northern California.* 5 May 2017 www.aclunc.org/blog/repeating-mistakes-past-anniversary-chinese-exclusion-act. (12 Jan. 2017).

Sontag, Susan. *On Photography.* New York: Farrar, Straus and Giroux, 1977.

Stedman, Alex. "Kellyanne Conway Apologizes for Bowling Green 'Massacre' Remarks, Spars with CNN's Jake Tapper." *Variety.com.* 7 February 2017. http://variety.com/2017/tv/news/kellyanne-conway-bowling-green-massacre-cnn-jake-tapper-1201980910/ (10 Jan. 2017).

Stinchcombe, William. "The Diplomacy of the WXYZ Affair." *William and Mary Quarterly* 34, no. 4 (1977): 590–617.

Stokols, Eli. "Trump Brings Up Vote Fraud Again, This Time in Meeting with Senators." *Politico.com.* 10 February 2017. www.politico.com/story/2017/02/trump-voter-fraud-senators-meeting-234909 (21 July 2017).

Strong, S. I. "Alternative Facts and the Post Truth Society: Meeting the Challenge." *University of Pennsylvania Law Review* 165, no. 137 (2017): 137–146.

Sullivan, Margaret. "The Post-Truth World of the Trump Administration Is Scarier Than You Think." *The Washington Post.* 4 December 2016. https://www.washingtonpost.com/lifestyle/style/the-post-truth-world-of-the-trump-administration-is-scarier-than-you-think/2016/12/02/ebda952a-b897-11e6-b994-f45a208f7a73_story.html?utm_term=.3fedc5a8c5e8 (10 Jan. 2018).

Tackett, Michael, and Wines, Michael. "Trump Disbands Commission on Voter Fraud." NYTimes.com. 3 January 2018. https://www.nytimes.com/2018/01/03/us/politics/trump-voter-fraud-commission.html (10 Feb. 2018).

Tani, Maxwell. "Man at Donald Trump Rally Tells Univision Anchor Jorge Ramos: 'Get out of my country.'" *Business Insider.* 26 August 2015. http://www.businessinsider.com/donald-trump-jorge-ramos-get-out-video-2015-8 (21 July 2017).

Taylor. Mark C. "About Religion: Economies of Faith in Virtual Culture." *Religion and Post-modernism,* edited by Mark C. Taylor. Chicago: University of Chicago Press, 1999.

_____. *Confidence Games: Money and Markets in a World Without Redemption.* Chicago: University of Chicago Press, 2004.

Tesich, Steve. "A Government of Lies." *The Nation.* 6 January 1992.

Thomsen, Jacqueline. "Twitter Reacts to Trump's 'Stable Genius' Tweet." *The Hill,* 6 January 2018.

Tonnies, Ferdinand. *Community and Association.* London: Routledge and Kegan Paul, 1955.

Trotta, Daniel. "Crowd Controversy: The Making of an Inauguration Day Photo." *Reueters.com.* 24 January 2017. https://www.reuters.com/article/us-usa-trump-inauguration-image/crowd-controversy-the-making-of-an-inauguration-day-photo-idUSKBN1572 VU (1 Feb. 2017).

Trump, Donald. *Crippled America: How to Make America Great Again.* New York: Simon & Schuster, 2015.

_____. By Hugh Hewitt, *The Hugh Hewitt Show,* "Donald Trump Makes a Return Visit," by Duane Patterson. www.hughhewitt.com/donald-trump-makes-return-visit/ (11 August 2016).

Trump, Donald (@realdonaldtrump)."Alec Baldwin, whose dying mediocre career was saved by his terrible impersonation of me on SNL, now says playing me was agony. Alec, it was agony for those who were forced to watch. Bring back Darrell Hammond, funnier and a far greater talent!" Twitter, March 2, 2018, 6:07 a.m. https://twitter.com/realdonaldtrump/status/969529668234829825.

_____. "@NBCNews is bad but Saturday Night Live is the worst of NBC. Not funny, cast is terrible, always a complete hit job. Really bad television!" Twitter, January 15, 2017, 2:46 p.m. https://twitter.com/realdonaldtrump/status/820764134857969666.

_____. "I watched parts of @nbcsnl Saturday Night Live last night. It is a totally one-sided, biased show—nothing funny at all. Equal time for us?" Twitter, November 20, 2016, 5:26 a.m. https://twitter.com/realdonaldtrump/status/800329364986626048.

_____. "Just tried watching Saturday Night Live—unwatchable! Totally biased, not funny and the Baldwin impersonation just can't get any worse. Sad." Twitter, December 3, 2016, 9:13 p.m. https://twitter.com/realdonaldtrump/status/805278955150471168.

_____. "Serious voter fraud in Virginia, New Hampshire and California—so why isn't the media reporting on this? Serious bias—big problem!" November 27, 2016, 7:31 p.m. Tweet.

_____. "Thank you to all of those who gave me such wonderful reviews for my performance on @nbcsnl Saturday Night Live. Best ratings in 4 years!" Twitter, November 8, 2015, 4:47 p.m. https://twitter.com/realdonaldtrump/status/663518286915702784.

_____. "Watched Saturday Night Live hit job on me.Time to retire the boring and unfunny show. Alec Baldwin portrayal stinks. Media rigging election!" @realdonaldtrump Twitter post. October 16, 2016, 4:14 a.m. https://twitter.com/realdonaldtrump/status/787612552654155776

Trump, Donald, with Tony Schwartz. *The Art of the Deal.* New York: Routledge, 1987.

Tsipursky, Glen. "Sometimes, Facts Can Actually Trump Ideology." *Scientific American.* 19 May 2017. https://blogs.scientificamerican.com/observations/sometimes-facts-can-actually-trump-ideology/ (21 July 2017).

Turner, Graeme. *Re-Inventing the Media.* London: Routledge, 2016.

United States Federal Elections Commission. *Official 2016 Presidential General Election Results.* Compiled by Public Records Branch, Public Disclosure and Media Relations Division, Office of Communications. Federal Election Commission. Washington, D.C., 30 January 2017, https://transition.fec.gov/pubrec/fe2016/2016presgeresults.pdf (21 July 2017).

Van Zoonen, Liesbet. "Audiences Reactions to Hollywood Politics." *Media Culture and Society* 29, no. 4 (2007): 531–547.

_____. *Entertaining the Citizen: When Politics and Popular Culture Converge.* Lanham, MD: Rowman & Littlefield, 2005.

Vitali, Ali, Kasie Hunt, and Frank Thorp, V. "Trump Referred to Haiti and African Nations as 'Shithole' Countries." *NBC News.* 12 January 2018. https://www.nbcnews.com/politics/white-house/trump-referred-haiti-african-countries-shithole-nations-n836946 (3 March 2018).

Wacquant, Loïc. "The Curious Eclipse of Prison Ethnograhpy in the Age of Mass Incarceration." *Ethnography* 3, no. 4 (2002): 371–397.

Wag the Dog. DVD. Directed by Barry Levison. Burbank: New Line Cinema, 1997.

Walker, Peter. "Kellyanne Conway Says She Is 'Not Inspector Gadget' or 'in job of having evidence' After Microwave Comments." *Independent.* 13 March 2017. http://www.independent.co.uk/news/world/americas/kellyanne-conway-microwave-comments-not-inspector-gadget-job-having-evidence-response-a7627441.html (10 Jan. 2018).

Wallace, Tim, Karen Yourish, and Troy Griggs. "Trump's Inauguration vs. Obama's: Comparing the Crowds." *New York Times.* 20 January 2017. https://www.nytimes.com/interactive/2017/01/20/us/politics/trump-inauguration-crowd.html (3 Jan. 2018).

Wang, Hansi Lo. "How America's Idea of Illegal Immigration Doesn't Always Match Reality." *NPR.org*. 8 March 2017. http://www.npr.org/sections/thetwo-way/2017/03/08/517561046/how-americas-idea-of-illegal-immigration-doesnt-always-match-reality (21 July 2017).
____. "Mexicans No Longer Make Up Majority of Immigrants in U.S. Illegally." *NPR.org*. 25 April 2017. http://wamu.org/story/17/04/25/mexicans-no-longer-make-up-majority-of-immigrants-in-u-s-illegally/ (21 July 2017).
Wang, Wendy. "The Rise of Intermarriage." *Pew Research Center*. 16 February 2012. http://www.pewsocialtrends.org/2012/02/16/the-rise-of-intermarriage/ (21 July 2017).
Washington, George, to Alexander Hamilton, July 29, 1795. *Founders on Line, National Archives*. https://founders.archives.gov/documents/Hamilton/01–18-02–0318.
Weston, Phippen J. "Asians Now Outpace Mexicans in Terms of Undocumented Growth." *The Atlantic*. 20 August 2015. https://www.theatlantic.com/politics/archive/2015/08/asians-now-outpace-mexicans-in-terms-of-undocumented-growth/432603/ (21 July 2017).
"What Is an Alternative Fact?" *English Language and Usage*. https://english.stackexchange.com/questions/369628/what-is-an-alternative-fact (12 Jan. 2018).
White, Hayden. *The Content of the Form: Narrative Discourse and Historical Representation*. Baltimore: Johns Hopkins University Press, 1987.
White House Office of the Press Secretary. "Executive Order: Border Security and Immigration Enforcement Improvements." *Whitehouse.gov*. 25 January 2017. https://www.whitehouse.gov/the-press-office/2017/01/25/executive-order-border-security-and-immigration-enforcement-improvements (17 Jan. 2018).
____. "Executive Order: Enhancing Public Safety in the Interior of the United States." *Whitehouse.gov*. 25 January 2017. https://www.whitehouse.gov/the-press-office/2017/01/25/presidential-executive-order-enhancing-public-safety-interior-united (17 Jan. 2018).
____. "Executive Order: Protecting the Nation from Foreign Terrorist Entry into the United States." *Whitehouse.gov*. 27 January 2017. https://www.whitehouse.gov/the-press-office/2017/01/27/executive-order-protecting-nation-foreign-terrorist-entry-united-states (26 June 2017).
Wilking, Rick. "Trump Proposes Ways to Make Mexico Pay for Immigrants." CBSNews.com. 1 August 2015. https://www.cbsnews.com/news/donald-trump-border-wall-immigration-plan-mexico-pay/ (21 July 2017).
Wilson, David A. *United Irishmen, United States: Immigrant Radicals in the Early Republic*. Ithaca: Cornell University Press, 1998.
Wolff, Michael. *Fire and Fury: Inside the Trump White House*. London: Little, Brown, 2018.
Woodward, Kathryn. *Concepts of identity and difference*. London: Sage, 1997.
Wooten, Sarah McIntosh. *Donald Trump: From Real Estate to Reality TV*. New York: Enslow 2009.
Wootson, Cleve R., Jr. "Trump Implied Frederick Douglass Was Alive. The Abolitionist's Family Offered a 'History Lesson,'" *Chicago Tribune*. 2 February 2017. http://www.chicagotribune.com/news/nationworld/ct-trump-frederick-douglass-remark-20170202-story.html (4 Feb. 2017).
Young, Louise. *Japan's Total Empire*. Berkeley: University of California Press, 1998.
Yourish, Karen, and Troy Griggs. "Tracking the President's Visits to Trump Properties." *New York Times*. 25 June 2017. https://www.nytimes.com/interactive/2017/04/05/us/politics/tracking-trumps-visits-to-his-branded-properties.html (10 Jan. 2018).
Zadrozny, Brandy. "The Man Behind 'Journalist. Rope. Tree.'" *The Daily Beast*. 8 November 2016. https://www.thedailybeast.com/the-man-behind-journalist-rope-tree (26 Dec. 2017).
Zannettou, Savvas, Tristan Caulifeld, Emilio De Cristofaro, Nicolas Kourttellis, Illias Leontidis, Michael Sirivanos, Gianluca Stringhini, and Jeremy Blackburn. "The Web Centipede: Understanding How Web Communities Influence Each Other Through the Lens of Mainstream and Alternative News Sources." *ArXiv Preprint ArXiv:1705.06947*, 19 May 2017, https://arxiv.org/abs/1705.06947 (1 June 2017).
Zelizer, Barbie. *About to Die: How News Images Move the Public*. Oxford: Oxford University Press, 2010.

Index